The Complete Dictionary of
SHAKESPEARE QUOTATIONS

The Complete Dictionary of
SHAKESPEARE QUOTATIONS

Compiled by
D. C. Browning
M. A. (Glasgow), B.A., B.Litt.(Oxon).

NEW ORCHARD EDITIONS
POOLE · NEW YORK · SYDNEY

Published by arrangement with J. M. Dent & Sons Ltd

This Edition published by
New Orchard Editions Ltd
Robert Rogers House
New Orchard
Poole, Dorset BH15 1LU

ISBN 1 85079 014 0

Printed in Portugal by
Printer Portugesa, Lisbon

INTRODUCTION

It is just over two centuries since the publication of the first collection of Shakespearian extracts, Dr Dodd's once popular *Beauties of Shakespeare*. Since then there have been so many Shakespearian anthologies of all shapes and sizes that some apology might seem necessary for adding yet another to the number. But the present volume is much more than just a collection of pleasant and interesting extracts from and about Shakespeare. It aims at providing within moderate compass what will be at once an anthology of all that is greatest in Shakespeare's writings, a reference work to the plays and poems and to Shakespeare allusions, and a companion and guide to Shakespeare's works, enabling the reader to find his way about them and to enjoy their choicest riches without having to quarry for them himself.

General Scheme

The general scheme of the volume is simple. The main part is a collection of quotations from Shakespeare's plays and poems, arranged according to the usual order of the works, the extracts from each play being prefaced by a brief summary of the plot. Then follows a smaller section consisting of passages which throw light on Shakespeare's life and career, and of tributes that have been paid to his genius. These two sections contain nearly four thousand quotations. Finally, a very full index enables the reader to turn at once to any quotation or extract which he wishes to look up.

Principle of Selection

The selection of quotations has been made as carefully as possible, each play having been specially studied with that aim in view, and the collections of general dictionaries of quotations having been gone through to ensure that no famous passage is omitted. But, of course, any choice must be to some extent arbitrary, when it is remembered that nearly every line of such a play as *Hamlet* must have been quoted at one time or another. In this connection it is of interest to reckon up the proportion of the whole play which appears in the dictionary. *Hamlet* contains 3,929 lines, and of these the dictionary includes some 1,700, or not far short of half. With such a generous selection it may be hoped that the book has practically every Shakespearian passage which is really memorable.

Comparative Figures

It may be instructive to note the relative 'quotability' of the plays as indicated by the number of extracts which have been included. The four great tragedies are at the top of the list, *Hamlet*, as one might expect, being easily first with nearly 350 extracts; its pre-eminence is partly accounted for by its length, for it is not far short of twice the length of *Macbeth*, which supplies 175 quotations. A little above the 200 mark appears *King Lear*, and a little below it *Othello*, with *As You Like It* between them. The popularity of this comedy which blends sunshine and whimsical philosophy bears out Hazlitt's observation that 'there is hardly any of Shakespeare's plays that contains a greater number of passages that have been quoted in books of extracts, or a greater number of phrases that have become in a manner proverbial.'

Following the great tragedies there is a distinct gap till we approach the 150 mark, round which clusters a group of five plays which have less sublimity but are models of composition and stagecraft. They comprise two tragedies, *Romeo and Juliet* and *Julius Caesar*; two comedies, *Twelfth Night* and *The Merchant of Venice*; and the historical play, *Henry IV, Part I*. The historical plays in general make a smaller contribution of memorable extracts than the tragedies and the comedies, but *1 Henry IV* holds an outstanding position because of the great Eastcheap scenes and the inimitable Falstaff; the lower figures for *2 Henry IV* and *Henry V* reflect the fat knight's waning popularity and death, though *Henry V*, because of its magnificent long speeches, has a higher quotation value than its score of an even hundred would suggest. The same may be said of *A Midsummer Night's Dream*, which with its long poetical passages ranks second of the comedies if the size as well as the number of quotations is taken into account.

A little over the hundred mark are the two witty comedies of *Love's Labour's Lost* and *Much Ado About Nothing*, together with that mature tragedy, *Antony and Cleopatra*. Just under the hundred are the 'romantic plays' of *The Tempest* and *The Winter's Tale*, the former, in spite of its popularity, being relegated to this low position by its brevity, for it is shorter even than *Macbeth*. After this comes a run mainly of historical plays, *Richard II* and *Richard III* both appearing in the eighties, *King John* and *Henry VIII* in the fifties, while the two farces, *The Taming of the Shrew* and *The Merry Wives of Windsor*, are just below that mark. Lowest in the list is the crude tragedy of *Titus Andronicus*, with the doubtful play of *Pericles* and that short prentice work, *The Comedy of Errors*, a little above it.

When dealing with the Sonnets, the main difficulty is to keep the selection within reasonable bounds. As it is, a dozen have been given in their entirety, since any other way of presentation would have impaired the unity of thought and expression; while the total of the extracts amounts to 450 lines—well over one-fifth of the whole. From the longer poems, *Venus and Adonis* and *Lucrece*, only a small number of quotations have been taken, for these works of Shakespeare's youth have not now the popularity which they enjoyed on publication. The dedications with which they were headed have been inserted, because of their biographical interest, in the next section of the quotations, where also will be found his epitaph and an epigram said to be by his hand.

Summaries of the Plots

After every quotation the speaker's name is given in brackets; and, with a view to identifying the various characters and indicating the part taken by each, a short synopsis of the plot has been inserted before the selections from each play. These summaries have been deliberately made as short as possible, so that they may provide a thumb-nail conspectus of the story, enabling readers to refresh their memories by seeing its main outlines at a glance. In the case of the historical plays a brief indication is also given of the period which they cover.

Shakespeare's Life

The section of the dictionary containing quotations not from but about Shakespeare follows the same general scheme. A very brief outline giving the known facts about Shakespeare's life is prefaced to the main items of what an eminent critic once called 'a scrapheap of considerable dimensions' containing facts and traditions about him. The playwright's will is given in full, along with the 'lives' by Fuller and Aubrey and substantial extracts from that by Rowe. This being a popular work, the spelling of these extracts has been modernized, just as the spelling of the plays themselves is in modern editions. Two chronological tables have been supplied, one giving the principal events of Shakespeare's life, along with a few contemporary happenings which may serve as landmarks; the other supplying the approximate dates of composition and publication of the different works.

Tributes to Shakespeare

Of tributes to Shakespeare a large volume could be and indeed has been made. In this selection only the most famous and familiar have been included, such as Heminge and Condell's preface to the First Folio, a number of the tributes paid by Ben Jonson and by his namesake the great Doctor, the sonnets of Milton and of Matthew Arnold, and other passages of similar calibre. In order that what one might term the *advocatus diaboli* may have his say, a final page of disparaging criticism has been compiled, ranging from the backbiting of the contemporary playwright Greene through Pepys, Chesterfield, and George III to the irrepressible Bernard Shaw.

Index

Containing over 8,000 references, the index provided here should suffice for all but the specialist as an effective Shakespeare concordance. Every effort has been made to choose the most suitable reference words for each extract, so that the reader who remembers only a fragment of a quotation, or even its subject merely, may be able to trace the entire passage with the minimum of trouble. The index should also serve as a guide to Shakespeare's reflections on different topics. By looking up (for example) such words as 'love,' 'death,' 'mercy,' one can review at a glance what he has said on these themes, while his patriotic passages can easily be traced under 'England.' Similarly, by looking up 'Shakespeare' in the index one can obtain a condensed impression of the man himself and of the way in which he inspired others.

Acknowledgments

The numbering of acts, scenes, and lines follows that of the well-known *Cambridge Shakespeare* of Clark and Wright as reproduced in the Globe edition, which has been used by many other books of reference, and has come to be regarded more or less as a standard. The text also follows the Cambridge editors for the most part, but in a number of cases where the readings of later editions have come to be generally accepted, or have the visible stamp of authenticity, they have been inserted in preference. For these and also for information given in the summaries of the plays use has been made of M. R. Ridley's New Temple edition of the works. The figures for the lengths of the plays, given on page 464, are taken from Sir Edmund K. Chambers's *William Shakespeare*. The index is arranged on the 'nothing-before-something' system set out in the pamphlet on Alphabetical Arrangement published by the British Standards Institution; proper names mentioned in Shakespearian documents and the titles of his works have been entered and set out in full.

D. C. B.

For the new edition the whole volume has been gone through afresh and a round dozen of slips or misprints have been corrected.

D. C. B.

CONTENTS

CONTENTS

COMEDIES

THE TEMPEST

The scene is an enchanted island where Prospero, the exiled Duke of Milan, has lived for twelve years alone with his daughter Miranda, after having been driven from his dukedom by his brother Antonio. Through his magic arts Prospero has made servants of Ariel, an airy spirit, and Caliban, a brutish monster. On the island a tempest throws Antonio and his confederate Alonso, King of Naples, along with Alonso's brother Sebastian and the attendant lords Gonzalo, Adrian, and Francisco. Ferdinand, Alonso's son, who has been washed ashore apart from the others, meets and falls in love with Miranda. Meanwhile Prospero uses his magic spells to terrify into repentance those who have usurped his place and wronged him. In another part of the island Caliban meets with two servants of the party, Stephano, a butler, and Trinculo, a jester, and there is much ludicrous drunken fooling, followed by a childish plot which Prospero easily foils. After a masque in which Juno and Ceres pronounce blessings on Ferdinand and Miranda, the play ends with Prospero forswearing his magic arts in a speech which is sometimes taken as Shakespeare's farewell to the stage, and the island is abandoned to Caliban. Ariel's songs are among Shakespeare's most beautiful lyrics.

Blow, till thou burst thy wind, if room enough!   I. i. 8
              (*Boatswain*)

What cares these roarers for the name of king?   18
              (*Boatswain*)

    I have great comfort from this fellow: methinks he hath   30
no drowning mark upon him; his complexion is perfect
gallows.   (*Gonzalo*)

What, must our mouths be cold?   (*Boatswain*)   56

            Would thou mightst lie drowning   60
The washing of ten tides!   (*Antonio*)

    Now would I give a thousand furlongs of sea for an   68
acre of barren ground, long heath, brown furze, any
thing.   The wills above be done! but I would fain die a
dry death.   (*Gonzalo*)

The sky, it seems, would pour down stinking pitch,   I ii. 3
But that the sea, mounting to the welkin's cheek,
Dashes the fire out.   (*Miranda*)

          What seest thou else   49
In the dark backward and abysm of time?   (*Prospero*)

I, thus neglecting worldly ends, all dedicated   89
To closeness and the bettering of my mind.   (*Prospero*)

             Like one   99
Who having into truth, by telling of it,
Made such a sinner of his memory,
To credit his own lie.   (*Prospero*)

         Me, poor man, my library   109
Was dukedom large enough.   (*Prospero*)

          I should sin   118
To think but nobly of my grandmother:
Good wombs have borne bad sons.   (*Miranda*)

A rotten carcass of a butt, not rigg'd,   146
Nor tackle, sail, nor mast; the very rats
Instinctively have quit it.   (*Prospero*)

Knowing I loved my books, he furnish'd me   I. ii. 166
From mine own library with volumes that
I prize above my dukedom.   (*Prospero*)

                   I come   189
To answer thy best pleasure; be 't to fly,
To swim, to dive into the fire, to ride
On the curl'd clouds, to thy strong bidding task
Ariel and all his quality.   (*Ariel*)

           The fire and cracks   203
Of sulphurous roaring the most mighty Neptune
Seem to besiege and make his bold waves tremble,
Yea, his dread trident shake.   (*Ariel*)

           The king's son, Ferdinand,   212
With hair up-staring—then like reeds, not hair,—
Was the first man that leap'd; cried, 'Hell is empty,
And all the devils are here.'   (*Ariel*)

           Cooling of the air with sighs   222
In an odd angle of the isle and sitting,
His arms in this sad knot.   (*Ariel*)

           Safely in harbour   226
Is the king's ship; in the deep nook, where once
Thou call'dst me up at midnight to fetch dew
From the still-vex'd Bermoothes, there she 's hid.
                         (*Ariel*)

I will be correspondent to command   297
And do my spiriting gently.   (*Ariel*)

As wicked dew as e'er my mother brush'd   321
With raven's feather from unwholesome fen
Drop on you both! a south-west blow on ye
And blister you all o'er!   (*Caliban*)

For this, be sure, to-night thou shalt have cramps,   325
Side-stitches that shall pen thy breath up; urchins
Shall, for the vast of night that they may work
All exercise on thee.   (*Prospero*)

You taught me language; and my profit on 't   363
Is, I know how to curse.   The red plague rid you
For learning me your language.   (*Caliban*)

           Come unto these yellow sands,   376
               And then take hands:
           Courtsied when you have and kiss'd
               The wild waves whist,

Foot it featly here and there;   I. ii. 380
And, sweet sprites, the burthen bear.
  Hark, hark!
   Bow-wow.
  The watch-dogs bark:
   Bow-wow.
  Hark, hark!   I hear
  The strain of strutting chanticleer
  Cry, Cock-a-diddle-dow.   (*Ariel, sings*)

      Sitting on a bank,   389
Weeping again the king my father's wreck,
This music crept by me upon the waters,
Allaying both their fury and my passion
With its sweet air.   (*Ferdinand*)

  Full fathom five thy father lies;   396
   Of his bones are coral made;
  Those are pearls that were his eyes:
   Nothing of him that doth fade
  But doth suffer a sea-change
  Into something rich and strange.
  Sea-nymphs hourly ring his knell:
      Ding-dong.
  Hark! now I hear them,—Ding-dong, bell.
       (*Ariel, sings*)

The fringed curtains of thine eye advance   408
And say what thou seest yond.   (*Prospero*)

Grief that's beauty's canker.   (*Prospero*)   415

I am the best of them that speak this speech,   429
Were I but where 'tis spoken.   (*Ferdinand*)

    At the first sight   440
They have changed eyes.   (*Prospero*)

There's nothing ill can dwell in such a temple: 457
If the ill spirit have so fair a house,
Good things will strive to dwell with't.   (*Miranda*)

He receives comfort like cold porridge.   (*Sebastian*)   II. i. 10

 Look, he's winding up the watch of his wit; by and by   12
it will strike.   (*Sebastian*)

Fie, what a spendthrift is he of his tongue!   (*Antonio*)   24

I saw him beat the surges under him,
And ride upon their backs; he trod the water,
Whose enmity he flung aside, and breasted
The surge most swoln that met him; his bold head
'Bove the contentious waves he kept, and oar'd
Himself with his good arms in lusty stroke
To the shore, that o'er his wave-worn basis bow'd,
As stooping to relieve him.   (*Francisco*)

Had I plantation of this isle, my lord,—   143

And were the king on't, what would I do?   145

I' the commonwealth I would by contraries   147
Execute all things; for no kind of traffic
Would I admit; no name of magistrate;
Letters should not be known; riches, poverty,
And use of service, none; contract, succession,
Bourn, bound of land, tilth, vineyard, none;
No use of metal, corn, or wine, or oil;
No occupation; all men idle, all;
And women too, but innocent and pure;
No sovereignty;—   (*Gonzalo*)

The latter end of his commonwealth forgets the beginning.   157
                                                   (*Antonio*)

All things in common nature should produce   159
Without sweat or endeavour: treason, felony,
Sword, pike, knife, gun, or need of any engine,
Would I not have; but nature should bring forth,
Of it own kind, all foison, all abundance,
To feed my innocent people.   (*Gonzalo*)

I would with such perfection govern, sir,   167
To excel the golden age.   (*Gonzalo*)

This is a strange repose, to be asleep   213
With eyes wide open; standing, speaking, moving,
And yet so fast asleep.   (*Sebastian*)

She that is queen of Tunis; she that dwells   246
Ten leagues beyond man's life; she that from Naples
Can have no note, unless the sun were post—
The man i' the moon's too slow—till new-born chins
Be rough and razorable.   (*Antonio*)

          There be that can rule Naples   262
As well as he that sleeps; lords that can prate
As amply and unnecessarily

As this Gonzalo; I myself could make   II. i. 265
A chough of as deep chat.   (*Antonio*)

All the infections that the sun sucks up   II. ii. 1
From bogs, fens, flats, on Prosper fall and make him
By inch-meal a disease.   (*Caliban*)

A very ancient and fish-like smell.   (*Trinculo*)   27

    Were I in England now, as once I was, and had but this   29
fish painted, not a holiday fool there but would give a
piece of silver: there would this monster make a man; any
strange beast there makes a man; when they will not give
a doit to relieve a lame beggar, they will lay out ten to see
a dead Indian.   (*Trinculo*)

Misery acquaints a man with strange bed-fellows.   41
                             (*Trinculo*)

Stephano.   I shall no more to sea, to sea,   44
          Here shall I die ashore—
This is a very scurvy tune to sing at a man's funeral: well,
here's my comfort.   [*Drinks.*]

    The master, the swabber, the boatswain and I,   48
        The gunner and his mate
Loved Mall, Meg and Marian and Margery,
        But none of us cared for Kate;
        For she had a tongue with a tang,
        Would cry to a sailor, Go hang!
She loved not the savour of tar nor of pitch,
Yet a tailor might scratch her where'er she did itch:
        Then to sea, boys, and let her go hang!
                    (*Stephano, sings*)

Four legs and two voices: a most delicate monster!   93
                        (*Stephano*)

    This is a devil and no monster: I will leave him; I have   102
no long spoon.   (*Stephano*)

    Prithee, do not turn me about; my stomach is not   118
constant.   (*Stephano*)

That's a brave god and bears celestial liquor.   (*Caliban*)   121

    Come, swear to that; kiss the book: I will furnish it   145
anon with new contents; swear.   (*Stephano*)

I prithee, let me bring thee where crabs grow;   II. ii. 171
And I with my long nails will dig thee pig-nuts;
Show thee a jay's nest and instruct thee how
To snare the nimble marmoset; I'll bring thee
To clustering filberts and sometimes I'll get thee
Young scamels from the rock.   (*Caliban*)

       No more dams I'll make for fish;   184
          Nor fetch firing
          At requiring;
       Nor scrape trencher, nor wash dish·
         'Ban, 'Ban, Cacaliban
         Has a new master: get a new man.
             (*Caliban, sings*)

O brave monster!   (*Stephano*)   192

There be some sports are painful, and their labour   III. i. 1
Delight in them sets off: some kinds of baseness
Are nobly undergone and most poor matters
Point to rich ends.   This my mean task
Would be as heavy to me as odious, but
The mistress which I serve quickens what's dead
And makes my labours pleasures: O she is
Ten times more gentle than her father's crabbed,
And he's composed of harshness.   I must remove
Some thousands of these logs and pile them up,
Upon a sore injunction: my sweet mistress
Weeps when she sees me work, and says, such baseness
Had never like executor.   I forget:
But these sweet thoughts do even refresh my labours,
Most busy lest, when I do it.   (*Ferdinand*)

I had rather crack my sinews, break my back,   26
Than you should such dishonour undergo,
While I sit lazy by.   (*Ferdinand*)

Poor worm, thou art infected.   (*Prospero*)   31

        'Tis fresh morning with me   33
When you are by at night.   (*Ferdinand*)

              Admired Miranda!   37
Indeed the top of admiration! worth
What's dearest to the world!   Full many a lady
I have eyed with best regard and many a time
The harmony of their tongues hath into bondage
Brought my too diligent ear: for several virtues
Have I liked several women; never any
With so full soul, but some defect in her

9

Did quarrel with the noblest grace she owed   III. i. 45
And put it to the foil: but you, O you,
So perfect and so peerless, are created
Of every creature's best!   (*Ferdinand*)

      Hence, bashful cunning!   81
And prompt me, plain and holy innocence!   (*Miranda*)

Ferdinand. Here's my hand.   89
Miranda. And mine, with my heart in 't.

 Drink, servant-monster, when I bid thee: thy eyes are   III. ii. 9
almost set in thy head.   (*Stephano*)

I am in case to justle a constable.   (*Trinculo*)   30

What a pied ninny's this!   (*Caliban*)   71

    Flout 'em and scout 'em,   130
    And scout 'em and flout 'em;
     Thought is free.   (*Stephano, sings*)

He that dies pays all debts.   (*Stephano*)   140

Be not afeard; the isle is full of noises,   144
Sounds and sweet airs, that give delight and hurt not.
Sometimes a thousand twangling instruments
Will hum about mine ears, and sometimes voices
That, if I then had waked after long sleep,
Will make me sleep again: and then, in dreaming,
The clouds methought would open and show riches
Ready to drop upon me, that, when I waked,
I cried to dream again.   (*Caliban*)

    Here's a maze trod indeed   III. iii. 2
Through forth-rights and meanders!   (*Gonzalo*)

    When we were boys,   43
Who would believe that there were mountaineers
Dew-lapped like bulls, whose throats had hanging at 'em
Wallets of flesh? or that there were such men
Whose heads stood in their breasts? which now we find
Each putter-out of five for one will bring us
Good warrant of.   (*Gonzalo*)

    You fools! I and my fellows   60
Are ministers of Fate: the elements,
Of whom your swords are temper'd, may as well
Wound the loud winds, or with bemock'd-at stabs
Kill the still-closing waters, as diminish
One dowle that's in my plume.   (*Ariel*)

        O, it is monstrous, monstrous!   III. iii. 95
Methought the billows spoke and told me of it;
The winds did sing it to me, and the thunder,
That deep and dreadful organ-pipe, pronounced
The name of Prosper. (*Alonso*)

             But one fiend at a time,   102
I 'll fight their legions o'er. (*Sebastian*)

Do not smile at me that I boast her off,   IV. i. 9
For thou shalt find she will outstrip all praise
And make it halt behind her. (*Prospero*)

Ceres, most bounteous lady, thy rich leas   60
Of wheat, rye, barley, vetches, oats and pease;
Thy turfy mountains, where live nibbling sheep,
And flat meads thatch'd with stover, them to keep;
Thy banks with pioned and twilled brims,
Which spongy April at thy hest betrims,
To make cold nymphs chaste crowns; and thy broom-
    groves,
Whose shadow the dismissed bachelor loves,
Being lass-lorn; thy pole-clipt vineyard;
And thy sea-marge, sterile and rocky-hard,
Where thou thyself dost air;—the queen o' the sky
Whose watery arch and messenger am I,
Bids thee leave these. (*Iris*)

        Earth's increase, foison plenty,   110
        Barns and garners never empty,
        Vines with clustering bunches growing,
        Plants with goodly burthen bowing;

        Spring come to you at the farthest
        In the very end of harvest!
        Scarcity and want shall shun you;
        Ceres' blessing so is on you. (*Ceres, sings*)

Our revels now are ended. These our actors,   148
As I foretold you, were all spirits and
Are melted into air, into thin air:
And like the baseless fabric of this vision,
The cloud-capp'd towers, the gorgeous palaces,
The solemn temples, the great globe itself,
Yea, all which it inherit, shall dissolve
And, like this insubstantial pageant faded,
Leave not a rack behind. We are such stuff
As dreams are made on, and our little life
Is rounded with a sleep. (*Prospero*)

They were red-hot with drinking;   iv. i. 171
So full of valour that they smote the air
For breathing in their faces; beat the ground
For kissing of their feet. (*Ariel*)

Give me thy hand.   I do begin to have bloody thoughts.   220
(*Stephano*)

We shall lose our time,   248
And all be turn'd to barnacles, or to apes
With foreheads villainous low. (*Caliban*)

Now does my project gather to a head. (*Prospero*)   v. i. 1

The rarer action is   27
In virtue than in vengeance. (*Prospero*)

Ye elves of hills, brooks, standing lakes and groves,   33
And ye that on the sands with printless foot
Do chase the ebbing Neptune and do fly him
When he comes back; you demi-puppets that
By moonshine do the green sour ringlets make,
Whereof the ewe not bites, and you whose pastime
Is to make midnight mushrooms, that rejoice
To hear the solemn curfew; by whose aid,
Weak masters though ye be, I have bedimm'd
The noontide sun, call'd forth the mutinous winds,
And 'twixt the green sea and the azured vault
Set roaring war: to the dread rattling thunder
Have I given fire and rifted Jove's stout oak
With his own bolt; the strong-based promontory
Have I made shake and by the spurs pluck'd up
The pine and cedar: graves at my command
Have waked their sleepers, oped, and let 'em forth
By my so potent art.   But this rough magic
I here abjure, and, when I have required
Some heavenly music, which even now I do,
To work mine end upon their senses that
This airy charm is for, I 'll break my staff,
Bury it certain fathoms in the earth,
And deeper than did ever plummet sound
I 'll drown my book. (*Prospero*)

Where the bee sucks, there suck I: 88
In a cowslip's bell I lie;
There I couch when owls do cry.
On the bat's back I do fly
After summer merrily.
Merrily, merrily shall I live now
Under the blossom that hangs on the bough.
(*Ariel, sings*)

Why, that's my dainty Ariel!   (*Prospero*)   v. i. 95

Yes, for a score of kingdoms you should wrangle,   174
And I would call it fair play.   (*Miranda*)

                                   O wonder!   181
How many goodly creatures are there here!
How beauteous mankind is!   O brave new world,
That has such people in't!   (*Miranda*)

Let us not burden our remembrance with   199
A heaviness that's gone.   (*Prospero*)

                          Look down, you gods,   201
And on this couple drop a blessed crown.   (*Gonzalo*)

   Every man shift for all the rest, and let no man take   256
care for himself.   (*Stephano*)

And Trinculo is reeling ripe: where should they   279
Find this grand liquor that hath gilded 'em?   (*Alonso*)

And thence retire me to my Milan, where   310
Every third thought shall be my grave.   (*Prospero*)

       Now my charms are all o'erthrown,   *Epilogue*, 1
       And what strength I have's mine own,
       Which is most faint.   (*Prospero*)

THE TWO GENTLEMEN OF VERONA

Two friends, Valentine and Proteus, when on a visit from Verona to Milan, both fall in love with the Duke's daughter Silvia, though she is already affianced to Thurio. Proteus's former sweetheart, Julia, follows him disguised as a boy, and takes service with him as a page. Through Proteus's treachery the Duke is induced to banish Valentine, and he becomes captain of a band of brigands, who subsequently capture Silvia. A rescue party, including the Duke, Thurio, Proteus, and Julia, locates her, but Thurio shows such poor spirit that the Duke gives Silvia to Valentine; Proteus discovers Julia's identity and renews his vows to her. The play contains two clowns, Valentine's servant Speed and Proteus's man Launce, whose devotion to his ill-trained dog Crab has become famous. Minor characters are Antonio, Proteus's father, his servant Panthino, and Julia's maid Lucetta.

14

Home-keeping youth have ever homely wits. (*Valentine*)   I. i. 2

I rather would entreat thy company   5
To see the wonders of the world abroad
Than, living daily sluggardized at home,
Wear out thy youth with shapeless idleness. (*Valentine*)

To be in love, where scorn is bought with groans;   29
Coy looks with heart-sore sighs; one fading moment's
  mirth
With twenty watchful, weary, tedious nights:
If haply won, perhaps a hapless gain;
If lost, why then a grievous labour won;
However, but a folly bought with wit,
Or else a wit by folly vanquished. (*Valentine*)

Go, go, be gone, to save your ship from wreck,   157
Which cannot perish having thee aboard,
Being destined to a drier death on shore. (*Proteus*)

I have no other but a woman's reason;   I. ii. 23
I think him so because I think him so. (*Lucetta*)

While other men, of slender reputation,   I. iii. 6
Put forth their sons to seek preferment out:
Some to the wars, to try their fortune there;
Some to discover islands far away;
Some to the studious universities. (*Panthino*)

Experience is by industry achieved   22
And perfected by the swift course of time. (*Antonio*)

O, how this spring of love resembleth   84
  The uncertain glory of an April day,
Which now shows all the beauty of the sun,
  And by and by a cloud takes all away! (*Proteus*)

Valentine. Why, how know you that I am in love?   II. i. 17
Speed. Marry, by these special marks: first, you have
learned, like Sir Proteus, to wreathe your arms, like a
malecontent; to relish a love-song, like a robin-red-
breast; to walk alone, like one that had the pestilence;
to sigh, like a schoolboy that had lost his A B C; to weep,
like a young wench that had buried her grandam; to fast,
like one that takes diet; to watch, like one that fears
robbing; to speak puling, like a beggar at Hallowmas.

Though the chameleon Love can feed on air, I am one   II. i. 178
that am nourished by my victuals and would fain have
meat. (*Speed*)

I think Crab my dog be the sourest-natured dog that   II. iii. 5
lives: my mother weeping, my father wailing, my sister
crying, our maid howling, our cat wringing her hands,
and all our house in a great perplexity, yet did not this
cruel-hearted cur shed one tear. (*Launce*)

A fine volley of words, gentlemen, and quickly shot off.   II. iv. 33
(*Silvia*)

His years but young, but his experience old;   69
His head unmellow'd, but his judgment ripe. (*Valentine*)

Why, man, she is mine own,   168
And I as rich in having such a jewel
As twenty seas, if all their sand were pearl,
The water nectar and the rocks pure gold. (*Valentine*)

Even as one heat another heat expels,   192
Or as one nail by strength drives out another,
So the remembrance of my former love
Is by a newer object quite forgotten. (*Proteus*)

The current that with gentle murmur glides,   II. vii. 25
Thou know'st, being stopp'd, impatiently doth rage;
But when his fair course is not hindered,
He makes sweet music with the enamell'd stones,
Giving a gentle kiss to every sedge
He overtaketh in his pilgrimage,
And so by many winding nooks he strays
With willing sport to the wild ocean. (*Julia*)

Then let her beauty be her wedding-dower. (*Duke*)   III. i. 78

Win her with gifts, if she respect not words: 89
Dumb jewels often in their silent kind
More than quick words do move a woman's mind.
(*Valentine*)

That man that hath a tongue, I say, is no man,   104
If with his tongue he cannot win a woman. (*Valentine*)

What light is light, if Silvia be not seen?   174
What joy is joy, if Silvia be not by?
Unless it be to think that she is by,
And feed upon the shadow of perfection.
Except I be by Silvia in the night,
There is no music in the nightingale;

Unless I look on Silvia in the day,   III. i. 180
There is no day for me to look upon;
She is my essence, and I leave to be,
If I be not by her fair influence
Foster'd, illumined, cherish'd, kept alive.   (*Valentine*)

Time is the nurse and breeder of all good.   (*Proteus*)   243

This weak impress of love is as a figure   III. ii. 6
Trenched in ice, which with an hour's heat
Dissolves to water and doth lose his form.   (*Duke*)

You must lay lime to tangle her desires   68
By wailful sonnets, whose composed rhymes
Should be full-fraught with serviceable vows.   (*Proteus*)

Valentine. My friends,—   IV. i. 7
First Outlaw. That's not so, sir: we are your enemies.
Second Outlaw. Peace! we'll hear him.
Third Outlaw. Ay, by my beard, will we, for he's a proper
man.

To make a virtue of necessity.   (*Second Outlaw*)   62

                              You know that love   IV. ii. 19
Will creep in service where it cannot go.   (*Proteus*)

            Who is Silvia? what is she,   39
                That all our swains commend her?
            Holy, fair and wise is she;
                The heavens such grace did lend her,
            That she might admired be.

            Is she kind as she is fair?
                For beauty lives with kindness.
            Love doth to her eyes repair,
                To help him of his blindness,
            And being help'd, inhabits there.

            Then to Silvia let us sing,
                That Silvia is excelling;
            She excels each mortal thing
                Upon the dull earth dwelling:
            To her let us garlands bring.   (*Song*)

Thou subtle, perjured, false, disloyal man!   95
Think'st thou I am so shallow, so conceitless,
To be seduced by thy flattery,
That hast deceived so many with thy vows?
Return, return, and make thy love amends.
For me, by this pale queen of night I swear,

I am so far from granting thy request   IV. ii. 101
That I despise thee for thy wrongful suit,
And by and by intend to chide myself
Even for this time I spend in talking to thee.   (*Silvia*)

Madam, if your heart be so obdurate,   120
Vouchsafe me yet your picture for my love,
The picture that is hanging in your chamber;
To that I'll speak, to that I'll sigh and weep:
For since the substance of your perfect self
Is else devoted, I am but a shadow;
And to your shadow will I make true love.   (*Proteus*)

                    A heart   IV. iii. 33
As full of sorrows as the sea of sands.   (*Silvia*)

   I have taught him, even as one would say precisely,   IV. iv. 5
'thus I would teach a dog.'   (*Launce*)

She hath been fairer, madam, than she is: 154
When she did think my master loved her well,
She, in my judgment, was as fair as you;
But since she did neglect her looking-glass
And threw her sun-expelling mask away,
The air hath starved the roses in her cheeks
And pinch'd the lily-tincture of her face,
That now she is become as black as I.   (*Julia*)

The sun begins to gild the western sky.   (*Eglamour*)   v. i. 1

How use doth breed a habit in a man!   v. iv. 1
This shadowy desert, unfrequented woods,
I better brook than flourishing peopled towns:
Here can I sit alone, unseen of any,
And to the nightingale's complaining notes
Tune my distresses and record my woes.   (*Valentine*)

It is the lesser blot, modesty finds,   108
Women to change their shapes than men their minds.
                         (*Julia*)

               O heaven! were man   110
But constant, he were perfect.   That one error
Fills him with faults; makes him run through all the sins:
Inconstancy falls off ere it begins.   (*Proteus*)

I hold him but a fool that will endanger   133
His body for a girl that loves him not.   (*Thurio*)

I think the boy hath grace in him; he blushes.   (*Duke*)   165

       Our day of marriage shall be yours;   172
One feast, one house, one mutual happiness.   (*Valentine*)

THE MERRY WIVES OF WINDSOR

Falstaff, with a view to sponging on them, sends love-letters to Mistress Ford and Mistress Page. But the 'merry wives' compare notes, and determine to teach him a lesson for his baseness. At a first assignation, he is nearly caught by Ford, the husband, and escapes in a basket of foul linen, only to be thrown into the river; from a second he escapes in the garb of an old woman but is soundly beaten in this character by Ford; at a third, in Windsor Park, after being chivvied and pinched by a crowd of pretended fairies, he is finally unmasked and ridiculed. An amusing sub-plot is provided in the wooing of Page's daughter Anne by three suitors—Slender, an amorous ninny, Doctor Caius, whose servant is Mistress Quickly, and Fenton, a wild young gentleman. In spite of machinations in Slender's favour by his cousin Justice Shallow and Sir Hugh Evans, a Welsh parson, Fenton wins her love and elopes with her. Falstaff's boon companions Pistol and Bardolph appear in the play, which is said to have been written at the request of Queen Elizabeth, who wanted to see Falstaff in love.

Shallow. I will make a Star-chamber matter of it; if I. i. I.
he were twenty Sir John Falstaffs, he shall not abuse
Robert Shallow, esquire.
Slender. In the county of Gloucester, justice of peace and
'Coram.'
Shallow. Ay, cousin Slender, and 'Custalorum.'
Slender. Ay, and 'Rato-lorum' too.

The dozen white louses do become an old coat well; it 19
agrees well, passant; it is a familiar beast to man, and
signifies love. (*Evans*)

Slender. I know the young gentlewoman; she has good 63
gifts.
Evans. Seven hundred pounds and possibilities is goot
gifts.

I combat challenge of this latten bilbo. 166
Word of denial in thy labras here!
Word of denial: froth and scum, thou liest! (*Pistol*)

For my part, I say the gentleman had drunk himself out 178
of his five sentences. (*Bardolph*)

And being fap, sir, was, as they say, cashiered. 183
                                            (*Bardolph*)

Come, gentlemen, I hope we shall drink down all un- 203
kindness. (*Page*)

I had rather than forty shillings I had my Book of 205
Songs and Sonnets here. (*Slender*)

What says my bully-rook? speak scholarly and wisely. I. iii. 2
                                            (*Host*)

O base Hungarian wight! wilt thou the spigot wield? 23
                                            (*Pistol*)

'Convey' the wise it call. 'Steal!' foh! a fico for the 32
phrase! (*Pistol*)

I ken the wight: he is of substance good. (*Pistol*) 40

Falstaff. My honest lads, I will tell you what I am about. 42
Pistol. Two yards, and more.

Let vultures gripe thy guts! for gourd and fullam holds,   I. iii. 94
And high and low beguiles the rich and poor:
Tester I'll have in pouch when thou shalt lack,
Base Phrygian Turk!   (*Pistol*)

Here will be an old abusing of God's patience and the   I. iv. 5
king's English.   (*Mistress Quickly*)

His worst fault is, that he is given to prayer; he is some-   13
thing peevish that way: but nobody but has his fault.
                                             (*Mistress Quickly*)

I would have sworn his disposition would have gone to   II. i. 60
the truth of his words; but they do no more adhere and
keep place together than the Hundredth Psalm to the
tune of 'Green Sleeves.'   (*Mistress Ford*)

Why then the world's mine oyster,   II. ii. 2
Which I with sword will open.   (*Pistol*)

Thinkest thou I'll endanger my soul gratis?   (*Falstaff*)   16

Marry, this is the short and the long of it.   60
                                             (*Mistress Quickly*)

'Love like a shadow flies when substance love pursues;   216
Pursuing that that flies, and flying what pursues.' (*Ford*)

Keep a gamester from the dice, and a good student   III. i. 37
from his book, and it is wonderful.   (*Shallow*)

I cannot tell what the dickens his name is.   III. ii. 19
                                             (*Mistress Page*)

What say you to young Master Fenton? he capers, he   67
dances, he has eyes of youth, he writes verses, he speaks
holiday, he smells April and May.   (*Host*)

Have I caught thee, my heavenly jewel?   (*Falstaff*)   III. iii. 45

Albeit I will confess thy father's wealth   III. iv. 13
Was the first motive that I woo'd thee, Anne:
Yet, wooing thee, I found thee of more value
Than stamps in gold or sums in sealed bags;
And 'tis the very riches of thyself
That now I aim at.   (*Fenton*)

O, what a world of vile ill-favour'd faults   32
Looks handsome in three hundred pounds a-year!   (*Anne*)

Anne. What is your will?   III. iv. 58
Slender. My will! 'od's heartlings, that's a pretty jest
indeed! I ne'er made my will yet, I thank heaven; I
am not such a sickly creature, I give heaven praise.

If it be my luck, so: if not, happy man be his dole!   67
                                              (*Slender*)

Alas, I had rather be set quick i' the earth   90
And bowl'd to death with turnips! (*Anne*)

    You may know by my size that I have a kind of alacrity   III. v. 12
in sinking; if the bottom were as deep as hell, I should
down. (*Falstaff*)

    Rammed me in with foul shirts and smocks, socks, foul   90
stockings, greasy napkins; that, Master Brook, there was
the rankest compound of villainous smell that ever
offended nostril. (*Falstaff*)

Evans. What is your genitive case plural, William?   IV. i. 59
William. Genitive case!
Evans. Ay.
William. Genitive—horum, harum, horum.
Mistress Quickly. Vengeance of Jenny's case! fie on her!
never name her, child, if she be a whore.

I am glad the fat knight is not here. (*Mistress Page*)   IV. ii. 28

We'll leave a proof, by that which we will do,   104
Wives may be merry, and yet honest too:
We do not act that often jest and laugh;
'Tis old, but true, still swine eats all the draff.
                                          (*Mistress Page*)

Be not as extreme in submission   IV. iv. 11
As in offence. (*Page*)

I was beaten myself into all the colours of the rainbow.   IV. v. 118
                                              (*Falstaff*)

    This is the third time; I hope good luck lies in odd   v. i. 2
numbers. Away! go. They say there is divinity in odd
numbers, either in nativity, chance, or death. (*Falstaff*)

    Since I plucked geese, played truant and whipped top,   26
I knew not what 'twas to be beaten till lately. (*Falstaff*)

    I come to her in white, and cry 'mum'; she cries   v. ii. 6
'budget'; and by that we know one another. (*Slender*)

Let the sky rain potatoes; let it thunder to the tune of   v. v. 20
Green Sleeves, hail kissing-confits and snow eringoes.
> *(Falstaff)*

Fairies, black, grey, green, and white,   41
You moonshine revellers, and shades of night.
> *(Mistress Quickly)*

Elves, list your names; silence, you airy toys,   46
Cricket, to Windsor chimneys shalt thou leap:
Where fires thou find'st unraked and hearths unswept,
There pinch the maids as blue as bilberry:
Our radiant queen hates sluts and sluttery.   *(Pistol)*

Search Windsor Castle, elves, within and out: 60
Strew good luck, ouphes, on every sacred room:
That it may stand till the perpetual doom,
In state as wholesome as in state 'tis fit,
Worthy the owner, and the owner it.
The several chairs of order look you scour
With juice of balm and every precious flower:
Each fair instalment, coat, and several crest,
With loyal blazon, evermore be blest!
And nightly, meadow-fairies, look you sing,
Like to the Garter's compass, in a ring:
The expressure that it bears, green let it be,
More fertile-fresh than all the field to see;
And 'Honi soit qui mal y pense' write
As emerald tufts, flowers purple, blue, and white;
Like sapphire, pearl and rich embroidery,
Buckled below fair knighthood's bending knee:
Fairies use flowers for their charactery.
> *(Mistress Quickly)*

Pinch him, fairies, mutually;   103
Pinch him for his villainy;
Pinch him, and burn him, and turn him about,
Till candles and starlight and moonshine be out.   *(Song)*

I do begin to perceive that I am made an ass.   *(Falstaff)*   124

Good husband, let us every one go home,   255
And laugh this sport o'er by a country fire.
> *(Mistress Page)*

MEASURE FOR MEASURE

The Duke of Vienna, wishing to have the city's laws against unchastity more strictly enforced without being himself taxed with severity, hands over the government to Angelo and pretends to go abroad, but really remains a secret looker-on in the disguise of a friar.   Claudio, convicted of having seduced Juliet, is condemned to death.   When his sister Isabella goes to intercede for him, Angelo offers to remit the penalty if she will become his mistress, but in spite of her brother's unmanly pleading she indignantly refuses.   The disguised Duke, hearing of what has passed, persuades Isabella to pretend assent and then let her place at the assignation be taken by Mariana, Angelo's formerly promised wife.   The scheme is successful, but Angelo breaks his word and gives orders for Claudio's execution, which, however, is prevented by the Duke, who then returns in his own person to demand an account of his deputy.   Isabella tells her story, Angelo's villainy is unmasked, and he does his duty by marrying Mariana, while Claudio marries Juliet and the Duke claims the hand of Isabella.   This is one of the so-called 'dark comedies,' but a certain amount of comic relief is supplied by the disreputable Mistress Overdone, her servant Pompey, and Elbow the constable.   Escalus, an old lord, and Lucio, a garrulous courtier, are contrasting types.

Heaven doth with us as we with torches do,   I. i. 33
Not light them for themselves; for if our virtues
Did not go forth of us, 'twere all alike
As if we had them not.   Spirits are not finely touch'd
But to fine issues, nor Nature never lends
The smallest scruple of her excellence
But, like a thrifty goddess, she determines
Herself the glory of a creditor,
Both thanks and use.   (*Duke*)

                  I love the people,   68
But do not like to stage me in their eyes:
Though it do well, I do not relish well
Their loud applause and Aves vehement;
Nor do I think the man of safe discretion
That does affect it.   (*Duke*)

Three thousand dolours a year.   (*Second Gentleman*)   I. ii. 50

   How now! which of your hips has the most profound   60
sciatica?   (*First Gentleman*)

Mistress Overdone. What's his offence?   90
Pompey. Groping for trouts in a peculiar river.

Thus can the demigod Authority   124
Make us pay down for our offence by weight
The words of heaven.   (*Claudio*)

As surfeit is the father of much fast,   130
So every scope by the immoderate use
Turns to restraint.   Our natures do pursue,
Like rats that ravin down their proper bane,
A thirsty evil; and when we drink we die.   (*Claudio*)

   I had as lief have the foppery of freedom as the morality   136
of imprisonment.   (*Lucio*)

How I have ever loved the life removed   I. iii. 8
And held in idle price to haunt assemblies
Where youth, and cost, and witless bravery keeps.
                      (*Duke*)

A man of stricture and firm abstinence.   (*Duke*)   12

                              Our decrees,   I. iii. 27
Dead to infliction, to themselves are dead;
And liberty plucks justice by the nose;
The baby beats the nurse, and quite athwart
Goes all decorum.   (*Duke*)

I would not—though 'tis my familiar sin   I. iv. 31
With maids to seem the lapwing and to jest,
Tongue far from heart—play with all virgins so:
I hold you as a thing ensky'd and sainted,
By your renouncement an immortal spirit,
And to be talk'd with in sincerity,
As with a saint.   (*Lucio*)

Lucio. Is she your cousin?   46
Isabella. Adoptedly; as school-maids change their names
By vain though apt affection.

                         A man whose blood   57
Is very snow-broth; one who never feels
The wanton stings and motions of the sense,
But doth rebate and blunt his natural edge
With profits of the mind, study and fast.   (*Lucio*)

                         Our doubts are traitors   77
And make us lose the good we oft might win
By fearing to attempt.   (*Lucio*)

                         When maidens sue,   80
Men give like gods; but when they weep and kneel,
All their petitions are as freely theirs
As they themselves would owe them.   (*Lucio*)

I'll see what I can do.   (*Isabella*)   84

We must not make a scarecrow of the law,   II. i. 1
Setting it up to fear the birds of prey,
And let it keep one shape, till custom make it
Their perch and not their terror.   (*Angelo*)

'Tis one thing to be tempted, Escalus,   17
Another thing to fall.   I not deny,
The jury, passing on the prisoner's life,
May in the sworn twelve have a thief or two
Guiltier than him they try.   (*Angelo*)

Some rise by sin, and some by virtue fall.   (*Escalus*)   38

    I do lean upon justice, sir, and do bring in here before   47
your good honour two notorious benefactors.   (*Elbow*)

This will last out a night in Russia,   II. i. 139
When nights are longest there. (*Angelo*)

Mercy is not itself, that oft looks so;   296
Pardon is still the nurse of second woe. (*Escalus*)

Condemn the fault, and not the actor of it?   II. ii. 37
Why, every fault's condemn'd ere it be done:
Mine were the very cipher of a function,
To fine the faults whose fine stands in record,
And let go by the actor. (*Angelo*)

You are too cold; if you should need a pin,   45
You could not with more tame a tongue desire it.
                    (*Lucio*)

No ceremony that to great ones 'longs,   59
Not the king's crown, nor the deputed sword,
The marshal's truncheon, nor the judge's robe,
Become them with one half so good a grace
As mercy does. (*Isabella*)

Why, all the souls that were were forfeit once;   73
And He that might the vantage best have took
Found out the remedy.   How would you be
If He, which is the top of judgment, should
But judge you as you are?   O, think on that;
And mercy then will breathe within your lips,
Like man new made. (*Isabella*)

It is the law, not I, condemn your brother. (*Angelo*)   80

The law hath not been dead, though it hath slept.   90
                    (*Angelo*)

Isabella. Yet show some pity.   99
Angelo. I show it most of all when I do justice;
For then I pity those I do not know,
Which a dismiss'd offence would after gall:
And do him right that, answering one foul wrong,
Lives not to act another.

               O, it is excellent   107
To have a giant's strength; but it is tyrannous
To use it like a giant. (*Isabella*)

                    Man, proud man,   117
Drest in a little brief authority,
Most ignorant of what he's most assured,
His glassy essence, like an angry ape,

Plays such fantastic tricks before high heaven   II. ii. 121
As make the angels weep.   (*Isabella*)

That in the captain's but a choleric word,   130
Which in the soldier is flat blasphemy.   (*Isabella*)

Not with fond shekels of the tested gold,   149
Or stones whose rates are either rich or poor
As fancy values them; but with true prayers
That shall be up at heaven and enter there
Ere sun-rise, prayers from preserved souls,
From fasting maids whose minds are dedicate
To nothing temporal.   (*Isabella*)

                         What, do I love her,   177
That I desire to hear her speak again,
And feast upon her eyes?   What is 't I dream on?
O cunning enemy, that, to catch a saint,
With saints dost bait thy hook!   Most dangerous
Is that temptation that doth goad us on
To sin in loving virtue.   (*Angelo*)

I 'll teach you how you shall arraign your conscience,   II. iii. 21
And try your penitence, if it be sound,
Or hollowly put on.   (*Duke*)

                     It oft falls out,   II. iv. 117
To have what we would have, we speak not what we mean.
                            (*Isabella*)

Women!   Help Heaven! men their creation mar   127
In profiting by them.   Nay, call us ten times frail;
For we are soft as our complexions are,
And credulous to false prints.   (*Isabella*)

Say what you can, my false o'erweighs your true.   170
                            (*Angelo*)

The miserable have no other medicine   III. i. 2
But only hope.   (*Claudio*)

Be absolute for death; either death or life   5
Shall thereby be the sweeter.   Reason thus with life:
If I do lose thee, I do lose a thing
That none but fools would keep: a breath thou art,
Servile to all the skyey influences,
That dost this habitation, where thou keep'st,
Hourly afflict: merely, thou art death's fool;
For him thou labour'st by thy flight to shun
And yet runn'st toward him still.   Thou art not noble;
For all the accommodations that thou bear'st

Are nursed by baseness. Thou 'rt by no means valiant;   III. i. 15
For thou dost fear the soft and tender fork
Of a poor worm. Thy best of rest is sleep,
And that thou oft provokest; yet grossly fear'st
Thy death, which is no more. Thou art not thyself;
For thou exist'st on many a thousand grains
That issue out of dust. Happy thou art not;
For what thou hast not, still thou strivest to get,
And what thou hast, forget'st. Thou art not certain;
For thy complexion shifts to strange effects,
After the moon. If thou art rich, thou 'rt poor;
For, like an ass whose back with ingots bows,
Thou bear'st thy heavy riches but a journey,
And death unloads thee. (*Duke*)

         When thou art old and rich,   36
Thou hast neither heat, affection, limb, nor beauty,
To make thy riches pleasant. (*Duke*)

The sense of death is most in apprehension;   78
And the poor beetle that we tread upon,
In corporal sufferance finds a pang as great
As when a giant dies. (*Isabella*)

           If I must die,   83
I will encounter darkness as a bride,
And hug it in mine arms. (*Claudio*)

Ay, but to die, and go we know not where;   118
To lie in cold obstruction and to rot;
This sensible warm motion to become
A kneaded clod; and the delighted spirit
To bathe in fiery floods, or to reside
In thrilling region of thick-ribbed ice;
To be imprison'd in the viewless winds,
And blown with reckless violence round about
The pendent world; or to be worse than worst
Of those that lawless and incertain thought
Imagine howling: 'tis too horrible!
The weariest and most loathed worldly life
That age, ache, penury and imprisonment
Can lay on nature is a paradise
To what we fear of death. (*Claudio*)

What sin you do to save a brother's life,   134
Nature dispenses with the deed so far
That it becomes a virtue. (*Claudio*)

Virtue is bold, and goodness never fearful. (*Duke*)   215

There, at the moated grange, resides this dejected   III. i 280
Mariana. (*Duke*)

No might nor greatness in mortality   III. ii. 196
Can censure 'scape; back-wounding calumny
The whitest virtue strikes. What king so strong
Can tie the gall up in the slanderous tongue? (*Duke*)

Take, O take those lips away,   IV. i. 1
   That so sweetly were forsworn;
And those eyes, the break of day,
   Lights that do mislead the morn:
But my kisses bring again, bring again;
Seals of love, but seal'd in vain, seal'd in vain. (*Song*)

         Music oft hath such a charm   14
To make bad good, and good provoke to harm. (*Duke*)

A bawd, sir? fie upon him! he will discredit our   IV. ii. 29
mystery. (*Abhorson, the executioner*)

Every true man's apparel fits your thief. (*Abhorson*)   46

Look, here's the warrant, Claudio, for thy death: 66
'Tis now dead midnight, and by eight to-morrow
Thou must be made immortal. (*Provost*)

Look, the unfolding star calls up the shepherd. (*Duke*)   219

Then have we here young Dizy, and young Master   IV. iii. 13
Deep-vow, and Master Copper-spur, and Master Starve-
lackey the rapier and dagger man, and young Drop-heir
that killed lusty Pudding, and Master Forthright the
tilter, and brave Master Shooty the great traveller, and
wild Half-can that stabbed Pots, and, I think, forty more;
all great doers in our trade, and are now 'for the Lord's
sake.' (*Pompey*)

I have been drinking hard all night, and I will have   54
more time to prepare me, or they shall beat my brains out
with billets: I will not consent to die this day, that's
certain. (*Barnardine, a condemned criminal*)

Alack, when once our grace we have forgot,   IV. iv. 36
Nothing goes right: we would, and we would not.
                       (*Angelo*)

O, your desert speaks loud; and I should wrong it,   v. i. 9
To lock it in the wards of covert bosom,
When it deserves, with characters of brass,
A forted residence 'gainst the tooth of time
And razure of oblivion. (*Duke*)

Respect to your great place! and let the devil   v. i. 294
Be sometime honour'd for his burning throne!   (*Duke*)

Hast thou or word or wit, or impudence,   368
That yet can do thee office? (*Duke*)

Haste still pays haste, and leisure answers leisure;   415
Like doth quit like, and MEASURE still FOR MEASURE. (*Duke*)

They say, best men are moulded out of faults: 444
And, for the most, become much more the better,
For being a little bad.   (*Mariana*)

THE COMEDY OF ERRORS

Twin sons of Aegeon and Aemilia, both named Antipholus, have each a servant named Dromio, the Dromios also being twins. Shipwrecked in infancy, the brothers were rescued and brought up separately, one at Syracuse and the other at Ephesus. Aegeon, searching for his son in Ephesus, is arrested as an alien. Antipholus of Syracuse also comes to Ephesus in search of his brother and there follows a series of ludicrous situations due to mistaken identity, culminating in Adriana, wife of the Ephesian Antipholus, laying an information before the duke. The abbess of a convent where Antipholus of Syracuse has taken refuge turns out to be his mother Aemilia. The two brothers confront each other, the confusion is cleared up, and Aegeon is pardoned and the whole family reunited. A minor character is Luciana, Adriana's sister.

The pleasing punishment that women bear.   (*Aegeon*)   I. i. 47

We may pity, though not pardon thee.   (*Duke*)   98

I will go lose myself   I. ii. 30
And wander up and down to view the city.
(Antipholus of Syracuse)

The capon burns, the pig falls from the spit,   44
The clock hath strucken twelve upon the bell;
My mistress made it one upon my cheek:
She is so hot because the meat is cold;
The meat is cold because you come not home;
You come not home because you have no stomach;
You have no stomach having broke your fast;
But we that know what 'tis to fast and pray
Are penitent for your default to-day.
(Dromio of Ephesus)

Methinks your maw, like mine, should be your clock   66
And strike you home without a messenger.
(Dromio of Ephesus)

There's nothing situate under heaven's eye   II. i. 16
But hath his bound, in earth, in sea, in sky:
The beasts, the fishes and the winged fowls
Are their males' subjects and at their controls:
Men, more divine, the masters of all these,
Lords of the wide world and wild watery seas,
Indued with intellectual sense and souls,
Of more pre-eminence than fish and fowls,
Are masters to their females, and their lords:
Then let your will attend on their accords.   (*Luciana*)

A wretched soul, bruised with adversity,   34
We bid be quiet when we hear it cry;
But were we burden'd with like weight of pain,
As much or more we should ourselves complain.
(Adriana)

Am I so round with you as you with me,   82
That like a football you do spurn me thus?
(Dromio of Ephesus)

The time was once when thou unurged wouldst vow   II. ii. 115
That never words were music to thine ear,
That never object pleasing in thine eye,
That never touch well welcome to thy hand,
That never meat sweet-savour'd in thy taste,
Unless I spake, or look'd, or touch'd, or carved to thee.
                                              (*Adriana*)

Thou art an elm, my husband, I a vine,   176
Whose weakness married to thy stronger state
Makes me with thy strength to communicate:
If aught possess thee from me, it is dross,
Usurping ivy, brier, or idle moss;
Who, all for want of pruning, with intrusion
Infect thy sap and live on thy confusion.   (*Adriana*)

My wife is shrewish when I keep not hours.   III. i. 2
                          (*Antipholus of Ephesus*)

Antipholus of Ephesus. But, soft! my door is lock'd.   Go   30
    bid them let us in.
Dromio of Ephesus. Maud, Bridget, Marian, Cicely,
    Gillian, Ginn!
Dromio of Syracuse. [*Within.*] Mome, malt-horse, capon,
    coxcomb, patch!
Either get thee from the door or sit down at the hatch.

If you did wed my sister for her wealth,   III. ii. 5
Then for her wealth's sake use her with more kindness.
                                        (*Luciana*)

Ill deeds are doubled with an evil word.   (*Luciana*)   20

He is deformed, crooked, old and sere,   IV. ii. 19
Ill-faced, worse bodied, shapeless everywhere;
Vicious, ungentle, foolish, blunt, unkind,
Stigmatical in making, worse in mind.   (*Adriana*)

My heart prays for him, though my tongue do curse.   28
                                        (*Adriana*)

                          Hath not else his eye   v. i. 50
Stray'd his affection in unlawful love?
A sin prevailing much in youthful men,
Who give their eyes the liberty of gazing.   (*Abbess*)

In bed he slept not for my urging it;   63
At board he fed not for my urging it;
Alone, it was the subject of my theme;
In company I often glanced it;
Still did I tell him it was vile and bad.   (*Adriana*)

The venom clamours of a jealous woman   v. i. 69
Poisons more deadly than a mad dog's tooth.
It seems his sleeps were hinder'd by thy railing,
And thereof comes it that his head is light.
Thou say'st his meat was sauced with thy upbraidings:
Unquiet meals make ill digestions;
Thereof the raging fire of fever bred;
And what's a fever but a fit of madness?
Thou say'st his sports were hinder'd by thy brawls:
Sweet recreation barr'd, what doth ensue
But moody and dull melancholy,
Kinsman to grim and comfortless despair,
And at her heels a huge infectious troop
Of pale distemperatures and foes to life?
In food, in sport and life-preserving rest
To be disturb'd, would mad or man or beast:
The consequence is then thy jealous fits
Have scared thy husband from the use of wits.

                                        (*Abbess*)

                    Along with them   237
They brought one Pinch, a hungry lean-faced villain,
A mere anatomy, a mountebank,
A threadbare juggler and a fortune-teller,
A needy, hollow-eyed, sharp-looking wretch,
A living-dead man.   (*Antipholus of Ephesus*)

O, grief hath changed me since you saw me last,   297
And careful hours with time's deformed hand
Have written strange defeatures in my face.   (*Aegeon*)

MUCH ADO ABOUT NOTHING

The chief attraction of this play lies in the romance between Benedick, a confirmed bachelor, and Beatrice, a professed man-hater. These two never meet without 'a skirmish of wit,' and their friends conspire to make a match between them by letting each overhear apparently secret conversations in which it is revealed that the other is cherishing a hopeless passion for the hearer. The plot is successful and they are finally betrothed, each still protesting that the step is taken only out of pity for the other. The main plot of the play is a sordid affair. Hero, daughter of Leonato, is engaged to marry Claudio, and Don John, wishing to disgrace her, gets Hero's maid Margaret to dress up as Hero and show herself in a compromising situation. Claudio retaliates for Hero's supposed faithlessness by repudiating her at the marriage ceremony; she faints with the shock and it is given out that she is dead. The conspiracy is revealed when Conrade and Borachio, two of Don John's followers, are overheard discussing it, and the matter is reported to Don Pedro, the Prince, by the constables Dogberry and Verges. Full of remorse, Claudio agrees, by way of amendment, to marry Hero's cousin, but at the ceremony finds that his bride is Hero herself, who was not dead after all. Benedick, Beatrice, and Dogberry are among Shakespeare's greatest creations.

A victory is twice itself when the achiever brings home   I. i. 8
full numbers. (*Leonato*)

He hath indeed better bettered expectation than you   15
must expect of me to tell you how. (*Messenger*)

He is a very valiant trencherman. (*Beatrice*)   51

They never meet but there's a skirmish of wit between   63
them. (*Leonato*)

He wears his faith but as the fashion of his hat. (*Beatrice*)   75

I see, lady, the gentleman is not in your books.   78
(*Messenger*)

Beatrice. I wonder that you will still be talking, Signior   117
Benedick: nobody marks you.
Benedick. What, my dear Lady Disdain! are you yet
living?

I had rather hear my dog bark at a crow than a man   133
swear he loves me. (*Beatrice*)

Shall I never see a bachelor of threescore again?   202
(*Benedick*)

'In time the savage bull doth bear the yoke.'   263
(*Don Pedro*)

Here you may see Benedick the married man.   269
(*Benedick*)

Thou wilt be like a lover presently   308
And tire the hearer with a book of words. (*Don Pedro*)

Thou wilt never get thee a husband, if thou be so   II. i. 19
shrewd of thy tongue. (*Leonato*)

Lord, I could not endure a husband with a beard on his   31
face: I had rather lie in the woollen. (*Beatrice*)

Would it not grieve a woman to be overmastered with a   63
piece of valiant dust? to make an account of her life to a
clod of wayward marl? (*Beatrice*)

Wooing, wedding, and repenting, is as a Scotch jig, a   II. i. 76
measure, and a cinque pace: the first suit is hot and hasty,
like a Scotch jig, and full as fantastical; the wedding,
mannerly-modest, as a measure, full of state and ancientry;
and then comes repentance and, with his bad legs, falls
into the cinque pace faster and faster, till he sink into his
grave. (*Beatrice*)

I have a good eye, uncle; I can see a church by daylight.   86
                                          (*Beatrice*)

Speak low, if you speak love. (*Don Pedro*)   103

I know you by the waggling of your head. (*Ursula*)   119

Friendship is constant in all other things   182
Save in the office and affairs of love:
Therefore all hearts in love use their own tongues;
Let every eye negotiate for itself
And trust no agent. (*Claudio*)

O, she misused me past the endurance of a block! an oak   246
but with one green leaf on it would have answered her.
                                          (*Benedick*)

She speaks poniards, and every word stabs; if her   255
breath were as terrible as her terminations, there were no
living near her; she would infect to the north star.
                                          (*Benedick*)

Will your grace command me any service to the world's   271
end? I will go on the slightest errand now to the Anti-
podes that you can devise to send me on; I will fetch you a
toothpicker now from the furthest inch of Asia, bring you
the length of Prester John's foot, fetch you a hair off the
great Cham's beard, do you any embassage to the Pigmies,
rather than hold three words' conference with this harpy.
                                          (*Benedick*)

Here's a dish I love not: I cannot endure my Lady   283
Tongue. (*Benedick*)

Silence is the perfectest herald of joy: I were but little   316
happy, if I could say how much. (*Claudio*)

Speak, cousin; or, if you cannot, stop his mouth with a   321
kiss. (*Beatrice*)

Don Pedro. Will you have me, lady?   339
Beatrice. No, my lord, unless I might have another for
working-days: your grace is too costly to wear every day.

There was a star danced, and under that I was born. II. i. 349
                               (Beatrice)

I have heard my daughter say she hath often dreamed of 359
unhappiness and waked herself with laughing.
                               (Leonato)

She mocks all her wooers out of suit.   *(Leonato)* 364

Till all graces be in one woman, one woman shall not II. iii. 29
come in my grace.   Rich she shall be, that's certain; wise,
or I'll none; virtuous, or I'll never cheapen her; fair, or
I'll never look on her; mild, or come not near me; noble,
or not I for an angel; of good discourse, an excellent
musician, and her hair shall be of what colour it please
God.   *(Benedick)*

Is it not strange that sheeps' guts should hale souls 61
out of men's bodies?   *(Benedick)*

      Sigh no more, ladies, sigh no more, 64
          Men were deceivers ever,
      One foot in sea and one on shore,
          To one thing constant never:
      Then sigh not so, but let them go,
          And be you blithe and bonny,
      Converting all your sounds of woe
          Into Hey nonny, nonny.

      Sing no more ditties, sing no moe,
          Of dumps so dull and heavy;
      The fraud of men was ever so,
          Since summer first was leavy:
      Then sigh not so, but let them go,
          And be you blithe and bonny,
      Converting all your sounds of woe
          Into Hey nonny, nonny.
                   (Balthasar, sings)

Sits the wind in that corner?   *(Benedick)* 102

In the managing of quarrels you may say he is wise; for 196
either he avoids them with great discretion, or undertakes
them with a most Christian-like fear.   *(Don Pedro)*

I may chance have some odd quirks and remnants of wit 244
broken on me, because I have railed so long against marriage: but doth not the appetite alter? a man loves the meat
in his youth that he cannot endure in his age.   Shall
quips and sentences and these paper bullets of the brain

awe a man from the career of his humour? No, the world   II. iii. 249
must be peopled. When I said I would die a bachelor, I
did not think I should live till I were married.

(*Benedick*)

    By this day! she's a fair lady: I do spy some marks of   253
love in her.   (*Benedick*)

For look where Beatrice, like a lapwing, runs,   III. i. 24
Close by the ground, to hear our conference.   (*Hero*)

The pleasant'st angling is to see the fish   26
Cut with her golden oars the silver stream,
And greedily devour the treacherous bait.   (*Ursula*)

            She is too disdainful;   34
I know her spirits are as coy and wild
As haggards of the rock.   (*Hero*)

Disdain and scorn ride sparkling in her eyes,   51
Misprising what they look on.   (*Hero*)

          It were not good   57
She knew his love, lest she make sport at it.   (*Hero*)

           I never yet saw man,   59
How wise, how noble, young, how rarely featured,
But she would spell him backward: if fair-faced,
She would swear the gentleman should be her sister;
If black, why, Nature, drawing of an antique,
Made a foul blot; if tall, a lance ill-headed;
If low, an agate very vilely cut;
If speaking, why, a vane blown with all winds;
If silent, why, a block moved with none.
So turns she every man the wrong side out
And never gives to truth and virtue that
Which simpleness and merit purchaseth.   (*Hero*)

           If I should speak,   74
She would mock me into air; O, she would laugh me
Out of myself, press me to death with wit.
Therefore let Benedick, like cover'd fire,
Consume away in sighs, waste inwardly:
It were a better death than die with mocks,
Which is as bad as die with tickling.   (*Hero*)

         I'll devise some honest slanders   84
To stain my cousin with: one doth not know
How much an ill word may empoison liking.   (*Hero*)

What fire is in mine ears? Can this be true? iii. i. 107
 Stand I condemn'd for pride and scorn so much!
Contempt, farewell! and maiden pride, adieu!
 No glory lives behind the back of such.
And, Benedick, love on; I will requite thee,
 Taming my wild heart to thy loving hand.
          (Beatrice)

Every one can master a grief but he that has it. iii. ii. 28
          (Benedick)

 If he be not in love with some woman, there is no be- 40
lieving old signs: a' brushes his hat o' mornings; what
should that bode? *(Claudio)*

 The barber's man hath been seen with him, and the old 45
ornament of his cheek hath already stuffed tennis-balls.
          (Claudio)

Leonato's Hero, your Hero, every man's Hero. 109
        (Don John)

Dogberry. Are you good men and true? iii. iii. 1
Verges. Yea, or else it were pity but they should suffer
salvation, body and soul.

 To be a well-favoured man is the gift of fortune; but 14
to write and read comes by nature. *(Dogberry)*

 You are thought here to be the most senseless and fit 22
man for the constable of the watch. *(Dogberry)*

Dogberry. This is your charge: you shall comprehend all 25
vagrom men; you are to bid any man stand, in the
prince's name.
Second Watchman. How if a' will not stand?
Dogberry. Why, then, take no note of him, but let him go;
and presently call the rest of the watch together and
thank God you are rid of a knave.

 You shall also make no noise in the streets; for for the 35
watch to babble and to talk is most tolerable and not to be
endured. *(Dogberry)*

Dogberry. If you meet a thief, you may suspect him, by 53
virtue of your office, to be no true man; and, for such
kind of men, the less you meddle or make with them,
why, the more is for your honesty.
Watchman. If we know him to be a thief, shall we not lay
hands on him?

Dogberry. Truly, by your office, you may; but I think they   III. iii. 59
that touch pitch will be defiled: the most peaceable way
for you, if you do take a thief, is to let him show himself
what he is and steal out of your company.

Borachio. Seest thou not what a deformed thief this   131
fashion is?
Watchman. [*Aside.*] I know that Deformed; a' has been a
vile thief this seven year; a' goes up and down like a
gentleman: I remember his name.

Margaret. I saw the Duchess of Milan's gown that they   III. iv. 15
praise so.
Hero. O, that exceeds, they say.
Margaret. By my troth, 's but a night-gown in respect of
yours: cloth o' gold, and cuts, and laced with silver, set
with pearls, down sleeves, side sleeves, and skirts, round
underborne with a bluish tinsel: but for a fine, quaint,
graceful and excellent fashion, yours is worth ten on 't.

Methinks you look with your eyes as other women do.   91
                                     (*Margaret*)

    I would have some confidence with you that decerns   III. v. 3
you nearly.   (*Dogberry*)

Dogberry. Goodman Verges, sir, speaks a little off the   10
matter: an old man, sir, and his wits are not so blunt as,
God help, I would desire they were; but, in faith, honest
as the skin between his brows.
Verges. Yes, I thank God I am as honest as any man living
that is an old man and no honester than I.

Comparisons are odorous.   (*Dogberry*)   18

Leonato. Neighbours, you are tedious.   20
Dogberry. It pleases your worship to say so, but we are the
poor duke's officers; but truly, for mine own part, if I
were as tedious as a king, I could find it in my heart to
bestow it all of your worship.

    A good old man, sir; he will be talking: as they say,   37
When the age is in, the wit is out.   (*Dogberry*)

    Our watch, sir, have indeed comprehended two as-   50
picious persons.   (*Dogberry*)

    O, what men dare do! what men may do! what men   IV. i. 19
daily do, not knowing what they do!   (*Claudio*)

There, Leonato, take her back again: IV. i. 32
Give not this rotten orange to your friend:
She's but the sign and semblance of her honour.
                                        (Claudio)

I never tempted her with word too large: 53
But, as a brother to his sister, show'd
Bashful sincerity and comely love.   (Claudio)

O, God defend me! how am I beset!   78
What kind of catechising call you this?   (Hero)

But fare thee well, most foul, most fair, farewell,   104
Thou pure impiety and impious purity!
For thee I'll lock up all the gates of love,
And on my eyelids shall conjecture hang,
To turn all beauty into thoughts of harm,
And never shall it more be gracious.   (Claudio)

Why ever wast thou lovely in my eyes?   (Leonato)   132

                    Why, she, O she is fallen   141
Into a pit of ink, that the wide sea
Hath drops too few to wash her clean again
And salt too little which may season give
To her foul-tainted flesh!   (Leonato)

                    I have mark'd   160
A thousand blushing apparitions
To start into her face, a thousand innocent shames
In angel whiteness beat away those blushes.   (Friar)

Maintain a mourning ostentation,   207
And on your family's old monument
Hang mournful epitaphs and do all rites
That appertain unto a burial.   (Friar)

                    It so falls out   219
That what we have we prize not to the worth
Whiles we enjoy it, but being lack'd and lost,
Why, then we rack the value, then we find
The virtue that possession would not show us
Whiles it was ours.   (Friar)

The idea of her life shall sweetly creep   226
Into his study of imagination,
And every lovely organ of her life
Shall come apparell'd in more precious habit,
More moving-delicate and full of life,
Into the eye and prospect of his soul,
Than when she lived indeed.   (Friar)

Benedick. Come, bid me do any thing for thee.   IV. i. 290
Beatrice. Kill Claudio.

O that I were a man!   (*Beatrice*)   304

O that I were a man for his sake! or that I had any   319
friend would be a man for my sake! But manhood is
melted into courtesies, valour into compliment, and men
are only turned into tongue, and trim ones too: he is now
as valiant as Hercules that only tells a lie and swears it.

                                        (*Beatrice*)

Write down, that they hope they serve God: and write   IV. ii. 20
God first; for God defend but God should go before such
villains! Masters, it is proved already that you are little
better than false knaves; and it will go near to be thought
so shortly. (*Dogberry*)

Flat burglary as ever was committed.   (*Dogberry*)   52

O villain! thou wilt be condemned into everlasting   58
redemption for this.   (*Dogberry*)

Conrade. Away! you are an ass, you are an ass.   75
Dogberry. Dost thou not suspect my place? dost thou not
suspect my years? O that he were here to write me
down an ass! But, masters, remember that I am an
ass; though it be not written down, yet forget not that I
am an ass. No, thou villain, thou art full of piety, as
shall be proved upon thee by good witness. I am a wise
fellow, and, which is more, an officer, and, which is
more, a householder, and, which is more, as pretty a
piece of flesh as any is in Messina, and one that knows
the law, go to; and a rich fellow enough, go to; and a
fellow that hath had losses, and one that hath two gowns
and every thing handsome about him. Bring him away.
O that I had been writ down an ass!

Antonio. If you go on thus you will kill yourself;   v. i. 1
And 'tis not wisdom thus to second grief
Against yourself.
Leonato.   I pray thee, cease thy counsel,
Which falls into mine ears as profitless
As water in a sieve: give not me counsel;
Nor let no comforter delight mine ear
But such a one whose wrongs do suit with mine.

Patch grief with proverbs.   (*Leonato*)   17

                                    Men
Can counsel and speak comfort to that grief
Which they themselves not feel; but, tasting it,
Their counsel turns to passion, which before
Would give preceptial medicine to rage,
Fetter strong madness in a silken thread,
Charm ache with air and agony with words:
No, no; 'tis all men's office to speak patience
To those that wring under the load of sorrow,
But no man's virtue nor sufficiency
To be so moral when he shall endure
The like himself.   (*Leonato*)

For there was never yet philosopher   35
That could endure the toothache patiently,
However they have writ the style of gods
And made a push at chance and sufferance.   (*Leonato*)

Tush, tush, man; never fleer and jest at me: 58
I speak not like a dotard nor a fool,
As under privilege of age to brag
What I have done being young, or what would do
Were I not old.   (*Leonato*)

I'll prove it on his body, if he dare,   74
Despite his nice fence and his active practice,
His May of youth and bloom of lustihood.   (*Leonato*)

Win me and wear me.   (*Antonio*)   82

Boys, apes, braggarts, Jacks, milksops!   (*Antonio*)   91

Scambling, out-facing, fashion-monging boys,   94
That lie and cog and flout, deprave and slander,
Go anticly, show outward hideousness,
And speak off half a dozen dangerous words,
How they might hurt their enemies, if they durst;
And this is all.   (*Antonio*)

You are almost come to part almost a fray.   (*Don Pedro*)   113

     What though care killed a cat, thou hast mettle enough   132
in thee to kill care.   (*Claudio*)

Don Pedro. Officers, what offence have these men done?   223
Dogberry. Marry, sir, they have committed false report:
moreover, they have spoken untruths; secondarily, they
are slanders; sixth and lastly, they have belied a lady;
thirdly, they have verified unjust things; and, to con-
clude, they are lying knaves.

Runs not this speech like iron through your blood?   v. i. 252
                               (*Don Pedro*)

He is composed and framed of treachery.   (*Don Pedro*)   257

Which is the villain? let me see his eyes,   269
That, when I note another man like him,
I may avoid him.   (*Leonato*)

    I can find out no rhyme to 'lady' but 'baby,' an inno-   v. ii. 36
cent rhyme; for 'scorn,' 'horn,' a hard rhyme; for
'school,' 'fool,' a babbling rhyme; very ominous endings.
                                    (*Benedick*)

    I pray thee now, tell me for which of my bad parts didst   60
thou first fall in love with me?   (*Benedick*)

    For which of my good parts did you first suffer love for   65
me?   (*Beatrice*)

Thou and I are too wise to woo peacefully.   (*Benedick*)   73

    Done to death by slanderous tongues   v. iii. 3
        Was the Hero that here lies:
    Death, in guerdon of her wrongs,
        Gives her fame which never dies.
    So the life that died with shame
    Lives in death with glorious fame.
                     (*Claudio, reads*)

    Pardon, goddess of the night,   12
    Those that slew thy virgin knight;
    For the which, with songs of woe,
    Round about her tomb they go.
        Midnight, assist our moan;
        Help us to sigh and groan,
            Heavily, heavily:
    Graves, yawn and yield your dead,
    Till death be uttered,
        Heavily, heavily.   (*Song*)

                  Look, the gentle day,   25
Before the wheels of Phoebus, round about
  Dapples the drowsy east with spots of grey.
                      (*Don Pedro*)

But, for my will, my will is your good will   v. iv. 28
May stand with ours, this day to be conjoin'd
In the state of honourable marriage.   (*Benedick*)

46

Why, what's the matter,   v. iv. 40
That you have such a February face,
So full of frost, of storm and cloudiness?

(*Don Pedro*)

Benedick. Do you not love me?   74
Beatrice. Why, no; no more than reason.

Benedick. Come, I will have thee; but, by this light, I take   92
thee for pity.
Beatrice. I would not deny you; but, by this good day, I
yield upon great persuasion; and partly to save your life,
for I was told you were in a consumption.
Benedick. Peace! I will stop your mouth.   [*Kissing her.*]
Don Pedro. How dost thou, Benedick, the married man?

LOVE'S LABOUR'S LOST

Ferdinand, King of Navarre, and his attendant lords, Biron, Longaville, and Dumain, have made a vow to live an ascetic life of study for three years, forswearing all women's society. But they have overlooked the visit, already arranged, of the Princess of France, with her train consisting of the ladies Rosaline, Maria, and Katharine, and the lords Boyet and Mercade. While the visitors are accommodated in the royal park, the king and his lords fall in love severally with the princess and her ladies, a great contest of wit and badinage ensuing while they more or less reluctantly break their vows of asceticism. A burlesque of affected culture is provided in Don Adriano de Armado, who courts the country maid Jaquenetta with most flowery speeches; his pert page Moth and the clown Costard supply comic relief; while the talk of Holofernes, the schoolmaster, with Sir Nathaniel, the curate, and the constable Dull ridicules the scholastic pedantry of the time. This is one of the gayest and most light-hearted of the plays, and has many passages of exquisite poetry.

Let fame, that all hunt after in their lives,   I. i. 1
Live register'd upon our brazen tombs
And then grace us in the disgrace of death;
When, spite of cormorant devouring Time,
The endeavour of this present breath may buy
That honour which shall bate his scythe's keen edge
And make us heirs of all eternity.
Therefore, brave conquerors,—for so you are,
That war against your own affections
And the huge army of the world's desires,—
Our late edict shall strongly stand in force:
Navarre shall be the wonder of the world;
Our court shall be a little Academe,
Still and contemplative in living art.   (*King*)

The mind shall banquet, though the body pine: 25
Fat paunches have lean pates, and dainty bits
Make rich the ribs, but bankrupt quite the wits.
                                   (*Longaville*)

The grosser manner of these world's delights   29
He throws upon the gross world's baser slaves:
To love, to wealth, to pomp, I pine and die;
With all these living in philosophy.   (*Dumain*)

Biron. What is the end of study? let me know.   55
King. Why, that to know, which else we should not know.
Biron. Things hid and barr'd, you mean, from common
    sense?
King. Ay, that is study's god-like recompense.
Biron. Come on, then; I will swear to study so,
To know the thing I am forbid to know:
As thus,—to study where I well may dine,
   When I to feast expressly am forbid;
Or study where to meet some mistress fine,
   When mistresses from common sense are hid;
Or, having sworn too hard a keeping oath,
Study to break it and not break my troth.

King. These be the stops that hinder study quite   70
And train our intellects to vain delight.
Biron. Why, all delights are vain; but that most vain,
Which with pain purchased doth inherit pain:
As, painfully to pore upon a book

c   49

To seek the light of truth; while truth the while
Doth falsely blind the eyesight of his look:
  Light seeking light doth light of light beguile:
So, ere you find where light in darkness lies,
Your light grows dark by losing of your eyes.
Study me how to please the eye indeed
  By fixing it upon a fairer eye,
Who dazzling so, that eye shall be his heed
  And give him light that it was blinded by.
Study is like the heaven's glorious sun
  That will not be deep-search'd with saucy looks:
Small have continual plodders ever won
  Save base authority from other's books.
These earthly godfathers of heaven's lights
  That give a name to every fixed star
Have no more profit of their shining nights
  Than those that walk and wot not what they are.
Too much to know is to know nought but fame;
And every godfather can give a name.

King. How well he's read, to reason against reading!   94
Dumain. Proceeded well, to stop all good proceeding!
Longaville. He weeds the corn and still lets grow the
    weeding.
Biron. The spring is near when green geese are a-
    breeding.

King. Biron is like an envious sneaping frost   100
  That bites the first-born infants of the spring.
Biron. Well, say I am; why should proud summer boast
  Before the birds have any cause to sing?
Why should I joy in any abortive birth?
At Christmas I no more desire a rose
Than wish a snow in May's new-fangled shows:
But like of each thing that in season grows.
So you, to study now it is too late,
Climb o'er the house to unlock the little gate.

A maid of grace and complete majesty.   (*Biron*)   137

If I break faith, this word shall speak for me;   154
I am forsworn on 'mere necessity.'   (*Biron*)

A man of fire-new words, fashion's own knight.   179
                           (*Biron*)

  'So it is, besieged with sable-coloured melancholy, I   233
did commend the black-oppressing humour to the most
wholesome physic of thy health-giving air; and, as I am
a gentleman, betook myself to walk. The time when?

About the sixth hour; when beasts most graze, birds best   I. i. 237
peck, and men sit down to that nourishment which is
called supper; so much for the time when.'
(King, reading Armado's letter)

King. [*Reads.*] 'But to the place where; it standeth north-   246
north-east and by east from the west corner of thy
curious-knotted garden: there did I see that low-spirited
swain, that base minnow of thy mirth,'—
Costard. Me?
King. [*Reads.*] 'that unlettered small-knowing soul,'—
Costard. Me?
King. [*Reads.*] 'that shallow vassal,'—
Costard. Still me?
King. [*Reads.*] 'which, as I remember, hight Costard,'—
Costard. O, me!

King. Sir, I will pronounce your sentence: you shall fast   302
a week with bran and water.
Costard. I had rather pray a month with mutton and
porridge.

Armado. How canst thou part sadness and melancholy,   I. ii. 7
my tender juvenal?
Moth. By a familiar demonstration of working, my tough
senior.

Moth. How many is one thrice told?   41
Armado. I am ill at reckoning; it fitteth the spirit of a
tapster.

Moth. You know how much the gross sum of deuce-ace   48
amounts to.
Armado. It doth amount to one more than two.
Moth. Which the base vulgar call three.
Armado. True.

Moth. My father's wit and my mother's tongue, assist me.   101
Armado. Sweet invocation of a child; most pretty and
pathetical.
Moth.   If she be made of white and red,
     Her faults will ne'er be known,
   For blushing cheeks by faults are bred
     And fears by pale white shown:
   Then if she fear, or be to blame,
     By this you shall not know,
   For still her cheeks possess the same
     Which native she doth owe.
   A dangerous rhyme, master, against the reason of white
and red.

Armado. Is there not a ballad, boy, of the King and the   i. ii. 114
Beggar?
Moth. The world was very guilty of such a ballad some
three ages since: but I think now 'tis not to be found;
or, if it were, it would neither serve for the writing nor
the tune.

Armado. Maid!   138
Jaquenetta. Man!
Armado. I will visit thee at the lodge.
Jaquenetta. That's hereby.
Armado. I know where it is situate.
Jaquenetta. Lord, how wise you are!
Armado. I will tell thee wonders.
Jaquenetta. With that face?
Armado. I love thee.
Jaquenetta. So I heard you say.
Armado. And so, farewell.
Jaquenetta. Fair weather after you!

I do affect the very ground, which is base, where her   172
shoe, which is baser, guided by her foot, which is basest,
doth tread. (*Armado*)

Assist me, some extemporal god of rhyme, for I am sure   189
I shall turn sonnet. Devise, wit; write, pen; for I am for
whole volumes in folio. (*Armado*)

Boyet. Be now as prodigal of all dear grace   II. i. 9
As Nature was in making graces dear
When she did starve the general world beside
And prodigally gave them all to you.
Princess. Good Lord Boyet, my beauty, though but mean,
Needs not the painted flourish of your praise:
Beauty is bought by judgment of the eye,
Not utter'd by base sale of chapmen's tongues.

A man of sovereign parts he is esteem'd;   44
Well fitted in arts, glorious in arms:
Nothing becomes him ill that he would well. (*Maria*)

For he hath wit to make an ill shape good,   59
And shape to win grace though he had no wit.
                                        (*Katharine*)

Biron they call him; but a merrier man,   66
Within the limit of becoming mirth,
I never spent an hour's talk withal:
His eye begets occasion for his wit;
For every object that the one doth catch

The other turns to a mirth-moving jest,   II. i. 71
Which his fair tongue, conceit's expositor,
Delivers in such apt and gracious words
That aged ears play truant at his tales
And younger hearings are quite ravished;
So sweet and voluble is his discourse.   (*Rosaline*)

Your wit's too hot, it speeds too fast, 'twill tire.   (*Biron*)   120

Maria. That last is Biron, the merry mad-cap lord: 215
Not a word with him but a jest.
Boyet. And every jest but a word.

My lips are no common, though several they be.   (*Maria*)   223

With your hat penthouse-like o'er the shop of your   III. i. 17
eyes; with your arms crossed on your thin-belly doublet
like a rabbit on a spit; or your hands in your pocket like
a man after the old painting.   (*Moth*)

Armado. How hast thou purchased this experience?   27
Moth. By my penny of observation.

Moth. I will add the l'envoy.   Say the moral again.   89
Armado.   The fox, the ape, and the humble-bee,
       Were still at odds, being but three.
Moth.   Until the goose came out of door,
       And stay'd the odds by adding four.

Now will I look at his remuneration.   Remuneration!   135
O, that's the Latin word for three farthings: three far-
things—remuneration.—'What's the price of this inkle?'
—'One penny.'—'No, I'll give you a remuneration': why,
it carries it.   Remuneration! why, it is a fairer name than
French crown.   I will never buy and sell out of the word.
                              (*Costard*)

Biron. There's thy guerdon; go.   170
                 [*Giving him a shilling.*]
Costard. Gardon, O sweet gardon! better than remunera-
tion, a 'leven-pence farthing better: most sweet gardon!
I will do it, sir, in print.   Gardon!   Remuneration!

And I, forsooth, in love!   I, that have been love's whip;   176
A very beadle to a humorous sigh:
A critic, nay, a night-watch constable;
A domineering pedant o'er the boy;
Than whom no mortal so magnificent!
This wimpled, whining, purblind, wayward boy;
This senior-junior, giant-dwarf, Dan Cupid;

Regent of love-rhymes, lord of folded arms,   III. i. 183
The anointed sovereign of sighs and groans,
Liege of all loiterers and malcontents. (*Biron*)

What, I! I love! I sue! I seek a wife!   191
A woman, that is like a German clock,
Still a-repairing, ever out of frame,
And never going aright, being a watch,
But being watch'd that it may still go right!
Nay, to be perjured, which is worst of all;
And, among three, to love the worst of all;
A wightly wanton with a velvet brow,
With two pitch-balls stuck in her face for eyes. (*Biron*)

                         Go to; it is a plague   203
That Cupid will impose for my neglect
Of his almighty dreadful little might.
Well, I will love, write, sigh, pray, sue and groan:
Some men must love my lady and some Joan. (*Biron*)

And out of question so it is sometimes,   IV. i. 30
Glory grows guilty of detested crimes.
When, for fame's sake, for praise, an outward part,
We bend to that the working of the heart. (*Princess*)

    'Shall I command thy love? I may: shall I enforce   81
thy love? I could: shall I entreat thy love? I will.
What shalt thou exchange for rags? robes; for tittles?
titles; for thyself? me. Thus, expecting thy reply, I
profane my lips on thy foot, my eyes on thy picture, and
my heart on thy every part. Thine, in the dearest design
of industry,
                    DON ADRIANO DE ARMADO.'
Thus dost thou hear the Nemean lion roar
    'Gainst thee, thou lamb, that standest as his prey.
Submissive fall his princely feet before,
    And he from forage will incline to play:
But if thou strive, poor soul, what art thou then?
Food for his rage, repasture for his den. (*Boyet*)

    The deer was, as you know, sanguis, in blood; ripe as   IV. ii. 3
the pomewater, who now hangeth like a jewel in the ear
of caelo, the sky, the welkin, the heaven; and anon falleth
like a crab on the face of terra, the soil, the land, the
earth. (*Holofernes*)

Sir Nathaniel. I assure ye, it was a buck of the first head.   9
Holofernes. Sir Nathaniel, haud credo.
Dull. 'Twas not a haud credo; 'twas a pricket.

Holofernes. Twice-sod simplicity, bis coctus!   IV. ii. 23
O thou monster Ignorance, how deformed dost thou look!
Sir Nathaniel. Sir, he hath never fed of the dainties that
are bred in a book; he hath not eat paper, as it were; he
hath not drunk ink; his intellect is not replenished; he is
only an animal, only sensible in the duller parts.

Many can brook the weather that love not the wind.   34
                              (*Sir Nathaniel*)

Dull. You two are book-men: can you tell me by your wit   35
What was a month old at Cain's birth, that's not five
weeks old as yet?
Holofernes. Dictynna, goodman Dull; Dictynna, good-
man Dull.
Dull. What is Dictynna?
Sir Nathaniel. A title to Phoebe, to Luna, to the moon.

I will something affect the letter, for it argues facility.   56
The preyful princess pierced and prick'd a pretty pleasing
    pricket. (*Holofernes*)

Fauste, precor gelida quando pecus omne sub umbra   95
Ruminat,—and so forth.   Ah, good old Mantuan!   I may
speak of thee as the traveller doth of Venice;
            Venetia, Venetia,
            Chi non ti vede non ti pretia.
Old Mantuan, old Mantuan! who understandeth thee not,
loves thee not.   (*Holofernes*)

Let me hear a staff, a stanze, a verse.   (*Holofernes*)   108

You find not the apostrophas, and so miss the accent: 123
let me supervise the canzonet.   Here are only numbers
ratified; but, for the elegancy, facility, and golden cadence
of poesy, caret. (*Holofernes*)

By heaven, I do love: and it hath taught me to rhyme   IV. iii. 13
and to be melancholy. (*Biron*)

So sweet a kiss the golden sun gives not   26
    To those fresh morning drops upon the rose,
As thy eye-beams, when their fresh rays have smote
    The night of dew that on my cheeks down flows.
                              (*King, reads*)

King. In love, I hope; sweet fellowship in shame.   49
Biron. One drunkard loves another of the name.

The heavenly rhetoric of thine eye.   (*Longaville, reads*)   IV. iii. 60

        What fool is not so wise   72
To lose an oath to win a paradise?   (*Longaville, reads*)

        On a day—alack the day!—   101
        Love, whose month is ever May,
        Spied a blossom passing fair
        Playing in the wanton air:
        Through the velvet leaves the wind,
        All unseen, can passage find;
        That the lover, sick to death,
        Wish himself the heaven's breath.
        Air, quoth he, thy cheeks may blow;
        Air, would I might triumph so!
        But, alack, my hand is sworn
        Ne'er to pluck thee from thy thorn;
        Vow, alack, for youth unmeet,
        Youth so apt to pluck a sweet!
        Do not call it sin in me,
        That I am forsworn for thee;
        Thou for whom Jove would swear
        Juno but an Ethiope were;
        And deny himself for Jove,
        Turning mortal for thy love.

                    (*Dumain, reads*)

Now step I forth to whip hypocrisy.   (*Biron*)   151

O me, with what strict patience have I sat,   165
To see a king transformed to a gnat!
To see great Hercules whipping a gig,
And profound Solomon to tune a jig,
And Nestor play at push-pin with the boys,
And critic Timon laugh at idle toys!   (*Biron*)

The sea will ebb and flow, heaven show his face;   216
  Young blood doth not obey an old decree.   (*Biron*)

A wither'd hermit, five-score winters worn,   242
  Might shake off fifty, looking in her eye:
Beauty doth varnish age, as if new-born,
  And gives the crutch the cradle's infancy.   (*Biron*)

Biron. No face is fair that is not full so black.   253
King. O paradox!   Black is the badge of hell,
The hue of dungeons and the suit of night.

Dumain. To look like her are chimney-sweepers black.   266
Longaville. And since her time are colliers counted bright.

King. And Ethiopes of their sweet complexion crack.   IV. iii. 268
Dumain. Dark needs no candles now, for dark is light.

Your mistresses dare never come in rain,   270
For fear their colours should be wash'd away.   (*Biron*)

Some tricks, some quillets, how to cheat the devil.   288
                           (*Longaville*)

But love, first learned in a lady's eyes,   327
Lives not alone immured in the brain;
But, with the motion of all elements,
Courses as swift as thought in every power,
And gives to every power a double power,
Above their functions and their offices.
It adds a precious seeing to the eye;
A lover's eyes will gaze an eagle blind;
A lover's ear will hear the lowest sound,
When the suspicious head of theft is stopp'd:
Love's feeling is more soft and sensible
Than are the tender horns of cockled snails;
Love's tongue proves dainty Bacchus gross in taste:
For valour, is not Love a Hercules,
Still climbing trees in the Hesperides?
Subtle as Sphinx; as sweet and musical
As bright Apollo's lute, strung with his hair;
And when Love speaks, the voice of all the gods
Make heaven drowsy with the harmony.
Never durst poet touch a pen to write
Until his ink were temper'd with Love's sighs;
O, then his lines would ravish savage ears
And plant in tyrants mild humility.
From women's eyes this doctrine I derive:
They sparkle still the right Promethean fire;
They are the books, the arts, the academes,
That show, contain and nourish all the world:
Else none at all in aught proves excellent.   (*Biron*)

For revels, dances, masks and merry hours   379
Forerun fair Love, strewing her way with flowers.
                           (*Biron*)

Your reasons at dinner have been sharp and sententious: v. i. 2
pleasant without scurrility, witty without affection, audacious without impudency, learned without opinion, and
strange without heresy.   (*Sir Nathaniel*)

Holofernes. His humour is lofty, his discourse peremp-   10
tory, his tongue filed, his eye ambitious, his gait majestical,
and his general behaviour vain, ridiculous, and thrasoni-
cal. He is too picked, too spruce, too affected, too odd,

as it were, too peregrinate, as I may call it.   v. i. 14
Sir Nathaniel. A most singular and choice epithet.
Holofernes. He draweth out the thread of his verbosity
finer than the staple of his argument.

Sir Nathaniel. Laus Deo, bene intelligo.   30
Holofernes. Bon, bon, fort bon! Priscian a little
scratched, 'twill serve.

Moth. They have been at a great feast of languages, and   38
stolen the scraps.
Costard. O, they have lived long on the alms-basket of
words. I marvel thy master hath not eaten thee for a
word; for thou art not so long by the head as honorifi-
cabilitudinitatibus.

Now, by the salt wave of the Mediterraneum, a sweet   61
touch, a quick venue of wit! snip, snap, quick and home!
it rejoiceth my intellect: true wit!   (*Armado*)

Thou disputest like an infant: go, whip thy gig.   69
                                              (*Holofernes*)

An I had but one penny in the world, thou shouldst   74
have it to buy gingerbread: hold, there is the very remuneration I had of thy master, thou halfpenny purse of
wit, thou pigeon-egg of discretion.   (*Costard*)

Armado. Do you not educate youth at the charge-house on   85
the top of the mountain?
Holofernes. Or mons, the hill.

The posteriors of this day, which the rude multitude   94
call the afternoon.   (*Armado*)

It will please his grace, by the world, sometime to lean   107
upon my poor shoulder, and with his royal finger, thus,
dally with my excrement, my mustachio; but, sweet heart,
let that pass.   (*Armado*)

Holofernes. Via, goodman Dull! thou hast spoken no word   156
all this while.
Dull. Nor understood none neither, sir.

He made her melancholy, sad, and heavy;   v. ii. 14
And so she died: had she been light, like you,
Of such a merry, nimble, stirring spirit,
She might ha' been a grandam ere she died:
And so may you; for a light heart lives long.
                                              (*Katharine*)

Well bandied both; a set of wit well play'd. (*Princess*)   v. ii. 29

Fair as a text B in a copy-book. (*Katharine*)   42

This and those pearls to me sent Longaville;   53
The letter is too long by half a mile. (*Maria*)

Princess. We are wise girls to mock our lovers so.   58
Rosaline. They are worse fools to purchase mocking so.

How I would make him fawn and beg and seek   62
And wait the season and observe the times
And spend his prodigal wits in bootless rhymes
And shape his service wholly to my hests
And make him proud to make me proud that jests!
                                              (*Rosaline*)

The blood of youth burns not with such excess   73
As gravity's revolt to wantonness. (*Rosaline*)

Folly in fools bears not so strong a note   75
As foolery in the wise, when wit doth dote. (*Maria*)

They do it but in mocking merriment;   139
And mock for mock is only my intent. (*Princess*)

There's no such sport as sport by sport o'erthrown.   153
                                              (*Princess*)

Biron. White-handed mistress, one sweet word with thee.   230
Princess. Honey, and milk, and sugar; there is three.

The tongues of mocking wenches are as keen   256
   As is the razor's edge invisible,
Cutting a smaller hair than may be seen,
   Above the sense of sense; so sensible
Seemeth their conference; their conceits have wings
Fleeter than arrows, bullets, wind, thought, swifter
   things. (*Boyet*)

Farewell, mad wenches; you have simple wits. (*King*)   264

This fellow pecks up wit as pigeons pease,   315
And utters it again when God doth please:
He is wit's pedler, and retails his wares
At wakes and wassails, meetings, markets, fairs;
And we that sell by gross, the Lord doth know,
Have not the grace to grace it with such show.
This gallant pins the wenches on his sleeve;
Had he been Adam, he had tempted Eve;

A' can carve too, and lisp: why, this is he   v. ii. 323
That kiss'd his hand away in courtesy;
This is the ape of form, monsieur the nice,
That, when he played at tables, chides the dice
In honourable terms: nay, he can sing
A mean most meanly; and in ushering
Mend him who can: the ladies call him sweet;
The stairs, as he treads on them, kiss his feet:
This is the flower that smiles on every one,
To show his teeth as white as whale's bone;
And consciences, that will not die in debt,
Pay him the due of honey-tongued Boyet.   (*Biron*)

Trim gallants, full of courtship and of state.   (*Princess*)   363

I dare not call them fools; but this I think,   371
When they are thirsty, fools would fain have drink.
                                        (*Rosaline*)

It were a fault to snatch words from my tongue.   382
                                        (*Rosaline*)

    Can any face of brass hold longer out?   395
Here stand I; lady, dart thy skill at me;
    Bruise me with scorn, confound me with a flout;
Thrust thy sharp wit quite through my ignorance;
    Cut me to pieces with thy keen conceit.   (*Biron*)

O, never will I trust to speeches penn'd,   402
    Nor to the motion of a schoolboy's tongue,
Nor never come in vizard to my friend,
    Nor woo in rhyme, like a blind harper's song!
Taffeta phrases, silken terms precise,
    Three-piled hyperboles, spruce affectation,
Figures pedantical; these summer-flies
    Have blown me full of maggot ostentation:
I do forswear them; and I here protest,
    By this white glove,—how white the hand, God
        knows!—
Henceforth my wooing mind shall be express'd
    In russet yeas and honest kersey noes.   (*Biron*)

Some carry-tale, some please-man, some slight zany,   463
Some mumble-news, some trencher-knight, some Dick,
That smiles his cheek in years and knows the trick
To make my lady laugh when she's disposed,
Told our intents before.   (*Biron*)

It pleased them to think me worthy of Pompion the Great.   506
                                        (*Costard*)

That sport best pleases that doth least know how.   v. ii. 517
                                        (*Princess*)

I protest, the schoolmaster is exceeding fantastical; too   531
too vain, too too vain.   (*Armado*)

A foolish mild man; an honest man, look you, and soon   548
dashed.   He is a marvellous good neighbour, faith, and a
very good bowler: but, for Alisander,—alas, you see how
'tis,—a little o'erparted.   (*Costard*)

Armado. I do adore thy sweet grace's slipper.   672
Boyet. [*Aside.*] Loves her by the foot.

If a' have no more man's blood in 's belly than will sup   697
a flea.   (*Biron*)

He wore none but a dishclout of Jaquenetta's, and that   720
a' wears next his heart for a favour.   (*Boyet*)

Mercade.   The news I bring   726
Is heavy in my tongue.   The king your father—
Princess. Dead, for my life!
Mercade. Even so; my tale is told.

I have seen the day of wrong through the little hole of   732
discretion, and I will right myself like a soldier.   (*Armado*)

A heavy heart bears not a nimble tongue.   (*Princess*)   747

                    To wail friends lost   759
Is not by much so wholesome-profitable
As to rejoice at friends but newly found.   (*King*)

Honest plain words best pierce the ear of grief.   (*Biron*)   763

                    A time, methinks, too short,   798
To make a world-without-end bargain in.   (*Princess*)

                    The world's large tongue   852
Proclaims you for a man replete with mocks,
Full of comparisons and wounding flouts,
Which you on all estates will execute
That lie within the mercy of your wit.   (*Rosaline*)

To move wild laughter in the throat of death?   865
It cannot be; it is impossible:
Mirth cannot move a soul in agony.   (*Biron*)

A jest's prosperity lies in the ear   871
Of him that hears it, never in the tongue
Of him that makes it.   (*Rosaline*)

SPRING

When daisies pied and violets blue   v. ii. 904
  And lady-smocks all silver-white
And cuckoo-buds of yellow hue
  Do paint the meadows with delight,
The cuckoo then, on every tree,
Mocks married men; for thus sings he,
              Cuckoo;
Cuckoo, cuckoo: O word of fear,
Unpleasing to a married ear!

When shepherds pipe on oaten straws
  And merry larks are ploughmen's clocks
And turtles tread, and rooks and daws,
  And maidens bleach their summer smocks.
The cuckoo then, on every tree,
Mocks married men; for thus sings he,
              Cuckoo;
Cuckoo, cuckoo: O word of fear,
Unpleasing to a married ear!   (Song)

WINTER

When icicles hang by the wall   922
  And Dick the shepherd blows his nail
And Tom bears logs into the hall
  And milk comes frozen home in pail,
When blood is nipp'd and ways be foul,
Then nightly sings the staring owl,
              Tu-whit;
Tu-who, a merry note,
While greasy Joan doth keel the pot.

When all around the wind doth blow
  And coughing drowns the parson's saw
And birds sit brooding in the snow
  And Marian's nose looks red and raw,
When roasted crabs hiss in the bowl,
Then nightly sings the staring owl,
              Tu-whit;
Tu-who, a merry note,
While greasy Joan doth keel the pot.   (Song)

The words of Mercury are harsh after the songs of   940
Apollo.   (Armado)

A MIDSUMMER NIGHT'S DREAM

This play is a fairy fantasy in which Oberon, king of the fairies, and his mischievous attendant Puck, work enchantments by means of the juice of a magic herb, which when sprinkled on the eyes of a sleeper causes the victim to fall in love with the first creature caught sight of on awaking. By its means Oberon plans to straighten out a human love-tangle. Hermia loves Lysander, but has been promised to Demetrius by her father Egeus, and by Athenian law the penalty for disobedience is death; so she and Lysander plan to elope. Hermia's friend Helena, who loves Demetrius, betrays the project to him, and they follow the pair into a magic wood. Oberon intends to use his charm to make Demetrius love Helena, but it is wrongly applied, with the result that now both Demetrius and Lysander woo Helena, who is enraged at what she regards as their mockery. After a great deal of wrangling a later application of the spell puts things right. Meanwhile, to teach Titania, the fairy queen, a lesson, Oberon has used the magic on her so that she falls in love with Bottom, a weaver, whom Puck has bewitched so that he has an ass's head. This spell too is lifted once it has served its turn and Bottom proceeds with his fellow artisans Quince, Snug, Flute, Snout, and Starveling to perform the play of 'Pyramus and Thisbe' which they have earlier rehearsed for the wedding celebrations of Theseus and Hippolyta, which form a background to the whole play. This amateur performance is a nonsensical burlesque of the most lurid dramas of the time and provides a ludicrous contrast to the delicate fairy poetry of the main plot.

O, methinks, how slow   i. i. 3
This old moon wanes! she lingers my desires,
Like to a step-dame or a dowager
Long withering out a young man's revenue.

         (*Theseus*)

The moon, like to a silver bow   9
New-bent in heaven. (*Hippolyta*)

This man hath bewitch'd the bosom of my child: 27
Thou, thou, Lysander, thou hast given her rhymes
And interchanged love-tokens with my child:
Thou hast by moonlight at her window sung
With feigning voice verses of feigning love,
And stolen the impression of her fantasy
With bracelets of thy hair, rings, gawds, conceits,
Knacks, trifles, nosegays, sweetmeats, messengers
Of strong prevailment in unharden'd youth. (*Egeus*)

To you your father should be as a god;   47
One that composed your beauties, yea, and one
To whom you are but as a form in wax
By him imprinted and within his power
To leave the figure or disfigure it. (*Theseus*)

Whether, if you yield not to your father's choice,   69
You can endure the livery of a nun,
For aye to be in shady cloister mew'd,
To live a barren sister all your life,
Chanting faint hymns to the cold fruitless moon.
Thrice-blessed they that master so their blood,
To undergo such maiden pilgrimage;
But earthlier happy is the rose distill'd,
Than that which withering on the virgin thorn
Grows, lives and dies in single blessedness. (*Theseus*)

She, sweet lady, dotes,   108
Devoutly dotes, dotes in idolatry,
Upon this spotted and inconstant man. (*Lysander*)

How now, my love! why is your cheek so pale?   128
How chance the roses there do fade so fast?

         (*Lysander*)

Lysander. Ay me! for aught that I could ever read,   I. i. 132
Could ever hear by tale or history,
The course of true love never did run smooth;
But either it was different in blood,—
Hermia. O cross! too high to be enthrall'd to low.
Lysander. Or else misgraffed in respect of years,—
Hermia. O spite! too old to be engaged to young.
Lysander. Or else it stood upon the choice of friends,—
Hermia. O hell! to choose love by another's eyes.
Lysander. Or, if there were a sympathy in choice,
War, death, or sickness did lay siege to it,
Making it momentany as a sound,
Swift as a shadow, short as any dream;
Brief as the lightning in the collied night,
That, in a spleen, unfolds both heaven and earth,
And ere a man hath power to say, 'Behold!'
The jaws of darkness do devour it up:
So quick bright things come to confusion.

           A customary cross,   153
As due to love as thoughts and dreams and sighs,
Wishes and tears, poor fancy's followers.   (*Hermia*)

                O happy fair!   182
Your eyes are lode-stars; and your tongue's sweet air
More tuneable than lark to shepherd's ear,
When wheat is green, when hawthorn buds appear.
                         (*Helena*)

To-morrow night, when Phoebe doth behold   209
Her silver visage in the watery glass,
Decking with liquid pearl the bladed grass,
A time that lovers' flights doth still conceal.
                      (*Lysander*)

      In the wood, where often you and I,   214
Upon faint primrose-beds were wont to lie,
Emptying our bosoms of their counsel sweet.
                      (*Hermia*)

Things base and vile, holding no quantity,   232
Love can transpose to form and dignity:
Love looks not with the eyes, but with the mind;
And therefore is wing'd Cupid painted blind:
Nor hath Love's mind of any judgment taste;
Wings and no eyes figure unheedy haste:
And therefore is Love said to be a child,
Because in choice he is so oft beguiled.
As waggish boys in game themselves forswear,
So the boy Love is perjured every where.   (*Helena*)

The most lamentable comedy, and most cruel death of   I. ii. 11
Pyramus and Thisby. (*Quince*)

Masters, spread yourselves. (*Bottom*)   16

My chief humour is for a tyrant: I could play Ercles   30
rarely, or a part to tear a cat in, to make all split.

> The raging rocks
> And shivering shocks
> Shall break the locks
>   Of prison gates;
> And Phibbus' car
> Shall shine from far
> And make and mar
>   The foolish Fates.

This was lofty! . . . This is Ercles' vein, the tyrant's
vein; a lover is more condoling. (*Bottom*)

Let not me play a woman; I have a beard coming.   49
                                                        (*Flute*)

An I may hide my face, let me play Thisby too, I 'll   54
speak in a monstrous little voice; thisne, thisne; 'Ah
Pyramus, my lover dear! thy Thisby dear, and lady dear!'
                                                     (*Bottom*)

Snug. Have you the lion's part written? pray you, if it be,   68
give it me, for I am slow of study.
Quince. You may do it extempore, for it is nothing but
roaring.
Bottom. Let me play the lion too: I will roar, that I will do
any man's heart good to hear me; I will roar, that I will
make the duke say, 'Let him roar again, let him roar again.'

That would hang us, every mother's son. (*All*)   80

I will aggravate my voice so that I will roar you as   83
gently as any sucking dove; I will roar you as 'twere any
nightingale. (*Bottom*)

You can play no part but Pyramus; for Pyramus is a   87
sweet-faced man; a proper man, as one shall see in a
summer's day; a most lovely gentleman-like man: therefore you must needs play Pyramus. (*Quince*)

I will discharge it in either your straw-colour beard,   95
your orange-tawny beard, your purple-in-grain beard, or
your French-crown-colour beard, your perfect yellow.
                                                     (*Bottom*)

Hold or cut bow-strings.   *(Bottom)*   I. ii. 110

Puck. How now, spirit! whither wander you?   II. i. 1
Fairy.   Over hill, over dale,
        Thorough bush, thorough brier,
     Over park, over pale,
        Thorough flood, thorough fire,
     I do wander every where,
     Swifter than the moon's sphere;
     And I serve the fairy queen,
     To dew her orbs upon the green.
     The cowslips tall her pensioners be:
     In their gold coats spots you see;
     Those be rubies, fairy favours,
     In those freckles live their savours:
I must go seek some dewdrops here
And hang a pearl in every cowslip's ear.

And now they never meet in grove or green,   28
By fountain clear, or spangled starlight sheen,
But they do square, that all their elves for fear
Creep into acorn-cups and hide them there.   *(Puck)*

Fairy. Either I mistake your shape and making quite,   32
Or else you are that shrewd and knavish sprite
Call'd Robin Goodfellow: are not you he
That frights the maidens of the villagery;
Skim milk, and sometimes labour in the quern
And bootless make the breathless housewife churn;
And sometimes make the drink to bear no barm;
Mislead night-wanderers, laughing at their harm?
Those that Hobgoblin call you and sweet Puck,
You do their work, and they shall have good luck:
Are not you he?
Puck.   Thou speak'st aright;
I am that merry wanderer of the night.
I jest to Oberon and make him smile
When I a fat and bean-fed horse beguile,
Neighing in likeness of a filly foal:
And sometime lurk I in a gossip's bowl,
In very likeness of a roasted crab,
And when she drinks, against her lips I bob
And on her wither'd dewlap pour the ale.
The wisest aunt, telling the saddest tale,
Sometime for three-foot stool mistaketh me;
Then slip I from her bum, down topples she,
And 'tailor' cries, and falls into a cough;
And then the whole quire hold their hips and laugh,
And waxen in their mirth and neeze and swear
A merrier hour was never wasted there.

And never, since the middle summer's spring,   II. i. 82
Met we on hill, in dale, forest or mead,
By paved fountain or by rushy brook,
Or in the beached margent of the sea,
To dance our ringlets to the whistling wind,
But with thy brawls thou hast disturb'd our sport.
Therefore the winds, piping to us in vain,
As in revenge, have suck'd up from the sea
Contagious fogs; which falling in the land
Have every pelting river made so proud
That they have overborne their continents:
The ox hath therefore stretch'd his yoke in vain.
The ploughman lost his sweat, and the green corn
Hath rotted ere his youth attain'd a beard;
The fold stands empty in the drowned field,
And crows are fatted with the murrion flock;
The nine men's morris is fill'd up with mud,
And the quaint mazes in the wanton green
For lack of tread are undistinguishable:
The human mortals want their winter here;
No night is now with hymn or carol blest:
Therefore the moon, the governess of floods,
Pale in her anger, washes all the air,
That rheumatic diseases do abound:
And thorough this distemperature we see
The seasons alter: hoary-headed frosts
Fall in the fresh lap of the crimson rose,
And on old Hiems' thin and icy crown
An odorous chaplet of sweet summer buds
Is, as in mockery, set: the spring, the summer,
The chiding autumn, angry winter, change
Their wonted liveries, and the mazed world
By their increase, now knows not which is which.

                                        (*Titania*)

                        Thou rememberest   148
Since once I sat upon a promontory,
And heard a mermaid on a dolphin's back
Utter such dulcet and harmonious breath
That the rude sea grew civil at her song
And certain stars shot madly from their spheres,
To hear the sea-maid's music.   (*Oberon*)

That very time I saw, but thou couldst not,   155
Flying between the cold moon and the earth,
Cupid all arm'd: a certain aim he took
At a fair vestal throned by the west,
And loosed his love-shaft smartly from his bow,
As it should pierce a hundred thousand hearts;
But I might see young Cupid's fiery shaft

Quench'd in the chaste beams of the watery moon,   II. i. 162
And the imperial votaress passed on,
In maiden meditation, fancy-free.
Yet mark'd I where the bolt of Cupid fell:
It fell upon a little western flower,
Before milk-white, now purple with love's wound,
And maidens call it love-in-idleness.   (*Oberon*)

I 'll put a girdle round about the earth   175
In forty minutes.   (*Puck*)

I am your spaniel; and, Demetrius,   203
The more you beat me, I will fawn on you.   (*Helena*)

Run when you will, the story shall be changed: 230
Apollo flies, and Daphne holds the chase;
The dove pursues the griffin; the mild hind
Makes speed to catch the tiger; bootless speed,
When cowardice pursues and valour flies.   (*Helena*)

We cannot fight for love, as men may do;   241
We should be woo'd, and were not made to woo.
                                          (*Helena*)

I know a bank where the wild thyme blows,   249
Where oxlips and the nodding violet grows,
Quite over-canopied with luscious woodbine,
With sweet musk-roses and with eglantine:
There sleeps Titania sometime of the night,
Lull'd in these flowers with dances and delight;
And there the snake throws her enamell'd skin,
Weed wide enough to wrap a fairy in.   (*Oberon*)

Come, now a roundel and a fairy song;   II. ii. 1
Then, for the third part of a minute, hence;
Some to kill cankers in the musk-rose buds,
Some war with rere-mice for their leathern wings,
To make my small elves coats, and some keep back
The clamorous owl that nightly hoots and wonders
At our quaint spirits. (*Titania*)

    You spotted snakes with double tongue,   9
        Thorny hedgehogs, be not seen:
    Newts and blind-worms, do no wrong,
        Come not near our fairy queen.
        Philomel, with melody
        Sing in our sweet lullaby;
    Lulla, lulla, lullaby, lulla, lulla, lullaby:
        Never harm,
        Nor spell nor charm,

Come our lovely lady nigh;   II. ii. 18
So, good night, with lullaby.

Weaving spiders, come not here;
  Hence, you long-legg'd spinners, hence!
Beetles black, approach not near;
  Worm nor snail, do no offence.
Philomel, with melody
  Sing in our sweet lullaby;
Lulla, lulla, lullaby, lulla, lulla, lullaby:
    Never harm,
    Nor spell nor charm,
Come our lovely lady nigh;
  So, good night, with lullaby.

(Fairies, sing)

And here the maiden, sleeping sound,   74
On the dank and dirty ground.
Pretty soul! she durst not lie
Near this lack-love, this kill-courtesy. *(Puck)*

O, wilt thou darkling leave me? do not so. *(Helena)*   86

Run through fire I will for thy sweet sake. *(Lysander)*   103

Who will not change a raven for a dove? *(Lysander)*   114

And touching now the point of human skill,   119
Reason becomes the marshal to my will
And leads me to your eyes, where I o'erlook
Love's stories written in love's richest book.

(Lysander)

As a surfeit of the sweetest things   137
The deepest loathing to the stomach brings,
Or as the heresies that men do leave
Are hated most of those they did deceive. *(Lysander)*

Bottom. Are we all met?   III. i. 1
Quince. Pat, pat; and here's a marvellous convenient
place for our rehearsal. This green plot shall be our
stage, this hawthorn-brake our tiring-house.

Starveling. I believe we must leave the killing out, when   15
all is done.
Bottom. Not a whit: I have a device to make all well.
Write me a prologue; and let the prologue seem to say,
we will do no harm with our swords and that Pyramus
is not killed indeed; and, for the more better assurance,
tell them that I Pyramus am not Pyramus, but Bottom
the weaver; this will put them out of fear.

Snout. Will not the ladies be afeard of the lion?   III. i. 27
Starveling. I fear it, I promise you.
Bottom. Masters, you ought to consider with yourselves:
to bring in—God shield us!—a lion among ladies, is a
most dreadful thing; for there is not a more fearful wild-
fowl than your lion living.

Snout. Doth the moon shine that night we play our play?   52
Bottom. A calendar, a calendar! Look in the almanac;
find out moonshine, find out moonshine.

What hempen homespuns have we swaggering here,   79
So near the cradle of the fairy queen?
What, a play toward! I'll be an auditor;
An actor too perhaps, if I see cause.   (*Puck*)

Bottom. Thisby, the flowers of odious savours sweet,—   84
Quince. Odours, odours.
Bottom. —odours savours sweet:
So hath thy breath, my dearest Thisby dear.

Flute. Must I speak now?   91
Quince. Ay, marry, must you; for you must understand
he goes but to see a noise that he heard, and is to come
again.
Flute. Most radiant Pyramus, most lily-white of hue,
  Of colour like the red rose on triumphant brier,
Most brisky juvenal and eke most lovely Jew,
  As true as truest horse that yet would never tire.

I'll follow you, I'll lead you about a round,   109
  Through bog, through bush, through brake, through
    brier:
Sometime a horse I'll be, sometime a hound,
  A hog, a headless bear, sometime a fire;
And neigh, and bark, and grunt, and roar, and burn,
Like horse, hound, hog, bear, fire, at every turn.
                              (*Puck*)

Bless thee, Bottom! bless thee! thou art translated.   121
                            (*Quince*)

Bottom. [*Sings.*] The ousel cock so black of hue,   128
        With orange-tawny bill,
      The throstle with his note so true,
        The wren with little quill,—
Titania. [*Awakening.*] What angel wakes me from my
  flowery bed?
Bottom. [*Sings.*] The finch, the sparrow and the lark,
        The plain-song cuckoo gray,
      Whose notes full many a man doth mark,
        And dares not answer nay.

Out of this wood do not desire to go: III. i. 155
Thou shalt remain here whether thou wilt or no.
I am a spirit of no common rate:
The summer still doth tend upon my state;
And I do love thee: therefore, go with me;
I'll give thee fairies to attend on thee,
And they shall fetch thee jewels from the deep,
And sing while thou on pressed flowers dost sleep:
And I will purge thy mortal grossness so
That thou shalt like an airy spirit go.
Peaseblossom! Cobweb! Moth! and Mustardseed!
                                        (*Titania*)

Be kind and courteous to this gentleman;   167
Hop in his walks and gambol in his eyes;
Feed him with apricocks and dewberries,
With purple grapes, green figs, and mulberries;
The honey-bags steal from the humble-bees,
And for night-tapers crop their waxen thighs
And light them at the fiery glow-worm's eyes,
To have my love to bed and to arise;
And pluck the wings from painted butterflies
To fan the moonbeams from his sleeping eyes:
Nod to him, elves, and do him courtesies.   (*Titania*)

    The moon, methinks, looks with a watery eye;   203
And when she weeps, weeps every little flower,
    Lamenting some enforced chastity.   (*Titania*)

A crew of patches, rude mechanicals.   (*Puck*)   III. ii. 9

The shallowest thick-skin of that barren sort.   (*Puck*)   13

As wild geese that the creeping fowler eye,   20
Or russet-pated choughs, many in sort,
Rising and cawing at the gun's report,
Sever themselves and madly sweep the sky,
So, at his sight, away his fellows fly.   (*Puck*)

Their sense thus weak, lost with their fears thus strong, 27
Made senseless things begin to do them wrong;
For briers and thorns at their apparel snatch;
Some sleeves, some hats, from yielders all things catch.
                                        (*Puck*)

Titania waked and straightway loved an ass.   (*Puck*)   34

It cannot be but thou hast murder'd him;   56
So should a murderer look, so dread, so grim.
                                        (*Hermia*)

And hast thou kill'd him sleeping? O brave touch!   III. ii. 70
Could not a worm, an adder do so much? (*Hermia*)

I go, I go; look how I go,   100
Swifter than arrow from the Tartar's bow. (*Puck*)

Lord, what fools these mortals be! (*Puck*)   115

> Then will two at once woo one;   118
> That must needs be sport alone;
> And those things do best please me
> That befal preposterously. (*Puck*)

Demetrius. [*Awaking*]. O Helen, goddess, nymph, perfect,   137
    divine!
To what, my love, shall I compare thine eyne?
Crystal is muddy. O, how ripe in show
Thy lips, those kissing cherries, tempting grow!
That pure congealed white, high Taurus' snow,
Fann'd with the eastern wind, turns to a crow
When thou hold'st up thy hand: O, let me kiss
This princess of pure white, this seal of bliss!
Helena. O spite! O hell! I see you all are bent
To set against me for your merriment:
If you were civil and knew courtesy,
You would not do me thus much injury.
Can you not hate me, as I know you do,
But you must join in souls to mock me too?
If you were men, as men you are in show,
You would not use a gentle lady so.

A trim exploit, a manly enterprise,   157
To conjure tears up in a poor maid's eyes
With your derision! (*Helena*)

Dark night, that from the eye his function takes,   177
The ear more quick of apprehension makes. (*Hermia*)

Fair Helena, who more engilds the night   187
Than all yon fiery oes and eyes of light. (*Lysander*)

Is all the counsel that we two have shared,   198
The sisters' vows, the hours that we have spent,
When we have chid the hasty-footed time
For parting us,—O, is all forgot?
All school-days' friendship, childhood innocence?
We, Hermia, like two artificial gods,
Have with our needles created both one flower,
Both on one sampler, sitting on one cushion,
Both warbling of one song, both in one key,

As if our hands, our sides, voices and minds,   III. ii. 207
Had been incorporate.   So we grew together,
Like to a double cherry, seeming parted,
But yet an union in partition;
Two lovely berries moulded on one stem;
So, with two seeming bodies, but one heart;
Two of the first, like coats in heraldry,
Due but to one and crowned with one crest.   (*Helena*)

Away, you Ethiope!   (*Lysander*)   257

Hang off, thou cat, thou burr! vile thing, let loose,   260
Or I will shake thee from me like a serpent!
                                        (*Lysander*)

                    Out, tawny Tartar, out!   263
Out, loathed medicine! hated potion, hence!
                                        (*Lysander*)

Helena. Fie, fie! you counterfeit, you puppet, you!   288
Hermia. Puppet? why so? ay, that way goes the game.
Now I perceive that she hath made compare
Between our statures; she hath urged her height;
And with her personage, her tall personage,
Her height, forsooth, she hath prevail'd with him.
And are you grown so high in his esteem,
Because I am so dwarfish and so low?
How low am I, thou painted maypole? speak;
How low am I? I am not yet so low
But that my nails can reach unto thine eyes.

I have no gift at all in shrewishness;   301
I am a right maid for my cowardice.   (*Helena*)

O, when she's angry, she is keen and shrewd!   323
She was a vixen when she went to school;
And though she be but little, she is fierce.   (*Helena*)

                    Get you gone, you dwarf;   328
You minimus, of hindering knot-grass made;
You bead, you acorn.   (*Lysander*)

Your hands than mine are quicker for a fray,   342
My legs are longer though, to run away.   (*Helena*)

Till o'er their brows death-counterfeiting sleep   364
With leaden legs and batty wings doth creep.   (*Oberon*)

For night's swift dragons cut the clouds full fast,   379
And yonder shines Aurora's harbinger.   (*Puck*)

But we are spirits of another sort: III. ii. 388
I with the morning's love have oft made sport,
And, like a forester, the groves may tread,
Even till the eastern gate, all fiery-red,
Opening on Neptune with fair blessed beams,
Turns into yellow gold his salt green streams.

(Oberon)

Up and down, up and down,   396
I will lead them up and down.   *(Puck)*

And sleep, that sometimes shuts up sorrow's eye,   435
Steal me awhile from mine own company.   *(Helena)*

Cupid is a knavish lad,   440
Thus to make poor females mad.   *(Puck)*

Jack shall have Jill;
Nought shall go ill;
The man shall have his mare again, and all shall be well.

(Puck)

Come, sit thee down upon this flowery bed,   IV. i. 1
   While I thy amiable cheeks do coy,
And stick musk-roses in thy sleek smooth head,
   And kiss thy fair large ears, my gentle joy.   *(Titania)*

Mounsieur Cobweb, good mounsieur, get your   10
weapons in your hand, and kill me a red-hipped humble-
bee on the top of a thistle; and, good mounsieur, bring me
the honey-bag.   *(Bottom)*

I must to the barber's mounsieur; for methinks I am   25
marvellous hairy about the face.   *(Bottom)*

Titania. What, wilt thou hear some music, my sweet love?   29
Bottom. I have a reasonable good ear in music. Let's
have the tongs and the bones.
Titania. Or say, sweet love, what thou desirest to eat.
Bottom. Truly, a peck of provender: I could munch your
good dry oats. Methinks I have a great desire to a
bottle of hay: good hay, sweet hay, hath no fellow.

Bottom. I pray you, let none of your people stir me: I   40
have an exposition of sleep come upon me.
Titania. Sleep thou, and I will wind thee in my arms.
Fairies, be gone, and be all ways away.
So doth the woodbine the sweet honeysuckle
Gentle entwist; the female ivy so
Enrings the barky fingers of the elm.

And that same dew, which sometime on the buds   IV. i. 56
Was wont to swell like round and orient pearls,
Stood now within the pretty flowerets' eyes
Like tears that did their own disgrace bewail. (*Oberon*)

Methought I was enamour'd of an ass.   (*Titania*)   80

　　　Then, my queen, in silence sad,   99
　　　Trip we after night's shade:
　　　We the globe can compass soon,
　　　Swifter than the wandering moon.   (*Oberon*)

Hippolyta. I was with Hercules and Cadmus once,   116
When in a wood of Crete they bay'd the bear
With hounds of Sparta: never did I hear
Such gallant chiding; for, besides the groves,
The skies, the fountains, every region near
Seem'd all one mutual cry: I never heard
So musical a discord, such sweet thunder.
Theseus. My hounds are bred out of the Spartan kind,
So flew'd, so sanded, and their heads are hung
With ears that sweep away the morning dew;
Crook-knee'd, and dew-lapp'd like Thessalian bulls;
Slow in pursuit, but match'd in mouth like bells,
Each under each.   A cry more tuneable
Was never holla'd to, nor cheer'd with horn,
In Crete, in Sparta, nor in Thessaly.

　　　　　My love to Hermia,   169
Melted as the snow, seems to me now
As the remembrance of an idle gawd
Which in my childhood I did dote upon.   (*Demetrius*)

These things seem small and undistinguishable,   191
Like far-off mountains turned into clouds.
　　　　　　　　　(*Demetrius*)

　I have had a most rare vision.   I have had a dream, past   209
the wit of man to say what dream it was: man is but an ass,
if he go about to expound this dream.   Methought I was
—there is no man can tell what.   Methought I was,—and
methought I had,—but man is but a patched fool, if he
will offer to say what methought I had.   The eye of man
hath not heard, the ear of man hath not seen, man's hand is
not able to taste, his tongue to conceive, nor his heart to
report, what my dream was.   I will get Peter Quince to
write a ballad of this dream: it shall be called Bottom's
Dream, because it hath no bottom. (*Bottom*)

Quince. He is a very paramour for a sweet voice.   IV. ii. 11
Flute. You must say 'paragon': a paramour is, God bless
us, a thing of naught.

Bottom! O most courageous day! O most happy hour!   27
           (*Quince*)

 Let Thisby have clean linen; and let not him that plays   40
the lion pare his nails, for they shall hang out for the
lion's claws. And, most dear actors, eat no onions nor
garlic, for we are to utter sweet breath. (*Bottom*)

         I never may believe   v. i. 2
These antique fables, nor these fairy toys.
Lovers and madmen have such seething brains,
Such shaping fantasies, that apprehend
More than cool reason ever comprehends.
The lunatic, the lover and the poet
Are of imagination all compact:
One sees more devils than vast hell can hold,
That is, the madman: the lover, all as frantic,
Sees Helen's beauty in a brow of Egypt:
The poet's eye, in a fine frenzy rolling,
Doth glance from heaven to earth, from earth to heaven;
And as imagination bodies forth
The forms of things unknown, the poet's pen
Turns them to shapes and gives to airy nothing
A local habitation and a name.
Such tricks hath strong imagination,
That, if it would but apprehend some joy,
It comprehends some bringer of that joy;
Or in the night, imagining some fear,
How easy is a bush supposed a bear! (*Theseus*)

Come now; what masques, what dances shall we have,   32
To wear away this long age of three hours
Between our after-supper and bed-time? (*Theseus*)

'A tedious brief scene of young Pyramus   56
And his love Thisbe; very tragical mirth.'
Merry and tragical! tedious and brief!
That is, hot ice and wondrous strange snow. (*Theseus*)

For never anything can be amiss,   82
When simpleness and duty tender it. (*Theseus*)

Where I have come, great clerks have purposed   93
To greet me with premeditated welcomes;
Where I have seen them shiver and look pale,
Make periods in the midst of sentences,

Throttle their practised accent in their fears   v. i. 97
And in conclusion dumbly have broke off,
Not paying me a welcome.   Trust me, sweet,
Out of this silence yet I pick'd a welcome;
And in the modesty of fearful duty
I read as much as from the rattling tongue
Of saucy and audacious eloquence.
Love, therefore, and tongue-tied simplicity
In least speak most, to my capacity.   (*Theseus*)

If we offend, it is with our good will.   108
    That you should think, we come not to offend,
But with good will.   To show our simple skill,
    That is the true beginning of our end.
Consider then we come but in despite.
    We do not come as minding to content you,
Our true intent is.   All for your delight
    We are not here.   That you should here repent you,
The actors are at hand and by their show,
You shall know all that you are like to know.
                                (*Quince as Prologue*)

    His speech was like a tangled chain; nothing impaired,   126
but all disordered.   (*Theseus*)

This grisly beast, which Lion hight by name,   140
The trusty Thisby, coming first by night,
Did scare away, or rather did affright;
And, as she fled, her mantle she did fall,
    Which Lion vile with bloody mouth did stain.
Anon comes Pyramus, sweet youth and tall,
    And finds his trusty Thisby's mantle slain:
Whereat, with blade, with bloody blameful blade,
    He bravely broach'd his boiling bloody breast;
And Thisby, tarrying in mulberry shade,
    His dagger drew, and died.   (*Prologue*)

Hippolyta. This is the silliest stuff that ever I heard.   212
Theseus. The best in this kind are but shadows; and the
worst are no worse, if imagination amend them.

Lion. You, ladies, you, whose gentle hearts do fear   222
    The smallest monstrous mouse that creeps on floor,
May now perchance both quake and tremble here,
    When lion rough in wildest rage doth roar.
Then know that I, one Snug the joiner, am
A lion-fell, nor else no lion's dam;
For, if I should as lion come in strife
Into this place, 'twere pity on my life.
Theseus. A very gentle beast, and of a good conscience.

Demetrius. Well roared, Lion.   v. i. 270
Theseus. Well run, Thisbe.
Hippolyta. Well shone, Moon.   Truly, the moon shines
with a good grace.

Pyramus.   But stay, O spite!   281
                   But mark, poor knight,
          What dreadful dole is here!
                   Eyes, do you see?
                   How can it be?
          O dainty duck!   O dear!
                   Thy mantle good,
          What, stain'd with blood!
          Approach, ye Furies fell!
                   O Fates, come, come,
                   Cut thread and thrum;
          Quail, crush, conclude, and quell!
Theseus. This passion, and the death of a dear friend,
would go near to make a man look sad.

Pyramus.   Come, tears, confound: 300
                   Out, sword, and wound
          The pap of Pyramus;
                   Ay, that left pap,
                   Where heart doth hop: [*Stabs himself.*]
          Thus die I, thus, thus, thus.
                   Now am I dead,
                   Now am I fled;
          My soul is in the sky:
                   Tongue, lose thy light;
                   Moon, take thy flight: [*Exit Moonshine.*]
          Now die, die, die, die, die.   [*Dies*]

Thisbe.   Asleep, my love?   331
                   What, dead, my dove?
          O Pyramus, arise!
                   Speak, speak.   Quite dumb?
                   Dead, dead?   A tomb
          Must cover thy sweet eyes.
                   These lily lips,
                   This cherry nose,
          These yellow cowslip cheeks,
                   Are gone, are gone:
                   Lovers, make moan:
          His eyes were green as leeks.
                   O Sisters Three,
                   Come, come to me,
          With hands as pale as milk;
                   Lay them in gore,
                   Since you have shore

With shears his thread of silk.   v. i. 348
   Tongue, not a word:
   Come, trusty sword;
Come, blade, my breast imbrue: [*Stabs herself.*]
   And, farewell, friends;
   Thus Thisby ends:
Adieu, adieu, adieu.   [*Dies.*]
Theseus. Moonshine and Lion are left to bury the dead.
Demetrius. Ay, and Wall too.

No epilogue, I pray you; for your play needs no excuse.   362
Never excuse; for when the players are all dead, there need
none to be blamed.   (*Theseus*)

The iron tongue of midnight hath told twelve: 370
Lovers, to bed; 'tis almost fairy time.   (*Theseus*)

Now the hungry lion roars,   378
   And the wolf behowls the moon;
Whilst the heavy ploughman snores,
   All with weary task fordone.
Now the wasted brands do glow,
   Whilst the screech-owl, screeching loud,
Puts the wretch that lies in woe
   In remembrance of a shroud.
Now it is the time of night
   That the graves all gaping wide,
Every one lets forth his sprite,
   In the church-way paths to glide:
And we fairies, that do run
   By the triple Hecate's team,
From the presence of the sun,
   Following darkness like a dream,
Now are frolic: not a mouse
Shall disturb this hallow'd house:
I am sent with broom before,
To sweep the dust behind the door.   (*Puck*)

Through the house give glimmering light   398
   By the dead and drowsy fire:
Every elf and fairy sprite
   Hop as light as bird from brier.   (*Oberon*)

Trip away; make no stay;   428
Meet me all by break of day.   (*Oberon*)

THE MERCHANT OF VENICE

Antonio, a Venetian merchant, borrows from Shylock, a Jewish usurer, to enable his friend Bassanio to go courting a wealthy heiress named Portia, whose hand is to go to whichever of her suitors makes the right choice among three caskets of gold, silver, and lead. After other suitors, the Princes of Morocco and of Arragon have failed, Bassanio wins her by choosing the leaden casket. Meanwhile at Venice Antonio is in peril of his life, for he is unable to repay the Jew and by the terms of the contract should in that case forfeit a pound of his flesh. Bassanio hurries home and Portia, without his knowledge, disguises herself as a lawyer and intervenes in the case when it comes before the Duke of Venice. By the legal quibble that the pound of flesh must contain no blood she turns Shylock's inhuman bond against himself and all ends happily. The play is one of the best-known comedies and one of the most successful theatrically, a most famous passage being Portia's speech on mercy. Minor characters are the Venetians Gratiano, Salanio, Salarino, and Lorenzo, Portia's maid Nerissa, the clown Launce-lot Gobbo and his old father. A charming sub-plot contains the love-story of Lorenzo and Shylock's daughter Jessica.

In sooth, I know not why I am so sad: I. i. I
It wearies me; you say it wearies you;
But how I caught it, found it, or came by it,
What stuff 'tis made of, whereof it is born,
I am to learn;
And such a want-wit sadness makes of me,
That I have much ado to know myself. (*Antonio*)

Your mind is tossing on the ocean;   8
There, where your argosies with portly sail,
Like signiors and rich burghers on the flood,
Or, as it were, the pageants of the sea,
Do overpeer the petty traffickers,
That curtsy to them, do them reverence,
As they fly by them with their woven wings. (*Salarino*)

Plucking the grass to know where sits the wind,   18
Peering in maps for ports and piers and roads. (*Salanio*)

        My wind cooling my broth   22
Would blow me to an ague, when I thought
What harm a wind too great at sea might do.
I should not see the sandy hour-glass run,
But I should think of shallows and of flats,
And see my wealthy Andrew dock'd in sand,
Vailing her high-top lower than her ribs
To kiss her burial. (*Salarino*)

        But even now worth this,   35
And now worth nothing. (*Salarino*)

My ventures are not in one bottom trusted,   42
Nor to one place; nor is my whole estate
Upon the fortune of the present year. (*Antonio*)

Nature hath framed strange fellows in her time: 51
Some that will evermore peep through their eyes
And laugh like parrots at a bag-piper,
And other of such vinegar aspect
That they'll not show their teeth in way of smile,
Though Nestor swear the jest be laughable. (*Salarino*)

I hold the world but as the world, Gratiano;   77
A stage where every man must play a part,
And mine a sad one. (*Antonio*)

Let me play the fool: I. i. 79
With mirth and laughter let old wrinkles come,
And let my liver rather heat with wine
Than my heart cool with mortifying groans.
Why should a man, whose blood is warm within,
Sit like his grandsire cut in alabaster?
Sleep when he wakes and creep into the jaundice
By being peevish? (*Gratiano*)

There are a sort of men whose visages   88
Do cream and mantle like a standing pond,
And do a wilful stillness entertain,
With purpose to be dress'd in an opinion
Of wisdom, gravity, profound conceit,
As who should say 'I am Sir Oracle,
And when I ope my lips let no dog bark!' (*Gratiano*)

But fish not, with this melancholy bait,   101
For this fool gudgeon, this opinion. (*Gratiano*)

Well, keep me company but two years moe,   108
Thou shalt not know the sound of thine own tongue.
                    (*Gratiano*)

Silence is only commendable   111
In a neat's tongue dried and a maid not vendible.
                    (*Gratiano*)

Gratiano speaks an infinite deal of nothing, more than   114
any man in all Venice.   His reasons are as two grains of
wheat hid in two bushels of chaff: you shall seek all day ere
you find them, and when you have them, they are not
worth the search. (*Bassanio*)

How much I have disabled mine estate,   123
By something showing a more swelling port
Than my faint means would grant continuance.
                    (*Bassanio*)

To you, Antonio,   130
I owe the most, in money and in love. (*Bassanio*)

My purse, my person, my extremest means,   138
Lie all unlock'd to your occasions. (*Antonio*)

In my school-days, when I had lost one shaft,   140
I shot his fellow of the self-same flight
The self-same way with more advised watch,
To find the other forth, and by adventuring both
I oft found both. (*Bassanio*)

You know me well, and herein spend but time   I. i. 153
To wind about my love with circumstance. (*Antonio*)

                Sometimes from her eyes   163
I did receive fair speechless messages. (*Bassanio*)

Nor is the wide world ignorant of her worth,   167
For the four winds blow in from every coast
Renowned suitors, and her sunny locks
Hang on her temples like a golden fleece;
Which makes her seat of Belmont Colchos' strand,
And many Jasons come in quest of her. (*Bassanio*)

They are as sick that surfeit with too much as they that   I. ii. 6
starve with nothing. (*Nerissa*)

Superfluity comes sooner by white hairs, but com-   9
petency lives longer. (*Nerissa*)

If to do were as easy as to know what were good to do,   13
chapels had been churches and poor men's cottages
princes' palaces.   It is a good divine that follows his own
instructions: I can easier teach twenty what were good
to be done, than be one of the twenty to follow mine own
teaching. (*Portia*)

He doth nothing but talk of his horse. (*Portia*)   44

God made him, and therefore let him pass for a man.   60
                              (*Portia*)

He will fence with his own shadow. (*Portia*)   66

How oddly he is suited!   I think he bought his doublet   79
in Italy, his round hose in France, his bonnet in Germany
and his behaviour every where. (*Portia*)

Nerissa. How like you the young German, the Duke of   90
Saxony's nephew?
Portia. Very vilely in the morning, when he is sober, and
most vilely in the afternoon, when he is drunk: when
he is best, he is a little worse than a man, and when he is
worst, he is little better than a beast.

I will do any thing, Nerissa, ere I'll be married to a   107
sponge. (*Portia*)

I dote on his very absence. (*Portia*)   120

Shylock. Antonio is a good man.   I. iii. 12
Bassanio. Have you heard any imputation to the contrary?

Ships are but boards, sailors but men: there be land-   I. iii. 22
rats and water-rats, water-thieves and land-thieves, I mean
pirates.   (*Shylock*)

I will buy with you, sell with you, talk with you, walk   36
with you, and so following, but I will not eat with you,
drink with you, nor pray with you.   (*Shylock*)

How like a fawning publican he looks!   42
I hate him for he is a Christian,
But more for that in low simplicity
He lends out money gratis and brings down
The rate of usance here with us in Venice.
If I can catch him once upon the hip,
I will feed fat the ancient grudge I bear him.
He hates our sacred nation, and he rails,
Even there where merchants most do congregate,
On me, my bargains and my well-won thrift,
Which he calls interest.   (*Shylock, aside*)

The devil can cite Scripture for his purpose.   99
An evil soul producing holy witness
Is like a villain with a smiling cheek,
A goodly apple rotten at the heart:
O, what a goodly outside falsehood hath!   (*Antonio*)

Three thousand ducats; 'tis a good round sum.   104
                                          (*Shylock*)

Signior Antonio, many a time and oft   107
In the Rialto you have rated me
About my moneys and my usances:
Still have I borne it with a patient shrug,
For sufferance is the badge of all our tribe.
You call me misbeliever, cut-throat dog,
And spit upon my Jewish gaberdine,
And all for use of that which is mine own.
Well then, it now appears you need my help:
Go to, then; you come to me, and you say
'Shylock, we would have moneys': you say so;
You, that did void your rheum upon my beard
And foot me as you spurn a stranger cur
Over your threshold: moneys is your suit.
What should I say to you?   Should I not say
'Hath a dog moneys? is it possible
A cur can lend three thousand ducats'?   Or
Shall I bend low and in a bondman's key,
With bated breath and whispering humbleness,
Say this:
'Fair sir, you spit on me on Wednesday last;

You spurn'd me such a day; another time   I. iii. 128
You call'd me dog; and for these courtesies
I'll lend you thus much moneys'?   (*Shylock*)

O father Abram, what these Christians are,   153
Whose own hard dealings teaches them suspect
The thoughts of others!   (*Shylock*)

I like not fair terms and a villain's mind.   (*Bassanio*)   181

Mislike me not for my complexion,   II. i. 1
The shadow'd livery of the burnish'd sun.   (*Morocco*)

I would outstare the sternest eyes that look,   27
Outbrave the heart most daring on the earth,
Pluck the young sucking cubs from the she-bear,
Yea, mock the lion when he roars for prey,
To win thee, lady.   (*Morocco*)

  My conscience says 'Launcelot, budge not.' 'Budge,'   II. ii.19
says the fiend. 'Budge not,' says my conscience.
                              (*Launcelot*)

O heavens, this is my true-begotten father!   36
                              (*Launcelot*)

I will try confusions with him.   (*Launcelot*)   38

It is a wise father that knows his own child.   80
                              (*Launcelot*)

  I am famished in his service; you may tell every finger   113
I have with my ribs.   (*Launcelot*)

Thou art too wild, too rude and bold of voice: 190
Parts that become thee happily enough
And in such eyes as ours appear not faults;
But where thou art not known, why, there they show
Something too liberal.   Pray thee, take pain
To allay with some cold drops of modesty
Thy skipping spirit, lest through thy wild behaviour
I be misconstrued in the place I go to
And lose my hopes.   (*Bassanio*)

Our house is hell, and thou, a merry devil,   II. iii. 2
Didst rob it of some taste of tediousness.   (*Jessica*)

Tears exhibit my tongue.   (*Launcelot*)   10

I know the hand: in faith, 'tis a fair hand;   II. iv. 12
And whiter than the paper it writ on
Is the fair hand that writ.   (*Lorenzo*)

There is some ill a-brewing towards my rest,   II. v. 17
For I did dream of money-bags to-night.   (*Shylock*)

Lock up my doors; and when you hear the drum   29
And the vile squealing of the wry-neck'd fife,
Clamber not you up to the casements then,
Nor thrust your head into the public street
To gaze on Christian fools with varnish'd faces.
                                        (*Shylock*)

The patch is kind enough, but a huge feeder;
Snail-slow in profit, and he sleeps by day
More than the wild-cat: drones hive not with me;   46
Therefore I part with him.   (*Shylock*)

Fast bind, fast find;   54
A proverb never stale in thrifty mind.   (*Shylock*)

O, ten times faster Venus' pigeons fly   II. vi. 5
To seal love's bonds new-made, than they are wont
To keep obliged faith unforfeited!   (*Salarino*)

                        All things that are,   12
Are with more spirit chased than enjoy'd.   (*Gratiano*)

How like a younker or a prodigal   14
The scarfed bark puts from her native bay,
Hugg'd and embraced by the strumpet wind!
How like the prodigal doth she return,
With over-weather'd ribs and ragged sails,
Lean, rent and beggar'd by the strumpet wind!
                                        (*Gratiano*)

But love is blind and lovers cannot see   36
The pretty follies that themselves commit;
For if they could, Cupid himself would blush
To see me thus transformed to a boy.   (*Jessica*)

What, must I hold a candle to my shames?   (*Jessica*)   41

Beshrew me but I love her heartily;   52
For she is wise, if I can judge of her,
And fair she is, if that mine eyes be true,
And true she is, as she hath proved herself,
And therefore, like herself, wise, fair and true,
Shall she be placed in my constant soul.   (*Lorenzo*)

The first, of gold, who this inscription bears,   II. vii. 4
'Who chooseth me shall gain what many men desire';
The second, silver, which this promise carries,
'Who chooseth me shall get as much as he deserves';
This third, dull lead, with warning all as blunt,
'Who chooseth me must give and hazard all he hath.'
                                        (*Morocco*)

A golden mind stoops not to shows of dross.   (*Morocco*)   20

From the four corners of the earth they come,   39
To kiss this shrine, this mortal-breathing saint.
                                        (*Morocco*)

A gentle riddance.   Draw the curtains, go.   78
Let all of his complexion choose me so.   (*Portia*)

My daughter!   O my ducats!   O my daughter!   II. viii. 15
Fled with a Christian!   O my Christian ducats!
Justice! the law! my ducats, and my daughter!
                                        (*Shylock*)

Why, all the boys in Venice follow him,   23
Crying, his stones, his daughter, and his ducats.
                                        (*Salarino*)

What many men desire! that 'many' may be meant   II. ix. 25
By the fool multitude, that choose by show,
Not learning more than the fond eye doth teach.
                                        (*Arragon*)

I will not choose what many men desire,   31
Because I will not jump with common spirits
And rank me with the barbarous multitudes.   (*Arragon*)

What's here? the portrait of a blinking idiot,   54
Presenting me a schedule!   (*Arragon*)

The ancient saying is no heresy,   82
Hanging and wiving goes by destiny.   (*Nerissa*)

   The Goodwins, I think they call the place; a very   III. i. 4
dangerous flat and fatal, where the carcases of many a tall
ship lie buried, as they say, if my gossip Report be an
honest woman of her word.   (*Salarino*)

Let him look to his bond.   (*Shylock*)   49

Hath not a Jew eyes? hath not a Jew hands, organs,   III. i. 62
dimensions, senses, affections, passions? fed with the same
food, hurt with the same weapons, subject to the same
diseases, healed by the same means, warmed and cooled
by the same winter and summer, as a Christian is?   If you
prick us, do we not bleed? if you tickle us, do we not
laugh? if you poison us, do we not die? and if you wrong
us, shall we not revenge?   (*Shylock*)

The villainy you teach me, I will execute, and it shall   76
go hard but I will better the instruction.   (*Shylock*)

I would my daughter were dead at my foot, and the   92
jewels in her ear! would she were hearsed at my foot, and
the ducats in her coffin!   (*Shylock*)

It was my turquoise; I had it of Leah when I was a   126
bachelor: I would not have given it for a wilderness of
monkeys.   (*Shylock*)

One half of me is yours, the other half yours,   III. ii. 16
Mine own, I would say; but if mine, then yours,
And so all yours.   (*Portia*)

Let music sound while he doth make his choice;   43
Then, if he lose, he makes a swan-like end,
Fading in music.   (*Portia*)

       Tell me where is fancy bred,   63
       Or in the heart or in the head?
       How begot, how nourished?
          Reply, reply.
       It is engender'd in the eyes,
       With gazing fed; and fancy dies
       In the cradle where it lies.
          Let us all ring fancy's knell:
          I'll begin it,—Ding, dong, bell.   (*Song*)

The world is still deceived with ornament.   74
In law, what plea so tainted and corrupt
But, being season'd with a gracious voice,
Obscures the show of evil?   In religion
What damned error, but some sober brow
Will bless it and approve it with a text,
Hiding the grossness with fair ornament?
There is no vice so simple but assumes
Some mark of virtue on his outward parts.   (*Bassanio*)

Thus ornament is but the guiled shore   III. ii 97
To a most dangerous sea; the beauteous scarf
Veiling an Indian beauty; in a word,
The seeming truth which cunning times put on
To entrap the wisest. (*Bassanio*)

How all the other passions fleet to air   108
As doubtful thoughts, and rash-embraced despair,
And shuddering fear, and green-eyed jealousy.   (*Portia*)

You see me, Lord Bassanio, where I stand,   150
Such as I am: though for myself alone
I would not be ambitious in my wish,
To wish myself much better; yet, for you
I would be trebled twenty times myself;
A thousand times more fair, ten thousand times
More rich;
That only to stand high in your account,
I might in virtues, beauties, livings, friends,
Exceed account: but the full sum of me
Is sum of something, which, to term in gross,
Is an unlesson'd girl, unschool'd, unpractised;
Happy in this, she is not yet so old
But she may learn; happier than this,
She is not bred so dull but she can learn;
Happiest of all is that her gentle spirit
Commits itself to yours to be directed,
As from her lord, her governor, her king.   (*Portia*)

Here are a few of the unpleasant'st words   254
That ever blotted paper! (*Bassanio*)

Thou call'dst me dog before thou hadst a cause;   III. iii. 6
But, since I am a dog, beware my fangs.   (*Shylock*)

I never did repent for doing good,   III. iv. 10
Nor shall not now. (*Portia*)

When we are both accoutred like young men,   63
I'll prove the prettier fellow of the two,
And wear my dagger with the braver grace,
And speak between the change of man and boy
With a reed voice, and turn two mincing steps
Into a manly stride, and speak of frays
Like a fine bragging youth, and tell quaint lies,
How honourable ladies sought my love,
Which I denying, they fell sick and died.   (*Portia*)

A stony adversary, an unhuman wretch   IV. i. 4
Uncapable of pity, void and empty
From any dram of mercy. (*Duke*)

As there is no firm reason to be render'd,   IV. i. 53
Why he cannot abide a gaping pig;
Why he, a harmless necessary cat;
Why he, a woollen bag-pipe.   (*Shylock*)

I am not bound to please thee with my answers.   65
                               (*Shylock*)

What, wouldst thou have a serpent sting thee twice?   69
                               (*Shylock*)

You may as well go stand upon the beach   71
And bid the main flood bate his usual height;
You may as well use question with the wolf
Why he hath made the ewe bleat for the lamb;
You may as well forbid the mountain pines
To wag their high tops and to make no noise,
When they are fretten with the gusts of heaven;
You may as well do any thing most hard,
As seek to soften that—than which what's harder?—
His Jewish heart.   (*Antonio*)

If every ducat in six thousand ducats   85
Were in six parts and every part a ducat,
I would not draw them; I would have my bond.
                        (*Shylock*)

How shalt thou hope for mercy, rendering none?   (*Duke*)   88

What judgment shall I dread, doing no wrong? (*Shylock*)   89

I am a tainted wether of the flock,   114
Meetest for death: the weakest kind of fruit
Drops earliest to the ground; and so let me.   (*Antonio*)

Not on thy sole, but on thy soul, harsh Jew,   123
Thou makest thy knife keen.   (*Gratiano*)

Thou almost makest me waver in my faith   130
To hold opinion with Pythagoras,
That souls of animals infuse themselves
Into the trunks of men.   (*Gratiano*)

The quality of mercy is not strain'd,   184
It droppeth as the gentle rain from heaven
Upon the place beneath: it is twice blest;
It blesseth him that gives and him that takes:
'Tis mightiest in the mightiest: it becomes
The throned monarch better than his crown;
His sceptre shows the force of temporal power,

The attribute to awe and majesty,   IV. i. 191
Wherein doth sit the dread and fear of kings;
But mercy is above this sceptred sway;
It is enthroned in the hearts of kings.
It is an attribute to God himself;
And earthly power doth then show likest God's
When mercy seasons justice.   Therefore, Jew,
Though justice be thy plea, consider this,
That, in the course of justice, none of us
Should see salvation: we do pray for mercy;
And that same prayer doth teach us all to render
The deeds of mercy.   (*Portia*)

Wrest once the law to your authority: 215
To do a great right, do a little wrong.   (*Bassanio*)

'Twill be recorded for a precedent,   220
And many an error by the same example
Will rush into the state: it cannot be.   (*Portia*)

A Daniel come to judgment! yea, a Daniel!   (*Shylock*)   223

An oath, an oath, I have an oath in heaven: 228
Shall I lay perjury upon my soul?   (*Shylock*)

Take thrice thy money; bid me tear the bond.   (*Portia*)   234

               I charge you by the law,   238
Whereof you are a well-deserving pillar,
Proceed to judgment.   (*Shylock*)

O noble judge!   O excellent young man!   (*Shylock*)   246

               O wise and upright judge!   250
How much more elder art thou than thy looks!
                       (*Shylock*)

'Twere good you do so much for charity.   (*Portia*)   261

For, as thou urgest justice, be assured   315
Thou shalt have justice, more than thou desirest.
                       (*Portia*)

A second Daniel, a Daniel, Jew!   333
Now, infidel, I have you on the hip.   (*Gratiano*)

A Daniel, still say I, a second Daniel!   340
I thank thee, Jew, for teaching me that word.   (*Gratiano*)

Nay, take my life and all: pardon not that: IV. i. 374
You take my house when you do take the prop
That doth sustain my house; you take my life
When you do take the means whereby I live. (*Shylock*)

He is well paid that is well satisfied. (*Portia*)   415

I see, sir, you are liberal in offers: 438
You taught me first to beg; and now methinks
You teach me how a beggar should be answer'd.
            (*Portia*)

But we'll outface them and outswear them too. (*Portia*) IV. ii. 18

The moon shines bright: in such a night as this,   V. i. 1
When the sweet wind did gently kiss the trees
And they did make no noise, in such a night
Troilus methinks mounted the Troyan walls
And sigh'd his soul towards the Grecian tents,
Where Cressid lay that night. (*Lorenzo*)

       In such a night   6
Did Thisbe fearfully o'ertrip the dew
And saw the lion's shadow ere himself
And ran dismay'd away. (*Jessica*)

       In such a night   9
Stood Dido with a willow in her hand
Upon the wild sea banks and waft her love
To come again to Carthage. (*Lorenzo*)

       In such a night   12
Medea gather'd the enchanted herbs
That did renew old Aeson. (*Jessica*)

       In such a night   20
Did pretty Jessica, like a little shrew,
Slander her love, and he forgave it her. (*Lorenzo*)

Who comes so fast in silence of the night? (*Lorenzo*)   25

How sweet the moonlight sleeps upon this bank!   54
Here will we sit and let the sounds of music
Creep in our ears: soft stillness and the night
Become the touches of sweet harmony. (*Lorenzo*)

    Look how the floor of heaven   58
Is thick inlaid with patines of bright gold:
There's not the smallest orb which thou behold'st
But in his motion like an angel sings,

Still quiring to the young-eyed cherubins;   v. i. 62
Such harmony is in immortal souls;
But whilst this muddy vesture of decay
Doth grossly close it in, we cannot hear it.   (*Lorenzo*)

Come, ho, and wake Diana with a hymn: 66
With sweetest touches pierce your mistress' ear
And draw her home with music.   (*Lorenzo*)

I am never merry when I hear sweet music.   (*Jessica*)   69

      Do but note a wild and wanton herd,   71
Or race of youthful and unhandled colts,
Fetching mad bounds, bellowing and neighing loud,
Which is the hot condition of their blood;
If they but hear perchance a trumpet sound,
Or any air of music touch their ears,
You shall perceive them make a mutual stand,
Their savage eyes turn'd to a modest gaze
By the sweet power of music.   (*Lorenzo*)

      Nought so stockish, hard and full of rage,   81
But music for the time doth change his nature.
The man that hath no music in himself,
Nor is not moved with concord of sweet sounds,
Is fit for treasons, stratagems and spoils;
The motions of his spirit are dull as night
And his affections dark as Erebus:
Let no such man be trusted.   (*Lorenzo*)

How far that little candle throws his beams!   90
So shines a good deed in a naughty world.   (*Portia*)

So doth the greater glory dim the less.   (*Portia*)   93

The crow doth sing as sweetly as the lark   102
When neither is attended, and I think
The nightingale, if she should sing by day,
When every goose is cackling, would be thought
No better a musician than the wren.   (*Portia*)

How many things by season season'd are   107
To their right praise and true perfection!   (*Portia*)

Peace, ho! the moon sleeps with Endymion   109
And would not be awaked.   (*Portia*)

He knows me as the blind man knows the cuckoo,   112
By the bad voice.   (*Portia*)

This night methinks is but the daylight sick.   (*Portia*)   124

For a light wife doth make a heavy husband. (*Portia*)   v. i. 130

If you had known the virtue of the ring,   199
Or half her worthiness that gave the ring,
Or your own honour to contain the ring,
You would not then have parted with the ring. (*Portia*)

I am the unhappy subject of these quarrels. (*Antonio*)   238

You shall not know by what strange accident   278
I chanced on this letter. (*Portia*)

AS YOU LIKE IT

After the opening of the play, the scene is set in the Forest of Arden, where the old Duke ('Duke Senior') has gone to live the simple life after his place has been usurped by his brother Frederick. To the forest goes Rosalind, the old Duke's daughter, when she is banished in turn. Her bosom friend Celia, Frederick's daughter, insists on going with her, and Touchstone, the court jester, bears them company. To the forest also goes young Orlando, with whom Rosalind fell in love (and he with her) when she saw him overthrow Frederick's wrestler Charles. Rosalind has disguised herself as a boy and obtained lodging from a shepherd, Corin. Meeting Orlando, who does not recognize her, she persuades him, as a frolic, to court her as Rosalind. The mock wooing proceeds with a lot of merriment, and matters are complicated by the fact that Phebe, a disdainful shepherdess loved to distraction by the shepherd Silvius, falls in love with the supposed boy. Touchstone also finds himself a mate, Audrey, displacing her rustic admirer William; and Orlando's brother Oliver, who has come seeking him, falls in love with Celia. At the end, Rosalind sorts out the couples and shows herself in her true guise, and they all pair off. A mock-serious background to this happiest of all the comedies is provided by the philosophical musings of Jaques, one of the old Duke's followers.

Report speaks goldenly of his profit. *(Orlando)* 1. i. 6

Is 'old dog' my reward? Most true, I have lost my teeth in your service. *(Adam)* 87

What's the new news at the new court? *(Oliver)* 101

Fleet the time carelessly, as they did in the golden world. *(Charles)* 124

Love no man in good earnest, nor no further in sport neither, than with safety of a pure blush thou mayst in honour come off again. *(Celia)* 1. ii. 30

Let us sit and mock the good housewife Fortune from her wheel, that her gifts may henceforth be bestowed equally. *(Celia)* 35

Rosalind. The bountiful blind woman doth most mistake in her gifts to women.
Celia. 'Tis true; for those that she makes fair she scarce makes honest, and those that she makes honest she makes very ill-favouredly. 39

How now, wit! whither wander you? *(Celia)* 58

A certain knight that swore by his honour they were good pancakes and swore by his honour the mustard was naught: now I'll stand to it, the pancakes were naught and the mustard was good, and yet was not the knight forsworn. *(Touchstone)* 66

Now unmuzzle your wisdom. *(Rosalind)* 74

Le Beau. How shall I answer you? 108
Rosalind. As wit and fortune will.
Touchstone. Or as the Destinies decree.
Celia. Well said: that was laid on with a trowel.

It is the first time that ever I heard breaking of ribs was sport for ladies. *(Touchstone)* 146

If I be foiled, there is but one shamed that was never gracious; if killed, but one dead that is willing to be so: I shall do my friends no wrong, for I have none to lament me, the world no injury, for in it I have nothing. 199
(Orlando)

Wear this for me, one out of suits with fortune,   I. ii. 258
That could give more, but that her hand lacks means.
                                  (Rosalind)

My pride fell with my fortunes.   *(Rosalind)*   264

Sir, you have wrestled well and overthrown   266
More than your enemies.   *(Rosalind)*

What passion hangs these weights upon my tongue?   269
                                (Orlando)

                    Sir, fare you well: 295
Hereafter, in a better world than this,
I shall desire more love and knowledge of you.
                              (Le Beau)

Thus must I from the smoke into the smother;   299
From tyrant duke unto a tyrant brother.   *(Orlando)*

Celia. Why, cousin! why, Rosalind!   Cupid have mercy!   I. iii. 1
not a word?
Rosalind. Not one to throw at a dog.

O, how full of briers is this working-day world!   12
                                (Rosalind)

Come, come, wrestle with thy affections.   *(Celia)*   21

Mistress, dispatch you with your safest haste   42
And get you from our court.   *(Duke Frederick)*

Never so much as in a thought unborn   53
Did I offend your highness.   *(Rosalind)*

Treason is not inherited, my lord.   *(Rosalind)*   63

                  We still have slept together,   75
Rose at an instant, learn'd, play'd, eat together,
And wheresoe'er we went, like Juno's swans,
Still we went coupled and inseparable.   *(Celia)*

Alas, what danger will it be to us,   110
Maids as we are, to travel forth so far!
Beauty provoketh thieves sooner than gold.   *(Rosalind)*

                  Were it not better,   116
Because that I am more than common tall,
That I did suit me all points like a man?
A gallant curtle-axe upon my thigh,

A boar-spear in my hand; and—in my heart   I. iii. 120
Lie there what hidden woman's fear there will—
We'll have a swashing and a martial outside,
As many other mannish cowards have
That do outface it with their semblances.   (*Rosalind*)

He'll go along o'er the wide world with me;   134
Leave me alone to woo him.   (*Celia*)

Now, my co-mates and brothers in exile,   II. i. 1
Hath not old custom made this life more sweet
Than that of painted pomp?   Are not these woods
More free from peril than the envious court?
Here feel we but the penalty of Adam,
The seasons' difference, as the icy fang
And churlish chiding of the winter's wind,
Which, when it bites and blows upon my body
Even till I shrink with cold, I smile and say
'This is no flattery: these are counsellors
That feelingly persuade me what I am.'
Sweet are the uses of adversity,
Which, like the toad, ugly and venomous,
Wears yet a precious jewel in its head;
And this our life exempt from public haunt
Finds tongues in trees, books in the running brooks,
Sermons in stones and good in every thing.
(*Duke Senior*)

Happy is your grace,   18
That can translate the stubbornness of fortune
Into so quiet and so sweet a style.   (*Amiens*)

It irks me the poor dappled fools,   22
Being native burghers of this desert city,
Should in their own confines with forked heads
Have their round haunches gored.   (*Duke Senior*)

As he lay along   30
Under an oak whose antique root peeps out
Upon the brook that brawls along this wood.   (*First Lord*)

The wretched animal heaved forth such groans   36
That their discharge did stretch his leathern coat
Almost to bursting, and the big round tears
Coursed one another down his innocent nose
In piteous chase.   (*First Lord*)

First, for his weeping into the needless stream;   47
'Poor deer,' quoth he, 'thou makest a testament
As worldlings do, giving thy sum of more

To that which had too much': then, being there alone,   II. i. 50
Left and abandon'd of his velvet friends,
''Tis right,' quoth he, 'thus misery doth part
The flux of company': anon a careless herd,
Full of the pasture, jumps along by him
And never stays to greet him; 'Ay,' quoth Jaques,
'Sweep on, you fat and greasy citizens;
'Tis just the fashion: wherefore do you look
Upon that poor and broken bankrupt there?'
                                        (First Lord)

I love to cope him in these sullen fits,   67
For then he's full of matter. *(Duke Senior)*

              In the morning early   II. ii. 6
They found the bed untreasured of their mistress.
                                        (First Lord)

Why would you be so fond to overcome   II. iii. 7
The bonny priser of the humorous duke? *(Adam)*

Know you not, master, to some kind of men   10
Their graces serve them but as enemies?
No more do yours: your virtues, gentle master,
Are sanctified and holy traitors to you.
O, what a world is this, when what is comely
Envenoms him that bears it! *(Adam)*

What, wouldst thou have me go and beg my food?   31
Or with a base and boisterous sword enforce
A thievish living on the common road? *(Orlando)*

               I have five hundred crowns,   38
The thrifty hire I saved under your father,
Which I did store to be my foster-nurse
When service should in my old limbs lie lame
And unregarded age in corners thrown:
Take that, and He that doth the ravens feed,
Yea, providently caters for the sparrow,
Be comfort to my age! *(Adam)*

Though I look old, yet I am strong and lusty;   47
For in my youth I never did apply
Hot and rebellious liquors in my blood,
Nor did not with unbashful forehead woo
The means of weakness and debility;
Therefore my age is as a lusty winter,
Frosty but kindly. *(Adam)*

O good old man, how well in thee appears   II. iii. 56
The constant service of the antique world,
When service sweat for duty, not for meed!
Thou art not for the fashion of these times,
Where none will sweat but for promotion,
And, doing that, do choke their service up
Even with the having: it is not so with thee.   (*Orlando*)

Master, go on, and I will follow thee,   69
To the last gasp, with truth and loyalty.
From seventeen years till now almost fourscore
Here lived I, but now live here no more.
At seventeen years many their fortunes seek;
But at fourscore it is too late a week:
Yet fortune cannot recompense me better
Than to die well and not my master's debtor.   (*Adam*)

Rosalind. O Jupiter, how weary are my spirits!   II. iv. 1
Touchstone. I care not for my spirits, if my legs were not
weary.

I must comfort the weaker vessel, as doublet and hose   5
ought to show itself courageous to petticoat.   (*Rosalind*)

Ay, now am I in Arden: the more fool I; when I was at   16
home, I was in a better place: but travellers must be
content.   (*Touchstone*)

Though in thy youth thou wast as true a lover   26
As ever sigh'd upon a midnight pillow.   (*Silvius*)

If thou remember'st not the slightest folly   34
That ever love did make thee run into,
Thou hast not loved:
Or if thou hast not sat as I do now,
Wearying thy hearer in thy mistress' praise,
Thou hast not loved:
Or if thou hast not broke from company
Abruptly, as my passion now makes me,
Thou hast not loved.   (*Silvius*)

Alas, poor shepherd! searching of thy wound,   44
I have by hard adventure found mine own.   (*Rosalind*)

I remember, when I was in love, I broke my sword upon   47
a stone and bid him take that for coming a-night to Jane
Smile; and I remember the kissing of her batlet and the
cow's dugs that her pretty chopt hands had milked; and I
remember the wooing of a peascod instead of her, from
whom I took two cods and, giving them her again, said

with weeping tears 'Wear these for my sake.'   We that are   II. iv. 53
true lovers run into strange capers; but as all is mortal in
nature, so is all nature in love mortal in folly.

                                      (*Touchstone*)

            I am shepherd to another man   78
And do not shear the fleeces that I graze:
My master is of churlish disposition
And little recks to find the way to heaven
By doing deeds of hospitality.   (*Corin*)

                          I like this place,   94
And willingly could waste my time in it.   (*Celia*)

                Under the greenwood tree   II. v. 1
                Who loves to lie with me,
                And turn his merry note
                Unto the sweet bird's throat,
        Come hither, come hither, come hither:
                Here shall he see
                No enemy
        But winter and rough weather.   (*Amiens, sings*)

      I can suck melancholy out of a song, as a weasel sucks   12
eggs. (*Jaques*)

Amiens. My voice is ragged: I know I cannot please you.   15
Jaques. I do not desire you to please me; I do desire you
to sing.   Come, more; another stanzo: call you 'em
stanzos?

                Who doth ambition shun   40
                And loves to live i' the sun,
                Seeking the food he eats
                And pleased with what he gets,
        Come hither, come hither, come hither:
                Here shall he see
                No enemy
        But winter and rough weather.   (*All sing*)

Jaques.   If it do come to pass   52
                That any man turn ass,
                Leaving his wealth and ease,
                A stubborn will to please,
        Ducdame, ducdame, ducdame:
                Here shall he see
                Gross fools as he,
           An if he will come to me.
Amiens.   What's that 'ducdame'?
Jaques.   'Tis a Greek invocation, to call fools into a circle.

Why, how now, Adam! no greater heart in thee? Live   II. vi. 4
a little, comfort a little; cheer thyself a little. If this
uncouth forest yield any thing savage, I will either be
food for it or bring it for food to thee.   (*Orlando*)

If he, compact of jars, grow musical,   II. vii. 5
We shall have shortly discord in the spheres.
                            (*Duke Senior*)

A fool, a fool! I met a fool i' the forest,   12
A motley fool; a miserable world!
As I do live by food, I met a fool;
Who laid him down and bask'd him in the sun,
And rail'd on Lady Fortune in good terms,
In good set terms and yet a motley fool.
'Good morrow, fool,' quoth I. 'No, sir,' quoth he,
'Call me not fool till heaven hath sent me fortune':
And then he drew a dial from his poke,
And, looking on it with lack-lustre eye,
Says very wisely, 'It is ten o'clock:
Thus we may see,' quoth he, 'how the world wags:
'Tis but an hour ago since it was nine,
And after one hour more 'twill be eleven;
And so, from hour to hour, we ripe and ripe,
And then, from hour to hour, we rot and rot;
And thereby hangs a tale.' When I did hear
The motley fool thus moral on the time,
My lungs began to crow like chanticleer,
That fools should be so deep-contemplative,
And I did laugh sans intermission
An hour by his dial. O noble fool!
A worthy fool! Motley's the only wear.   (*Jaques*)

Jaques.   One that hath been a courtier,   36
And says, if ladies be but young and fair,
They have the gift to know it: and in his brain,
Which is as dry as the remainder biscuit
After a voyage, he hath strange places cramm'd
With observation, the which he vents
In mangled forms. O that I were a fool!
I am ambitious for a motley coat.
Duke Senior. Thou shalt have one.
Jaques.   It is my only suit.

            I must have liberty   47
Withal, as large a charter as the wind,
To blow on whom I please; for so fools have;
And they that are most galled with my folly,
They most must laugh. And why, sir, must they so?
The 'why' is plain as way to parish church:
He that a fool doth very wisely hit

Doth very foolishly, although he smart,   II. vii. 54
Not to seem senseless of the bob: if not,
The wise man's folly is anatomized
Even by the squandering glances of the fool.
Invest me in my motley; give me leave
To speak my mind, and I will through and through
Cleanse the foul body of the infected world,
If they will patiently receive my medicine.   (*Jaques*)

Most mischievous foul sin, in chiding sin: 64
For thou thyself hast been a libertine,
As sensual as the brutish sting itself;
And all the embossed sores and headed evils,
That thou with license of free foot hast caught,
Wouldst thou disgorge into the general world.
                                        (*Duke Senior*)

Why, who cries out on pride,   70
That can therein tax any private party?
Doth it not flow as hugely as the sea,
Till that the weary very means do ebb?
What woman in the city do I name,
When that I say the city-woman bears
The cost of princes on unworthy shoulders?
Who can come in and say that I mean her,
When such a one as she such is her neighbour?
Or what is he of basest function
That says his bravery is not on my cost,
Thinking that I mean him, but therein suits
His folly to the mettle of my speech?
There then; how then? what then?   Let me see wherein
My tongue hath wrong'd him: if it do him right,
Then he hath wrong'd himself; if he be free,
Why then my taxing like a wild-goose flies,
Unclaim'd of any man. (*Jaques*)

                          The thorny point   94
Of bare distress hath ta'en from me the show
Of smooth civility: yet am I inland bred
And know some nurture.   (*Orlando*)

                          Your gentleness shall force   102
More than your force move us to gentleness.
                                        (*Duke Senior*)

                          Whate'er you are   109
That in this desert inaccessible
Under the shade of melancholy boughs,
Lose and neglect the creeping hours of time;
If ever you have look'd on better days,

If ever been where bells have knoll'd to church,   II. vii. 114
If ever sat at any good man's feast,
If ever from your eyelids wiped a tear
And know what 'tis to pity and be pitied,
Let gentleness my strong enforcement be:
In the which hope I blush, and hide my sword.

(Orlando)

This wide and universal theatre   137
Presents more woeful pageants than the scene
Wherein we play in.   (Duke Senior)

              All the world's a stage,   139
And all the men and women merely players:
They have their exits and their entrances;
And one man in his time plays many parts,
His acts being seven ages.   At first the infant,
Mewling and puking in the nurse's arms.
And then the whining school-boy, with his satchel
And shining morning face, creeping like snail
Unwillingly to school.   And then the lover,
Sighing like furnace, with a woeful ballad
Made to his mistress' eyebrow.   Then a soldier,
Full of strange oaths and bearded like the pard,
Jealous in honour, sudden and quick in quarrel,
Seeking the bubble reputation
Even in the cannon's mouth.   And then the justice,
In fair round belly with good capon lined,
With eyes severe and beard of formal cut,
Full of wise saws and modern instances;
And so he plays his part.   The sixth stage shifts
Into the lean and slipper'd pantaloon
With spectacles on nose and pouch on side,
His youthful hose, well saved, a world too wide
For his shrunk shank; and his big manly voice,
Turning again toward childish treble, pipes
And whistles in his sound.   Last scene of all,
That ends this strange eventful history,
Is second childishness and mere oblivion,
Sans teeth, sans eyes, sans taste, sans every thing.

(Jaques)

        Blow, blow, thou winter wind,   174
        Thou art not so unkind
          As man's ingratitude;
        Thy tooth is not so keen,
        Because thou art not seen,
          Although thy breath be rude.
Heigh-ho! sing, heigh-ho! unto the green holly:
Most friendship is feigning, most loving mere folly:

II. vii. 182

Then, heigh-ho, the holly!
This life is most jolly.

Freeze, freeze, thou bitter sky,
That dost not bite so nigh
As benefits forgot:
Though thou the waters warp,
Thy sting is not so sharp
As friend remember'd not.
Heigh-ho! sing, heigh-ho! unto the green holly:
Most friendship is feigning, most loving mere folly:
Then, heigh-ho, the holly!
This life is most jolly.

(Amiens, sings)

Seek him with candle; bring him dead or living
Within this twelvemonth.   *(Duke Frederick)*

III. i. 6

Hang there, my verse, in witness of my love:
And thou, thrice-crowned queen of night, survey
With thy chaste eye, from thy pale sphere above
Thy huntress' name that my full life doth sway.
(Orlando)

III. ii. 1

Run, run, Orlando, carve on every tree
The fair, the chaste and inexpressive she.   *(Orlando)*

9

Corin. And how like you this shepherd's life, Master
Touchstone?
Touchstone. Truly, shepherd, in respect of itself it is a
good life; but in respect that it is a shepherd's life, it is
naught. In respect that it is solitary, I like it very well;
but in respect that it is private, it is a very vile life. Now,
in respect it is in the fields, it pleaseth me well; but in
respect it is not in the court, it is tedious. As it is a spare
life, look you, it fits my humour well: but as there is no
more plenty in it, it goes much against my stomach.

11

Touchstone. Hast any philosophy in thee, shepherd?
Corin. No more but that I know the more one sickens the
worse at ease he is; and that he that wants money, means
and content is without three good friends; that the
property of rain is to wet and fire to burn; that good pasture makes fat sheep, and that a great cause of the night is
lack of the sun; that he that hath learned no wit by nature
nor art may complain of good breeding or comes of a very
dull kindred.

22

Touchstone. Truly, thou art damned, like an ill-roasted   III. ii. 38
egg all on one side.
Corin. For not being at court? Your reason.
Touchstone. Why, if thou never wast at court, thou never
sawest good manners; if thou never sawest good manners,
then thy manners must be wicked; and wickedness is sin,
and sin is damnation. Thou art in a parlous state,
shepherd.

Sir, I am a true labourer: I earn that I eat, get that   77
I wear, owe no man hate, envy no man's happiness, glad of
other men's good, content with my harm, and the
greatest of my pride is to see my ewes graze and my
lambs suck. *(Corin)*

Rosalind. [*Reads.*] From the east to western Ind,   93
    No jewel is like Rosalind.
Her worth, being mounted on the wind,
    Through all the world bears Rosalind.
All the pictures fairest lined
    Are but black to Rosalind.
Let no face be kept in mind
    But the fair of Rosalind.
Touchstone. I'll rhyme you so eight years together,
dinners and suppers and sleeping-hours excepted; it is the
right butter-women's rank to market.

This is the very false gallop of verses: why do you   119
infect yourself with them? *(Touchstone)*

Why should this a desert be?   133
    For it is unpeopled? No;
Tongues I'll hang on every tree,
    That shall civil sayings show:
Some, how brief the life of man
    Runs his erring pilgrimage,
That the stretching of a span
    Buckles in his sum of age.
Some, of violated vows
    'Twixt the souls of friend and friend.
                   (Celia, reads)

Therefore Heaven Nature charged   149
    That one body should be fill'd
With all graces wide-enlarged:
    Nature presently distill'd
Helen's cheek, but not her heart,
    Cleopatra's majesty,
Atalanta's better part,
    Sad Lucretia's modesty.

Thus Rosalind of many parts   III. ii. 157
By heavenly synod was devised,
Of many faces, eyes and hearts,
To have the touches dearest prized.
Heaven would that she these gifts should have,
And I to live and die her slave.   (*Celia, reads*)

Let us make an honourable retreat; though not with   169
bag and baggage, yet with scrip and scrippage.
                                         (*Touchstone*)

I was never so berhymed since Pythagoras' time, that I   186
was an Irish rat, which I can hardly remember.
                                         (*Rosalind*)

It is a hard matter for friends to meet; but mountains   194
may be removed with earthquakes and so encounter.
                                         (*Celia*)

O wonderful, wonderful, and most wonderful wonder-   201
ful! and yet again wonderful, and after that, out of all
hooping! (*Celia*)

One inch of delay more is a South-sea of discovery.   206
                                         (*Rosalind*)

Take the cork out of thy mouth that I may drink thy   213
tidings. (*Rosalind*)

What manner of man?   Is his head worth a hat, or his   217
chin worth a beard? (*Rosalind*)

Speak, sad brow and true maid.   (*Rosalind*)   227

Rosalind. What did he when thou sawest him?   What   232
said he? How looked he? Wherein went he? What
makes he here? Did he ask for me? Where remains
he? How parted he with thee? and when shalt thou see
him again? Answer me in one word.
Celia.   You must borrow me Gargantua's mouth first; 'tis
a word too great for any mouth of this age's size.

There lay he, stretched along, like a wounded knight.   253
                                         (*Celia*)

Do you not know I am a woman? when I think, I must   263
speak. (*Rosalind*)

Slink by, and note him.   (*Rosalind*)   267

Jaques. Let's meet as little as we can.   III. ii. 273
Orlando. I do desire we may be better strangers.

Jaques. What stature is she of?   285
Orlando. Just as high as my heart.

I answer you right painted cloth, from whence you have   290
studied your questions. (*Orlando*)

Jaques. You have a nimble wit: I think 'twas made of   293
Atalanta's heels.   Will you sit down with me? and we two
will rail against our mistress the world and all our misery.
Orlando. I will chide no breather in the world but myself,
against whom I know most faults.

Jaques. By my troth, I was seeking for a fool when I   303
found you.
Orlando. He is drowned in the brook: look but in, and
you shall see him.

Jaques. I'll tarry no longer with you: farewell, good   309
Signior Love.
Orlando. I am glad of your departure: adieu, good Mon-
sieur Melancholy.

Rosalind. I pray you, what is't o'clock?   317
Orlando. You should ask me what time o' day: there's no
clock in the forest.
Rosalind. Then there is no true lover in the forest; else
sighing every minute and groaning every hour would
detect the lazy foot of Time as well as a clock.

Time travels in divers paces with divers persons.   I'll   325
tell you who Time ambles withal, who Time trots withal,
who Time gallops withal and who he stands still withal.
                                        (*Rosalind*)

Orlando. Who doth he gallop withal?   344
Rosalind. With a thief to the gallows, for though he go as
softly as foot can fall, he thinks himself too soon there.
Orlando. Who stays it still withal?
Rosalind. With lawyers in the vacation; for they sleep
between term and term and then they perceive not how
Time moves.

Here in the skirts of the forest, like fringe upon a   353
petticoat. (*Rosalind*)

Orlando. Can you remember any of the principal evils   369
that he laid to the charge of women?

Rosalind. There were none principal; they were all like   III. ii. 371
one another as halfpence are, every one fault seeming
monstrous till his fellow-fault came to match it.

    A lean cheek, which you have not, a blue eye and   392
sunken, which you have not, an unquestionable spirit,
which you have not, a beard neglected, which you have
not; . . . then your hose should be ungartered, your
bonnet unbanded, your sleeve unbuttoned, your shoe
untied and every thing about you demonstrating a careless
desolation. (*Rosalind, describing a man in love*)

    Love is merely a madness, and, I tell you, deserves as   420
well a dark house and a whip as madmen do: and the
reason why they are not so punished and cured is, that
the lunacy is so ordinary that the whippers are in love too.
                                      (*Rosalind*)

    O knowledge ill-inhabited, worse than Jove in a   III. iii. 10
thatched house! (*Jaques*)

Touchstone. Truly, I would the gods had made thee   16
poetical.
Audrey. I do not know what 'poetical' is: is it honest in
deed and word? is it a true thing?
Touchstone. No, truly; for the truest poetry is the most
feigning; and lovers are given to poetry, and what they
swear in poetry may be said as lovers they do feign.

    Honesty coupled to beauty is to have honey a sauce to   30
sugar. (*Touchstone*)

Touchstone. To cast away honesty upon a foul slut were to   35
put good meat into an unclean dish.
Audrey. I am not a slut, though I thank the gods I am
foul.
Touchstone. Well, praised be the gods for thy foulness!
sluttishness may come hereafter.

Sir Oliver Martext. Is there none here to give the woman?   67
Touchstone. I will not take her on gift of any man.

    Good even, good Master What-ye-call't: how do you,   74
sir? You are very well met: God 'ild you for your last
company: I am very glad to see you: even a toy in hand
here, sir: nay, pray be covered. (*Touchstone*)

    As the ox hath his bow, sir, the horse his curb, and the   80
falcon her bells, so man hath his desires; and as pigeons
bill, so wedlock would be nibbling. (*Touchstone*)

Farewell, good Master Oliver: not,—   III. iii. 100

        O sweet Oliver,
        O brave Oliver,
    Leave me not behind thee:

but,—

        Wind away,
        Begone, I say,
    I will not to wedding with thee.   (*Touchstone*)

Rosalind. I' faith, his hair is of a good colour.   III. iv. 11
Celia. An excellent colour: your chestnut was ever the
only colour.

    O, that's a brave man! he writes brave verses, speaks   43
brave words, swears brave oaths and breaks them
bravely.   (*Celia*)

              A pageant truly play'd   55
Between the pale complexion of true love
And the red glow of scorn and proud disdain.   (*Corin*)

The sight of lovers feedeth those in love.   (*Rosalind*)   60

Say that you love me not, but say not so   III. v. ii
In bitterness.   The common executioner,
Whose heart the accustom'd sight of death makes hard,
Falls not the axe upon the humbled neck
But first begs pardon.   (*Silvius*)

Thou tell'st me there is murder in mine eye: 10
'Tis pretty, sure, and very probable,
That eyes, that are the frail'st and softest things,
Who shut their coward gates on atomies,
Should be call'd tyrants, butchers, murderers!   (*Phebe*)

Scratch thee but with a pin, and there remains   21
Some scar of it; lean but upon a rush,
The cicatrice and capable impressure
Thy palm some moment keeps.   (*Phebe*)

If ever,—as that ever may be near,—   28
You meet in some fresh cheek the power of fancy,
Then shall you know the wounds invisible
That love's keen arrows make.   (*Silvius*)

            Who might be your mother,   35
That you insult, exult, and all at once,
Over the wretched?   What though you have no beauty,—
As, by my faith, I see no more in you
Than without candle may go dark to bed—
Must you be therefore proud and pitiless?   (*Rosalind*)

I think she means to tangle my eyes too!   III. v. 42
No, faith, proud mistress, hope not after it:
'Tis not your inky brows, your black silk hair,
Your bugle eyeballs, nor your cheek of cream,
That can entame my spirits to your worship.   (*Rosalind*)

You foolish shepherd, wherefore do you follow her,   49
Like foggy south puffing with wind and rain?
You are a thousand times a properer man
Than she a woman: 'tis such fools as you
That makes the world full of ill-favour'd children:
'Tis not her glass, but you, that flatters her. (*Rosalind*)

But, mistress, know yourself: down on your knees,   57
And thank heaven, fasting, for a good man's love:
For I must tell you friendly in your ear,
Sell when you can: you are not for all markets:
Cry the man mercy; love him; take his offer:
Foul is most foul, being foul to be a scoffer. (*Rosalind*)

Sweet youth, I pray you, chide a year together: 64
I had rather hear you chide than this man woo.' (*Phebe*)

Rosalind. Why look you so upon me?   69
Phebe. For no ill will I bear you.
Rosalind. I pray you, do not fall in love with me,
For I am falser than vows made in wine:
Besides, I like you not.

Dead shepherd, now I find thy saw of might,   81
'Who ever loved that loved not at first sight?'   (*Phebe*)

So holy and so perfect is my love,   99
And I in such a poverty of grace,
That I shall think it a most plenteous crop
To glean the broken ears after the man
That the main harvest reaps: loose now and then
A scatter'd smile, and that I'll live upon.   (*Silvius*)

Think not I love him, though I ask for him;   109
'Tis but a peevish boy; yet he talks well;
But what care I for words? yet words do well
When he that speaks them pleases those that hear.
It is a pretty youth: not very pretty:
But, sure, he's proud, and yet his pride becomes him:
He'll make a proper man: the best thing in him
Is his complexion; and faster than his tongue
Did make offence his eye did heal it up.
He is not very tall; yet for his years he's tall:
His leg is but so so; and yet 'tis well:

There was a pretty redness in his lip,   III. v. 120
A little riper and more lusty red
Than that mix'd in his cheek; 'twas just the difference
Betwixt the constant red and mingled damask. (*Phebe*)

He said mine eyes were black and my hair black;   130
And, now I am remember'd, scorn'd at me:
I marvel why I answer'd not again:
But that's all one; omittance is no quittance.
I'll write to him a very taunting letter. (*Phebe*)

I will be bitter with him and passing short. (*Phebe*)   138

Rosalind. They say you are a melancholy fellow.   IV. i. 3
Jaques. I am so; I do love it better than laughing.

Jaques. Why, 'tis good to be sad and say nothing.   8
Rosalind. Why, then, 'tis good to be a post.

I have neither the scholar's melancholy, which is   10
emulation, nor the musician's, which is fantastical, nor
the courtier's, which is proud, nor the soldier's, which is
ambitious, nor the lawyer's, which is politic, nor the
lady's, which is nice, nor the lover's, which is all these: but
it is a melancholy of mine own, compounded of many
simples, extracted from many objects. (*Jaques*)

A traveller! By my faith, you have great reason to be   21
sad: I fear you have sold your own lands to see other
men's; then, to have seen much and to have nothing, is to
have rich eyes and poor hands. (*Rosalind*)

I had rather have a fool to make me merry than experi-   28
ence to make me sad; and to travel for it too! (*Rosalind*)

Orlando. Good day and happiness, dear Rosalind.   31
Jaques. Nay, then, God be wi' you, an you talk in blank
verse.

Farewell, Monsieur Traveller: look you lisp and wear   33
strange suits, disable all the benefits of your own country,
be out of love with your nativity and almost chide God for
making you that countenance you are, or I will scarce think
you have swam in a gondola. (*Rosalind*)

Break an hour's promise in love! He that will divide a   44
minute into a thousand parts and break but a part of the
thousandth part of a minute in the affairs of love, it may
be said of him that Cupid hath clapped him o' the
shoulder, but I'll warrant him heart-whole. (*Rosalind*)

E   113

Come, woo me, woo me, for now I am in a holiday   IV. i. 68
humour and like enough to consent. (*Rosalind*)

Rosalind. Very good orators, when they are out, they will   75
spit; and for lovers lacking—God warn us!—matter,
the cleanliest shift is to kiss.
Orlando. How if the kiss be denied?
Rosalind. Then she puts you to entreaty, and there begins
new matter.

The poor world is almost six thousand years old, and in   95
all this time there was not any man died in his own person,
videlicet, in a love-cause. (*Rosalind*)

Men have died from time to time and worms have eaten   106
them, but not for love. (*Rosalind*)

Orlando. I would not have my right Rosalind of this   108
mind, for, I protest, her frown might kill me.
Rosalind. By this hand, it will not kill a fly.

Orlando. Then love me, Rosalind.   115
Rosalind. Yes, faith, will I, Fridays and Saturdays and all.

Men are April when they woo, December when they   147
wed: maids are May when they are maids, but the sky
changes when they are wives. I will be more jealous
of thee than a Barbary cock-pigeon over his hen, more
clamorous than a parrot against rain, more new-fangled
than an ape, more giddy in my desires than a monkey: I
will weep for nothing, like Diana in the fountain, and I
will do that when you are disposed to be merry; I will
laugh like a hyen, and that when thou art inclined to sleep.
                                                (*Rosalind*)

Make the doors upon a woman's wit and it will out at   162
the casement; shut that and 'twill out at the key-hole;
stop that, 'twill fly with the smoke out at the chimney.
                                                (*Rosalind*)

You shall never take her without her answer, unless you   175
take her without her tongue. (*Rosalind*)

'Tis no matter how it be in tune, so it make noise   IV. ii. 9
enough. (*Jaques*)

What shall he have that kill'd the deer?   11
His leather skin and horns to wear.
Then sing him home; the rest shall bear
        This burden.

Take thou no scorn to wear the horn;   IV. ii. 15
It was a crest ere thou wast born:
  Thy father's father wore it,
  And thy father bore it:
The horn, the horn, the lusty horn
Is not a thing to laugh to scorn.   (*Foresters, sing*)

She says I am not fair, that I lack manners;   IV. iii. 15
She calls me proud, and that she could not love me,
Were man as rare as phoenix.   (*Rosalind*)

I saw her hand: she has a leathern hand,   24
A freestone-colour'd hand; I verily did think
That her old gloves were on, but 'twas her hands:
She has a huswife's hand.   (*Rosalind*)

                   Women's gentle brain   33
Could not drop forth such giant-rude invention,
Such Ethiope words, blacker in their effect
Than in their countenance.   (*Rosalind*)

  If the scorn of your bright eyne   50
  Have power to raise such love in mine,
  Alack, in me what strange effect
  Would they work in mild aspect!
  Whiles you chid me, I did love;
  How then might your prayers move!
             (*Rosalind, reads*)

  What, to make thee an instrument and play false strains   67
upon thee! not to be endured!   (*Rosalind*)

I see love hath made thee a tame snake.   (*Rosalind*)   70

The rank of osiers by the murmuring stream   80
Left on your right hand brings you to the place.   (*Celia*)

                Pacing through the forest,   101
Chewing the food of sweet and bitter fancy.   (*Oliver*)

Under an oak, whose boughs were moss'd with age,   105
And high top bald with dry antiquity.   (*Oliver*)

A lioness, with udders all drawn dry,   115
Lay couching, head on ground, with catlike watch,
When that the sleeping man should stir; for 'tis
The royal disposition of that beast
To prey on nothing that doth seem as dead.   (*Oliver*)

It is meat and drink to me to see a clown.   (*Touchstone*)   v. i. 11

Touchstone. Art rich?   v. i. 26
William. Faith, sir, so so.
Touchstone. 'So so' is good, very good, very excellent
good; and yet it is not; it is but so so.

To have, is to have; for it is a figure in rhetoric that   45
drink, being poured out of a cup into a glass, by filling the
one doth empty the other.   (*Touchstone*)

Therefore, you clown, abandon,—which is in the vulgar   52
leave,—the society,—which in the boorish is company,—
of this female,—which in the common is woman; which
together is, abandon the society of this female, or, clown,
thou perishest; or, to thy better understanding, diest; or,
to wit, I kill thee, make thee away, translate thy life into
death, thy liberty into bondage.   (*Touchstone*)

Trip, Audrey! trip, Audrey! I attend, I attend.   69
                                                (*Touchstone*)

Is 't possible that on so little acquaintance you should   v. ii. 1
like her? that but seeing you should love her? and loving
woo? and wooing, she should grant? and will you persever
to enjoy her?   (*Orlando*)

Rosalind. I thought thy heart had been wounded with the   24
claws of a lion.
Orlando. Wounded it is, but with the eyes of a lady.

Your brother and my sister no sooner met but they   35
looked, no sooner looked but they loved, no sooner loved
but they sighed, no sooner sighed but they asked one
another the reason, no sooner knew the reason but they
sought the remedy; and in these degrees have they made a
pair of stairs to marriage which they will climb incontinent, or else be incontinent before marriage: they are in
the very wrath of love and they will together; clubs cannot
part them.   (*Rosalind*)

O, how bitter a thing it is to look into happiness   47
through another man's eyes!   (*Orlando*)

Phebe. Good shepherd, tell this youth what 'tis to love.   89
Silvius. It is to be all made of sighs and tears;

It is to be all made of faith and service;   95

It is to be all made of fantasy,   100
All made of passion and all made of wishes,

All adoration, duty, and observance,   v. ii. 102
All humbleness, all patience, and impatience,
All purity, all trial, all observance.

If this be so, why blame you me to love you?   (*Silvius*)   111

   Pray you, no more of this; 'tis like the howling of Irish   119
wolves against the moon.   (*Rosalind*)

Touchstone. To-morrow is the joyful day, Audrey; to-   v. iii. 1
morrow will we be married.
Audrey. I do desire it with all my heart; and I hope it is
no dishonest desire to desire to be a woman of the world.

First Page. Shall we clap into 't roundly, without hawk-   11
ing or spitting or saying we are hoarse, which are only
prologues to a bad voice?
Second Page. I' faith, i' faith; and both in a tune, like two
gipsies on a horse.

     It was a lover and his lass,   17
      With a hey, and a ho, and a hey nonino,
    That o'er the green corn-field did pass
      In the spring time, the only pretty ring time,
    When birds do sing, hey ding a ding, ding:
      Sweet lovers love the spring.

     Between the acres of the rye,
      With a hey, and a ho, and a hey nonino,
    These pretty country folks would lie,
      In spring time, the only pretty ring time,
    When birds do sing, hey ding a ding, ding:
      Sweet lovers love the spring.

     This carol they began that hour,
      With a hey, and a ho, and a hey nonino,
    How that a life was but a flower
      In spring time, the only pretty ring time,
    When birds do sing, hey ding a ding, ding:
      Sweet lovers love the spring.

     And therefore take the present time,
      With a hey, and a ho, and a hey nonino;
    For love is crowned with the prime
      In spring time, the only pretty ring time,
    When birds do sing, hey ding a ding, ding:
      Sweet lovers love the spring.   (*Song*)

First Page. We kept time, we lost not our time.   38
Touchstone. By my troth, yes; I count it but time lost to
hear such a foolish song.

I sometimes do believe, and sometimes do not: v. iv. 3
As those that fear they hope, and know they fear.
                                        (*Orlando*)

Rosalind. You say, that you'll have Phebe, if she will?   16
Silvius. Though to have her and death were both one
thing.

    I have trod a measure; I have flattered a lady; I have   45
been politic with my friend, smooth with mine enemy; I
have undone three tailors; I have had four quarrels, and
like to have fought one.   (*Touchstone*)

Touchstone. A poor virgin, sir, an ill-favoured thing, sir,   60
but mine own; a poor humour of mine, sir, to take that
that no man else will: rich honesty dwells like a miser,
sir, in a poor house; as your pearl in your foul oyster.
Duke Senior. By my faith, he is very swift and sententious.
Touchstone. According to the fool's bolt, sir, and such
dulcet diseases.

Jaques. How did you find the quarrel on the seventh   69
cause?
Touchstone. Upon a lie seven times removed.

    I durst go no further than the Lie Circumstantial, nor   90
he durst not give me the Lie Direct; and so we measured
swords and parted.   (*Touchstone*)

    O sir, we quarrel in print, by the book; as you have   95
books for good manners: I will name you the degrees.
The first, the Retort Courteous; the second, the Quip
Modest; the third, the Reply Churlish; the fourth, the
Reproof Valiant; the fifth, the Countercheck Quarrelsome;
the sixth, the Lie with Circumstance; the seventh, the Lie
Direct.   All these you may avoid but the Lie Direct; and
you may avoid that too, with an If.   (*Touchstone*)

Your If is the only peace-maker; much virtue in If.   107
                                        (*Touchstone*)

Jaques. Is not this a rare fellow, my lord? he's as good   109
at any thing and yet a fool.
Duke Senior. He uses his folly like a stalking-horse and
under the presentation of that he shoots his wit.

Meantime, forget this new-fall'n dignity   182
And fall into our rustic revelry. (*Duke Senior*)

If it be true that good wine needs no bush, 'tis true that *Epilogue* 3
a good play needs no epilogue.   (*Rosalind*)

I charge you, O women, for the love you bear to men, to   13
like as much of this play as please you: and I charge you,
O men, for the love you bear to women—as I perceive by
your simpering, none of you hates them—that between
you and the women the play may please.   If I were a
woman I would kiss as many of you as had beards that
pleased me, complexions that liked me, and breaths that I
defied not.   (*Rosalind*)

THE TAMING OF THE SHREW

There is here a play within a play, for the opening scene shows how Christopher Sly, a tinker, is found dead drunk by a wealthy lord, who for a jest has him dressed in fine clothes and waited on when he wakes by obsequious attendants who keep assuring him that he is a nobleman who has been out of his wits. The play proper is then performed for his entertainment. Bianca, the modest daughter of Baptista, is courted by young Hortensio, old but wealthy Gremio, and Lucentio, a recent arrival. Their prospects are blighted by her elder sister Katharina, who scares all suitors away with her shrewish tongue; for Baptista insists that the elder daughter must be married before the younger. To them arrives Petruchio, who is attracted by Katharina and promises that he can deal with her. Two of Bianca's suitors disguise themselves to get access to her, Lucentio masquerading as a schoolmaster and Hortensio as a music-teacher. Petruchio meanwhile tames Katharina by disregarding her nagging and out-shouting her, while professing to be her ardent adorer, until she becomes his submissive wife. Lucentio wins Bianca and Hortensio consoles himself with a widow. A great part of the play is crude farce, but there are some shrewd comments by Lucentio's servant Tranio and Petruchio's man Grumio.

The Slys are no rogues; look in the chronicles; we came   *Induction,*
in with Richard Conqueror.   Therefore paucas pallabris;   i. 3
let the world slide: sessa!   (*Sly*)

Grim death, how foul and loathsome is thine image!   35
                      (*Lord*)

   Ne'er ask me what raiment I 'll wear; for I have no more   ii. 11
doublets than backs, no more stockings than legs, nor no
more shoes than feet.   (*Sly*)

Dost thou love pictures? we will fetch thee straight   51
Adonis painted by a running brook,
And Cytherea all in sedges hid,
Which seem to move and wanton with her breath,
Even as the waving sedges play with wind.
                    (*Second Servant*)

Why, sir, you know no house nor no such maid,   93
Nor no such men as you have reckon'd up,
As Stephen Sly and old John Naps of Greece
And Peter Turph and Henry Pimpernell
And twenty more such names and men as these
Which never were nor no man ever saw.
                   (*Third Servant*)

   Come, madam wife, sit by my side and let the world   146
slip: we shall ne'er be younger.   (*Sly*)

Let 's be no stoics nor no stocks, I pray;   I. i. 31
Or so devote to Aristotle's checks
As Ovid be an outcast quite abjured.   (*Tranio*)

No profit grows where is no pleasure ta'en: 39
In brief, sir, study what you most affect.   (*Tranio*)

To comb your noddle with a three legg'd stool.   64
                   (*Katharina*)

My books and instruments shall be my company,   82
On them to look and practise by myself.   (*Bianca*)

There's small choice in rotten apples.   (*Hortensio*)   138

Tranio, I saw her coral lips to move   179
And with her breath she did perfume the air:
Sacred and sweet was all I saw in her.   (*Lucio*)

   'Tis a very excellent piece of work, madam lady: would   258
'twere done.   (*Sly*)

*E   121

Crowns in my purse I have and goods at home,   I. ii. 57
And so am come abroad to see the world.   (*Petruchio*)

Nothing comes amiss, so money comes withal. (*Grumio*)   82

                         Though she chide as loud   95
As thunder when the clouds in autumn crack.
                                          (*Petruchio*)

    See, to beguile the old folks, how the young folks lay   138
their heads together! (*Grumio*)

Think you a little din can daunt mine ears?   200
Have I not in my time heard lions roar?
Have I not heard the sea puff'd up with winds
Rage like an angry boar chafed with sweat?
Have I not heard great ordnance in the field,
And heaven's artillery thunder in the skies?
Have I not in a pitched battle heard
Loud 'larums, neighing steeds, and trumpets' clang?
And do you tell me of a woman's tongue,
That gives not half so great a blow to hear
As will a chestnut in a farmer's fire?
Tush, tush! fear boys with bugs.   (*Petruchio*)

And do as adversaries do in law,   278
Strive mightily, but eat and drink as friends.
                                          (*Hortensio*)

She is your treasure, she must have a husband;   II. i. 32
I must dance barefoot on her wedding day
And for your love to her lead apes in hell.
                                          (*Katharina*)

I am as peremptory as she proud-minded;   132
And where two raging fires meet together
They do consume the thing that feeds their fury:
Though little fire grows great with little wind,
Yet extreme gusts will blow out fire and all:
So I to her and so she yields to me;
For I am rough and woo not like a babe. (*Petruchio*)

Now, by the world, it is a lusty wench;   161
I love her ten times more than e'er I did:
O, how I long to have some chat with her! (*Petruchio*)

Say that she rail; why then I'll tell her plain   171
She sings as sweetly as a nightingale:
Say that she frown; I'll say she looks as clear
As morning roses newly wash'd with dew:

Say she be mute and will not speak a word;   II. i. 175
Then I'll commend her volubility,
And say she uttereth piercing eloquence:
If she do bid me pack, I'll give her thanks,
As though she bid me stay by her a week:
If she deny to wed, I'll crave the day
When I shall ask the banns and when be married.

                           (*Petruchio*)

Katharine. They call me Katharine that do talk of me.   185
Petruchio. You lie, in faith; for you are call'd plain Kate,
And bonny Kate and sometimes Kate the curst;
And Kate, the prettiest Kate in Christendom,
Kate of Kate Hall, my super-dainty Kate,
For dainties are all Kates, and therefore, Kate,
Take this of me, Kate of my consolation;
Hearing thy mildness praised in every town,
Thy virtues spoke of, and thy beauty sounded,
Yet not so deeply as to thee belongs,
Myself am moved to woo thee for my wife.

If you strike me, you are no gentleman.   (*Katharina*)   223

Thou must be married to no man but me;   277
For I am he am born to tame you, Kate,
And bring you from a wild Kate to a Kate
Conformable as other household Kates.   (*Petruchio*)

A mad-cap ruffian and a swearing Jack,   290
That thinks with oaths to face the matter out.

                           (*Katharina*)

Sirrah young gamester, your father were a fool   402
To give thee all, and in his waning age
Set foot under thy table: tut, a toy!
An old Italian fox is not so kind, my boy.   (*Gremio*)

I am no breeching scholar in the schools;   III. i. 18
I'll not be tied to hours nor 'pointed times,
But learn my lessons as I please myself.   (*Bianca*)

Lucentio. 'Hic ibat,' as I told you before, 'Simois,' I am   31
Lucentio, 'hic est,' son unto Vincentio of Pisa, 'Sigeia
tellus,' disguised thus to get your love; 'Hic steterat,' and
that Lucentio that comes a-wooing, 'Priami,' is my man
Tranio, 'regia,' bearing my port, 'celsa senis,' that we
might beguile the old pantaloon.

        .   .   .   .   .

Bianca. Now let me see if I can construe it: 'Hic ibat   41
Simois,' I know you not, 'hic est Sigeia tellus,' I trust

you not; 'hic steterat Priami,' take heed he hear us not,   III. i. 43
'regia,' presume not, 'celsa senis,' despair not.

And wherefore gaze this goodly company,   III. ii. 96
As if they saw some wondrous monument,
Some comet or unusual prodigy ?   (*Petruchio*)

To me she's married, not unto my clothes.   (*Petruchio*)   119

This done, he took the bride about the neck   179
And kiss'd her lips with such a clamorous smack
That at the parting all the church did echo.   (*Gremio*)

The door is open, sir; there lies your way;   212
You may be jogging whiles your boots are green.
                                       (*Katharina*)

But for my bonny Kate, she must with me.   229
Nay, look not big, nor stamp, nor stare, nor fret;
I will be master of what is mine own.   (*Petruchio*)

A whoreson beetle-headed, flap-ear'd knave.   (*Petruchio*)   IV. i. 160

She eat no meat to-day, nor none shall eat;   200
Last night she slept not, nor to-night she shall not;
As with the meat, some undeserved fault
I'll find about the making of the bed;
And here I'll fling the pillow, there the bolster,
This way the coverlet, another way the sheets:
Ay, and amid this hurly I intend
That all is done in reverend care of her;
And in conclusion she shall watch all night:
And if she chance to nod I'll rail and brawl
And with the clamour keep her still awake.
This is a way to kill a wife with kindness;
And thus I'll curb her mad and headstrong humour.
                                       (*Petruchio*)

Kindness in women, not their beauteous looks,   IV. ii. 41
Shall win my love.   (*Hortensio*)

The poorest service is repaid with thanks.   (*Petruchio*)   IV. iii. 45

And revel it as bravely as the best,   54
With silken coats and caps and golden rings,
With ruffs and cuffs and fardingales and things;
With scarfs and fans and double change of bravery,
With amber bracelets, beads, and all this knavery.
                                       (*Petruchio*)

Thy gown? why, ay: come, tailor, let us see't.   IV. iii. 86
O mercy, God! what masquing stuff is here?
What's this? a sleeve? 'tis like a demi-cannon:
What, up and down, carved like an apple-tart?
Here's snip and nip and cut and slish and slash,
Like to a censer in a barber's shop:
Why, what, i' devil's name, tailor, call'st thou this?
                                                (*Petruchio*)

O monstrous arrogance! Thou liest, thou thread, thou   108
   thimble,
Thou yard, three-quarters, half-yard, quarter, nail!
Thou flea, thou nit, thou winter-cricket thou!
Braved in mine own house with a skein of thread?
Away, thou rag, thou quantity, thou remnant;
Or I shall so be-mete thee with thy yard
As thou shalt think on prating whilst thou livest!
                                                (*Petruchio*)

Our purses shall be proud, our garments poor;   173
For 'tis the mind that makes the body rich;
And as the sun breaks through the darkest clouds,
So honour peereth in the meanest habit.
What is the jay more precious than the lark,
Because his feathers are more beautiful?
Or is the adder better than the eel,
Because his painted skin contents the eye?   (*Petruchio*)

It shall be what o'clock I say it is.   (*Petruchio*)   197

   I knew a wench married in an afternoon as she went to   IV. iv. 99
the garden for parsley to stuff a rabbit.   (*Biondello*)

Such war of white and red within her cheeks! (*Petruchio*)   30

Nothing but sit and sit, and eat and eat!   (*Petruchio*)   V. ii. 12

He that is giddy thinks the world turns round.   (*Widow*)   20

Fie, fie! unknit that threatening unkind brow,   136
And dart not scornful glances from those eyes,
To wound thy lord, thy king, thy governor:
It blots thy beauty as frosts do bite the meads,
Confounds thy fame as whirlwinds shake fair buds,
And in no sense is meet or amiable.
A woman moved is like a fountain troubled,
Muddy, ill-seeming, thick, bereft of beauty;
And while it is so, none so dry or thirsty
Will deign to sip or touch one drop of it.
Thy husband is thy lord, thy life, thy keeper,
Thy head, thy sovereign; one that cares for thee,

And for thy maintenance commits his body   v. ii. 148
To painful labour both by sea and land,
To watch the night in storms, the day in cold,
Whilst thou liest warm at home, secure and safe;
And craves no other tribute at thy hands
But love, fair looks and true obedience;
Too little payment for so great a debt.
Such duty as the subject owes the prince
Even such a woman oweth to her husband;
And when she is froward, peevish, sullen, sour,
And not obedient to his honest will,
What is she but a foul contending rebel
And graceless traitor to her loving lord?
I am ashamed that women are so simple
To offer war where they should kneel for peace,
Or seek for rule, supremacy and sway,
When they are bound to serve, love and obey.
Why are our bodies soft and weak and smooth,
Unapt to toil and trouble in the world,
But that our soft conditions and our hearts
Should well agree with our external parts?
Come, come, you froward and unable worms!
My mind hath been as big as one of yours,
My heart as great, my reason haply more,
To bandy word for word and frown for frown;
But now I see our lances are but straws,
Our strength as weak, our weakness past compare,
That seeming to be most which we indeed least are.
Then vail your stomachs, for it is no boot,
And place your hands below your husband's foot.

                                        (*Katharina*)

ALL'S WELL THAT ENDS WELL

Helena, daughter of a famous physician, cherishes an unrequited love for the high-born Count Bertram, with whose mother she lives. Going to the court, she cures the king of a deadly disease and as a reward is allowed to choose a husband from the nobility. She names Bertram, who marries her but, thinking her beneath him, goes off to fight for the Duke of Florence, telling her that he will accept her as his wife only if she can obtain a ring from his finger. In Florence Bertram tries to seduce Diana, with whose mother Helena, who has gone there in the guise of a pilgrim, is lodging. It is arranged that Helena should take Diana's place at a midnight assignation, and she there obtains the ring which enables her to claim that she has satisfied Bertram's inhuman condition. Bertram then repents and accepts her. The sordid plot is somewhat relieved by the amusing knavery of Parolles, a cowardly braggart who is unmercifully hoaxed and ridiculed by his comrades-in-arms.

He hath abandoned his physicians, madam; under   I. i. 15
whose practices he hath persecuted time with hope, and
finds no other advantage in the process but only the losing
of hope by time. (*Lafeu, an old lord*)

Moderate lamentation is the right of the dead, excessive   64
grief the enemy of the living. (*Lafeu*)

                     Love all, trust a few,   73
Do wrong to none: be able for thine enemy
Rather in power than use, and keep thy friend
Under thy own life's key: be check'd for silence,
But never tax'd for speech. (*Countess*)

                     My imagination   93
Carries no favour in 't but Bertram's.
I am undone: there is no living, none,
If Bertram be away. 'Twere all one
That I should love a bright particular star
And think to wed it, he is so above me:
In his bright radiance and collateral light
Must I be comforted, not in his sphere.
The ambition in my love thus plagues itself:
The hind that would be mated by the lion
Must die for love. 'Twas pretty, though a plague,
To see him every hour; to sit and draw
His arched brows, his hawking eye, his curls,
In our heart's table; heart too capable
Of every line and trick of his sweet favour:
But now he's gone, and my idolatrous fancy
Must sanctify his reliques. (*Helena*)

                     Full oft we see   115
Cold wisdom waiting on superfluous folly. (*Helena*)

Our remedies oft in ourselves do lie,   231
Which we ascribe to heaven: the fated sky
Gives us free scope, only doth backward pull
Our slow designs when we ourselves are dull. (*Helena*)

But on us both did haggish age steal on   I. ii. 29
And wore us out of act. (*King*)

                     His honour,   38
Clock to itself, knew the true minute when
Exception bid him speak, and at this time
His tongue obey'd his hand: who were below him
He used as creatures of another place,

And bow'd his eminent top to their low ranks,   I. ii. 43
Making them proud of his humility,
In their poor praise he humbled. (*King*)

        'Let me not live,' quoth he,   55
'After my flame lacks oil, to be the snuff
Of younger spirits, whose apprehensive senses
All but new things disdain; whose judgments are
Mere fathers of their garments; whose constancies
Expire before their fashions.' (*King*)

He must needs go that the devil drives. (*Clown*)   I. iii. 31

    Among nine bad if one be good,   82
    There's yet one good in ten. (*Clown*)

Even so it was with me when I was young: 134
  If ever we are nature's, these are ours; this thorn
Doth to our rose of youth rightly belong;
  Our blood to us, this to our blood is born;
It is the show and seal of nature's truth,
Where love's strong passion is impress'd in youth:
By our remembrances of days foregone,
Such were our faults, or then we thought them none.
          (*Countess*)

My friends were poor, but honest; so's my love: 201
Be not offended; for it hurts not him
That he is loved of me: I follow him not
By any token of presumptuous suit;
Nor would I have him till I do deserve him;
Yet never know how that desert should be.
I know I love in vain, strive against hope;
Yet in this captious and intenible sieve
I still pour in the waters of my love
And lack not to lose still: thus, Indian-like,
Religious in mine error, I adore
The sun, that looks upon his worshipper,
But knows of him no more. (*Helena*)

Those girls of Italy, take heed of them: II. i. 19
They say, our French lack language to deny,
If they demand. (*King*)

I am commanded here, and kept a coil with   27
'Too young' and 'the next year' and ''tis too early.'
          (*Bertram*)

I shall stay here the forehorse to a smock,   30
Creaking my shoes on the plain masonry,
Till honour be bought up and no sword worn
But one to dance with! (*Bertram*)

He that of greatest works is finisher   II. i. 139
Oft does them by the weakest minister:
So holy writ in babes hath judgment shown,
When judges have been babes; great floods have flown
From simple sources, and great seas have dried
When miracles have by the greatest been denied.
Oft expectation fails and most oft there
Where most it promises, and oft it hits
Where hope is coldest and despair most fits.   (*Helena*)

It is not so with Him that all things knows   152
As 'tis with us that square our guess by shows;
But most it is presumption in us when
The help of heaven we count the act of men.   (*Helena*)

Ere twice the horses of the sun shall bring   164
Their fiery torcher his diurnal ring,
Ere twice in murk and occidental damp
Moist Hesperus hath quench'd his sleepy lamp,
Or four and twenty times the pilot's glass
Hath told the thievish minutes how they pass,
What is infirm from your sound parts shall fly,
Health shall live free and sickness freely die.   (*Helena*)

From lowest place when virtuous things proceed,   II. iii. 132
The place is dignified by the doer's deed.   (*King*)

                            War is no strife   308
To the dark house and the detested wife.   (*Bertram*)

A young man married is a man that's marred.   (*Parolles*)   315

Bertram.   Here comes my clog.   [*Enter Helena.*]   II. v. 58

                            Sir, I can nothing say,   76
But that I am your most obedient servant.   (*Helena*)

Strangers and foes do sunder, and not kiss.   (*Helena*)   91

There's nothing here that is too good for him   III. ii. 82
But only she; and she deserves a lord
That twenty such rude boys might tend upon
And call her hourly mistress.   (*Countess*)

A very tainted fellow, and full of wickedness.   (*Countess*)   89

Where death and danger dog the heels of worth.   III. iv. 15
                (*Steward, reading Helena's letter*)

What is 'pourquoi'? do or not do? I would I had   I. iii. 96
bestowed that time in the tongues that I have in fencing,
dancing, and bear-baiting: O, had I but followed the arts!
(*Sir Andrew*)

Sir Toby. What is thy excellence in a galliard, knight?   127
Sir Andrew. Faith, I can cut a caper.

Wherefore are these things hid? wherefore have these   133
gifts a curtain before 'em? (*Sir Toby*)

Is it a world to hide virtues in? (*Sir Toby*)   140

Thou know'st no less but all; I have unclasp'd   I. iv. 13
To thee the book even of my secret soul. (*Duke*)

                Stand at her doors,   16
And tell them, there thy fixed foot shall grow
Till thou have audience. (*Duke*)

For they shall yet belie thy happy years,   30
That say thou art a man: Diana's lip
Is not more smooth and rubious; thy small pipe
Is as the maiden's organ, shrill and sound,
And all is semblative a woman's part. (*Duke*)

Whoe'er I woo, myself would be his wife. (*Viola*)   45

Many a good hanging prevents a bad marriage. (*Clown*)   I. v. 20

What says Quinapalus? 'Better a witty fool than a   38
foolish wit.' (*Clown*)

Virtue that transgresses is but patched with sin; and   53
sin that amends is but patched with virtue. (*Clown*)

Beauty's a flower. (*Clown*)   57

Good my mouse of virtue, answer me. (*Clown*)   69

Olivia. What's a drunken man like, fool?   139
Clown. Like a drowned man, a fool and a mad man: one
draught above heat makes him a fool; the second mads
him; and a third drowns him.

Not yet old enough for a man, nor young enough for a   165
boy; as a squash is before 'tis a peascod, or a codling
when 'tis almost an apple: 'tis with him in standing water,
between boy and man. He is very well-favoured and he
speaks very shrewishly; one would think his mother's milk
were scarce out of him. (*Malvolio*)

Most radiant, exquisite and unmatchable beauty. (*Viola*)   I. v. 181

Some mollification for your giant, sweet lady. (*Viola*)   218

Olivia. Is 't not well done?   [*Unveiling.*]   253
Viola. Excellently done, if God did all.
Olivia. 'Tis in grain, sir; 'twill endure wind and
weather.

Viola. 'Tis beauty truly blent, whose red and white   257
Nature's own sweet and cunning hand laid on:
Lady, you are the cruell'st she alive,
If you will lead these graces to the grave
And leave the world no copy.
Olivia. O, sir, I will not be so hard-hearted; I will give
out divers schedules of my beauty: it shall be inven-
toried, and every particle and utensil labelled to my will:
as, item, two lips, indifferent red; item, two grey eyes,
with lids to them; item, one neck, one chin, and so forth.

I see you what you are, you are too proud;   269
But, if you were the devil, you are fair.
My lord and master loves you: O, such love
Could be but recompensed, though you were crown'd
The nonpareil of beauty. (*Viola*)

If I did love you in my master's flame,   283
With such a suffering, such a deadly life,
In your denial I would find no sense;
I would not understand it. (*Viola*)

Make me a willow cabin at your gate,   287
And call upon my soul within the house;
Write loyal cantons of contemned love
And sing them loud even in the dead of night;
Halloo your name to the reverberate hills
And make the babbling gossip of the air
Cry out 'Olivia!' (*Viola*)

Olivia. What is your parentage?   296
Viola. Above my fortunes, yet my state is well:
I am a gentleman.

I am no fee'd post, lady; keep your purse. (*Viola*)   303

Farewell, fair cruelty. (*Viola*)   307

'I am a gentleman.' I 'll be sworn thou art;   310
Thy tongue, thy face, thy limbs, actions and spirit,
Do give thee five-fold blazon. (*Olivia*)

She bore a mind that envy could not but call fair. II. i. 31
                                        (*Sebastian*)

Fortune forbid my outside have not charm'd her! (*Viola*) II. ii. 19

How easy is it for the proper-false   30
In women's waxen hearts to set their forms! (*Viola*)

O time! thou must untangle this, not I;   41
It is too hard a knot for me to untie! (*Viola*)

A false conclusion: I hate it as an unfilled can. To be II. iii. 6
up after midnight and to go to bed then, is early: so that to
go to bed after midnight is to go to bed betimes. (*Sir Toby*)

Thou wast in very gracious fooling last night, when   23
thou spokest of Pigrogromitus, of the Vapians passing the
equinoctial of Queubus: 'twas very good, i' faith.
                                        (*Sir Andrew*)

I did impeticos thy gratillity; for Malvolio's nose is no   29
whipstock: my lady has a white hand, and the Myrmidons
are no bottle-ale houses. (*Clown*)

Why, this is the best fooling, when all is done.   33
                                        (*Sir Andrew*)

Clown. Would you have a love-song, or a song of good   36
life?
Sir Toby. A love-song, a love-song.
Sir Andrew. Ay, ay: I care not for good life.

O mistress mine, where are you roaming?   40
O, stay and hear; your true love's coming,
    That can sing both high and low:
Trip no further, pretty sweeting;
Journeys end in lovers meeting
    Every wise man's son doth know. (*Clown, sings*)

What is love? 'tis not hereafter;   48
Present mirth hath present laughter;
    What's to come is still unsure:
In delay there lies no plenty;
Then come kiss me, sweet and twenty,
    Youth's a stuff will not endure. (*Clown, sings*)

Sir Andrew. A mellifluous voice, as I am true knight.   54
Sir Toby. A contagious breath.
Sir Andrew. Very sweet and contagious, i' faith.

137

Shall we rouse the night-owl in a catch that will draw   II. iii. 59
three souls out of one weaver?   (*Sir Toby*)

What a caterwauling do you keep here!   (*Maria*)   76

Clown. Beshrew me, the knight's in admirable fooling.   85
Sir Andrew. Ay, he does well enough if he be disposed,
and so do I too: he does it with a better grace, but I do it
more natural.

Sir Toby. Dost thou think, because thou art virtuous,   123
there shall be no more cakes and ale?
Clown. Yes, by Saint Anne, and ginger shall be hot i' the
mouth too.

Go, sir, rub your chain with crumbs.   (*Sir Toby*)   128

Maria. Marry, sir, sometimes he is a kind of puritan.   151
Sir Andrew. O, if I thought that, I 'ld beat him like a dog!

I have no exquisite reason for 't, but I have reason good   157
enough.   (*Sir Andrew*)

My purpose is, indeed, a horse of that colour.   (*Maria*)   181

That old and antique song we heard last night: II. iv. 3
Methought it did relieve my passion much,
More than light airs and recollected terms
Of these most brisk and giddy-pated times.   (*Duke*)

               If ever thou shalt love,   15
In the sweet pangs of it remember me;
For such as I am all true lovers are,
Unstaid and skittish in all motions else,
Save in the constant image of the creature
That is beloved.   (*Duke*)

Duke. How dost thou like this tune?   20
Viola. It gives a very echo to the seat
Where love is throned.

               Let still the woman take   30
An elder than herself; so wears she to him,
So sways she level in her husband's heart:
For, boy, however we do praise ourselves,
Our fancies are more giddy and unfirm,
More longing, wavering, sooner lost and worn,
Than women's are.   (*Duke*)

Then let thy love be younger than thyself,   II. iv. 37
Or thy affection cannot hold the bent;
For women are as roses, whose fair flower
Being once display'd, doth fall that very hour. (*Duke*)

O, fellow, come, the song we had last night.   43
Mark it, Cesario, it is old and plain;
The spinsters and the knitters in the sun
And the free maids that weave their thread with bones
Do use to chant it: it is silly sooth,
And dallies with the innocence of love,
Like the old age. (*Duke*)

        Come away, come away, death,   52
            And in sad cypress let me be laid;
        Fly away, fly away, breath;
            I am slain by a fair cruel maid.
        My shroud of white, stuck all with yew,
                O, prepare it!
        My part of death, no one so true
                Did share it.

        Not a flower, not a flower sweet,
            On my black coffin let there be strown;
        Not a friend, not a friend greet
            My poor corpse, where my bones shall be thrown:
        A thousand thousand sighs to save,
                Lay me, O, where
        Sad true lover never find my grave,
                To weep there! (*Clown, sings*)

Get thee to yond same sovereign cruelty: 83
Tell her, my love, more noble than the world,
Prizes not quantity of dirty lands;
The parts that fortune hath bestow'd upon her,
Tell her, I hold as giddily as fortune;
But 'tis that miracle and queen of gems
That nature pranks her in attracts my soul. (*Duke*)

There is no woman's sides   96
Can bide the beating of so strong a passion
As love doth give my heart; no woman's heart
So big, to hold so much: they lack retention.
Alas, their love may be call'd appetite,
No motion of the liver, but the palate,
That suffer surfeit, cloyment and revolt;
But mine is all as hungry as the sea,
And can digest as much. (*Duke*)

Duke.   And what's her history?   II. iv. 112
Viola. A blank, my lord.   She never told her love,
But let concealment, like a worm i' the bud,
Feed on her damask cheek: she pined in thought,
And with a green and yellow melancholy
She sat like patience on a monument,
Smiling at grief.   Was not this love indeed?
We men may say more, swear more: but indeed
Our shows are more than will; for still we prove
Much in our vows, but little in our love.

I am all the daughters of my father's house,   123
And all the brothers too.   (*Viola*)

He has been yonder i' the sun practising behaviour to   II. v. 19
his own shadow this half-hour.   (*Maria*)

Here comes the trout that must be caught with tickling.   25
                                    (*Maria*)

Contemplation makes a rare turkey-cock of him.   (*Fabian*)   35

There is example for't; the lady of the Strachy married   44
the yeoman of the wardrobe.   (*Malvolio*)

And then to have the humour of state; and after a   58
demure travel of regard, telling them I know my place as I
would they should do theirs.   (*Malvolio*)

I frown the while; and perchance wind up my watch, or   65
play with my—some rich jewel.   (*Malvolio*)

Malvolio. 'Besides, you waste the treasure of your time   85
with a foolish knight,'—
Sir Andrew. That's me, I warrant you.
Malvolio. 'One Sir Andrew,'—
Sir Andrew. I knew 'twas I; for many do call me fool.

Now is the woodcock near the gin.   (*Fabian*)   92

I may command where I adore;   115
    But silence, like a Lucrece knife,
With bloodless stroke my heart doth gore:
    M, O, A, I, doth sway my life.   (*Malvolio, reads*)

In my stars I am above thee; but be not afraid of great-   155
ness; some are born great, some achieve greatness, and
some have greatness thrust upon 'em.   (*Malvolio, reads*)

I will be strange, stout, in yellow stockings, and cross-   186
gartered, even with the swiftness of putting on.
                                    (*Malvolio*)

Clown. Now Jove, in his next commodity of hair, send   III. i. 50
thee a beard!
Viola. By my troth, I'll tell thee, I am almost sick for one;
[*Aside.*] though I would not have it grow on my chin.

This fellow is wise enough to play the fool;   67
And to do that well craves a kind of wit:
He must observe their mood on whom he jests,
The quality of persons, and the time,
And, like the haggard, check at every feather
That comes before his eye.   This is a practice
As full of labour as a wise man's art.   (*Viola*)

Taste your legs, sir; put them to motion.   (*Sir Toby*)   87

   Most excellent accomplished lady, the heavens rain   95
odours on you!   (*Viola*)

   'Odours,' 'pregnant,' and 'vouchsafed': I'll get 'em   101
all three all ready.   (*Sir Andrew*)

Viola. I pity you.   134
Olivia.   That's a degree to love.
Viola. No, not a grize; for 'tis a vulgar proof,
That very oft we pity enemies.

O world, how apt the poor are to be proud!   (*Olivia*)   138

The clock upbraids me with the waste of time.   (*Olivia*)   141

O, what a deal of scorn looks beautiful   157
In the contempt and anger of his lip!   (*Olivia*)

Cesario, by the roses of the spring,   161
By maidhood, honour, truth and every thing,
I love thee so, that, maugre all thy pride,
Nor wit nor reason can my passion hide.   (*Olivia*)

Love sought is good, but given unsought is better.   168
                                         (*Olivia*)

By innocence I swear, and by my youth,   169
I have one heart, one bosom, and one truth,
And that no woman has.   (*Viola*)

To awake your dormouse valour.   (*Fabian*)   III. ii. 19

You are now sailed into the north of my lady's opinion;   III. ii. 27
where you will hang like an icicle on a Dutchman's beard,
unless you do redeem it by some laudable attempt either
of valour or policy.   (*Fabian*)

Taunt him with the license of ink: if thou thou'st him   47
some thrice, it shall not be amiss; and as many lies as will
lie in thy sheet of paper, although the sheet were big
enough for the bed of Ware in England, set 'em down.
                                                (*Sir Toby*)

Let there be gall enough in thy ink, though thou write   52
with a goose-pen, no matter.   (*Sir Toby*)

He does smile his face into more lines than is in the new   84
map with the augmentation of the Indies: you have not
seen such a thing as 'tis. I can hardly forbear hurling
things at him.   (*Maria*)

I can no other answer make but thanks,   III. iii. 14
And thanks, and ever thanks; how oft good turns
Are shuffled off with such uncurrent pay. (*Sebastian*)

I pray you, let us satisfy our eyes   22
With the memorials and the things of fame
That do renown this city. (*Sebastian*)

In the south suburbs, at the Elephant,   39
Is best to lodge.   (*Antonio*)

Haply your eye shall light upon some toy   44
You have desire to purchase; and your store,
I think, is not for idle markets, sir.   (*Antonio*)

Where is Malvolio? he is sad and civil,   III. iv. 5
And suits well for a servant with my fortunes.   (*Olivia*)

Sweet lady, ho, ho.   (*Malvolio*)   18

Please one, and please all.   (*Malvolio*)   25

I think we do know the sweet Roman hand.   (*Malvolio*)   30

At your request! yes; nightingales answer daws.   38
                                                (*Malvolio*)

Why, this is very midsummer madness.   (*Olivia*)   61

What, man! defy the devil: consider, he's an enemy to   107
mankind.   (*Sir Toby*)

Why, how now, my bawcock! how dost thou, chuck?   III. iv. 125
                          (*Sir Toby*)

Get him to say his prayers, good Sir Toby, get him to   131
pray.   (*Maria*)

If this were played upon a stage now, I could condemn   140
it as an improbable fiction.   (*Fabian*)

Sir Toby. [*Reads.*] 'Youth, whatsoever thou art, thou art   161
but a scurvy fellow.'
Fabian. Good, and valiant.
Sir Toby. [*Reads.*] 'Wonder not, nor admire not in thy
mind, why I do call thee so, for I will show thee no reason
for 't.'
Fabian. A good note; that keeps you from the blow of the
law.
Sir Toby. [*Reads.*] 'Thou comest to the lady Olivia, and in
my sight she uses thee kindly: but thou liest in thy
throat; that is not the matter I challenge thee for.'
Fabian. Very brief, and to exceeding good sense—less.

Still you keep o' the windy side of the law.   (*Fabian*)   181

Sir Toby. [*Reads.*] 'Fare thee well; and God have mercy   183
upon one of our souls! He may have mercy upon mine;
but my hope is better, and so look to thyself. Thy friend,
as thou usest him, and thy sworn enemy,
                          ANDREW AGUECHEEK.'

So soon as ever thou seest him, draw; and, as thou   194
drawest, swear horrible; for it comes to pass oft that a
terrible oath, with a swaggering accent sharply twanged
off, gives manhood more approbation than ever proof
itself would have earned him.   (*Sir Toby*)

This will so fright them both that they will kill one   214
another by the look, like cockatrices.   (*Sir Toby*)

Here, wear this jewel for me, 'tis my picture;   228
Refuse it not; it hath no tongue to vex you.   (*Olivia*)

He is a devil in private brawl: souls and bodies hath   258
he divorced three.   (*Sir Toby*)

He is indeed, sir, the most skilful, bloody and fatal   292
opposite that you could possibly have found in any part of
Illyria. Will you walk towards him?   (*Fabian*)

An I thought he had been valiant and so cunning in   311
fence, I 'ld have seen him damned ere I 'ld have challenged
him.   (*Sir Andrew*)

Out of my lean and low ability   III. iv. 378
I 'll lend you something; my having is not much. (*Viola*)

I hate ingratitude more in a man   388
Than lying, vainness, babbling, drunkenness,
Or any taint of vice whose strong corruption
Inhabits our frail blood. (*Viola*)

In nature there 's no blemish but the mind;   401
None can be call'd deform'd but the unkind:
Virtue is beauty, but the beauteous evil
Are empty trunks o'erflourish'd by the devil. (*Antonio*)

I prithee, vent thy folly somewhere else. (*Sebastian*)   IV. i. 10

     I 'll have an action of battery against him, if there be   36
any law in Illyria: though I struck him first, yet it's no
matter for that. (*Sir Andrew*)

                         Ungracious wretch,   51
Fit for the mountains and the barbarous caves,
Where manners ne'er were preach'd! out of my sight!
                                              (*Olivia*)

     As the old hermit of Prague, that never saw pen and   IV. ii. 14
ink, very wittily said to a niece of King Gorboduc, 'That
that is is.' (*Clown*)

Clown. What is the opinion of Pythagoras concerning wild   54
fowl?
Malvolio. That the soul of our grandam might haply
inhabit a bird.
Clown. What thinkest thou of his opinion?
Malvolio. I think nobly of the soul, and no way approve
his opinion.

                    I am gone, sir,   130
                    And anon, sir,
                I 'll be with you again,
                    In a trice,
                    Like to the old Vice,
                Your need to sustain;
                Who, with dagger of lath,
                In his rage and his wrath,
                    Cries, Ah, ha! to the devil:
                Like a mad lad,
                Pare thy nails, dad;
                    Adieu, goodman devil. (*Clown, sings*)

Blame not this haste of mine.   If you mean well,   IV. iii. 22
Now go with me and with this holy man
Into the chantry by: there, before him
And underneath that consecrated roof,
Plight me the full assurance of your faith;
That my most jealous and too doubtful soul
May live at peace.   (*Olivia*)

That face of his I do remember well;   v. i. 54
Yet, when I saw it last, it was besmear'd
As black as Vulcan in the smoke of war:
A bawbling vessel was he captain of,
For shallow draught and bulk unprizable;
With which such scathful grapple did he make
With the most noble bottom of our fleet,
That very envy and the tongue of loss
Cried fame and honour on him.   (*Duke*)

Here comes the countess: now heaven walks on earth.   100
                                      (*Duke*)

Live you the marble-breasted tyrant still.   (*Duke*)   127

A contract of eternal bond of love,   159
Confirm'd by mutual joinder of your hands,
Attested by the holy close of lips,
Strengthen'd by interchangement of your rings;
And all the ceremony of this compact
Seal'd in my function, by my testimony.   (*Priest*)

O thou dissembling cub! what wilt thou be   167
When time hath sow'd a grizzle on thy case?   (*Duke*)

    We took him for a coward, but he's the very devil   184
incardinate.   (*Sir Andrew*)

    He's drunk, Sir Toby, an hour agone; his eyes were set   204
at eight i' the morning.   (*Clown*)

One face, one voice, one habit, and two persons,   223
A natural perspective, that is and is not!   (*Duke*)

Perpend, my princess, and give ear.   (*Clown*)   307

                    Madam, you have done me wrong,   336
Notorious wrong.   (*Malvolio*)

Thou shalt be both the plaintiff and the judge   362
Of thine own cause.   (*Olivia*)

Alas, poor fool, how have they baffled thee!   (*Olivia*)   377
F   145

Thus the whirligig of time brings in his revenges.   v. i. 385
                                                      (Clown)

I'll be revenged on the whole pack of you.   (Malvolio)   387

He hath been most notoriously abused.   (Olivia)   388

   When that I was and a little tiny boy,   398
     With hey, ho, the wind and the rain,
   A foolish thing was but a toy,
     For the rain it raineth every day.

   But when I came to man's estate,
     With hey, ho, the wind and the rain,
   'Gainst knaves and thieves men shut their gate,
     For the rain it raineth every day.

   But when I came, alas! to wive,
     With hey, ho, the wind and the rain,
   By swaggering could I never thrive,
     For the rain it raineth every day.

   But when I came unto my beds,
     With hey, ho, the wind and the rain,
   With toss-pots still had drunken heads,
     For the rain it raineth every day.

   A great while ago the world begun,
     With hey, ho, the wind and the rain,
   But that's all one, our play is done,
     And we'll strive to please you every day.
                                                  (Clown, sings)

THE WINTER'S TALE

Leontes, king of Sicilia, has a groundless suspicion that his queen Hermione has committed adultery with Polixenes, king of Bohemia, who is paying a prolonged visit to his court. Camillo, an old Sicilian lord, warns Polixenes, and flees with him to Bohemia. Leontes, taking this as proof of the queen's guilt, has her imprisoned. Later, in spite of the protests of his lords, he determines on the destruction of her newly born daughter, and Antigonus is commissioned to dispose of the child, named Perdita by her mother. After he leaves her on the barren coast of Bohemia, himself falling prey to a bear, Perdita is discovered and brought up by a shepherd. Meanwhile in Sicily Mamillius, Leontes's little son, is dead of grief at his mother's disgrace, and Paulina, Antigonus's wife, tells the king that the queen has also succumbed. Sixteen years now pass, and Florizel, the son of Polixenes, is found by his father courting Perdita; to escape his wrath the young couple flee to Sicily, aided by the exiled Camillo, who wants to return home. To save himself the old shepherd reveals the objects he found with Perdita, showing her to be the lost princess. Polixenes, who has followed his son, now approves his choice, and Paulina stages a final surprise by inviting Leontes to inspect a statue of Hermione, which turns out to be the queen herself, who had been hidden away. The disjointed plot is redeemed by some passages of beautiful poetry, and Autolycus, the pedlar, is an engaging rogue.

They that went on crutches ere he was born desire yet   I. i. 44
their life to see him a man. (*Camillo*)

Nine changes of the watery star. (*Polixenes*)   I. ii. I

There is no tongue that moves, none, none i' the world,   20
So soon as yours could win me. (*Polixenes*)

Two lads that thought there was no more behind   63
But such a day to-morrow as to-day,
And to be boy eternal. (*Polixenes*)

We were as twinn'd lambs that did frisk i' the sun,   67
And bleat the one at the other: what we changed
Was innocence for innocence; we knew not
The doctrine of ill-doing, nor dream'd
That any did. (*Polixenes*)

What! have I twice said well? when was 't before?   90
I prithee tell me; cram 's with praise, and make 's
As fat as tame things: one good deed dying tongueless
Slaughters a thousand waiting upon that.
Our praises are our wages: you may ride 's
With one soft kiss a thousand furlongs ere
With spur we heat an acre. (*Hermione*)

But to be paddling palms and pinching fingers,   115
As now they are, and making practised smiles,
As in a looking-glass, and then to sigh, as 'twere
The mort o' the deer; O, that is entertainment
My bosom likes not. (*Leontes*)

Why, that's my bawcock.   What, hast smutch'd thy nose?   121
They say it is a copy out of mine.   Come, captain,
We must be neat; not neat, but cleanly, captain.
                                        (*Leontes*)

                 Still virginalling   125
Upon his palm! (*Leontes*)

                 They say we are   129
Almost as like as eggs; women say so,
That will say any thing. (*Leontes*)

                 Looking on the lines   153
Of my boy's face, methought I did recoil
Twenty-three years, and saw myself unbreech'd,
In my green velvet coat, my dagger muzzled,
Lest it should bite its master, and so prove,
As ornaments oft do, too dangerous. (*Leontes*)

He's all my exercise, my mirth, my matter,   I. ii. 166
Now my sworn friend and then mine enemy,
My parasite, my soldier, statesman, all:
He makes a July's day short as December,
And with his varying childness cures in me
Thoughts that would thick my blood.   (*Polixenes*)

                       Should all despair   198
That have revolted wives, the tenth of mankind
Would hang themselves.   Physic for 't there is none;
It is a bawdy planet, that will strike
Where 'tis predominant.   (*Leontes*)

You never spoke what did become you less   282
Than this.   (*Camillo*)

                Is whispering nothing?   284
Is leaning cheek to cheek? is meeting noses?
Kissing with inside lip? stopping the career
Of laughter with a sigh?—a note infallible
Of breaking honesty?—horsing foot on foot?
Skulking in corners? wishing clocks more swift?
Hours, minutes? noon, midnight? and all eyes
Blind with the pin and web but theirs, theirs only,
That would unseen be wicked? is this nothing?

                       (*Leontes*)

              Bespice a cup,   316
To give mine enemy a lasting wink.   (*Leontes*)

            If I could find example   357
Of thousands that had struck anointed kings
And flourish'd after, I'ld not do't; but since
Nor brass nor stone nor parchment bears not one,
Let villany itself forswear't.   (*Camillo*)

             You may as well   426
Forbid the sea for to obey the moon
As or by oath remove or counsel shake
The fabric of his folly.   (*Camillo*)

Mamillius. What colour are your eyebrows?   II. i. 13
First Lady.   Blue, my lord.
Mamillius. Nay, that's a mock: I have seen a lady's nose
That has been blue, but not her eyebrows.

Hermione.   Pray you, sit by us,   22
And tell's a tale.
Mamillius.   Merry or sad shall't be?
Hermione. As merry as you will.
Mamillius. A sad tale's best for winter: I have one
Of sprites and goblins.

The silence often of pure innocence   II. ii. 41
Persuades when speaking fails. (*Paulina*)

A nest of traitors! (*Leontes*)   II. iii. 81

                                    Behold, my lords.   97
Although the print be little, the whole matter
And copy of the father, eye, nose, lip,
The trick of 's frown, his forehead, nay, the valley,
The pretty dimples of his chin and cheek, his smiles,
The very mould and frame of hand, nail, finger. (*Paulina*)

It is an heretic that makes the fire,   115
Not she which burns in 't. (*Paulina*)

I am a feather for each wind that blows. (*Leontes*)   154

The climate's delicate, the air most sweet,   III. i. 1
Fertile the isle, the temple much surpassing
The common praise it bears. (*Cleomenes*)

The bug which you would fright me with I seek.   III. ii. 93
To me can life be no commodity. (*Hermione*)

What studied torments, tyrant, hast for me?   176
What wheels? racks? fires? what flaying? boiling?
In leads or oils? what old or newer torture
Must I receive, whose every word deserves
To taste of thy most worst? Thy tyranny
Together working with thy jealousies,
Fancies too weak for boys, too green and idle
For girls of nine, O, think what they have done
And then run mad indeed, stark mad! (*Paulina*)

                    What's gone and what's past help   223
Should be past grief. (*Paulina*)

Thou art perfect then, our ship hath touch'd upon   III. iii. 1
The deserts of Bohemia? (*Antigonus*)

                    The skies look grimly,   3
And threaten present blusters. (*Mariner*)

Blossom, speed thee well! (*Antigonus*)   46

Antigonus.   I never saw   55
The heavens so dim by day. A savage clamour!
Well may I get aboard! This is the chase:
I am gone for ever   [*Exit, pursued by a bear.*]

I would there were no age between sixteen and three-   III. iii. 59
and-twenty, or that youth would sleep out the rest; for
there is nothing in the between but getting wenches with
child, wronging the ancientry, stealing, fighting.
(*Shepherd*)

This has been some stair-work, some trunk-work, some   75
behind-door-work.   (*Shepherd*)

Now the ship boring the moon with her main-mast, and   93
anon swallowed with yest and froth, as you'ld thrust a
cork into a hogshead.   (*Clown*)

The men are not yet cold under water, nor the bear   107
half dined on the gentleman: he's at it now.   (*Clown*)

When daffodils begin to peer,   IV. iii. 1
    With heigh! the doxy over the dale;
Why, then comes in the sweet o' the year;
    For the red blood reigns in the winter's pale.

The white sheet bleaching on the hedge,
    With heigh! the sweet birds, O, how they sing!
Doth set my pugging tooth on edge;
    For a quart of ale is a dish for a king.

The lark, that tirra-lyra chants,
    With heigh! with heigh! the thrush and the jay,
Are summer songs for me and my aunts,
    While we lie tumbling in the hay. (*Autolycus, sings*)

    But shall I go mourn for that, my dear?   15
        The pale moon shines by night:
    And when I wander here and there,
        I then do most go right. (*Autolycus, sings*)

My father named me Autolycus; who, being, as I am,   24
littered under Mercury, was likewise a snapper-up of
unconsidered trifles.   (*Autolycus*)

Offer me no money, I pray you; that kills my heart.   87
                              (*Autolycus*)

If you had but looked big and spit at him, he'ld have   113
run.   (*Clown*)

        Jog on, jog on, the foot-path way,   132
            And merrily hent the stile-a:
        A merry heart goes all the day,
            Your sad tires in a mile-a. (*Autolycus, sings*)

These your unusual weeds to each part of you   IV. iv. I
Do give a life: no shepherdess, but Flora
Peering in April's front. This your sheep-shearing
Is as a meeting of the petty gods,
And you the queen on 't. (*Florizel*)

When my old wife lived, upon   55
This day she was both pantler, butler, cook,
Both dame and servant; welcomed all, served all;
Would sing her song and dance her turn; now here,
At upper end o' the table, now i' the middle;
On his shoulder, and his; her face o' fire
With labour and the thing she took to quench it,
She would to each one sip. (*Shepherd*)

Reverend sirs,   73
For you there's rosemary and rue; these keep
Seeming and savour all the winter long. (*Perdita*)

The year groweth ancient,   79
Not yet on summer's death, nor on the birth
Of trembling winter, the fairest flowers o' the season
Are our carnations and streak'd gillyvors,
Which some call nature's bastards: of that kind
Our rustic garden's barren; and I care not
To get slips of them. (*Perdita*)

We marry   92
A gentler scion to the wildest stock,
And make conceive a bark of baser kind
By bud of nobler race: this is an art
Which does mend nature, change it rather, but
The art itself is nature. (*Polixenes*)

I'll not put   99
The dibble in earth to set one slip of them;
No more than were I painted I would wish
This youth would say 'twere well and only therefore
Desire to breed by me. Here's flowers for you;
Hot lavender, mints, savory, marjoram;
The marigold, that goes to bed wi' the sun
And with him rises weeping: these are flowers
Of middle summer, and I think they are given
To men of middle age. (*Perdita*)

I should leave grazing, were I of your flock,   109
And only live by gazing. (*Camillo*)

You'ld be so lean, that blasts of January   IV. iv. 111
Would blow you through and through.   (*Perdita*)

I would I had some flowers o' the spring that might   113
Become your time of day; and yours, and yours,
That wear upon your virgin branches yet
Your maidenheads growing: O Proserpina,
For the flowers now, that frighted thou let'st fall
From Dis's waggon! daffodils
That come before the swallow dares, and take
The winds of March with beauty; violets dim,
But sweeter than the lids of Juno's eyes
Or Cytherea's breath; pale primroses,
That die unmarried, ere they can behold
Bright Phoebus in his strength—a malady
Most incident to maids; bold oxlips and
The crown imperial; lilies of all kinds,
The flower-de-luce being one!   (*Perdita*)

Perdita. To strew him o'er and o'er!   129
Florizel.   What, like a corse?
Perdita. No, like a bank for love to lie and play on;
Not like a corse; or if, not to be buried,
But quick and in mine arms.

                              What you do   135
Still betters what is done.   When you speak, sweet,
I'ld have you do it ever: when you sing,
I'ld have you buy and sell so, so give alms,
Pray so; and, for the ordering your affairs,
To sing them too: when you do dance, I wish you
A wave o' the sea, that you might ever do
Nothing but that; move still, still so,
And own no other function: each your doing,
So singular in each particular,
Crowns what you are doing in the present deed,
That all your acts are queens.   (*Florizel*)

Your hand, my Perdita: so turtles pair,   154
That never mean to part.   (*Florizel*)

Polixenes. This is the prettiest low-born lass that ever 156
Ran on the green-sward: nothing she does or seems
But smacks of something greater than herself,
Too noble for this place.
Camillo.   He tells her something
That makes her blood look out: good sooth, she is
The queen of curds and cream.

     *F   153

He says he loves my daughter: IV. iv. 171
I think so too: for never gazed the moon
Upon the water as he'll stand and read
As 'twere my daughter's eyes: and, to be plain,
I think there is not half a kiss to choose
Who loves another best.   (*Shepherd*)

Polixenes.   She dances featly.   176
Shepherd. So she does any thing; though I report it
That should be silent.

Clown. I love a ballad but even too well, if it be doleful   188
matter merrily set down, or a very pleasant thing indeed
and sung lamentably.
Servant. He hath songs for man or woman, of all sizes; no
milliner can so fit his customers with gloves: he has the
prettiest love-songs for maids; so without bawdry, which
is strange; with such delicate burthens of dildos and
fadings, 'jump her and thump her'; and where some
stretch-mouthed rascal would, as it were, mean mischief
and break a foul gap into the matter, he makes the maid to
answer 'Whoop, do me no harm, good man.'

He hath ribbons of all the colours i' the rainbow.   206
                                          (*Servant*)

　　Lawn as white as driven snow;   220
　　Cyprus black as e'er was crow;
　　Gloves as sweet as damask roses;
　　Masks for faces and for noses;
　　Bugle bracelet, necklace amber,
　　Perfume for a lady's chamber;
　　Golden quoifs and stomachers,
　　For my lads to give their dears:
　　Pins and poking-sticks of steel,
　　What maids lack from head to heel:
　　Come buy of me, come; come buy, come buy;
　　Buy, lads, or else your lasses cry:
　　Come buy.   (*Autolycus, sings*)

There are cozeners abroad; therefore it behoves men to   256
be wary.   (*Autolycus*)

I love a ballad in print o' life, for then we are sure they   263
are true.   (*Mopsa*)

　　Will you buy any tape,   321
　　Or lace for your cape,
　　My dainty duck, my dear-a?
　　Any silk, any thread,
　　Any toys for your head,

Of the new'st and finest, finest wear-a?   IV. iv. 326
   Come to the pedlar;
   Money's a meddler,
That doth utter all men's ware-a.
                        (*Autolycus, sings*)

            I take thy hand, this hand,   372
As soft as dove's down and as white as it,
Or Ethiopian's tooth, or the fann'd snow that's bolted
By the northern blasts twice o'er.   (*Florizel*)

      Were I crown'd the most imperial monarch,   382
Thereof most worthy, were I the fairest youth
That ever made eye swerve, had force and knowledge
More than was ever man's, I would not prize them
Without her love; for her employ them all;
Commend them and condemn them to her service
Or to their own perdition.   (*Florizel*)

Take hands, a bargain!   (*Shepherd*)   393

         Reason my son   416
Should choose himself a wife, but as good reason
The father, all whose joy is nothing else
But fair posterity, should hold some counsel
In such a business.   (*Polixenes*)

           Thou a sceptre's heir,   429
That thus affects a sheep-hook!   (*Polixenes*)

I was not much afeard; for once or twice   452
I was about to speak and tell him plainly,
The selfsame sun that shines upon his court
Hides not his visage from our cottage but
Looks on alike.   (*Perdita*)

I'll queen it no inch farther.   (*Perdita*)   459

But as the unthought-on accident is guilty   548
To what we wildly do, so we profess
Ourselves to be the slaves of chance and flies
Of every wind that blows.   (*Florizel*)

Camillo. Prosperity's the very bond of love,   583
Whose fresh complexion and whose heart together
Affliction alters.
Perdita.   One of these is true:
I think affliction may subdue the cheek,
But not take in the mind.

Camillo.   I cannot say 'tis pity   iv. iv. 591
She lacks instructions, for she seems a mistress
To most that teach.
Perdita.   Your pardon, sir; for this
I'll blush you thanks.

I have sold all my trumpery; not a counterfeit stone,   607
not a ribbon, glass, pomander, brooch, table-book, ballad,
knife, tape, glove, shoe-tie, bracelet, horn-ring, to keep
my pack from fasting: they throng who should buy first, as
if my trinkets had been hallowed and brought a benediction to the buyer. (*Autolycus*)

Autolycus. I am a poor fellow, sir.   643
Camillo. Why, be so still; here's nobody will steal that
from thee.

To have an open ear, a quick eye, and a nimble hand, is   683
necessary for a cut-purse. (*Autolycus*)

Though I am not naturally honest, I am so sometimes   731
by chance. (*Autolycus*)

Let me have no lying: it becomes none but tradesmen.   743
                                                (*Autolycus*)

Advocate's the court word for a pheasant. (*Clown*)   767

How blessed are we that are not simple men!   771
Yet nature might have made me as these are.
Therefore I will not disdain. (*Autolycus*)

A great man, I'll warrant; I know by the picking on's   778
teeth. (*Clown*)

If I had a mind to be honest, I see Fortune would not   861
suffer me: she drops booties in my mouth. (*Autolycus*)

Do as the heavens have done, forget your evil;   v. i. 5
With them forgive yourself. (*Cleomenes*)

If, one by one, you wedded all the world,   13
Or from the all that are took something good,
To make a perfect woman, she you kill'd
Would be unparallel'd. (*Paulina*)

Women will love her, that she is a woman   110
More worth than any man; men that she is
The rarest of all women. (*Gentleman*)

Autolycus. I know you are now, sir, a gentleman born.   v. ii. 145
Clown. Ay, and have been so any time these four hours.

Clown. There was the first gentleman-like tears that ever   155
we shed.
Shepherd. We may live, son, to shed many more.
Clown. Ay; or else 'twere hard luck, being in so pre-
posterous estate as we are.

My lord, your sorrow was too sore laid on,   v. iii. 49
Which sixteen winters cannot blow away,
So many summers dry: scarce any joy
Did ever so long live; no sorrow
But kill'd itself much sooner.   (*Camillo*)

If this be magic, let it be an art   110
Lawful as eating.   (*Leontes*)

     You gods, look down   121
And from your sacred vials pour your graces
Upon my daughter's head!   (*Hermione*)

HISTORIES

KING JOHN

This play covers a period of some sixteen years, but takes considerable liberties with the order of events. The main characters are the treacherous usurper King John himself, his nephew Prince Arthur, whose rightful claim to the English throne is supported by King Philip of France, and Faulconbridge, styled throughout the Bastard, a supposed natural son of Richard Cœur-de-Lion. King John has the support of his mother, Queen Elinor, and Prince Arthur that of his mother Constance. War breaks out, the rival armies meet in France, and after an abortive peace King John captures Arthur and has him imprisoned in a castle with secret orders for his execution. Hubert de Burgh, who is entrusted with the task, relents at the young prince's pleadings, but Arthur is nevertheless killed when he jumps from the castle wall in an attempt to escape, and the whole English people are horrified when they hear the news. The French invade England, but are defeated, and the play ends with King John's death by poison. Cardinal Pandulph, the Pope's legate, takes an important part as a diplomat.

The which if he can prove, a' pops me out   I. i. 68
At least from fair five hundred pound a year.   (*Bastard*)

Whether hadst thou rather be a Faulconbridge   134
And like thy brother, to enjoy thy land,
Or the reputed son of Coeur-de-Lion,
Lord of thy presence and no land beside?
                                 (*Queen Elinor*)

Something about, a little from the right,   170
  In at the window, or else o'er the hatch:
Who dares not stir by day must walk by night,
  And have is have, however men do catch:
Near or far off, well won is still well shot,
And I am I, howe'er I was begot.   (*Bastard*)

And if his name be George, I'll call him Peter;   186
For new-made honour doth forget men's names.
                                     (*Bastard*)

Sweet, sweet, sweet poison for the age's tooth.   (*Bastard*)   213

Till Angiers and the right thou hast in France,   II. i. 22
Together with that pale, that white-faced shore,
Whose foot spurns back the ocean's roaring tides
And coops from other lands her islanders,
Even till that England, hedged in with the main,
That water-walled bulwark, still secure
And confident from foreign purposes,
Even till that utmost corner of the west
Salute thee for her king.   (*Duke of Austria*)

The peace of heaven is theirs that lift their swords   35
In such a just and charitable war.   (*Duke of Austria*)

Rash, inconsiderate, fiery voluntaries,   67
With ladies' faces and fierce dragons' spleens,
Have sold their fortunes at their native homes,
Bearing their birthrights proudly on their backs,
To make a hazard of new fortunes here.   (*Chatillon*)

For courage mounteth with occasion.   (*Duke of Austria*)   82

Queen Elinor.   Come to thy grandam, child.   159
Constance. Do, child, go to it grandam, child;
Give grandam kingdom, and it grandam will
Give it a plum, a cherry, and a fig:
There's a good grandam.

And now, instead of bullets wrapp'd in fire,   II. i. 227
To make a shaking fever in your walls,
They shoot but calm words folded up in smoke,
To make a faithless error in your ears.   (*King John*)

Saint George, that swinged the dragon, and e'er since   288
Sits on his horse back at mine hostess' door.   (*Bastard*)

Many a widow's husband grovelling lies,   305
Coldly embracing the discolour'd earth;
And victory, with little loss, doth play
Upon the dancing banners of the French.
                                    (*French Herald*)

Blood hath bought blood and blows have answer'd blows;   329
Strength match'd with strength, and power confronted
     power.   (*First Citizen*)

O, now doth Death line his dead chaps with steel;   352
The swords of soldiers are his teeth, his fangs;
And now he feasts, mousing the flesh of men.   (*Bastard*)

He is the half part of a blessed man,   437
Left to be finished by such as she;
And she a fair divided excellence,
Whose fulness of perfection lies in him.
O, two such silver currents, when they join,
Do glorify the banks that bound them in.
                                    (*First Citizen*)

          Here's a large mouth, indeed,   457
That spits forth death and mountains, rocks and seas,
Talks as familiarly of roaring lions
As maids of thirteen do of puppy-dogs!
What cannoneer begot this lusty blood?
He speaks plain cannon fire, and smoke and bounce;
He gives the bastinado with his tongue:
Our ears are cudgell'd: not a word of his
But buffets better than a fist of France:
Zounds! I was never so bethump'd with words
Since I first call'd my brother's father dad.   (*Bastard*)

Mad world! mad kings! mad composition!   (*Bastard*)   561

That smooth-faced gentleman, tickling Commodity,   573
Commodity, the bias of the world.   (*Bastard*)

Well, whiles I am a beggar, I will rail   593
And say there is no sin but to be rich;
And being rich, my virtue then shall be
To say there is no vice but beggary.   (*Bastard*)

Nature and Fortune join'd to make thee great. III. i. 52
(Constance)

I will instruct my sorrows to be proud; 68
For grief is proud and makes his owner stoop.
To me and to the state of my great grief
Let kings assemble; for my grief's so great
That no supporter but the huge firm earth
Can hold it up: here I and sorrows sit;
Here is my throne, bid kings come bow to it.
(Constance)

To solemnize this day the glorious sun 77
Stays in his course and plays the alchemist,
Turning with splendour of his precious eye
The meagre cloddy earth to glittering gold.
(King Philip)

Thou wear a lion's hide! doff it for shame, 128
And hang a calf's-skin on those recreant limbs.
(Constance)

The better act of purposes mistook 274
Is to mistake again; though indirect,
Yet indirection thereby grows direct,
And falsehood falsehood cures, as fire cools fire
Within the scorched veins of one new-burn'd.
(Pandulph)

Old Time the clock-setter, that bald sexton Time. 324
(Bastard)

Bell, book, and candle shall not drive me back, III. iii. 12
When gold and silver becks me to come on. (Bastard)

        I had a thing to say, 25
But I will fit it with some better time. (King John)

King John. Good Hubert, Hubert, Hubert, throw thine eye 59
On yon young boy: I'll tell thee what, my friend,
He is a very serpent in my way;
And wheresoe'er this foot of mine doth tread,
He lies before me: dost thou understand me?
Thou art his keeper.
Hubert.   And I'll keep him so,
That he shall not offend your majesty.
King John.   Death.
Hubert. My lord?
King John.   A grave.
Hubert.   He shall not live.
King John.   Enough.
I could be merry now.

Death, death; O amiable lovely death!   III. iv. 25
Thou odoriferous stench! sound rottenness!
Arise forth from the couch of lasting night,
Thou hate and terror to prosperity,
And I will kiss thy detestable bones
And put my eyeballs in thy vaulty brows
And ring these fingers with thy household worms
And stop this gap of breath with fulsome dust
And be a carrion monster like thyself:
Come, grin on me, and I will think thou smilest
And buss thee as thy wife.   Misery's love,
O, come to me!   (*Constance*)

I am not mad: I would to heaven I were!   48
For then, 'tis like I should forget myself.   (*Constance*)

Grief fills the room up of my absent child,   93
Lies in his bed, walks up and down with me,
Puts on his pretty looks, repeats his words,
Remembers me of all his gracious parts,
Stuffs out his vacant garments with his form;
Then, have I reason to be fond of grief?   (*Constance*)

There's nothing in this world can make me joy: 107
Life is as tedious as a twice-told tale
Vexing the dull ear of a drowsy man.   (*Lewis*)

        When Fortune means to men most good,   119
She looks upon them with a threatening eye.   (*Pandulph*)

And he that stands upon a slippery place   137
Makes nice of no vile hold to stay him up.   (*Pandulph*)

Heat me these irons hot.   (*Hubert*)   v. i. 1

Methinks no body should be sad but I: 13
Yet, I remember, when I was in France,
Young gentlemen would be as sad as night,
Only for wantonness.   (*Arthur*)

If I talk to him, with his innocent prate   25
He will awake my mercy which lies dead:
Therefore I will be sudden and dispatch.   (*Hubert*)

Have you the heart?   When your head did but ache,   41
I knit my handkercher about your brows,
The best I had, a princess wrought it me,
And I did never ask it you again;
And with my hand at midnight held your head,
And like the watchful minutes to the hour,

Still and anon cheer'd up the heavy time,   IV. i. 47
Saying, 'What lack you?' and 'Where lies your grief?'
Or 'What good love may I perform for you?'   (*Arthur*)

Alas, what need you be so boisterous-rough?   76
I will not struggle, I will stand stone-still.
For heaven sake, Hubert, let me not be bound!
Nay, hear me, Hubert, drive these men away,
And I will sit as quiet as a lamb;
I will not stir, nor wince, nor speak a word,
Now look upon the iron angerly. (*Arthur*)

Arthur. Lo, by my troth, the instrument is cold   104
And would not harm me.
Hubert.   I can heat it, boy.
Arthur. No, in good sooth; the fire is dead with grief,
Being create for comfort, to be used
In undeserved extremes: see else yourself;
There is no malice in this burning coal;
The breath of heaven hath blown his spirit out
And strew'd repentant ashes on his head.
Hubert. But with my breath I can revive it, boy.
Arthur. An if you do, you will but make it blush
And glow with shame of your proceedings, Hubert.

To gild refined gold, to paint the lily,   IV. ii. 11
To throw a perfume on the violet,
To smooth the ice, or add another hue
Unto the rainbow, or with taper-light
To seek the beauteous eye of heaven to garnish,
Is wasteful and ridiculous excess.   (*Salisbury*)

When workmen strive to do better than well,   28
They do confound their skill in covetousness;
And oftentimes excusing of a fault
Doth make the fault the worse by the excuse. (*Pembroke*)

There is no sure foundation set on blood,   104
No certain life achieved by others' death.   (*King John*)

The spirit of the time shall teach me speed.   (*Bastard*) 176

I saw a smith stand with his hammer, thus,   193
The whilst his iron did on the anvil cool,
With open mouth swallowing a tailor's news;
Who, with his shears and measure in his hand,
Standing on slippers, which his nimble haste
Had falsely thrust upon contrary feet,
Told of a many thousand warlike French
That were embattailed and rank'd in Kent. (*Hubert*)

Another lean unwash'd artificer.   *(Hubert)*   IV. ii. 201

How oft the sight of means to do ill deeds   219
Make deeds ill done!   Hadst thou not been by,
A fellow by the hand of nature mark'd,
Quoted and sign'd to do a deed of shame,
This murder had not come into my mind.   *(King John)*

Out of my sight, and never see me more!   *(King John)*   242

Whate'er you think, good words, I think, were best.   IV. iii. 28
                                          (Bastard)

                    If thou didst but consent   125
To this most cruel act, do but despair;
And if thou want'st a cord, the smallest thread
That ever spider twisted from her womb
Will serve to strangle thee; a rush will be a beam
To hang thee on; or wouldst thou drown thyself,
Put but a little water in a spoon,
And it shall be as all the ocean,
Enough to stifle such a villain up.   *(Bastard)*

Be great in act, as you have been in thought.   *(Bastard)*   V. i. 45

Unthread the rude eye of rebellion   V. iv. 11
And welcome home again discarded faith.   *(Melun)*

The day shall not be up so soon as I,   V. v. 21
To try the fair adventure of to-morrow.   *(Lewis)*

Ay, marry, now my soul hath elbow-room.   *(King John)*   V. vii. 28

I beg cold comfort; and you are so strait   42
And so ingrateful, you deny me that.   *(King John)*

This England never did, nor never shall,   112
Lie at the proud foot of a conqueror,
But when it first did help to wound itself.
Now these her princes are come home again,
Come the three corners of the world in arms,
And we shall shock them.   Nought shall make us rue,
If England to itself do rest but true.   *(Bastard)*

KING RICHARD II

This play deals with a period of two years, from 1398 to the beginning of 1400, at the end of Richard's reign. It opens with preparations for trial by combat between two great nobles, Henry Duke of Hereford, surnamed Bolingbroke, who is the son of John of Gaunt, Duke of Lancaster, and Thomas Mowbray, Duke of Norfolk. Just as they are ready to commence, Richard stops the contest and banishes them both; and on the death of John of Gaunt soon afterwards he confiscates the estates to which Bolingbroke would have fallen heir. The latter then takes the opportunity of the king's absence in Ireland to claim his estates by force of arms. Richard's supporters prove faithless and he has to submit to Bolingbroke, who deposes him and seizes the throne. Confined to Pomfret Castle, Richard is killed in a struggle with his jailers. The play has many passages of exquisite poetry, in particular John of Gaunt's famous panegyric on England.

Old John of Gaunt, time-honour'd Lancaster. I. i. 1
(*King Richard*)

'Tis not the trial of a woman's war, 48
The bitter clamour of two eager tongues,
Can arbitrate this cause betwixt us twain. (*Mowbray*)

Pierced to the soul with slander's venom'd spear. 171
(*Mowbray*)

Lions make leopards tame. (*King Richard*) 174

The purest treasure mortal times afford 177
Is spotless reputation: take that away,
Men are but gilded loam or painted clay.
A jewel in a ten-times-barr'd-up chest
Is a bold spirit in a loyal breast.
Mine honour is my life; both grow in one;
Take honour from me, and my life is done. (*Mowbray*)

We were not born to sue, but to command. 196
(*King Richard*)

That which in mean men we intitle patience I. ii. 33
Is pale cold cowardice in noble breasts.
(*Duchess of Gloucester*)

Lo, as at English feasts, so I regreet I. iii. 67
The daintiest last, to make the end most sweet.
(*Bolingbroke*)

Take from my mouth the wish of happy years. 94
(*Mowbray*)

Truth hath a quiet breast. (*Mowbray*) 96

This must my comfort be, 144
That sun that warms you here shall shine on me;
And those his golden beams to you here lent
Shall point on me and gild my banishment. (*Bolingbroke*)

The sly slow hours shall not determinate 150
The dateless limit of thy dear exile. (*King Richard*)

The language I have learn'd these forty years, 159
My native English, now I must forgo:
And now my tongue's use is to me no more
Than an unstringed viol or a harp. (*Mowbray*)

I am too old to fawn upon a nurse, 170
Too far in years to be a pupil now. (*Mowbray*)

Now no way can I stray;   I. iii. 206
Save back to England, all the world's my way.

(*Mowbray*)

How long a time lies in one little word!   213
Four lagging winters and four wanton springs
End in a word: such is the breath of kings.   (*Bolingbroke*)

Shorten my days thou canst with sullen sorrow,   227
And pluck nights from me, but not lend a morrow.

(*Gaunt*)

Things sweet to taste prove in digestion sour.   (*Gaunt*)   236

All places that the eye of heaven visits   275
Are to a wise man ports and happy havens.
Teach thy necessity to reason thus;
There is no virtue like necessity.   (*Gaunt*)

For gnarling sorrow hath less power to bite   292
The man that mocks at it and sets it light.   (*Gaunt*)

O, who can hold a fire in his hand   293
By thinking on the frosty Caucasus?
Or cloy the hungry edge of appetite
By bare imagination of a feast?
Or wallow naked in December snow
By thinking on fantastic summer's heat?
O, no! the apprehension of the good
Gives but the greater feeling to the worse.   (*Bolingbroke*)

Where'er I wander, boast of this I can,   308
Though banish'd, yet a trueborn Englishman.

(*Bolingbroke*)

King Richard. And say, what store of parting tears were   I. iv. 5
shed?
Aumerle. Faith, none for me; except the north-east wind,
Which then blew bitterly against our faces,
Awaked the sleeping rheum, and so by chance
Did grace our hollow parting with a tear.

Wooing poor craftsmen with the craft of smiles.   28

(*King Richard*)

Off goes his bonnet to an oyster-wench;   31
A brace of draymen bid God speed him well
And had the tribute of his supple knee,
With 'Thanks, my countrymen, my loving friends.'

(*King Richard*)

Now put it, God, in the physician's mind   I. iv. 59
To help him to his grave immediately! (*King Richard*)

Pray God we may make haste, and come too late!   64
                                        (*King Richard*)

O, but they say the tongues of dying men   II. i. 5
Enforce attention like deep harmony. (*Gaunt*)

Methinks I am a prophet new inspired   31
And thus expiring do foretell of him:
His rash fierce blaze of riot cannot last,
For violent fires soon burn out themselves;
Small showers last long, but sudden storms are short;
He tires betimes that spurs too fast betimes. (*Gaunt*)

This royal throne of kings, this scepter'd isle,   40
This earth of majesty, this seat of Mars,
This other Eden, demi-paradise,
This fortress built by Nature for herself
Against infection and the hand of war,
This happy breed of men, this little world,
This precious stone set in the silver sea,
Which serves it in the office of a wall
Or as a moat defensive to a house,
Against the envy of less happier lands,
This blessed plot, this earth, this realm, this England,
This nurse, this teeming womb of royal kings,
Fear'd by their breed and famous by their birth,
Renowned for their deeds as far from home,
For Christian service and true chivalry,
As is the sepulchre in stubborn Jewry
Of the world's ransom, blessed Mary's Son,
This land of such dear souls, this dear dear land,
Dear for her reputation through the world,
Is now leased out, I die pronouncing it,
Like to a tenement or pelting farm:
England, bound in with the triumphant sea,
Whose rocky shore beats back the envious siege
Of watery Neptune, is now bound in with shame,
With inky blots and rotten parchment bonds:
That England, that was wont to conquer others,
Hath made a shameful conquest of itself. (*Gaunt*)

Old Gaunt indeed, and gaunt in being old. (*Gaunt*)   74

King Richard. Can sick men play so nicely with their   94
   names?
Gaunt. No, misery makes sport to mock itself.

The ripest fruit first falls, and so doth he. (*King Richard*)   153

To lay aside life-harming heaviness   II. ii. 3
And entertain a cheerful disposition.   (*Bushy*)

Queen. Uncle, for God's sake, speak comfortable words.   76
York. Should I do so, I should belie my thoughts:
Comfort's in heaven; and we are on the earth,
Where nothing lives but crosses, cares and grief.

But time will not permit: all is uneven,   121
And every thing is left at six and seven.   (*York*)

Alas, poor duke! the task he undertakes   145
Is numbering sands and drinking oceans dry.   (*Green*)

I am a stranger here in Gloucestershire: II. iii. 3
These high wild hills and rough uneven ways
Draws out our miles, and makes them wearisome;
And yet your fair discourse hath been as sugar,
Making the hard way sweet and delectable.
                                (*Northumberland*)

I count myself in nothing else so happy   46
As in a soul remembering my good friends.
                                (*Bolingbroke*)

Bloody with spurring, fiery-red with haste.   58
                                (*Northumberland*)

Evermore thanks, the exchequer of the poor.   65
                                (*Bolingbroke*)

Grace me no grace, nor uncle me no uncle.   (*York*)   87

The caterpillars of the commonwealth,   166
Which I have sworn to weed and pluck away.
                                (*Bolingbroke*)

Things past redress are now with me past care.   (*York*)   171

The bay-trees in our country are all wither'd   II. iv. 8
And meteors fright the fixed stars of heaven;
The pale-faced moon looks bloody on the earth
And lean-look'd prophets whisper fearful change.
                                (*A Welsh Captain*)

Eating the bitter bread of banishment.   (*Bolingbroke*)   III. i. 21

The means that heaven yields must be embraced,   III. ii. 29
And not neglected.   (*Bishop of Carlisle*)

Not all the water in the rude rough sea   III. ii. 54
Can wash the balm off from an anointed king;
The breath of worldly men cannot depose
The deputy elected by the Lord:
For every man that Bolingbroke hath press'd
To lift shrewd steel against our golden crown,
God for his Richard hath in heavenly pay
A glorious angel: then, if angels fight,
Weak men must fall, for heaven still guards the right.
                                        (*King Richard*)

O, call back yesterday, bid time return!   (*Salisbury*)   69

Is not the king's name twenty thousand names?   85
                                        (*King Richard*)

Cry woe, destruction, ruin and decay;   102
The worst is death, and death will have his day.
                                        (*King Richard*)

Like an unseasonable stormy day,   106
Which makes the silver rivers drown their shores.
                                        (*Scroop*)

Aumerle. Where is the duke my father with his power?   143
King Richard. No matter where; of comfort no man speak:
Let's talk of graves, of worms and epitaphs;
Make dust our paper and with rainy eyes
Write sorrow on the bosom of the earth,
Let's choose executors and talk of wills.   (*King Richard*)

And nothing can we call our own but death   152
And that small model of the barren earth
Which serves as paste and cover to our bones.
                                        (*King Richard*)

For God's sake, let us sit upon the ground   155
And tell sad stories of the death of kings:
How some have been deposed; some slain in war;
Some haunted by the ghosts they have deposed;
Some poison'd by their wives; some sleeping kill'd;
All murder'd: for within the hollow crown
That rounds the mortal temples of a king
Keeps Death his court and there the antic sits,
Scoffing his state and grinning at his pomp,
Allowing him a breath, a little scene,
To monarchize, be fear'd and kill with looks,
Infusing him with self and vain conceit
As if this flesh which walls about our life
Were brass impregnable, and humour'd thus
Comes at the last and with a little pin
Bores through his castle wall, and farewell king!
                                        (*King Richard*)

Men judge by the complexion of the sky   III. ii. 194
   The state and inclination of the day:
So may you by my dull and heavy eye,
   My tongue hath but a heavier tale to say.
I play the torturer, by small and small
To lengthen out the worst that must be spoken.   (*Scroop*)

By heaven, I'll hate him everlastingly   207
That bids me be of comfort any more.   (*King Richard*)

See, see, King Richard doth himself appear,   III. iii. 62
As doth the blushing discontented sun
From out the fiery portal of the east.   (*Bolingbroke*)

What must the king do now? must he submit?   143
The king shall do it: must he be deposed?
The king shall be contented: must he lose
The name of king? o' God's name, let it go:
I'll give my jewels for a set of beads,
My gorgeous palace for a hermitage,
My gay apparel for an almsman's gown,
My figured goblets for a dish of wood,
My sceptre for a palmer's walking-staff,
My subjects for a pair of carved saints,
And my large kingdom for a little grave,
A little little grave, an obscure grave;
Or I'll be buried in the king's highway,
Some way of common trade, where subjects' feet
May hourly trample on their sovereign's head.
                              (*King Richard*)

Northumberland. My lord, in the base court he doth attend   176
To speak with you; may it please you to come down.
King Richard. Down, down I come; like glistering Phae-
   thon,
Wanting the manage of unruly jades.
In the base court?   Base court, where kings grow base,
To come at traitors' calls and do them grace.

               They well deserve to have,   200
That know the strong'st and surest way to get.
                       (*King Richard*)

When our sea-walled garden, the whole land,   III. iv. 43
Is full of weeds, her fairest flowers choked up,
Her fruit-trees all unpruned, her hedges ruin'd,
Her knots disorder'd and her wholesome herbs
Swarming with caterpillars.   (*Servant*)

Superfluous branches   III. iv. 63
We lop away, that bearing boughs may live.
                                        (*Gardener*)

Here did she fall a tear; here in this place   104
I 'll set a bank of rue, sour herb of grace:
Rue, even for ruth, here shortly shall be seen,
In the remembrance of a weeping queen.   (*Gardener*)

If I dare eat, or drink, or breathe, or live,   IV. i. 73
I dare meet Surrey in a wilderness,
And spit upon him, whilst I say he lies,
And lies, and lies.   (*Fitzwater*)

          And there at Venice gave   97
His body to that pleasant country's earth,
And his pure soul unto his captain Christ,
Under whose colours he had fought so long.
                                        (*Bishop of Carlisle*)

Peace shall go sleep with Turks and infidels,   139
And in this seat of peace tumultuous wars
Shall kin with kin and kind with kind confound.
                                        (*Bishop of Carlisle*)

You may my glories and my state depose,   192
But not my griefs; still am I king of those.
                                        (*King Richard*)

Now mark me, how I will undo myself.   203
I give this heavy weight from off my head
And this unwieldy sceptre from my hand,
The pride of kingly sway from out my heart;
With mine own tears I wash away my balm,
With mine own hands I give away my crown,
With mine own tongue deny my sacred state,
With mine own breath release all duty's rites:
All pomp and majesty I do forswear;
My manors, rents, revenues I forgo;
My acts, decrees and statutes I deny:
God pardon all oaths that are broke to me!
God keep all vows unbroke that swear to thee!
                                        (*King Richard*)

God save King Harry, unking'd Richard says,   220
And send him many years of sunshine days!
                                        (*King Richard*)

A mockery king of snow.   (*King Richard*)   260

The shadow of your sorrow hath destroy'd   IV. i. 292
The shadow of your face.   (*Bolingbroke*)

Bolingbroke. Go, some of you convey him to the Tower.   316
King Richard. O, good! convey? conveyers are you all,
That rise thus nimbly by a true king's fall.

Julius Caesar's ill-erected tower.   (*Queen*)   v. i. 2

But soft, but see, or rather do not see   7
My fair rose wither.   (*Queen*)

                I am sworn brother, sweet,   20
To grim Necessity, and he and I
Will keep a league till death.   (*King Richard*)

A king of beasts, indeed; if aught but beasts,   35
I had been still a happy king of men.   (*King Richard*)

In winter's tedious nights sit by the fire   40
With good old folks and let them tell thee tales
Of woeful ages long ago betid.   (*King Richard*)

                  The north,   76
Where shivering cold and sickness pines the clime.
               (*King Richard*)

Queen. And must we be divided? must we part?   81
King Richard. Ay, hand from hand, my love, and heart
   from heart.
Queen. Banish us both and send the king with me.
Northumberland. That were some love but little policy.

As in a theatre, the eyes of men,   v. ii. 23
After a well-graced actor leaves the stage,
Are idly bent on him that enters next,
Thinking his prattle to be tedious.   (*York*)

             Who are the violets now   46
That strew the green lap of the new come spring?
             (*Duchess of York*)

Fear, and not love, begets his penitence.   (*York*)   v. iii. 56

He prays but faintly and would be denied.   103
            (*Duchess of York*)

Duchess of York. No word like 'pardon' for kings' mouths   v. iii. 118
  so meet.
York. Speak it in French, king; say, 'pardonne moi.'
Duchess of York. Dost thou teach pardon pardon to
  destroy?

                   How sour sweet music is,   v. v. 42
When time is broke and no proportion kept!
So is it in the music of men's lives. (*King Richard*)

King Richard. Mount, mount, my soul! thy seat is up on   112
  high;
Whilst my gross flesh sinks downward, here to die.
                                [*Dies.*]

They love not poison that do poison need.   v. vi. 38
                      (*Bolingbroke*)

KING HENRY IV, PART I

Covering the events of a single year, from June 1402 to July 1403, the play tells of the rebellion of Henry Hotspur, Lord Percy, son of the Earl of Northumberland, assisted by Mortimer, Earl of March, Owen Glendower of Wales, and the Scottish Earl of Douglas. The rebels meet with a crushing reverse at the battle of Shrewsbury, where Hotspur is slain in single combat by the young Prince of Wales. The Prince also appears in the comic Eastcheap scenes, drinking and revelling with the disreputable Sir John Falstaff and his boon companions Poins, Gadshill, Peto, and Bardolph in the Boar's Head Tavern, where Mistress Quickly is hostess. To show up Falstaff's cowardice and humbug, the Prince and Poins disguise themselves and 'hijack' his party after they have robbed some travellers at Gadshill, subsequently exposing Falstaff's cock-and-bull story of having been set upon by eleven men in buckram. Unabashed, Falstaff joins with the Prince in giving burlesque imitations of the king reprimanding his graceless son, and at Shrewsbury tries to claim the credit of having killed Hotspur.

So shaken as we are, so wan with care. (*King*)   I. i. 1

No more the thirsty entrance of this soil   5
Shall daub her lips with her own children's blood. (*King*)

To chase these pagans in those holy fields   24
Over whose acres walk'd those blessed feet
Which fourteen hundred years ago were nail'd
For our advantage on the bitter cross. (*King*)

Sir Walter Blunt, new lighted from his horse,   63
Stain'd with the variation of each soil
Betwixt that Holmedon and this seat of ours. (*King*)

    Unless hours were cups of sack, and minutes capons,   I. ii. 8
and clocks the tongues of bawds, and dials the signs of
leaping-houses, and the blessed sun himself a fair hot
wench in flame-coloured taffeta, I see no reason why thou
shouldst be so superfluous to demand the time of the
day. (*Prince*)

    We that take purses go by the moon and the seven stars, 15
and not by Phoebus, he, 'that wandering knight so fair.'
                                    (*Falstaff*)

Falstaff. God save thy grace,—majesty I should say, for 18
grace thou wilt have none,—
Prince. What, none?
Falstaff. No, by my troth, not so much as will serve to be
prologue to an egg and butter.

    Let not us that are squires of the night's body be called 28
thieves of the day's beauty: let us be Diana's foresters,
gentlemen of the shade, minions of the moon. (*Falstaff*)

Falstaff. Is not my hostess of the tavern a most sweet 45
wench?
Prince. As the honey of Hybla, my old lad of the castle.
And is not a buff jerkin a most sweet robe of durance?
Falstaff. How now, how now, mad wag! what, in thy
quips and thy quiddities?

Old father antic the law. (*Falstaff*)   69

Falstaff. 'Sblood, I am as melancholy as a gib cat or a 82
lugged bear.
Prince. Or an old lion, or a lover's lute.
Falstaff. Yea, or the drone of a Lincolnshire bagpipe.

Prince. What sayest thou to a hare, or the melancholy of   I. ii. 86
Moor-ditch?
Falstaff. Thou hast the most unsavoury similes.

Falstaff. I would to God thou and I knew where a   92
commodity of good names were to be bought.   An old
lord of the council rated me the other day in the street
about you, sir, but I marked him not; and yet he talked
very wisely, but I regarded him not; and yet he talked
wisely, and in the street too.
Prince. Thou didst well; for wisdom cries out in the
streets, and no man regards it.
Falstaff. O, thou hast damnable iteration and art indeed
able to corrupt a saint.

Before I knew thee, Hal, I knew nothing; and now am I,   104
if a man should speak truly, little better than one of the
wicked.   (*Falstaff*)

Why, Hal, 'tis my vocation, Hal; 'tis no sin for a man   117
to labour in his vocation.   (*Falstaff*)

There's neither honesty, manhood, nor good fellowship   155
in thee, nor thou camest not of the blood royal, if thou
darest not stand for ten shillings.   (*Falstaff*)

Farewell, thou latter spring! farewell, All-hallown   177
summer!   (*Prince*)

I know you all, and will awhile uphold   218
The unyoked humour of your idleness:
Yet herein will I imitate the sun,
Who doth permit the base contagious clouds
To smother up his beauty from the world,
That, when he please again to be himself,
Being wanted, he may be more wonder'd at,
By breaking through the foul and ugly mists
Of vapours that did seem to strangle him.
If all the year were playing holidays,
To sport would be as tedious as to work;
But when they seldom come, they wish'd for come,
And nothing pleaseth but rare accidents.
So, when this loose behaviour I throw off
And pay the debt I never promised,
By how much better than my word I am,
By so much shall I falsify men's hopes;
And like bright metal on a sullen ground,
My reformation, glittering o'er my fault,
Shall show more goodly and attract more eyes
Than that which hath no foil to set it off.   (*Prince*)

Came there a certain lord, neat, and trimly dress'd,   I. iii. 33
Fresh as a bridegroom; and his chin new reap'd
Show'd like a stubble-land at harvest-home;
He was perfumed like a milliner;
And 'twixt his finger and his thumb he held
A pouncet-box, which ever and anon
He gave his nose and took 't away again;
Who therewith angry, when it next came there,
Took it in snuff; and still he smiled and talk'd,
And as the soldiers bore dead bodies by,
He call'd them untaught knaves, unmannerly,
To bring a slovenly unhandsome corse
Betwixt the wind and his nobility.
With many holiday and lady terms
He question'd me. (*Hotspur*)

To be so pester'd with a popinjay. (*Hotspur*)   50

                    He made me mad   53
To see him shine so brisk, and smell so sweet,
And talk so like a waiting-gentlewoman
Of guns and drums and wounds,—God save the mark!—
And telling me the sovereign'st thing on earth
Was parmaceti for an inward bruise;
And that it was great pity, so it was,
This villanous salt-petre should be digg'd
Out of the bowels of the harmless earth,
Which many a good tall fellow had destroy'd
So cowardly; and but for these vile guns,
He would himself have been a soldier. (*Hotspur*)

He durst as well have met the devil alone   116
As Owen Glendower for an enemy. (*King*)

To put down Richard, that sweet lovely rose,   175
And plant this thorn, this canker, Bolingbroke. (*Hotspur*)

I 'll read you matter deep and dangerous,   190
As full of peril and adventurous spirit
As to o'er-walk a current roaring loud
On the unsteadfast footing of a spear. (*Worcester*)

                    O, the blood more stirs   197
To rouse a lion than to start a hare! (*Hotspur*)

By heaven, methinks it were an easy leap,   201
To pluck bright honour from the pale-faced moon,
Or dive into the bottom of the deep,
Where fathom-line could never touch the ground,
And pluck up drowned honour by the locks. (*Hotspur*)

I would have him poison'd with a pot of ale. (*Hotspur*)   i. iii. 233

Why, what a candy deal of courtesy   251
This fawning greyhound then did proffer me! (*Hotspur*)

I know a trick worth two of that. (*First Carrier*)   ii. i. 40

Gadshill. What, ho! chamberlain!   53
Chamberlain. [*Within*.] At hand, quoth pick-purse.

   I am joined with no foot land-rakers, no long-staff six-   80
penny strikers, none of these mad mustachio purple-hued
malt-worms; but with nobility and tranquillity, burgo-
masters and great oneyers, such as can hold in, such as will
strike sooner than speak, and speak sooner than drink, and
drink sooner than pray. (*Gadshill*)

We have the receipt of fern-seed, we walk invisible.   96
                                (*Gadshill*)

   I have forsworn his company hourly any time this two   ii. ii. 16
and twenty years, and yet I am bewitched with the
rogue's company.   If the rascal have not given me medicines to make me love him, I'll be hanged; it could not be
else; I have drunk medicines. (*Falstaff*)

   Strike; down with them; cut the villains' throats: ah!   87
whoreson caterpillars! bacon-fed knaves! they hate us
youth: down with them; fleece them. (*Falstaff*)

   On, bacons, on!   What, ye knaves! young men must   95
live. (*Falstaff*)

   It would be argument for a week, laughter for a month   100
and a good jest for ever. (*Prince*)

Away, good Ned.   Falstaff sweats to death,   115
And lards the lean earth as he walks along. (*Prince*)

Out of this nettle, danger, we pluck this flower, safety.   ii. iii. 10
                                (*Hotspur*)

   Our plot is as good a plot as ever was laid; our friends   18
true and constant: a good plot, good friends, and full of
expectation; an excellent plot, very good friends.
                                (*Hotspur*)

I could brain him with his lady's fan. (*Hotspur*)   25

Come, come, you paraquito, answer me   ii. iii. 88
Directly unto this question that I ask:
In faith, I'll break thy little finger, Harry,
An if thou wilt not tell me all things true.   (*Lady Percy*)

Away, you trifler! Love! I love thee not,   93
I care not for thee, Kate: this is no world
To play with mammets and to tilt with lips:
We must have bloody noses and crack'd crowns,
And pass them current too.   (*Hotspur*)

I know you wise, but yet no farther wise   110
Than Harry Percy's wife: constant you are,
But yet a woman: and for secrecy,
No lady closer; for I well believe
Thou wilt not utter what thou dost not know;
And so far will I trust thee, gentle Kate.   (*Hotspur*)

Poins. Where hast been, Hal?   ii. iv. 3
Prince. With three or four loggerheads amongst three or
four score hogsheads.

A Corinthian, a lad of mettle, a good boy.   (*Prince*)   13

Prince. Wilt thou rob this leathern jerkin, crystal-   77
button, not-pated, agate-ring, puke-stocking, caddis-
garter, smooth-tongue, Spanish-pouch,—
Francis. O Lord, sir, who do you mean?
Prince. Why, then, your brown bastard is your only
drink; for look you, Francis, your white canvas doublet
will sully: in Barbary, sir, it cannot come to so much.

That ever this fellow should have fewer words than a   110
parrot, and yet the son of a woman!   (*Prince*)

I am not yet of Percy's mind, the Hotspur of the north;   114
he that kills me some six or seven dozen of Scots at a
breakfast, washes his hands, and says to his wife 'Fie
upon this quiet life! I want work.'   (*Prince*)

Didst thou never see Titan kiss a dish of butter?   134
pitiful-hearted Titan, that melted at the sweet tale of the
sun's? if thou didst, then behold that compound.
                                              (*Prince*)

There live not three good men unhanged in England;   143
and one of them is fat and grows old.   (*Falstaff*)

Falstaff. A plague of all cowards, I say still.   146
Prince. How now, wool-sack! what mutter you?

Why, you whoreson round man, what's the matter?   II. iv. 155
(*Prince*)

I call thee coward! I'll see thee damned ere I call   161
thee coward: but I would give a thousand pound I could
run as fast as thou canst. You are straight enough in the
shoulders, you care not who sees your back: call you that
backing of your friends? A plague upon such backing!
give me them that will face me. (*Falstaff*)

I have 'scaped by miracle. I am eight times thrust   184
through the doublet, four through the hose; my buckler
cut through and through; my sword hacked like a handsaw—ecce signum! (*Falstaff*)

I am a Jew else, an Ebrew Jew.   (*Falstaff*)   198

Falstaff. I have peppered two of them; two I am sure I   211
have paid, two rogues in buckram suits. I tell thee what,
Hal, if I tell thee a lie, spit in my face, call me horse.
Thou knowest my old ward; here I lay, and thus I bore
my point. Four rogues in buckram let drive at me—
Prince. What, four? thou saidst but two even now.
Falstaff. Four, Hal; I told thee four.
Poins. Ay, ay, he said four.
Falstaff. These four came all a-front, and mainly thrust
at me. I made me no more ado but took all their seven
points in my target, thus.

Falstaff. With a thought seven out of the eleven I paid.   242
Prince. O monstrous! eleven buckram men grown out of
two!
Falstaff. But, as the devil would have it, three misbe-
gotten knaves in Kendal green came at my back and let
drive at me; for it was so dark, Hal, that thou couldst not
see thy hand.
Prince. These lies are like their father that begets them;
gross as a mountain, open, palpable.

Give you a reason on compulsion! if reasons were as   263
plentiful as blackberries, I would give no man a reason
upon compulsion, I. (*Falstaff*)

Prince. This sanguine coward, this bed-presser, this   268
horseback-breaker, this huge hill of flesh,—
Falstaff. 'Sblood, you starveling, you elf-skin, you dried
neat's tongue, you bull's pizzle, you stock-fish! O for
breath to utter what is like thee! you tailor's yard, you
sheath, you bow-case, you vile standing-tuck—

Mark now, how a plain tale shall put you down. (*Prince*) II. iv. 281

Ah, no more of that, Hal, an thou lovest me! (*Falstaff*) 312

What doth gravity out of his bed at midnight? (*Falstaff*) 325

How now, my sweet creature of bombast! How long 359
is 't ago, Jack, since thou sawest thine own knee? (*Prince*)

A plague of sighing and grief! it blows a man up like a 365
bladder. (*Falstaff*)

Falstaff. That sprightly Scot of Scots, Douglas, that 377
runs o' horseback up a hill perpendicular,—
Prince. He that rides at high speed and with his pistol
kills a sparrow flying.
Falstaff. You have hit it.
Prince. So did he never the sparrow.

I must speak in passion, and I will do it in King 425
Cambyses' vein. (*Falstaff*)

Falstaff. For God's sake, lords, convey my tristful queen; 433
For tears do stop the flood-gates of her eyes.
Hostess. O Jesu, he doth it as like one of these harlotry
players as ever I see!

Peace, good pint-pot; peace, good tickle-brain. Harry, 437
I do not only marvel where thou spendest thy time, but
also how thou art accompanied: for though the camomile,
the more it is trodden on the faster it grows, yet youth, the
more it is wasted the sooner it wears. (*Falstaff*)

Shall the blessed sun of heaven prove a micher and eat 448
blackberries? a question not to be asked. Shall the son
of England prove a thief and take purses? a question to be
asked. (*Falstaff*)

For, Harry, now I do not speak to thee in drink but in 457
tears, not in pleasure but in passion, not in words only,
but in woes also. (*Falstaff*)

A goodly portly man, i' faith, and a corpulent. (*Falstaff*) 464

Swearest thou, ungracious boy? henceforth ne'er look 490
on me. Thou art violently carried away from grace: there
is a devil haunts thee in the likeness of an old fat man; a
tun of man is thy companion. Why dost thou converse
with that trunk of humours, that bolting-hutch of beast-
liness, that swollen parcel of dropsies, that huge bombard
of sack, that stuffed cloak-bag of guts, that roasted Man-
ningtree ox with the pudding in his belly, that reverend

*G   185

vice, that grey iniquity, that father ruffian, that vanity in   II. iv. 498
years? Wherein is he good, but to taste sack and drink it?
wherein neat and cleanly, but to carve a capon and eat it?
wherein cunning, but in craft? wherein crafty, but in
villany? wherein villanous, but in all things? wherein
worthy, but in nothing? (*Prince*)

If sack and sugar be a fault, God help the wicked! if to   516
be old and merry be a sin, then many an old host that I
know is damned: if to be fat be to be hated, then Pharaoh's
lean kine are to be loved. (*Falstaff*)

No, my good lord; banish Peto, banish Bardolph,   521
banish Poins: but for sweet Jack Falstaff, kind Jack
Falstaff, true Jack Falstaff, valiant Jack Falstaff, and
therefore more valiant, being, as he is, old Jack Falstaff,
banish not him thy Harry's company, banish not him thy
Harry's company: banish plump Jack, and banish all the
world. (*Falstaff*)

Play out the play. (*Falstaff*)   531

Sheriff. Good night, my noble lord.   572
Prince. I think it is good morrow, is it not?
Sheriff. Indeed, my lord, I think it be two o'clock.

Peto. [*Reads.*] Item, A capon,   2s. 2d.   585
    Item, Sauce,   4d.
    Item, Sack, two gallons,   5s. 8d.
    Item, Anchovies and sack after
      supper,   2s. 6d.
    Item, Bread,   0½d.
Prince. O monstrous! but one half-pennyworth of bread
to this intolerable deal of sack!

Glendower.   At my nativity   III. i. 13
The front of heaven was full of fiery shapes,
Of burning cressets; and at my birth
The frame and huge foundation of the earth
Shaked like a coward.
Hotspur. Why, so it would have done at the same season,
if your mother's cat had but kittened, though yourself
had never been born.

Diseased nature oftentimes breaks forth   27
In strange eruptions; oft the teeming earth
Is with a kind of colic pinch'd and vex'd
By the imprisoning of unruly wind
Within her womb; which, for enlargement striving,
Shakes the old beldam earth and topples down
Steeples and moss-grown towers. (*Hotspur*)

These signs have mark'd me extraordinary;   III. i. 41
And all the courses of my life do show
I am not in the roll of common men.   (*Glendower*)

Glendower. I can call spirits from the vasty deep.   53
Hotspur. Why, so can I, or so can any man;
But will they come when you do call for them?
Glendower. Why, I can teach you, cousin, to command
The devil.
Hotspur. And I can teach thee, coz, to shame the devil
By telling truth: tell truth and shame the devil.
If thou have power to raise him, bring him hither,
And I'll be sworn I have power to shame him hence.
O, while you live, tell truth and shame the devil!

Glendower. Three times hath Henry Bolingbroke made   64
   head
Against my power; thrice from the banks of Wye
And sandy-bottom'd Severn have I sent him
Bootless home and weather-beaten back.
Hotspur. Home without boots, and in foul weather too!
How 'scapes he agues, in the devil's name?

Methinks my moiety, north from Burton here,   96
In quantity equals not one of yours:
See how this river comes me cranking in,
And cuts me from the best of all my land
A huge half-moon, a monstrous cantle out.   (*Hotspur*)

I had rather be a kitten and cry mew   129
Than one of these same metre ballad-mongers;
I had rather hear a brazen canstick turn'd,
Or a dry wheel grate on the axle-tree;
And that would set my teeth nothing on edge,
Nothing so much as mincing poetry:
'Tis like the forced gait of a shuffling nag.   (*Hotspur*)

But in the way of bargain, mark ye me,   139
I'll cavil on the ninth part of a hair.   (*Hotspur*)

        Sometime he angers me   148
With telling me of the moldwarp and the ant,
Of the dreamer Merlin and his prophecies,
And of a dragon and a finless fish,
A clip-wing'd griffin and a moulten raven,
A couching lion and a ramping cat,
And such a deal of skimble-skamble stuff
As puts me from my faith.   (*Hotspur*)

O, he is as tedious   III. i. 159
As a tired horse, a railing wife;
Worse than a smoky house: I had rather live
With cheese and garlic in a windmill, far,
Than feed on cates and have him talk to me
In any summer-house in Christendom.   (*Hotspur*)

Well, I am school'd: good manners be your speed!   190
                                        (*Hotspur*)

My daughter weeps: she will not part with you;   193
She'll be a soldier, too, she'll to the wars. (*Glendower*)

I understand thy kisses and thou mine,   205
And that's a feeling disputation.   (*Mortimer*)

She bids you on the wanton rushes lay you down   214
And rest your gentle head upon her lap,
And she will sing the song that pleaseth you
And on your eyelids crown the god of sleep,
Charming your blood with pleasing heaviness,
Making such difference 'twixt wake and sleep,
As is the difference betwixt day and night
The hour before the heavenly-harness'd team
Begins his golden progress in the east.   (*Glendower*)

And those musicians that shall play to you   226
Hang in the air a thousand leagues from hence.
                                        (*Glendower*)

Hotspur. Come, Kate, thou art perfect in lying down: 229
come, quick, quick, that I may lay my head in thy lap.
Lady Percy. Go, ye giddy goose.

Now I perceive the devil understands Welsh;   233
And 'tis no marvel he is so humorous.   (*Hotspur*)

Hotspur. Come, Kate, I'll have your song too.   250
Lady Percy. Not mine, in good sooth.
Hotspur. Not yours, in good sooth!   Heart! you swear
like a comfit-maker's wife.   'Not you, in good sooth,'
and 'as true as I live,' and 'as God shall mend me,' and
'as sure as day,'
And givest such sarcenet surety for thy oaths,
As if thou never walk'st further than Finsbury.
Swear me, Kate, like a lady as thou art,
A good mouth-filling oath, and leave 'in sooth,'
And such protest of pepper-gingerbread,
To velvet-guards and Sunday-citizens.

By smiling pick-thanks and base newsmongers. (*Prince*)   III. ii. 25

The hope and expectation of thy time. (*King*)   III. ii. 36

Had I so lavish of my presence been,   39
So common-hackney'd in the eyes of men,
So stale and cheap to vulgar company,
Opinion, that did help me to the crown,
Had still kept loyal to possession
And left me in reputeless banishment,
A fellow of no mark nor likelihood.
By being seldom seen, I could not stir
But like a comet I was wonder'd at. (*King*)

The skipping king, he ambled up and down   60
With shallow jesters and rash bavin wits,
Soon kindled and soon burnt; carded his state,
Mingled his royalty with capering fools,
Had his great name profaned with their scorns
And gave his countenance, against his name,
To laugh at gibing boys and stand the push
Of every beardless vain comparative. (*King*)

To loathe the taste of sweetness, whereof a little   72
More than a little is by much too much. (*King*)

So when he had occasion to be seen,   74
He was but as the cuckoo is in June,
Heard, not regarded. (*King*)

Why, Harry, do I tell thee of my foes,   122
Which art my near'st and dearest enemy? (*King*)

Our hands are full of business: let's away;   179
Advantage feeds him fat, while men delay. (*King*)

My skin hangs about me like an old lady's loose gown;   III. iii. 3
I am withered like an old apple-john. (*Falstaff*)

Well, I 'll repent, and that suddenly, while I am in some   5
liking; I shall be out of heart shortly, and then I shall have
no strength to repent. An I have not forgotten what the
inside of a church is made of, I am a peppercorn, a
brewer's horse: the inside of a church! Company, vil-
anous company, hath been the spoil of me. (*Falstaff*)

Do thou amend thy face, and I 'll amend my life: thou   27
art our admiral, thou bearest the lantern in the poop, but
'tis in the nose of thee; thou art the Knight of the Burning
Lamp. (*Falstaff*)

Falstaff. Go to, you are a woman, go.   70
Hostess. Who, I? no; I defy thee: God's light, I was never
called so in mine own house before.

Shall I not take mine ease in mine inn but I shall have   III. iii. 92
my pocket picked? (*Falstaff*)

A trifle, some eight-penny matter.   (*Prince*)   119

Hostess. There's neither faith, truth, nor womanhood in   125
me else.
Falstaff. There's no more faith in thee than in a stewed
prune; nor no more truth in thee than in a drawn fox;
and for womanhood, Maid Marian may be the deputy's
wife of the ward to thee.   Go, you thing, go.
Hostess. Say, what thing? what thing?
Falstaff. What thing! why, a thing to thank God on.
Hostess. I am no thing to thank God on, I would thou
shouldst know it; I am an honest man's wife.

I have more flesh than another man, and therefore more   188
frailty. (*Falstaff*)

'Zounds! how has he the leisure to be sick   IV. i. 17
In such a justling time? (*Hotspur*)

The nimble-footed madcap Prince of Wales,   95
And his comrades, that daff'd the world aside,
And bid it pass. (*Hotspur*)

           All furnish'd, all in arms;   97
All plumed like estridges that with the wind
Baited like eagles having lately bathed;
Glittering in golden coats, like images;
As full of spirit as the month of May,
And gorgeous as the sun at midsummer;
Wanton as youthful goats, wild as young bulls.
I saw young Harry, with his beaver on,
His cuisses on his thighs, gallantly arm'd,
Rise from the ground like feather'd Mercury,
And vaulted with such ease into his seat,
As if an angel dropp'd down from the clouds,
To turn and wind a fiery Pegasus
And witch the world with noble horsemanship. (*Vernon*)

No more, no more: worse than the sun in March,   111
This praise doth nourish agues. (*Hotspur*)

Doomsday is near; die all, die merrily. (*Hotspur*)   134

     Such a commodity of warm slaves, as had as lieve hear   IV. ii. 19
the devil as a drum. (*Falstaff*)

A mad fellow met me on the way and told me I had un-   iv. ii. 39
loaded all the gibbets and pressed the dead bodies.   No
eye hath seen such scarecrows.   (*Falstaff*)

There's but a shirt and a half in all my company; and   46
the half shirt is two napkins tacked together and thrown
over the shoulders like a herald's coat without sleeves.
                                             (*Falstaff*)

How now, blown Jack! how now, quilt!   (*Prince*)   54

I am as vigilant as a cat to steal cream.   (*Falstaff*)   64

Prince. I did never see such pitiful rascals.   70
Falstaff. Tut, tut; good enough to toss; food for powder,
food for powder; they'll fill a pit as well as better: tush,
man, mortal men, mortal men.
Westmoreland. Ay, but, Sir John, methinks they are
exceeding poor and bare, too beggarly.
Falstaff. 'Faith, for their poverty, I know not where they
had that; and for their bareness, I am sure they never
learned that of me.

To the latter end of a fray and the beginning of a feast   85
Fits a dull fighter and a keen guest.   (*Falstaff*)

For mine own part, I could be well content   v. i. 23
To entertain the lag-end of my life
With quiet hours.   (*Worcester*)

To face the garment of rebellion   74
With some fine colour that may please the eye
Of fickle changelings and poor discontents,
Which gape and rub the elbow at the news
Of hurlyburly innovation.   (*King*)

I do not think a braver gentleman,   89
More active-valiant or more valiant-young,
More daring or more bold, is now alive
To grace this latter age with noble deeds.   (*Prince*)

I would 'twere bed-time, Hal, and all well.   (*Falstaff*)   125

Well, 'tis no matter; honour pricks me on.   Yea, but   130
how if honour prick me off when I come on? how then?
Can honour set to a leg? no: or an arm? no: or take away
the grief of a wound? no.   Honour hath no skill in sur-
gery, then? no.   What is honour? a word.   What is in that
word honour? what is that honour? air.   A trim reckoning!   Who hath it? he that died o' Wednesday.   Doth he

feel it? no.   Doth he hear it? no.   'Tis insensible, then?   v. i. 137
Yea, to the dead.   But will it not live with the living? no.
Why? detraction will not suffer it.   Therefore I'll none
of it.   Honour is a mere scutcheon: and so ends my
catechism.   (*Falstaff*)

For treason is but trusted like the fox,   v. ii. 9
Who, ne'er so tame, so cherish'd and lock'd up,
Will have a wild trick of his ancestors.   (*Worcester*)

O gentlemen, the time of life is short!   82
To spend that shortness basely were too long,
If life did ride upon a dial's point,
Still ending at the arrival of an hour.
An if we live, we live to tread on kings;
If die, brave death, when princes die with us!   (*Hotspur*)

I was not born a yielder, thou proud Scot.   (*Blunt*)   v. iii. 11

    I have led my ragamuffins where they are peppered: 36
there's not three of my hundred and fifty left alive; and
they are for the town's end, to beg during life.   (*Falstaff*)

I have paid Percy, I have made him sure.   (*Falstaff*)   47

And God forbid a shallow scratch should drive   v. iv. 11
The Prince of Wales from such a field as this.   (*Prince*)

Two stars keep not their motion in one sphere;   65
Nor can one England brook a double reign,
Of Harry Percy and the Prince of Wales.   (*Prince*)

Hotspur.   Percy, thou art dust,   85
And food for—   [*Dies.*]
Prince. For worms, brave Percy: fare thee well, great
   heart!
Ill-weaved ambition, how much art thou shrunk!
When that this body did contain a spirit,
A kingdom for it was too small a bound;
But now two paces of the vilest earth
Is room enough: this earth that bears thee dead
Bears not alive so stout a gentleman.

Prince. [*Spying Falstaff on the ground.*] What, old ac-   102
   quaintance! could not all this flesh
Keep in a little life?   Poor Jack, farewell!
I could have better spared a better man.

    The better part of valour is discretion; in the which   121
better part I have saved my life.   (*Falstaff*)

Come, brother John; full bravely hast thou flesh'd   v. iv. 133
Thy maiden sword.   (*Prince*)

Prince. Why, Percy I killed myself and saw thee dead.   148
Falstaff. Didst thou? Lord, Lord, how this world is
given to lying! I grant you I was down and out of
breath; and so was he: but we rose both at an instant
and fought a long hour by Shrewsbury clock.

Lancaster. This is the strangest tale that ever I heard.   158
Prince. This is the strangest fellow, brother John.

If I do grow great, I'll grow less; for I'll purge, and   167
leave sack, and live cleanly as a nobleman should do.
                                        (*Falstaff*)

KING HENRY IV, PART II

This continues the story of Part I to the accession of Henry V in 1413. The rebellion is carried on after Hotspur's death by Scroop, Archbishop of York, and the Lords Mowbray and Hastings, but while parleying with the king's younger son, Prince John of Lancaster, they are treacherously arrested and led off to execution. The king, at the point of death, has a moving interview with his son Henry, and advises him to start a foreign war to divert the attention of malcontents, while the Prince on his part promises to reform his wild ways. Shortly afterwards Henry IV dies and the Prince succeeds. In the Eastcheap scenes in this play Pistol, a blustering bully who mouths tags from contemporary melodramas, makes his appearance along with Bardolph, Peto, Poins, Mistress Quickly, and her gossip Doll Tearsheet. Falstaff, recruiting for the king's forces with the help of Shallow and Silence, country justices, makes great sport of the down-at-heel specimens he has to accept. When his fellow-roisterer the Prince becomes Henry V Falstaff thinks his fortune made, but he is quickly disillusioned, for the new king, sacrificing friendship to policy, repulses and imprisons him.

I, from the orient to the drooping west,   Induction 3
Making the wind my post-horse, still unfold
The acts commenced on this ball of earth:
Upon my tongues continual slanders ride,
The which in every language I pronounce,
Stuffing the ears of men with false reports.
I speak of peace, while covert enmity
Under the smile of safety wounds the world. (*Rumour*)

                    Every minute now   I. i. 7
Should be the father of some stratagem.
                   (*Northumberland*)

He told me that rebellion had bad luck   41
And that young Harry Percy's spur was cold. (*Travers*)

Yea, this man's brow, like to a title-leaf,   60
Foretells the nature of a tragic volume. (*Northumberland*)

Thou tremblest; and the whiteness in thy cheek   68
Is apter than thy tongue to tell thy errand.
Even such a man, so faint, so spiritless,
So dull, so dead in look, so woe-begone,
Drew Priam's curtain in the dead of night,
And would have told him half his Troy was burnt.
                   (*Northumberland*)

He that but fears the thing he would not know   85
Hath by instinct knowledge from others' eyes
That what he fear'd is chanced. (*Northumberland*)

Yet the first bringer of unwelcome news   100
Hath but a losing office, and his tongue
Sounds ever after as a sullen bell,
Remember'd tolling a departing friend. (*Northumberland*)

   I am not only witty in myself, but the cause that wit is in   I. ii. 11
other men. (*Falstaff*)

   I do here walk before thee like a sow that hath over-   12
whelmed all her litter but one. (*Falstaff*)

A rascally yea-forsooth knave. (*Falstaff*)   42

   I bought him in Paul's, and he'll buy me a horse in   58
Smithfield: an I could get me but a wife in the stews, I
were manned, horsed, and wived. (*Falstaff*)

This apoplexy is, as I take it, a kind of lethargy, an't   I. ii. 126
please your lordship; a kind of sleeping in the blood, a
whoreson tingling.   (*Falstaff*)

It is the disease of not listening, the malady of not   138
marking, that I am troubled withal.   (*Falstaff*)

I am as poor as Job, my lord, but not so patient.   144
                                        (*Falstaff*)

Chief Justice. Well, the truth is, Sir John, you live in   155
great infamy.
Falstaff. He that buckles him in my belt cannot live in
less.
Chief Justice. Your means are very slender, and your
waste is great.
Falstaff. I would it were otherwise; I would my means
were greater, and my waist slenderer.

Chief Justice. There is not a white hair on your face but   182
should have his effect of gravity.
Falstaff. His effect of gravy, gravy, gravy.

You that are old consider not the capacities of us that   195
are young.   (*Falstaff*)

We that are in the vaward of our youth.   (*Falstaff*)   198

Chief Justice. Have you not a moist eye? a dry hand?   203
a yellow cheek? a white beard? a decreasing leg? an in-
creasing belly? is not your voice broken? your wind
short? your chin double? your wit single? and every part
about you blasted with antiquity? and will you yet call
yourself young?   Fie, fie, fie, Sir John!
Falstaff. My lord, I was born about three of the clock in
the afternoon, with a white head and something a round
belly.   For my voice, I have lost it with halloing and singing of anthems.

It was alway yet the trick of our English nation, if they   241
have a good thing, to make it too common.   (*Falstaff*)

I were better to be eaten to death with a rust than to be   245
scoured to nothing with perpetual motion.   (*Falstaff*)

If I do, fillip me with a three-man beetle.   (*Falstaff*)   255

I can get no remedy against this consumption of the   264
purse: borrowing only lingers and lingers it out, but the
disease is incurable. (*Falstaff*)

                       When we mean to build,   I. iii. 41
We first survey the plot, then draw the model;
And when we see the figure of the house,
Then must we rate the cost of the erection.
                             (Lord Bardolph)

An habitation giddy and unsure   89
Hath he that buildeth on the vulgar heart.   *(Archbishop)*

Past and to come seems best; things present worst.   108
                               (Archbishop)

Fang (a sheriff's officer). A rescue! a rescue!   II. i. 61
Hostess. Good people, bring a rescue or two.

    Away, you scullion! you rampallian! you fustilarian!   65
I'll tickle your catastrophe.   *(Falstaff)*

Hostess. He is arrested at my suit.   77
Chief Justice. For what sum?
Hostess. It is more than for some, my lord; it is for all, all
I have.   He hath eaten me out of house and home; he hath
put all my substance into that fat belly of his.

    Thou didst swear to me upon a parcel-gilt goblet,   93
sitting in my Dolphin-chamber, at the round table, by a
sea-coal fire, upon Wednesday in Wheeson week, when the
prince broke thy head for liking his father to a singing-
man of Windsor, thou didst swear to me then, as I was
washing thy wound, to marry me and make me my lady
thy wife.   *(Hostess)*

    Glasses, glasses, is the only drinking: and for thy   155
walls, a pretty slight drollery, or the story of the Prodigal,
or the German hunting in water-work, is worth a thousand of these bed-hangings and these fly-bitten tapestries.
                               (Falstaff)

    This is the right fencing grace, my lord; tap for tap,   205
and so part fair.   *(Falstaff)*

Prince. Before God, I am exceeding weary.   II. ii. 1
Poins. Is't come to that?   I had thought weariness durst
not have attached one of so high blood.

Doth it not show vilely in me to desire small beer?   7
                         (Prince)

    What a disgrace is it to me to remember thy name! or   15
to know thy face to-morrow! or to take note how many

pair of silk stockings thou hast, viz. these, and those that   II. ii. 17
were thy peach-coloured ones! or to bear the inventory of
thy shirts, as, one for superfluity, and another for use!
                                    (*Prince*)

Thou art a blessed fellow to think as every man thinks: 61
never a man's thought in the world keeps the road-way
better than thine.   (*Prince*)

The boy that I gave Falstaff: a' had him from me   75
Christian; and look, if the fat villain have not transformed
him ape.   (*Prince*)

Away, you whoreson upright rabbit, away!   (*Bardolph*)   91

Thus we play the fools with the time, and the spirits   154
of the wise sit in the clouds and mock us.   (*Prince*)

Page. A proper gentlewoman, sir, and a kinswoman of my   169
master's.
Prince. Even such kin as the parish heifers are to the town
bull.

He was indeed the glass   II. iii. 21
Wherein the noble youth did dress themselves.
                                    (*Lady Percy*)

He was the mark and glass, copy and book,   31
That fashion'd others.   (*Lady Percy*)

You do draw my spirits from me   46
With new lamenting ancient oversights.
                                    (*Northumberland*)

'Tis with my mind   62
As with the tide swell'd up unto his height,
That makes a still-stand, running neither way.
                                    (*Northumberland*)

To serve bravely is to come halting off.   (*Falstaff*)   II. iv. 54

Shut the door; there comes no swaggerers here.   82
                                    (*Hostess*)

Away, you mouldy rogue, away!   I am meat for your   134
master.   (*Doll Tearsheet*)

Pistol. I'll see her damned first; to Pluto's damned lake,   169
by this hand, to the infernal deep, with Erebus and
tortures vile also.   Hold hook and line, say I.   Down,

down, dogs! down, faitors! Have we not Hiren here? II. iv. 172
Hostess. Good Captain Peesel, be quiet; 'tis very late,
i' faith: I beseek you now, aggravate your choler.

Pistol. These be good humours indeed! Shall pack- 177
 horses,
And hollow pamper'd jades of Asia,
Which cannot go but thirty mile a day,
Compare with Caesars, and with Cannibals,
And Trojan Greeks? nay, rather damn them with
King Cerberus; and let the welkin roar.
Shall we fall foul for toys?
Hostess. By my troth, captain, these are very bitter words.

Pistol. Die men like dogs! give crowns like pins! Have 188
we not Hiren here?
Hostess. O' my word, captain, there's none such here.
What the good-year! do you think I would deny her?
For God's sake, be quiet.
Pistol. Then feed, and be fat, my fair Calipolis.

Give me some sack: and, sweetheart, lie thou there. 197
    (*Pistol, laying down his sword*)

Bardolph. Come, get you down stairs. 209
Pistol. What! shall we have incision? shall we imbrue?
Then death rock me asleep, abridge my doleful days.
Why, then, let grievous, ghastly, gaping wounds
Untwine the Sisters Three! Come, Atropos, I say!

 Thou whoreson little tidy Bartholomew boar-pig, when 250
wilt thou leave fighting o' days and foining o' nights, and
begin to patch up thine old body for heaven?
    (*Doll Tearsheet*)

Doll. Sirrah, what humour's the prince of? 256
Falstaff. A good shallow young fellow: a' would have
made a good pantler, a' would ha' chipped bread well.

 Is it not strange that desire should so many years outlive 286
performance? (*Poins*)

Falstaff. I am old, I am old. 294
Doll. I love thee better than I love e'er a scurvy young boy
of them all.

    I feel me much to blame, 390
So idly to profane the precious time,
When tempest of commotion, like the south
Borne with black vapour, doth begin to melt
And drop upon our bare unarmed heads. (*Prince*)

Well, fare thee well: I have known thee these twenty-   II. iv. 412
nine years, come peascod-time; but an honester and truer-
hearted man,—well, fare thee well. (*Hostess*)

                    O sleep, O gentle sleep,   III. i. 5
Nature's soft nurse, how have I frighted thee,
That thou no more wilt weigh my eyelids down
And steep my senses in forgetfulness?
Why rather, sleep, liest thou in smoky cribs,
Upon uneasy pallets stretching thee
And hush'd with buzzing night-flies to thy slumber,
Than in the perfumed chambers of the great,
Under the canopies of costly state,
And lull'd with sound of sweetest melody? (*King*)

Wilt thou upon the high and giddy mast   18
Seal up the ship-boy's eyes, and rock his brains
In cradle of the rude imperious surge
And in the visitation of the winds,
Who take the ruffian billows by the top,
Curling their monstrous heads and hanging them
With deafening clamour in the slippery clouds,
That, with the hurly, death itself awakes?
Canst thou, O partial sleep, give thy repose
To the wet sea-boy in an hour so rude,
And in the calmest and most stillest night,
With all appliances and means to boot,
Deny it to a king? Then happy low, lie down!
Uneasy lies the head that wears a crown. (*King*)

O God! that one might read the book of fate,   45
And see the revolution of the times
Make mountains level, and the continent,
Weary of solid firmness, melt itself
Into the sea! and, other times, to see
The beachy girdle of the ocean
Too wide for Neptune's hips; how chances mock,
And changes fill the cup of alteration
With divers liquors! O, if this were seen,
The happiest youth, viewing his progress through,
What perils past, what crosses to ensue,
Would shut the book, and sit him down and die. (*King*)

There is a history in all men's lives,   80
Figuring the nature of the times deceased;
The which observed, a man may prophesy,
With a near aim, of the main chance of things
As yet not come to life, which in their seeds
And weak beginnings lie intreasured. (*Warwick*)

Shallow. I was once of Clement's Inn, where I think they   iii. ii. 15
will talk of mad Shallow yet.
Silence. You were called 'lusty Shallow' then, cousin.
Shallow. By the mass, I was called any thing; and I would
have done any thing indeed too, and roundly too.

Shallow. Jesu, Jesu, the mad days that I have spent! and   36
to see how many of my old acquaintance are dead!
Silence. We shall all follow, cousin.
Shallow. Certain, 'tis certain; very sure, very sure: death,
as the Psalmist saith, is certain to all; all shall die.
How a good yoke of bullocks at Stamford fair?

Shallow. Is old Double of your town living yet?   45
Silence. Dead, sir.
Shallow. Jesu, Jesu, dead! a' drew a good bow; and dead!
a' shot a fine shoot: John a Gaunt loved him well, and
betted much money on his head.

A soldier is better accommodated than with a wife.   72
                                        (*Bardolph*)

Phrase call you it? by this good day, I know not the   81
phrase; but I will maintain the word with my sword to be
a soldier-like word, and a word of exceeding good command, by heaven.   Accommodated; that is, when a man
is, as they say, accommodated; or when a man is, being,
whereby a' may be thought to be accommodated; which
is an excellent thing.   (*Bardolph*)

Thou wilt be as valiant as the wrathful dove or most   170
magnanimous mouse.   (*Falstaff*)

We have heard the chimes at midnight, Master Shallow.   228
                                        (*Falstaff*)

A man can die but once: we owe God a death: I'll ne'er   250
bear a base mind: an't be my destiny, so; an't be not, so:
no man's too good to serve's prince; and let it go which
way it will, he that dies this year is quit for the next.
                                        (*Feeble*)

Lord, Lord, how subject we old men are to this vice of   325
lying!   (*Falstaff*)

I do remember him at Clement's Inn like a man made   331
after supper of a cheese-paring: when a' was naked, he
was, for all the world, like a forked radish, with a head
fantastically carved upon it with a knife.   (*Falstaff*)

And now is this Vice's dagger become a squire, and   III. ii. 344
talks as familiarly of John a Gaunt as if he had been sworn
brother to him. (*Falstaff*)

Turning your books to graves, your ink to blood,   IV. i. 50
Your pens to lances and your tongue divine
To a loud trumpet and a point of war. (*Westmoreland*)

I have in equal balance justly weigh'd   67
What wrongs our arms may do, what wrongs we suffer,
And find our griefs heavier than our offences.
(*Archbishop*)

Our peace shall stand as firm as rocky mountains.   188
(*Hastings*)

Against ill chances men are ever merry;   IV. ii. 81
But heaviness foreruns the good event. (*Archbishop*)

A peace is of the nature of a conquest;   89
For then both parties nobly are subdued,
And neither party loser. (*Archbishop*)

                                    Like a school broke up,   104
Each hurries toward his home and sporting-place.
(*Hastings*)

An I had but a belly of any indifferency, I were simply   IV. iii. 22
the most active fellow in Europe: my womb, my womb,
my womb, undoes me. (*Falstaff*)

He saw me and yielded; that I may justly say, with the   44
hook-nosed fellow of Rome, 'I came, saw, and overcame.'
(*Falstaff*)

This same young sober-blooded boy doth not love me;   93
nor a man cannot make him laugh; but that's no marvel,
he drinks no wine. (*Falstaff*)

If I had a thousand sons, the first humane principle I   133
would teach them should be, to forswear thin potations
and to addict themselves to sack. (*Falstaff*)

He hath a tear for pity and a hand   IV. iv. 31
Open as day for melting charity. (*King*)

Most subject is the fattest soil to weeds. (*King*)   54

The blood weeps from my heart when I do shape   58
In forms imaginary the unguided days
And rotten times that you shall look upon
When I am sleeping with my ancestors. (*King*)

The prince but studies his companions   IV. iv. 68
Like a strange tongue, wherein, to gain the language,
'Tis needful that the most immodest word
Be look'd upon and learn'd; which once attain'd,
Your highness knows, comes to no further use
But to be known and hated.   (*Warwick*)

Will Fortune never come with both hands full,   103
But write her fair words still in foulest letters?
She either gives a stomach and no food;
Such are the poor, in health; or else a feast
And takes away the stomach; such are the rich,
That have abundance and enjoy it not.   (*King*)

The seasons change their manners, as the year   123
Had found some months asleep and leap'd them over.
                                  (*Gloucester*)

Why doth the crown lie there upon his pillow,   IV. v. 21
Being so troublesome a bedfellow?
O polish'd perturbation! golden care!
That keep'st the ports of slumber open wide
To many a watchful night! sleep with it now!
Yet not so sound and half so deeply sweet
As he whose brow with homely biggen bound
Snores out the watch of night.   (*Prince*)

How quickly nature falls into revolt   66
When gold becomes her object!   (*King*)

Prince. I never thought to hear you speak again.   92
King. Thy wish was father, Harry, to that thought.

Have you a ruffian that will swear, drink, dance,   125
Revel the night, rob, murder, and commit
The oldest sins the newest kind of ways?   (*King*)

               God knows, my son,   184
By what by-paths and indirect crook'd ways
I met this crown.   (*King*)

Be it thy course to busy giddy minds   214
With foreign quarrels; that action, hence borne out,
May waste the memory of the former days.   (*King*)

  Some pigeons, Davy, a couple of short-legged hens, a   v. i. 27
joint of mutton, and any pretty little tiny kickshaws.
                                  (*Shallow*)

A friend i' the court is better than a penny in purse.   33
                                  (*Shallow*)

It is certain that either wise bearing or ignorant carriage   v. i. 84
is caught, as men take diseases, one of another: therefore
let men take heed of their company.   (*Falstaff*)

You shall see him laugh till his face be like a wet cloak   94
ill laid up!   (*Falstaff*)

Chief Justice. How doth the king?   v. ii. 2
Warwick. Exceeding well; his cares are now all ended.
Chief Justice. I hope, not dead.
Warwick.   He's walk'd the way of nature.

And I dare swear you borrow not that face   28
Of seeming sorrow, it is sure your own.   (*Gloucester*)

Brothers, you mix your sadness with some fear: 46
This is the English, not the Turkish court;
Not Amurath an Amurath succeeds,
But Harry Harry.   (*King Henry V*)

Be merry, be merry, my wife has all;   v. iii. 35
For women are shrews, both short and tall:
'Tis merry in hall when beards wag all,
    And welcome merry Shrove-tide.
                (*Silence, sings.*)

Falstaff. I did not think Master Silence had been a man   40
of this mettle.
Silence. Who, I? I have been merry twice and once ere
now.

I hope to see London once ere I die.   (*Davy*)   64

        Do me right,   77
        And dub me knight:
           Samingo.   (*Silence, sings.*)

And helter-skelter have I rode to thee,   98
And tidings do I bring and lucky joys
And golden times and happy news of price.   (*Pistol*)

A foutre for the world and worldlings base!   103
I speak of Africa and golden joys.   (*Pistol*)

Shallow. I am, sir, under the king, in some authority.   117
Pistol. Under which king, Besonian? speak, or die.

Falstaff. What, is the old king dead?   126
Pistol. As nail in door.

Let us take any man's horses; the laws of England are   v. iii. 142
at my commandment.   (*Falstaff*)

Thy Doll, and Helen of thy noble thoughts,   v. v. 35
Is in base durance and contagious prison;
Haled thither
By most mechanical and dirty hand.   (*Pistol*)

Falstaff. God save thy grace, King Hal! my royal Hal!   44
Pistol. The heavens thee guard and keep, most royal imp
of fame!
Falstaff. God save thee, my sweet boy!
King. My lord chief justice, speak to that vain man.
Chief Justice. Have you your wits? know you what 'tis
you speak?
Falstaff. My king! my Jove! I speak to thee, my heart!
King. I know thee not, old man: fall to thy prayers;
How ill white hairs become a fool and jester!
I have long dream'd of such a kind of man,
So surfeit-swell'd, so old and so profane;
But, being awaked, I do despise my dream.

Presume not that I am the thing I was;   60
For God doth know, so shall the world perceive,
That I have turn'd away my former self;
So will I those that kept me company.   (*King*)

Master Shallow, I owe you a thousand pound.   (*Falstaff*)   77

If you be not too much cloyed with fat meat, our humble   Epilogue
author will continue the story, with Sir John in it, and   28
make you merry with fair Katharine of France; where, for
any thing I know, Falstaff shall die of a sweat, unless
already a' be killed with your hard opinions; for Oldcastle
died a martyr, and this is not the man.   My tongue is
weary; when my legs are too, I will bid you good night:
and so kneel down before you; but, indeed, to pray for the
queen.

KING HENRY V

This play covers the period from 1414 to 1420, and is mainly concerned with Henry V's expedition to France. First, however, comes the unmasking of Lord Scroop, Sir Thomas Grey, and the Earl of Cambridge, who are arrested for treason. Henry then crosses to France with his army, captures Harfleur, and after a magnificent 'pep talk' to his men wins the victory of Agincourt. The final scene shows him wooing and winning Princess Katharine, daughter of the French king. Three of the Eastcheap roisterers of the earlier plays, Pistol, Nym, and Bardolph, reappear in this one, together with a boy, and Mistress Quickly, now married to Pistol. Falstaff has died of a broken heart because of the king's treatment. Bardolph is hanged for looting and Pistol, shown up as an empty braggart by Fluellen, a Welsh captain whom he has insulted, plans to return to his old trade of cutpurse.

O for a Muse of fire, that would ascend   Prologue 1
The brightest heaven of invention,
A kingdom for a stage, princes to act
And monarchs to behold the swelling scene!
Then should the warlike Harry, like himself,
Assume the port of Mars; and at his heels,
Leash'd in like hounds, should famine, sword and fire
Crouch for employment.   (*Chorus*)

                 Can this cockpit hold   11
The vasty fields of France? or may we cram
Within this wooden O the very casques
That did affright the air at Agincourt?   (*Chorus*)

Piece out our imperfections with your thoughts;   23
Into a thousand parts divide one man,
And make imaginary puissance;
Think, when we talk of horses, that you see them
Printing their proud hoofs i' the receiving earth:
For 'tis your thoughts that now must deck our kings,
Carry them here and there; jumping o'er times,
Turning the accomplishment of many years
Into an hour-glass.   (*Chorus*)

Of indigent faint souls past corporal toil.   (*Canterbury*)   1. i. 16

Consideration, like an angel, came   28
And whipp'd the offending Adam out of him.   (*Canterbury*)

Hear him but reason in divinity,   38
And all-admiring with an inward wish
You would desire the king were made a prelate:
Hear him debate of commonwealth affairs,
You would say it hath been all in all his study:
List his discourse of war, and you shall hear
A fearful battle render'd you in music:
Turn him to any cause of policy,
The Gordian knot of it he will unloose,
Familiar as his garter: that, when he speaks,
The air, a charter'd libertine, is still,
And the mute wonder lurketh in men's ears,
To steal his sweet and honey'd sentences;
So that the art and practic part of life
Must be the mistress to this theoric.   (*Canterbury*)

The strawberry grows underneath the nettle   60
And wholesome berries thrive and ripen best
Neighbour'd by fruit of baser quality.   (*Bishop of Ely*)

God and his angels guard your sacred throne   I. ii. 7
And make you long become it!   (*Canterbury*)

O noble English, that could entertain   III
With half their forces the full pride of France
And let another half stand laughing by,
All out of work and cold for action!   (*Canterbury*)

When all her chivalry hath been in France   157
And she a mourning widow of her nobles,
She hath herself not only well defended
But taken and impounded as a stray
The King of Scots; whom she did send to France,
To fill King Edward's fame with prisoner kings
And make her chronicle as rich with praise
As is the ooze and bottom of the sea
With sunken wreck and sumless treasuries.

                                        (*Canterbury*)

But there's a saying very old and true,   166
        'If that you will France win,
        Then with Scotland first begin.'   (*Westmoreland*)

            Therefore doth heaven divide   183
The state of man in divers functions,
Setting endeavour in continual motion;
To which is fixed, as an aim or butt,
Obedience: for so work the honey-bees,
Creatures that by a rule in nature teach
The act of order to a peopled kingdom.
They have a king and officers of sorts;
Where some, like magistrates, correct at home,
Others, like merchants, venture trade abroad,
Others, like soldiers, armed in their stings,
Make boot upon the summer's velvet buds,
Which pillage they with merry march bring home
To the tent-royal of their emperor;
Who, busied in his majesty, surveys
The singing masons building roofs of gold,
The civil citizens kneading up the honey,
The poor mechanic porters crowding in
Their heavy burdens at the narrow gate,
The sad-eyed justice, with his surly hum,
Delivering o'er to executors pale
The lazy yawning drone.   (*Canterbury*)

As many arrows, loosed several ways,   207
Come to one mark; as many ways meet in one town;
As many fresh streams meet in one salt sea;
As many lines close in the dial's centre;

So may a thousand actions, once afoot,   I. ii. 211
End in one purpose, and be all well borne
Without defeat.   (*Canterbury*)

His present and your pains we thank you for: 260
When we have match'd our rackets to these balls,
We will, in France, by God's grace, play a set
Shall strike his father's crown into the hazard.
         (*King Henry*)

     'Tis ever common   271
That men are merriest when they are from home.
         (*King Henry*)

Now all the youth of England are on fire,   II. Prologue
And silken dalliance in the wardrobe lies: 1
Now thrive the armourers, and honour's thought
Reigns solely in the breast of every man:
They sell the pasture now to buy the horse,
Following the mirror of all Christian kings,
With winged heels, as English Mercuries.
For now sits Expectation in the air,
And hides a sword from hilts unto the point
With crowns imperial, crowns and coronets,
Promised to Harry and his followers.   (*Chorus*)

O England! model to thy inward greatness,   16
Like little body with a mighty heart,
What mightst thou do, that honour would thee do,
Were all thy children kind and natural!   (*Chorus*)

 I dare not fight; but I will wink and hold out mine iron: II. i. 7
it is a simple one; but what though? it will toast cheese,
and it will endure cold as another man's sword will: and
there's an end.   (*Nym*)

 I cannot tell: things must be as they may: men may   22
sleep, and they may have their throats about them at that
time; and some say knives have edges.   It must be as it
may: though patience be a tired mare, yet she will plod.
         (*Nym*)

Base tike, call'st thou me host?   31
Now, by this hand, I swear, I scorn the term;
Nor shall my Nell keep lodgers.   (*Pistol*)

Nym. Will you shog off? I would have you solus.   48
Pistol. 'Solus,' egregious dog?   O viper vile!
The 'solus' in thy most mervailous face;
The 'solus' in thy teeth, and in thy throat,

H   209

And in thy hateful lungs, yea, in thy maw, perdy,   II. i. 52
And, which is worse, within thy nasty mouth!
I do retort the 'solus' in thy bowels.

O braggart vile and damned furious wight!   64
The grave doth gape, and doting death is near;
Therefore exhale.   (*Pistol*)

Nym. I will cut thy throat, one time or other, in fair   73
terms: that is the humour of it.
Pistol. 'Couple a gorge!'
That is the word.   I thee defy again.
O hound of Crete, think'st thou my spouse to get?

Nym. You'll pay me the eight shillings I won of you at   98
betting?
Pistol. Base is the slave that pays.

Hostess. Come in quickly to Sir John.   Ah, poor heart!   122
he is so shaked of a burning quotidian tertian, that it is
most lamentable to behold.   Sweet men, come to him.
Nym. The king hath run bad humours on the knight;
that's the even of it.
Pistol. Nym, thou hast spoke the right;
His heart is fracted and corroborate.

Never was monarch better fear'd and loved   II. ii. 25
Than is your majesty.   (*Cambridge*)

Enlarge the man committed yesterday,   40
That rail'd against our person: we consider
It was excess of wine that set him on;
And on his more advice we pardon him.   (*King Henry*)

King Henry. O, let us yet be merciful.   47
Cambridge. So may your highness, and yet punish too.

The mercy that was quick in us but late,   79
By your own counsel is suppress'd and kill'd.
                    (*King Henry*)

Treason and murder ever kept together,   105
As two yoke-devils sworn to either's purpose.
                    (*King Henry*)

O, how hast thou with jealousy infected   126
The sweetness of affiance!   Show men dutiful?
Why, so didst thou: seem they grave and learned?
Why, so didst thou: come they of noble family?
Why, so didst thou: seem they religious?
Why, so didst thou: or are they spare in diet,

Free from gross passion or of mirth or anger,   II. ii. 132
Constant in spirit, not swerving with the blood,
Garnish'd and deck'd in modest complement,
Not working with the eye without the ear,
And but in purged judgment trusting neither?
Such and so finely bolted didst thou seem.

(King Henry)

Boy, bristle thy courage up; for Falstaff he is dead,   II. iii. 5
And we must yearn therefore.   (Pistol)

Nay, sure, he's not in hell: he's in Arthur's bosom, if   9
ever man went to Arthur's bosom.   A' made a finer end
and went away an it had been any christom child; a' parted
even just between twelve and one, even at the turning o'
the tide: for after I saw him fumble with the sheets and
play with flowers and smile upon his fingers' ends, I knew
there was but one way; for his nose was as sharp as a pen,
and a' babbled of green fields.   'How now, Sir John!'
quoth I: 'what, man! be o' good cheer.'   So a' cried out
'God, God, God!' three or four times.   Now I, to comfort him, bid him a' should not think of God; I hoped
there was no need to trouble himself with any such
thoughts yet.   (Hostess)

As cold as any stone.   (Hostess)   25

Nym. They say he cried out of sack.   29
Hostess. Ay, that a' did.
Bardolph. And of women.
Hostess. Nay, that a' did not.
Boy. Yes, that a' did; and said they were devils incarnate.
Hostess. A' never could abide carnation; 'twas a colour he
    never liked.

Do you not remember, a' saw a flea stick upon Bar-   42
dolph's nose, and a' said it was a black soul burning in
hell-fire?   (Boy)

Come, let's away.   My love, give me thy lips.   49
Look to my chattels and my movables:
Let senses rule; the word is 'Pitch and Pay:'
Trust none;
For oaths are straws, men's faiths are wafer-cakes,
And hold-fast is the only dog, my duck:
Therefore, Caveto be thy counsellor.   (Pistol)

How modest in exception, and withal   II. iv. 34
How terrible in constant resolution.

(Constable of France)

And you shall find his vanities forespent   II. iv. 36
Were but the outside of the Roman Brutus,
Covering discretion with a coat of folly;
As gardeners do with ordure hide those roots
That shall first spring and be most delicate.
                                     (*Constable of France*)

Self-love, my liege, is not so vile a sin   74
As self-neglecting.   (*Dauphin*)

'Tis no sinister nor no awkward claim,   85
Pick'd from the worm-holes of long-vanish'd days,
Nor from the dust of old oblivion raked.   (*Exeter*)

                                    Still be kind,   III. Pro-
And eke out our performance with your mind.   (*Chorus*)   logue 34

Once more unto the breach, dear friends, once more;   III. i. 1
Or close the wall up with our English dead.
In peace there's nothing so becomes a man
As modest stillness and humility:
But when the blast of war blows in our ears,
Then imitate the action of the tiger;
Stiffen the sinews, summon up the blood,
Disguise fair nature with hard-favour'd rage;
Then lend the eye a terrible aspect;
Let it pry through the portage of the head
Like the brass cannon; let the brow o'erwhelm it
As fearfully as doth a galled rock
O'erhang and jutty his confounded base,
Swill'd with the wild and wasteful ocean.
Now set the teeth and stretch the nostril wide,
Hold hard the breath and bend up every spirit
To his full height.   On, on, you noblest English,
Whose blood is fet from fathers of war-proof!
Fathers that, like so many Alexanders,
Have in these parts from morn till even fought
And sheathed their swords for lack of argument:
Dishonour not your mothers; now attest
That those whom you call'd fathers did beget you.
Be copy now to men of grosser blood,
And teach them how to war.   And you, good yeomen,
Whose limbs were made in England, show us here
The mettle of your pasture; let us swear
That you are worth your breeding; which I doubt not;
For there is none of you so mean and base,
That hath not noble lustre in your eyes.
I see you stand like greyhounds in the slips,
Straining upon the start.   The game's afoot:
Follow your spirit, and upon this charge
Cry 'God for Harry, England, and Saint George!'
                                     (*King Henry*)

Would I were in an alehouse in London!   I would give   III. ii. 12
all my fame for a pot of ale and safety.   (*Boy*)

For Nym, he hath heard that men of few words are the   37
best men; and therefore he scorns to say his prayers, lest
a' should be thought a coward.   (*Boy*)

They will steal any thing, and call it purchase.   (*Boy*)   44

Normans, but bastard Normans, Norman bastards!   III. v. 10
Mort de ma vie! if they march along
Unfought withal, but I will sell my dukedom,
To buy a slobbery and a dirty farm
In that nook-shotten isle of Albion.   (*Bourbon*)

Is not their climate foggy, raw and dull,   16
On whom, as in despite, the sun looks pale,
Killing their fruit with frowns?   (*Constable of France*)

By your patience, Aunchient Pistol.   Fortune is painted   III. vi. 31
blind, with a muffler afore her eyes, to signify to you that
Fortune is blind; and she is painted also with a wheel, to
signify to you, which is the moral of it, that she is turning,
and inconstant, and mutability, and variation: and her
foot, look you, is fixed upon a spherical stone, which rolls,
and rolls, and rolls.   (*Fluellen*)

Let gallows gape for dog; let man go free   44
And let not hemp his wind-pipe suffocate:
But Exeter hath given the doom of death
For pax of little price.   (*Pistol*)

Fluellen. Aunchient Pistol, I do partly understand your   52
     meaning.
Pistol. Why then, rejoice therefore.

What a beard of the general's cut and a horrid suit of   81
the camp will do among foaming bottles and ale-washed
wits, is wonderful to be thought on.   (*Gower*)

My people are with sickness much enfeebled,   154
My numbers lessen'd, and those few I have
Almost no better than so many French;
Who when they were in health, I tell thee, herald,
I thought upon one pair of English legs
Did march three Frenchmen.   (*King Henry*)

Rambures. He longs to eat the English.   III. vii. 99
Constable of France. I think he will eat all he kills.

That island of England breeds very valiant creatures;   III. vii. 150
their mastiffs are of unmatchable courage.   (*Rambures*)

You may as well say, that's a valiant flea that dare eat   155
his breakfast on the lip of a lion.   (*Orleans*)

Give them great meals of beef and iron and steel, they   161
will eat like wolves and fight like devils.
                         (*Constable of France*)

Now entertain conjecture of a time   IV. Pro-
When creeping murmur and the poring dark   logue 1
Fills the wide vessel of the universe.
From camp to camp through the foul womb of night
The hum of either army stilly sounds,
That the fix'd sentinels almost receive
The secret whispers of each other's watch:
Fire answers fire, and through their paly flames
Each battle sees the other's umber'd face;
Steed threatens steed, in high and boastful neighs
Piercing the night's dull ear; and from the tents
The armourers, accomplishing the knights,
With busy hammers closing rivets up,
Give dreadful note of preparation.   (*Chorus*)

A little touch of Harry in the night.   (*Chorus*)   47

Gloucester, 'tis true that we are in great danger;   IV. i. 1
The greater therefore should our courage be.
                      (*King Henry*)

There is some soul of goodness in things evil,   4
Would men observingly distil it out.   (*King Henry*)

Thus may we gather honey from the weed,   11
And make a moral of the devil himself.   (*King Henry*)

Pistol. Discuss unto me; art thou officer?   37
Or art thou base, common and popular?
King Henry. I am a gentleman of a company.
Pistol. Trail'st thou the puissant pike?

The king's a bawcock, and a heart of gold,   44
A lad of life, an imp of fame;
Of parents good, of fist most valiant:
I kiss his dirty shoe, and from heart-string
I love the lovely bully.   (*Pistol*)

If you would take the pains but to examine the wars of   69
Pompey the Great, you shall find, I warrant you, that
there is no tiddle taddle nor pibble pabble in Pompey's
camp.   (*Fluellen*)

If the enemy is an ass and a fool and a prating coxcomb,   IV. i. 79
is it meet, think you, that we should also, look you, be an
ass and a fool and a prating coxcomb? *(Fluellen)*

Though it appear a little out of fashion,   85
There is much care and valour in this Welshman.
                   (King Henry)

I think the king is but a man, as I am: the violet smells   105
to him as it doth to me. *(King Henry)*

Every subject's duty is the king's; but every subject's   185
soul is his own. *(King Henry)*

               What infinite heart's-ease   253
Must kings neglect, that private men enjoy!
And what have kings, that privates have not too,
Save ceremony, save general ceremony? *(King Henry)*

'Tis not the balm, the sceptre and the ball,   277
The sword, the mace, the crown imperial,
The intertissued robe of gold and pearl,
The farced title running 'fore the king,
The throne he sits on, nor the tide of pomp
That beats upon the high shore of this world,
No, not all these, thrice-gorgeous ceremony,
Not all these, laid in bed majestical,
Can sleep so soundly as the wretched slave,
Who with a body fill'd and vacant mind
Gets him to rest, cramm'd with distressful bread;
Never sees horrid night, the child of hell,
But, like a lackey, from the rise to set
Sweats in the eye of Phoebus and all night
Sleeps in Elysium; next day after dawn
Doth rise and help Hyperion to his horse,
And follows so the ever-running year,
With profitable labour, to his grave:
And, but for ceremony, such a wretch,
Winding up days with toil and nights with sleep,
Had the fore-hand and vantage of a king. *(King Henry)*

O God of battles! steel my soldiers' hearts;   306
Possess them not with fear; take from them now
The sense of reckoning, if the opposed numbers
Pluck their hearts from them. Not to-day, O Lord,
O, not to-day, think not upon the fault
My father made in compassing the crown!
                   (King Henry)

Big Mars seems bankrupt in their beggar'd host   IV. ii. 43
And faintly through a rusty beaver peeps.   *(Grandpré)*

He is as full of valour as of kindness;   IV. iii. 15
Princely in both.   *(Bedford)*

            O that we now had here   16
But one ten thousand of those men in England
That do no work to-day!   *(Westmoreland)*

If we are mark'd to die, we are enow   20
To do our country loss; and if to live,
The fewer men, the greater share of honour.
God's will!   I pray thee, wish not one man more.
By Jove, I am not covetous for gold,
Nor care I who doth feed upon my cost;
It yearns me not if men my garments wear;
Such outward things dwell not in my desires:
But if it be a sin to covet honour,
I am the most offending soul alive.   *(King Henry)*

This day is call'd the feast of Crispian: 40
He that outlives this day, and comes safe home,
Will stand a tip-toe when this day is named,
And rouse him at the name of Crispian.
He that shall live this day, and see old age,
Will yearly on the vigil feast his neighbours,
And say 'To-morrow is Saint Crispian:'
Then will he strip his sleeve and show his scars,
And say 'These wounds I had on Crispin's day.'
Old men forget; yet all shall be forgot,
But he'll remember with advantages
What feats he did that day: then shall our names,
Familiar in his mouth as household words,
Harry the king, Bedford and Exeter,
Warwick and Talbot, Salisbury and Gloucester,
Be in their flowing cups freshly remember'd.
This story shall the good man teach his son;
And Crispin Crispian shall ne'er go by,
From this day to the ending of the world,
But we in it shall be remembered:
We few, we happy few, we band of brothers;
For he to-day that sheds his blood with me
Shall be my brother; be he ne'er so vile,
This day shall gentle his condition:
And gentlemen in England now a-bed
Shall think themselves accursed they were not here,
And hold their manhoods cheap whiles any speaks
That fought with us upon Saint Crispin's day.
                           (King Henry)

The man that once did sell the lion's skin   VI. iii. 93
While the beast lived, was killed with hunting him.
                                        (King Henry)

We are but warriors for the working-day;   109
Our gayness and our gilt are all besmirch'd
With rainy marching in the painful field.   (King Henry)

Pistol. What is thy name? discuss.   IV. iv. 5
French Soldier. O Seigneur Dieu!
Pistol. O, Signieur Dew should be a gentleman:
Perpend my words, O Signieur Dew, and mark;
O Signieur Dew, thou diest on point of fox,
Except, O signieur, thou do give to me
Egregious ransom.

French Soldier. Est-il impossible d'échapper la force de   18
ton bras?
Pistol. Brass, cur!
Thou damned and luxurious mountain goat,
Offer'st me brass?

    I did never know so full a voice issue from so empty a   71
heart: but the saying is true, 'The empty vessel makes
the greatest sound.'   (Boy)

Mort de ma vie! all is confounded, all!   IV. v. 3
Reproach and everlasting shame
Sits mocking in our plumes.   (Dauphin)

And all my mother came into mine eyes   IV. vi. 31
And gave me up to tears.   (Exeter)

    I tell you, captain, if you look in the maps of the 'orld,   IV. vii. 24
I warrant you sall find, in the comparisons between Mace-
don and Monmouth, that the situations, look you, is both
alike.   There is a river in Macedon; and there is also
moreover a river at Monmouth: it is called Wye at Monmouth; but it is out of my prains what is the name of the
other river; but 'tis all one, 'tis alike as my fingers is to my
fingers, and there is salmons in both.   (Fluellen)

    There is occasions and causes why and wherefore in all   v. i. 3
things.   (Fluellen)

    By this leek, I will most horribly revenge: I eat and eat,   49
I swear—   (Pistol)

All hell shall stir for this.   (Pistol)   72

To England will I steal, and there I'll steal: v. i. 92
And patches will I get unto these cudgell'd scars,
And swear I got them in the Gallia wars.   (*Pistol*)

Why that the naked, poor and mangled Peace,   v. ii. 34
Dear nurse of arts, plenties and joyful births,
Should not in this best garden of the world,
Our fertile France, put up her lovely visage?

                                                (*Burgundy*)

Her vine, the merry cheerer of the heart,   41
Unpruned dies; her hedges even-pleach'd,
Like prisoners wildly over-grown with hair,
Put forth disorder'd twigs; her fallow leas
The darnel, hemlock and rank fumitory
Doth root upon, while that the coulter rusts
That should deracinate such savagery;
The even mead, that erst brought sweetly forth
The freckled cowslip, burnet and green clover,
Wanting the scythe, all uncorrected, rank,
Conceives by idleness and nothing teems
But hateful docks, rough thistles, kecksies, burs,
Losing both beauty and utility.   (*Burgundy*)

King Henry. Do you like me, Kate?   107
Katharine. Pardonnez-moi, I cannot tell vat is 'like me.'
King Henry. An angel is like you, Kate, and you are like
an angel.

   I know no ways to mince it in love, but directly to say   129
'I love you': then if you urge me farther than to say 'do
you in faith?' I wear out my suit.   Give me your answer;
i' faith, do: and so clap hands and a bargain: how say you,
lady?   (*King Henry*)

   If I could win a lady at leap-frog, or by vaulting into   143
my saddle with my armour on my back, under the cor-
rection of bragging be it spoken, I should quickly leap into
a wife.   (*King Henry*)

   While thou livest, dear Kate, take a fellow of plain and   159
uncoined constancy; for he perforce must do thee right,
because he hath not the gift to woo in other places: for
these fellows of infinite tongue, that can rhyme themselves
into ladies' favours, they do always reason themselves out
again.   (*King Henry*)

   A good leg will fall; a straight back will stoop; a black   165
beard will turn white; a curled pate will grow bald; a fair
face will wither; a full eye will wax hollow: but a good

heart, Kate, is the sun and the moon; or rather the sun   v. ii. 168
and not the moon; for it shines bright and never changes,
but keeps his course truly. (*King Henry*)

My comfort is, that old age, that ill layer up of beauty,   246
can do no more spoil upon my face. (*King Henry*)

Henry Plantagenet is thine; who, though I speak it   258
before his face, if he be not fellow with the best king, thou
shalt find the best king of good fellows. (*King Henry*)

O Kate, nice customs curtsy to great kings. Dear   294
Kate, you and I cannot be confined within the weak list
of a country's fashion: we are the makers of manners,
Kate. (*King Henry*)

God, the best maker of all marriages,   387
Combine your hearts in one, your realms in one!
                            (*Queen of France*)

KING HENRY VI, PART I

The three parts of *Henry VI* form a trilogy of chronicle plays which can hardly claim to have a plot, being simply a succession of episodes. Part I covers the period from the death of Henry V in 1422 to the marriage alliance of Henry VI and Margaret, daughter to Reignier, Duke of Anjou, in 1444. It opens with the news of English defeats in France and the loss of extensive territory. As the play proceeds, Joan of Arc relieves Orleans, Lord Talbot, who was besieging it, is killed, and the English are driven out. But Joan, who is depicted unsympathetically as a devil-inspired harlot, is taken and burned. Meanwhile in England, the king being a minor, there are incessant squabbles between his uncle, the Duke of Gloucester, who is Lord Protector, and his great-uncle Henry Beaufort, Bishop of Winchester; while a scene in the Temple garden, where the Duke of York's faction choose the white rose for their emblem, and the Earl of Somerset's choose the red rose, marks the beginning of the disastrous Wars of the Roses. Other leading characters are, on the English side, the Duke of Bedford, the Earls of Warwick and Suffolk, Richard Plantagenet, afterwards Duke of York, and Edmund Mortimer; on the French side Charles the Dauphin, afterwards King of France. The authorship of this play is disputed.

Hung be the heavens with black, yield day to night!   I. i. 1
                (*Bedford*)

I think, by some odd gimmors of device   I. ii. 41
Their arms are set like clocks, still to strike on;
Else ne'er could they hold out so as they do.
                (*Reignier*)

Expect Saint Martin's summer, halcyon days.   (*Joan*)   131

Glory is like a circle in the water,   133
Which never ceaseth to enlarge itself
Till by broad spreading it disperse to nought.   (*Joan*)

Thy promises are like Adonis' gardens   I. vi. 6
That one day bloom'd and fruitful were the next.
                (*Charles*)

And I have heard it said, unbidden guests   II. ii. 55
Are often welcomest when they are gone.   (*Bedford*)

Faith, I have been a truant in the law,   II. iv. 7
And never yet could frame my will to it;
And therefore frame the law unto my will.   (*Suffolk*)

Between two hawks, which flies the higher pitch;   11
Between two dogs, which hath the deeper mouth;
Between two blades, which bears the better temper:
Between two horses, which doth bear him best;
Between two girls, which hath the merriest eye;
I have perhaps some shallow spirit of judgment;
But in these nice sharp quillets of the law,
Good faith, I am no wiser than a daw.   (*Warwick*)

I'll note you in my book of memory.   (*Plantagenet*)   101

These eyes, like lamps whose wasting oil is spent,   II. v. 8
Wax dim, as drawing to their exigent.   (*Mortimer*)

Just death, kind umpire of men's miseries,   29
With sweet enlargement doth dismiss me hence.
                (*Mortimer*)

Comest thou with deep premeditated lines,   III. i. 1
With written pamphlets studiously devised?
                (*Winchester*)

For friendly counsel cuts off many foes.   (*King*)   185

Undaunted spirit in a dying breast!   (*Talbot*)   III. ii. 99

Care is no cure, but rather corrosive,   III. iii. 3
For things that are not to be remedied.   (*Joan*)

When first this order was ordain'd, my lords,   IV. i. 33
Knights of the garter were of noble birth,
Valiant and virtuous, full of haughty courage,
Such as were grown to credit by the wars;
Not fearing death, nor shrinking for distress,
But always resolute in most extremes.
He then that is not furnish'd in this sort
Doth but usurp the sacred name of knight,
Profaning this most honourable order.   (*Talbot*)

I owe him little duty, and less love.   (*Somerset*)   IV. iv. 34

Him that thou magnifiest with all these titles   IV. vii. 75
Stinking and fly-blown lies here at our feet.   (*Joan*)

Marriage, uncle! alas, my years are young!   v. i. 21
And fitter is my study and my books
Than wanton dalliance with a paramour.   (*King*)

Of all base passions, fear is most accursed.   (*Joan*)   v. ii. 18

She's beautiful and therefore to be woo'd;   v. iii. 78
She is a woman, therefore to be won.   (*Suffolk*)

For what is wedlock forced but a hell,   v. v. 62
An age of discord and continual strife?
Whereas the contrary bringeth bliss,
And is a pattern of celestial peace.   (*Suffolk*)

KING HENRY VI, PART II

Treating of Henry's reign in the years 1445 to 1455, this play opens with his marriage to Princess Margaret of Anjou. The political intrigues among the powerful nobles continue, the Duke of York being the most determined and dangerous, while rival parties support the king's uncle, Duke Humphrey of Gloucester, who has the title of Lord Protector, and Cardinal Beaufort, the king's great-uncle. The Duke of Gloucester, disgraced and accused of treason, is found dead in suspicious circumstances, and subsequently his enemy the Cardinal dies raving out what seems a confession of guilt. The play concludes with the Duke of York's triumph over the king's forces at the battle of St Albans. Comic relief is supplied by the scenes depicting Jack Cade's revolt, his naïve promises to his simple-minded followers, and his suspicion and hatred of anything connected with learning or education.

O Lord, that lends me life,   I. i. 19
Lend me a heart replete with thankfulness! (*King*)

For Suffolk's duke, may he be suffocate,   124
That dims the honour of this warlike isle! (*York*)

While these do labour for their own preferment,   181
Behoves it us to labour for the realm. (*Salisbury*)

Pirates may make cheap pennyworths of their pillage.   222
                                        (*York*)

She bears a duke's revenues on her back,   I. iii. 83
And in her heart she scorns our poverty. (*Queen*)

Could I come near your beauty with my nails,   144
I'ld set my ten commandments in your face.
                 (*Duchess of Gloucester*)

Deep night, dark night, the silent of the night,   I. iv. 19
The time of night when Troy was set on fire;
The time when screech-owls cry and ban-dogs howl
And spirits walk and ghosts break up their graves,
That time best fits the work we have in hand.
                          (*Bolingbroke*)

Thus sometimes hath the brightest day a cloud;   II. iv. 1
And after summer evermore succeeds
Barren winter, with his wrathful nipping cold:
So cares and joys abound, as seasons fleet. (*Gloucester*)

Small curs are not regarded when they grin;   III. i. 18
But great men tremble when the lion roars. (*Queen*)

Now 'tis the spring, and weeds are shallow-rooted;   31
Suffer them now, and they'll o'ergrow the garden
And choke the herbs for want of husbandry. (*Queen*)

Smooth runs the water where the brook is deep. (*Suffolk*)   53

Henry my lord is cold in great affairs,   224
Too full of foolish pity, and Gloucester's show
Beguiles him as the mournful crocodile
With sorrow snares relenting passengers,
Or as the snake roll'd in a flowering bank,
With shining checker'd slough, doth sting a child
That for the beauty thinks it excellent. (*Queen*)

Faster than spring-time showers comes thought on   337
   thought. (*York*)

What stronger breastplate than a heart untainted!   III. ii. 232
Thrice is he arm'd that hath his quarrel just,
And he but naked, though lock'd up in steel,
Whose conscience with injustice is corrupted.   (King)

Well could I curse away a winter's night,   335
Though standing naked on a mountain top,
Where biting cold would never let grass grow,
And think it but a minute spent in sport.   (Suffolk)

Ah, what a sign it is of evil life,   III. iii. 5
Where death's approach is seen so terrible!   (King)

He dies, and makes no sign.   (King)   29

Forbear to judge, for we are sinners all.   31
Close up his eyes and draw the curtain close;
And let us all to meditation.   (King)

The gaudy, blabbing and remorseful day   IV. i. 1
Is crept into the bosom of the sea.   (Captain)

Small things make base men proud.   (Suffolk)   106

True nobility is exempt from fear: 129
More can I bear than you dare execute.   (Suffolk)

Great men oft die by vile bezonians: 134
A Roman sworder and banditto slave
Murder'd sweet Tully; Brutus' bastard hand
Stabb'd Julius Caesar; savage islanders
Pompey the Great; and Suffolk dies by pirates.   (Suffolk)

Your captain is brave, and vows reformation.   There   IV. ii. 70
shall be in England seven halfpenny loaves sold for a
penny: the three-hooped pot shall have ten hoops; and I
will make it felony to drink small beer.   (Cade)

Dick. The first thing we do, let's kill all the lawyers.   82
Cade. Nay, that I mean to do.   Is not this a lamentable
thing, that of the skin of an innocent lamb should be
made parchment? that parchment, being scribbled o'er,
should undo a man?

Clerk. Sir, I thank God, I have been so well brought up   112
that I can write my name.
All. He hath confessed: away with him! he's a villain
and a traitor.
Cade. Away with him, I say! hang him with his pen and
ink-horn about his neck.

Sir, he made a chimney in my father's house, and the   IV. ii. 156
bricks are alive at this day to testify it; therefore deny it
not.   (*Smith*)

We will not leave one lord, one gentleman: 194
Spare none but such as go in clouted shoon;
For they are thrifty honest men and such
As would, but that they dare not, take our parts.
                                              (*Cade*)

The trust I have is in mine innocence,   IV. iv. 59
And therefore am I bold and resolute.   (*Say*)

Thou hast most traitorously corrupted the youth of the   IV. vii. 35
realm in erecting a grammar school: and whereas, before,
our forefathers had no other books but the score and the
tally, thou hast caused printing to be used, and, contrary
to the king, his crown and dignity, thou hast built a paper-
mill.   It will be proved to thy face that thou hast men
about thee that usually talk of a noun and a verb, and such
abominable words as no Christian ear can endure to hear.
                                              (*Cade*)

Away with him, away with him! he speaks Latin.   (*Cade*)   63

Kent, in the Commentaries Caesar writ,   66
Is term'd the civil'st place of all this isle:
Sweet is the country, because full of riches;
The people liberal, valiant, active, wealthy.   (*Say*)

Was ever feather so lightly blown to and fro as this   IV. viii 57
multitude?   (*Cade*)

Was never subject long'd to be a king   IV. ix. 5
As I do long and wish to be a subject.   (*King*)

Lord, who would live turmoiled in the court,   IV. x. 18
And may enjoy such quiet walks as these?   (*Iden*)

To lose thy youth in peace, and to achieve   v. ii. 46
The silver livery of advised age,
And, in thy reverence and thy chair-days, thus
To die in ruffian battle.   (*Young Clifford*)

KING HENRY VI, PART III

This continues the reign from 1455 to its end in 1471. Henry weakly concedes to Richard, Duke of York, the right of succeeding him on the throne, but the duke is killed after his defeat at the battle of Wakefield and his son Edward carries on the struggle. After varying fortunes Henry is defeated at Towton and flees to Scotland, the young Duke of York being proclaimed king as Edward IV. Returning from exile, Henry is captured and imprisoned. Meanwhile the Earl of Warwick, nicknamed the kingmaker, is sent to France to negotiate a marriage between Edward and the sister of the French king, but in his absence Edward marries Lady Grey, and Warwick, incensed at being put in a false position, changes sides, invades England with French help, releases Henry, and restores him to the throne. Edward rallies his followers and at the battle of Barnet Warwick is killed. Henry, once more imprisoned, is foully murdered by the Duke of Gloucester, Edward's brother.

Patience is for poltroons. (*Clifford*) I. i. 62

How sweet a thing it is to wear a crown; I ii. 29
Within whose circuit is Elysium
And all that poets feign of bliss and joy. (*Richard*)

The sands are number'd that make up my life. (*York*) I. iv. 25

'Tis beauty that doth oft make women proud; 128
But, God he knows, thy share thereof is small. (*York*)

O tiger's heart wrapt in a woman's hide! (*York*) 137

See how the morning opes her golden gates, II. i. 21
And takes her farewell of the glorious sun! (*Richard*)

And many strokes, though with a little axe, 54
Hew down and fell the hardest-timber'd oak. (*Messenger*)

The smallest worm will turn being trodden on, II. ii. 17
And doves will peck in safeguard of their brood.
(*Clifford*)

Didst thou never hear 45
That things ill-got had ever bad success?
And happy always was it for that son
Whose father for his hoarding went to hell?
(*King Henry*)

Thou setter up and plucker down of kings. (*Edward*) II. iii. 37

This battle fares like to the morning's war, II. v. 1
When dying clouds contend with growing light,
What time the shepherd, blowing of his nails,
Can neither call it perfect day nor night. (*King Henry*)

Would I were dead! if God's good will were so; 19
For what is in this world but grief and woe?
(*King Henry*)

O God! methinks it were a happy life, 21
To be no better than a homely swain;
To sit upon a hill, as I do now,
To carve out dials quaintly, point by point,
Thereby to see the minutes how they run,
How many make the hour full complete;
How many hours bring about the day;
How many days will finish up the year;
How many years a mortal man may live.
When this is known, then to divide the times:

So many hours must I tend my flock;   II. v. 31
So many hours must I take my rest;
So many hours must I contemplate;
So many hours must I sport myself;
So many days my ewes have been with young;
So many weeks ere the poor fools will ean;
So many years ere I shall shear the fleece:
So minutes, hours, days, months, and years,
Pass'd over to the end they were created,
Would bring white hairs unto a quiet grave.
Ah, what a life were this! how sweet! how lovely!
Gives not the hawthorn-bush a sweeter shade
To shepherds looking on their silly sheep,
Than doth a rich embroider'd canopy
To kings that fear their subjects' treachery?
O, yes, it doth; a thousand-fold it doth.   (*King Henry*)

Ill blows the wind that profits nobody.   (*Soldier Son*)   55

Second Keeper. But, if thou be a king, where is thy crown?   III. i. 61
King Henry. My crown is in my heart, not on my head;
Not deck'd with diamonds and Indian stones,
Nor to be seen: my crown is called content:
A crown it is that seldom kings enjoy.

Like one that stands upon a promontory,   III. ii. 135
And spies a far-off shore where he would tread,
Wishing his foot were equal with his eye.   (*Gloucester*)

I 'll drown more sailors than the mermaid shall;   186
I 'll slay more gazers than the basilisk;
I 'll play the orator as well as Nestor,
Deceive more slily than Ulysses could,
And, like a Sinon, take another Troy.   (*Gloucester*)

                    Yield not thy neck   III. iii. 16
To fortune's yoke, but let thy dauntless mind
Still ride in triumph over all mischance.   (*King Lewis*)

For how can tyrants safely govern home,   69
Unless abroad they purchase great alliance?
                    (*Queen Margaret*)

Yet hasty marriage seldom proveth well.   (*Gloucester*)   IV. i. 18

Let us be back'd with God and with the seas   43
Which He hath given for fence impregnable.   (*Hastings*)

I hear, yet say not much, but think the more.   83
                    (*Gloucester, aside*)

What fates impose, that men must needs abide;   IV. iii. 58
It boots not to resist both wind and tide.
(King Edward)

This pretty lad will prove our country's bliss.   IV. vi. 70
His looks are full of peaceful majesty,
His head by nature framed to wear a crown,
His hand to wield a sceptre, and himself
Likely in time to bless a regal throne.
(King Henry, speaking of young Richmond)

A little fire is quickly trodden out;   IV. viii. 7
Which, being suffer'd, rivers cannot quench. (Clarence)

Like to his island girt in with the ocean. (Warwick)   20

But, whiles he thought to steal the single ten,   V. i. 43
The king was slily finger'd from the deck! (Gloucester)

The harder match'd, the greater victory.   (King Edward)   70

Why, what is pomp, rule, reign, but earth and dust?   V. ii. 27
And, live we how we can, yet die we must. (Warwick)

For every cloud engenders not a storm. (Clarence)   V. iii. 13

Great lords, wise men ne'er sit and wail their loss,   V. iv. 1
But cheerly seek how to redress their harms.
What though the mast be now blown overboard,
The cable broke, the holding-anchor lost,
And half our sailors swallow'd in the flood?
Yet lives our pilot still.   (Queen Margaret)

What cannot be avoided   37
'Twere childish weakness to lament or fear.
(Queen Margaret)

So part we sadly in this troublous world,   V. v. 7
To meet with joy in sweet Jerusalem. (Queen Margaret)

Suspicion always haunts the guilty mind,   V. vi. 11
The thief doth fear each bush an officer.   (Gloucester)

Down, down to hell; and say I sent thee thither.   67
(Gloucester, stabbing King Henry)

KING RICHARD III

This play covers the years 1471 to 1485 and shows how Richard, the infamous Crookback, wades through slaughter to a throne and then to destruction. First he has his own brother Clarence committed to the Tower on a charge of treason, and drowned in a butt of malmsey wine. On the death of Edward IV Richard sets himself to get rid of all who are loyal to the king's party, executing Earl Rivers and the Lords Grey and Hastings, and then having the boy king Edward V and his brother smothered in the Tower. The Duke of Buckingham, Richard's accomplice, turns against him, but is captured and executed. Meanwhile Richard has triumphed over his physical deformity and his evil reputation by wooing and marrying Anne, widow of the dead son of Henry VI, whom he had murdered. Poisoning her after she has served her turn, he starts negotiations for an alliance with Edward IV's daughter Elizabeth. But retribution at last overtakes him at Bosworth, near Leicester, where Henry, Earl of Richmond, defeats and kills him to succeed as Henry VII.

Now is the winter of our discontent   I. i. I
Made glorious summer by this sun of York;
And all the clouds that lour'd upon our house
In the deep bosom of the ocean buried.
Now are our brows bound with victorious wreaths;
Our bruised arms hung up for monuments;
Our stern alarums changed to merry meetings,
Our dreadful marches to delightful measures.
Grim-visaged war hath smooth'd his wrinkled front;
And now, instead of mounting barbed steeds
To fright the souls of fearful adversaries,
He capers nimbly in a lady's chamber
To the lascivious pleasing of a lute.   (*Gloucester*)

I, that am curtail'd of this fair proportion,   18
Cheated of feature by dissembling nature,
Deform'd, unfinish'd, sent before my time
Into this breathing world, scarce half made up,
And that so lamely and unfashionable
That dogs bark at me as I halt by them.   (*Gloucester*)

In this weak piping time of peace.   (*Gloucester*)   24

And therefore, since I cannot prove a lover,   28
To entertain these fair well-spoken days,
I am determined to prove a villain
And hate the idle pleasures of these days.   (*Gloucester*)

Simple, plain Clarence! I do love thee so,   118
That I will shortly send thy soul to heaven.   (*Gloucester*)

With lies well steel'd with weighty arguments.   148
                (*Gloucester*)

Gloucester. Villains, set down the corse; or, by Saint Paul,   I. ii. 36
I'll make a corse of him that disobeys.
Gentleman. My lord, stand back, and let the coffin pass.

No beast so fierce but knows some touch of pity.   (*Anne*)   71

Vouchsafe, divine perfection of a woman.   (*Gloucester*)   75

Vouchsafe, defused infection of a man.   (*Anne*)   78

Anne. O, he was gentle, mild, and virtuous!   104
Gloucester. The fitter for the King of heaven, that hath him.

It is a quarrel most unnatural   134
To be revenged on him that loveth you.   (*Gloucester*)

That all the standers-by had wet their cheeks,   I. ii. 163
Like trees bedash'd with rain. (*Gloucester*)

Look, how this ring encompasseth thy finger,   204
Even so thy breast encloseth my poor heart. (*Gloucester*)

Was ever woman in this humour woo'd?   228
Was ever woman in this humour won? (*Gloucester*)

A sweeter and a lovelier gentleman,   243
Framed in the prodigality of nature,
Young, valiant, wise, and, no doubt, right royal,
The spacious world cannot again afford. (*Gloucester*)

Because I cannot flatter and speak fair,   I. iii. 47
Smile in men's faces, smooth, deceive and cog,
Duck with French nods and apish courtesy,
I must be held a rancorous enemy.
Cannot a plain man live and think no harm,
But thus his simple truth must be abused
By silken, sly, insinuating Jacks? (*Gloucester*)

                    The world is grown so bad,   70
That wrens make prey where eagles dare not perch:
Since every Jack became a gentleman,
There's many a gentle person made a Jack. (*Gloucester*)

I was a pack-horse in his great affairs. (*Gloucester*)   122

Hear me, you wrangling pirates, that fall out   158
In sharing that which you have pill'd from me!
                    (*Queen Margaret*)

Why strew'st thou sugar on that bottled spider,   242
Whose deadly web ensnareth thee about?
                    (*Queen Margaret*)

Dispute not with her; she is lunatic. (*Dorset*)   254

They that stand high have many blasts to shake them;   259
And if they fall, they dash themselves to pieces.
                    (*Queen Margaret*)

Buckingham.   Curses never pass   285
The lips of those that breathe them in the air.
Queen Margaret. I'll not believe but they ascend the sky,
And there awake God's gentle-sleeping peace.

The secret mischiefs that I set abroach   325
I lay unto the grievous charge of others. (*Gloucester*)
                              233

And thus I clothe my naked villany   I. iii. 336
With old odd ends stolen out of holy writ;
And seem a saint, when most I play the devil.
                                        (*Gloucester*)

Talkers are no good doers.   (*First Murderer*)   352

O, I have pass'd a miserable night,   I. iv. 2
So full of ugly sights, of ghastly dreams,
That, as I am a Christian faithful man,
I would not spend another such a night,
Though 'twere to buy a world of happy days,
So full of dismal terror was the time!   (*Clarence*)

Lord, Lord! methought, what pain it was to drown!   21
What dreadful noise of waters in mine ears!
What ugly sights of death within mine eyes!
Methought I saw a thousand fearful wrecks;
Ten thousand men that fishes gnaw'd upon;
Wedges of gold, great anchors, heaps of pearl,
Inestimable stones, unvalued jewels,
All scatter'd in the bottom of the sea:
Some lay in dead men's skulls; and in those holes
Where eyes did once inhabit, there were crept,
As 'twere in scorn of eyes, reflecting gems,
Which woo'd the slimy bottom of the deep,
And mock'd the dead bones that lay scatter'd by.
                                          (*Clarence*)

O, then began the tempest to my soul,   44
Who pass'd, methought, the melancholy flood,
With that grim ferryman which poets write of,
Unto the kingdom of perpetual night.   (*Clarence*)

Clarence is come; false, fleeting, perjured Clarence.   55
                                          (*Clarence*)

Sorrow breaks seasons and reposing hours,   76
Makes the night morning, and the noon-tide night.
                                        (*Brakenbury*)

Second Murderer. I pray thee, stay a while: I hope my   120
holy humour will change; 'twas wont to hold me but
while one would tell twenty.
First Murderer. How dost thou feel thyself now?
Second Murderer. 'Faith, some certain dregs of conscience are yet within me.
First Murderer. Remember our reward, when the deed is
done.
Second Murderer. 'Zounds, he dies: I had forgot the
reward.

I'll not meddle with it: it is a dangerous thing: it   i. iv. 137
makes a man a coward: a man cannot steal, but it
accuseth him; he cannot swear, but it checks him; he
cannot lie with his neighbour's wife, but it detects him:
'tis a blushing shamefast spirit that mutinies in a man's
bosom; it fills one full of obstacles: it made me once
restore a purse of gold that I found; it beggars any man
that keeps it: it is turned out of all towns and cities for a
dangerous thing; and every man that means to live well
endeavours to trust to himself and to live without it.
       (*Second Murderer, speaking of conscience*)

First Murderer. Relent! 'tis cowardly and womanish.   264
Clarence. Not to relent is beastly, savage, devilish.

It were lost sorrow to wail one that's lost.   ii. ii. 11
       (*Duchess of York*)

Oh, that deceit should steal such gentle shapes,   27
And with a virtuous vizard hide foul guile!
       (*Duchess of York*)

God bless thee; and put meekness in thy mind,   107
Love, charity, obedience, and true duty!
       (*Duchess of York*)

Woe to that land that's govern'd by a child!   ii. iii. 11
       (*Third Citizen*)

When clouds appear, wise men put on their cloaks;   32
When great leaves fall, the winter is at hand;
When the sun sets, who doth not look for night?
       (*Third Citizen*)

Small herbs have grace, great weeds do grow apace.   ii. iv. 13
       (*Young Duke of York, quoting Gloucester*)

So wise so young, they say, do never live long.   iii. i. 79
       (*Gloucester*)

I moralize two meanings in one word.   (*Gloucester*)   83

God keep the prince from all the pack of you!   iii. iii. 5
A knot you are of damned blood-suckers.   (*Grey*)

Tellest thou me of 'ifs'?   Thou art a traitor: iii. iv. 77
Off with his head!   (*Gloucester*)

Tut, I can counterfeit the deep tragedian;   iii. v. 5
Speak and look back, and pry on every side,

Tremble and start at wagging of a straw,   III. v. 7
Intending deep suspicion: ghastly looks
Are at my service, like enforced smiles;
And both are ready in their offices,
At any time, to grace my stratagems.   (*Buckingham*)

Made him my book, wherein my soul recorded   27
The history of all her secret thoughts.   (*Gloucester*)

Play the maid's part, still answer nay, and take it.   III. vii. 51
                                    (*Buckingham*)

A beauty-waning and distressed widow,   185
Even in the afternoon of her best days.   (*Buckingham*)

Eighty odd years of sorrow have I seen,   IV. i. 96
And each hour's joy wreck'd with a week of teen.
                                    (*Duchess of York*)

High-reaching Buckingham grows circumspect.   IV. ii. 31
                                    (*King Richard*)

Gold were as good as twenty orators.   (*Page*)   37

I am not in the giving vein to-day.   (*King Richard*)   119

Thou troublest me; I am not in the vein.   122
                                    (*King Richard*)

'Lo, thus,' quoth Dighton, 'lay those tender babes:'   IV. iii. 9
'Thus, thus,' quoth Forrest, 'girdling one another
Within their innocent alabaster arms:
Their lips were four red roses on a stalk,
Which in their summer beauty kiss'd each other.'
                                    (*Tyrrel*)

            We smothered   17
The most replenished sweet work of nature,
That from the prime creation e'er she framed.
                            (*Tyrrel, quoting Dighton*)

The sons of Edward sleep in Abraham's bosom,   38
And Anne my wife hath bid the world good night.
                                    (*King Richard*)

Come, I have heard that fearful commenting   51
Is leaden servitor to dull delay.   (*King Richard*)

Let not the heavens hear these tell-tale women   IV. iv. 149
Rail on the Lord's anointed.   (*King Richard*)

Tetchy and wayward was thy infancy;   IV. iv. 168
Thy school-days frightful, desperate, wild and furious,
Thy prime of manhood daring, bold and venturous,
Thy age confirm'd, proud, subtle, bloody, treacherous,
More mild, but yet more harmful, kind in hatred.
                                   (*Duchess of York*)

Look, what is done cannot be now amended: 291
Men shall deal unadvisedly sometimes,
Which after hours give leisure to repent.
                                   (*King Richard*)

An honest tale speeds best being plainly told.   358
                        (*Queen Elizabeth*)

Harp not on that string, madam.   (*King Richard*)   364

Queen Elizabeth. Shall I be tempted of the devil thus?   418
King Richard. Ay, if the devil tempt thee to do good.

Relenting fool, and shallow, changing woman!   431
                                   (*King Richard*)

Thus doth he force the swords of wicked men   v. i. 23
To turn their own points on their masters' bosoms.
                                   (*Buckingham*)

To reap the harvest of perpetual peace   v. ii. 15
By this one bloody trial of sharp war.   (*Richmond*)

True hope is swift, and flies with swallow's wings;   23
Kings it makes gods, and meaner creatures kings.
                                   (*Richmond*)

The weary sun hath made a golden set,   v. iii. 19
And, by the bright track of his fiery car,
Gives signal of a goodly day to-morrow.   (*Richmond*)

I have not that alacrity of spirit,   73
Nor cheer of mind, that I was wont to have.
                                   (*King Richard*)

O coward conscience, how dost thou afflict me!   179
                                   (*King Richard*)

My conscience hath a thousand several tongues,   193
And every tongue brings in a several tale,
And every tale condemns me for a villain.
                                   (*King Richard*)

I shall despair.   There is no creature loves me;   v. iii. 200
And if I die, no soul shall pity me:
Nay, wherefore should they, since that I myself
Find in myself no pity to myself?   (*King Richard*)

By the apostle Paul, shadows to-night   216
Have struck more terror to the soul of Richard
Than can the substance of ten thousand soldiers
Armed in proof, and led by shallow Richmond.
                                        (*King Richard*)

God and our good cause fight upon our side.   240
                                        (*Richmond*)

A thing devised by the enemy.   (*King Richard*)   306

Conscience is but a word that cowards use,   309
Devised at first to keep the strong in awe.
                                        (*King Richard*)

A milk-sop, one that never in his life   325
Felt so much cold as over shoes in snow.
                                        (*King Richard*)

Fight, gentlemen of England! fight, bold yeomen!   338
Draw, archers, draw your arrows to the head!
                                        (*King Richard*)

A horse! a horse! my kingdom for a horse!   v. iv. 7
                                        (*King Richard*)   and 13

Slave, I have set my life upon a cast,   9
And I will stand the hazard of the die:
I think there be six Richmonds in the field;
Five have I slain to-day instead of him.
                                        (*King Richard*)

KING HENRY VIII

The gorgeous pageantry of this play presents the events of Henry's reign from the Field of the Cloth of Gold in 1520 to the birth of the Princess Elizabeth in 1533. The principal characters are the king, his first wife, Katharine of Aragon, his second wife, Anne Bullen, and Cardinal Wolsey. The execution of the Duke of Buckingham, brought about by Wolsey's scheming, is followed by the Cardinal's own downfall, when the miscarrying of a letter reveals to the king his plots with the Pope. Meanwhile Queen Katharine has been brought to trial and the king chooses the beautiful Anne to be her successor. Archbishop Cranmer is shown triumphing over his enemies through the king's favour, and presiding at the baptism of Elizabeth, the future queen, who is the subject, together with her successor James, of a final panegyric. It is generally agreed that the greater part of this play is not by Shakespeare, but by John Fletcher, another famous Elizabethan dramatist.

Those that come to see   Prologue 9
Only a show or two, and so agree
The play may pass, if they be still and willing,
I 'll undertake may see away their shilling
Richly in two short hours.

To-day the French,   I. i. 18
All clinquant, all in gold, like heathen gods,
Shone down the English; and, to-morrow, they
Made Britain India: every man that stood
Show'd like a mine.   (*Norfolk*)

The devil speed him! no man's pie is freed   52
From his ambitious finger.   (*Buckingham*)

The force of his own merit makes his way.   (*Norfolk*)   64

And let your reason with your choler question   130
What 'tis you go about.   (*Norfolk*)

Heat not a furnace for your foe so hot   140
That it do singe yourself: we may outrun
By violent swiftness, that which we run at,
And lose by over-running.   (*Norfolk*)

What we oft do best,   I. ii. 81
By sick interpreters, once weak ones, is
Not ours, or not allow'd; what worst, as oft,
Hitting a grosser quality, is cried up
For our best act.   (*Wolsey*)

The gentleman is learn'd, and a most rare speaker.   (*King*)   III

New customs,   I. iii. 2
Though they be never so ridiculous,
Nay, let 'em be unmanly, yet are follow'd.   (*Lord Sands*)

Two women placed together makes cold weather.   I. iv. 22
(*Lord Chamberlain*)

By heaven, she is a dainty one.   Sweetheart,   94
I were unmannerly to take you out,
And not to kiss you.   (*King*)

The mirror of all courtesy.   (*Second Gentleman*)   II. i. 53

The law I bear no malice for my death;   62
'T has done, upon the premises, but justice:
But those that sought it I could wish more Christians.
(*Buckingham*)

Chamberlain. It seems the marriage with his brother's   II. ii. 17
  wife
Has crept too near his conscience.
Suffolk.   No, his conscience
Has crept too near another lady.

This bold bad man.   (*Chamberlain*)   44

        'Tis better to be lowly born,   II. iii. 19
And range with humble livers in content,
Than to be perk'd up in a glistering grief,
And wear a golden sorrow.   (*Anne Bullen*)

Old Lady.   You would not be a queen?   34
Anne Bullen. No, not for all the riches under heaven.

Beauty and honour in her are so mingled   76
That they have caught the king.   (*Chamberlain*)

I have been to you a true and humble wife,   II. iv. 23
At all times to your will conformable. (*Queen Katharine*)

You sign your place and calling, in full seeming,   108
With meekness and humility; but your heart
Is cramm'd with arrogancy, spleen, and pride.
                            (*Queen Katharine*)

        Orpheus with his lute made trees,   III. i. 3
        And the mountain tops that freeze,
          Bow themselves when he did sing:
        To his music plants and flowers
        Ever sprung; as sun and showers
          There had made a lasting spring.

        Every thing that heard him play,
        Even the billows of the sea,
          Hung their heads, and then lay by.
        In sweet music is such art,
        Killing care and grief of heart
          Fall asleep, or hearing die.   (*Song*)

Wolsey. Tanta est erga te mentis integritas, regina   40
serenissima,—
Queen Katharine. O, good my lord, no Latin.

Heaven is above all yet; there sits a judge   100
That no king can corrupt.   (*Queen Katharine*)

I am the most unhappy woman living.   147
                            (*Queen Katharine*)

I   241

                  Like the lily,   III. i. 151
That once was mistress of the field and flourish'd,
I'll hang my head and perish.   (*Queen Katharine*)

              'Tis well said again;   III. ii. 152
And 'tis a kind of good deed to say well:
And yet words are no deeds.   (*King*)

                 My endeavours   169
Have ever come too short of my desires. (*Wolsey*)

                 Read o'er this;   201
And after, this: and then to breakfast with
What appetite you have.   (*King*)

I have touch'd the highest point of all my greatness;   223
And, from that full meridian of my glory,
I haste now to my setting: I shall fall
Like a bright exhalation in the evening,
And no man see me more.   (*Wolsey*)

I dare your worst objections: if I blush,   307
It is to see a nobleman want manners. (*Wolsey*)

And so we'll leave you to your meditations   345
How to live better.   (*Norfolk*)

Farewell! a long farewell to all my greatness!   351
This is the state of man: to-day he puts forth
The tender leaves of hopes; to-morrow blossoms,
And bears his blushing honours thick upon him;
The third day comes a frost, a killing frost,
And, when he thinks, good easy man, full surely
His greatness is a-ripening, nips his root,
And then he falls, as I do.   I have ventured,
Like little wanton boys that swim on bladders,
This many summers in a sea of glory,
But far beyond my depth: my high-blown pride
At length broke under me and now has left me,
Weary and old with service, to the mercy
Of a rude stream, that must for ever hide me.
Vain pomp and glory of this world, I hate ye:
I feel my heart new open'd.   O, how wretched
Is that poor man that hangs on princes' favours!
There is, betwixt that smile we would aspire to,
That sweet aspect of princes, and their ruin,
More pangs and fears than wars or women have:
And when he falls, he falls like Lucifer,
Never to hope again.   (*Wolsey*)

I know myself now; and I feel within me   III. ii. 378
A peace above all earthly dignities,
A still and quiet conscience. (*Wolsey*)

A load would sink a navy. (*Wolsey*)   383

Cromwell, I did not think to shed a tear   428
In all my miseries; but thou hast forced me,
Out of thy honest truth, to play the woman.
Let's dry our eyes: and thus far hear me, Cromwell;
And, when I am forgotten, as I shall be,
And sleep in dull cold marble, where no mention
Of me more must be heard of, say I taught thee,
Say Wolsey, that once trod the ways of glory,
And sounded all the depths and shoals of honour,
Found thee a way, out of his wreck, to rise in;
A sure and safe one, though thy master miss'd it.
Mark but my fall, and that that ruin'd me.
Cromwell, I charge thee, fling away ambition:
By that sin fell the angels; how can man, then,
The image of his Maker, hope to win by it?
Love thyself last: cherish those hearts that hate thee;
Corruption wins not more than honesty.
Still in thy right hand carry gentle peace,
To silence envious tongues.   Be just, and fear not:
Let all the ends thou aim'st at be thy country's,
Thy God's, and truth's; then if thou fall'st, O Cromwell,
Thou fall'st a blessed martyr! (*Wolsey*)

Had I but served my God with half the zeal   455
I served my king, he would not in mine age
Have left me naked to mine enemies.   (*Wolsey*)

An old man, broken with the storms of state,   IV. ii. 21
Is come to lay his weary bones among ye.
                    (*Griffith, quoting Wolsey*)

                              Full of repentance,   27
Continual meditations, tears, and sorrows,
He gave his honours to the world again,
His blessed part to heaven, and slept in peace. (*Griffith*)

So may he rest; his faults lie gently on him!   31
                              (*Katharine*)

                              He was a man   33
Of an unbounded stomach, ever ranking
Himself with princes; one that, by suggestion,
Tied all the kingdom: simony was fair-play;
                              243

His own opinion was his law: i' the presence   IV. ii. 37
He would say untruths, and be ever double
Both in his words and meaning: he was never,
But where he meant to ruin, pitiful:
His promises were, as he then was, mighty;
But his performance, as he is now, nothing.
                                        (Katharine)

Men's evil manners live in brass; their virtues   45
We write in water.   (Griffith)

He was a scholar, and a ripe and good one;   51
Exceeding wise, fair-spoken, and persuading:
Lofty and sour to them that loved him not;
But to those men that sought him sweet as summer.
And though he were unsatisfied in getting,
Which was a sin, yet in bestowing, madam,
He was most princely: ever witness for him
Those twins of learning that he raised in you,
Ipswich and Oxford.   (Griffith)

After my death I wish no other herald,   69
No other speaker of my living actions,
To keep mine honour from corruption,
But such an honest chronicler as Griffith. (Katharine)

O my good lord, that comfort comes too late;   120
'Tis like a pardon after execution.   (Katharine)

King. I guess thy message.   Is the queen deliver'd?   v. i. 162
Say, ay; and of a boy.
Old Lady.   Ay, ay, my liege;
And of a lovely boy: the God of heaven
Both now and ever bless her! 'tis a girl,
Promises boys hereafter.   Sir, your queen
Desires your visitation, and to be
Acquainted with this stranger: 'tis as like you
As cherry is to cherry.

                                        To suffer   v. ii. 29
A man of his place, and so near our favour,
To dance attendance on their lordships' pleasures.
                                        (King)

                    Love and meekness, lord,   v. iii. 62
Become a churchman better than ambition.   (Cranmer)

                              'Tis a cruelty   76
To load a falling man.   (Cromwell)
                    244

You play the spaniel,   v. iii. 126
And think with wagging of your tongue to win me.
                                                    (*King*)

These are the youths that thunder at a playhouse, and   v. iv. 63
fight for bitten apples; that no audience but the tribula-
tion of Tower-hill, or the limbs of Limehouse, their dear
brothers, are able to endure.   (*Porter*)

This royal infant—heaven still move about her!—   v. v. 18
Though in her cradle, yet now promises
Upon this land a thousand thousand blessings,
Which time shall bring to ripeness: she shall be—
But few now living can behold that goodness—
A pattern to all princes living with her,
And all that shall succeed; Saba was never
More covetous of wisdom and fair virtue
Than this pure soul shall be: all princely graces,
That mould up such a mighty piece as this is,
With all the virtues that attend the good,
Shall still be doubled on her: truth shall nurse her,
Holy and heavenly thoughts still counsel her:
She shall be loved and fear'd: her own shall bless her;
Her foes shake like a field of beaten corn,
And hang their heads with sorrow: good grows with her:
In her days every man shall eat in safety,
Under his own vine, what he plants; and sing
The merry songs of peace to all his neighbours:
God shall be truly known; and those about her
From her shall read the perfect ways of honour.
                                                    (*Cranmer*)

Wherever the bright sun of heaven shall shine,   51
His honour and the greatness of his name
Shall be, and make new nations.   (*Cranmer*)

'Tis ten to one this play can never please   Epilogue 1
All that are here: some come to take their ease,
And sleep an act or two.

TRAGEDIES

TROILUS AND CRESSIDA

The setting of this play is the city of Troy during its famous siege, and most of the well-known heroes appear in course of the action; on the Greek side, Agamemnon, the leader, the sulky Achilles with his friend Patroclus, the wronged Menelaus, the crafty Ulysses, wise old Nestor, the warriors Ajax and Diomedes, and the scurrilous Thersites; on the Trojan side King Priam with his sons Hector, Paris, and Troilus, his daughter Cassandra, and Helen, Menelaus's unfaithful wife. The main plot is the liaison between Troilus and Cressida, a Trojan girl whose father has joined the Greeks. By the aid of her uncle Pandarus, Troilus obtains his desires, but soon afterwards there is an exchange of prisoners and Cressida, transferred to the Greek camp, forgets Troilus and gives her favours to Diomedes. In the background is the story of the campaign, with Ulysses devising a stratagem to bring about a contest between Achilles and Hector, the greatest warriors on either side, and Achilles eventually slaying his rival by treachery. Thersites forms a sort of sardonic chorus, pointing out the futility of it all.

The princes orgulous. *Prologue* 2

But I am weaker than a woman's tear, I. i. 9
Tamer than sleep, fonder than ignorance,
Less valiant than the virgin in the night,
And skilless as unpractised infancy. (*Troilus*)

                          Her hand, 55
In whose comparison all whites are ink,
Writing their own reproach, to whose soft seizure
The cygnet's down is harsh, and spirit of sense
Hard as the palm of ploughman. (*Troilus*)

I have had my labour for my travail. (*Pandarus*) 71

They say he is a very man per se, I. ii. 15
And stands alone. (*Alexander, a servant*)

Yet hold I off. Women are angels, wooing: 312
Things won are done; joy's soul lies in the doing.
That she beloved knows nought that knows not this:
Men prize the thing ungain'd more than it is:
That she was never yet that ever knew
Love got so sweet as when desire did sue. (*Cressida*)

             In the reproof of chance I. iii. 33
Lies the true proof of men: the sea being smooth,
How many shallow bauble boats dare sail
Upon her patient breast, making their way
With those of nobler bulk! (*Nestor*)

The heavens themselves, the planets and this centre 85
Observe degree, priority and place,
Insisture, course, proportion, season, form,
Office and custom, in all line of order. (*Ulysses*)

          O, when degree is shaked, 101
Which is the ladder to all high designs,
The enterprise is sick! (*Ulysses*)

Take but degree away, untune that string, 109
And, hark, what discord follows! each thing meets
In mere oppugnancy: the bounded waters
Should lift their bosoms higher than the shores
And make a sop of all this solid globe:
Strength should be lord of imbecility,
And the rude son should strike his father dead:
Force should be right; or rather, right and wrong,
Between whose endless jar justice resides,
Should lose their names, and so should justice too. (*Ulysses*)

      Like a strutting player, whose conceit   I. iii. 153
Lies in his hamstring, and doth think it rich
To hear the wooden dialogue and sound
'Twixt his stretch'd footing and the scaffoldage.

                               (*Ulysses*)

A slave whose gall coins slanders like a mint.   (*Nestor*)   193

They tax our policy, and call it cowardice,   197
Count wisdom as no member of the war,
Forestall prescience and esteem no act
But that of hand.   (*Ulysses*)

And in such indexes, although small pricks   343
To their subsequent volumes, there is seen
The baby figure of the giant mass
Of things to come at large.   (*Nestor*)

Let us, like merchants, show our foulest wares,   359
And think, perchance, they'll sell; if not,
The lustre of the better yet to show,
Shall show the better.   (*Ulysses*)

Thou mongrel beef-witted lord!   (*Thersites*)   II. i. 13

      Ajax, who wears his wit in his belly and his guts in his   79
head.   (*Thersites*)

               Modest doubt is call'd   II. ii. 15
The beacon of the wise, the tent that searches
To the bottom of the worst.   (*Hector*)

But value dwells not in particular will;
It holds his estimate and dignity   53
As well wherein 'tis precious of itself
As in the prizer: 'tis mad idolatry
To make the service greater than the god.   (*Hector*)

Well may we fight for her whom, we know well,   161
The world's large spaces cannot parallel.   (*Paris*)

Unlike young men, whom Aristotle thought   166
Unfit to hear moral philosophy.   (*Hector*)

She is a theme of honour and renown,   199
A spur to valiant and magnanimous deeds,
Whose present courage may beat down our foes,
And fame in time to come canonize us.   (*Troilus*)

The elephant hath joints, but none for courtesy: his   II. iii. 113
legs are legs for necessity, not for flexure.   (*Ulysses*)

A stirring dwarf we do allowance give   146
Before a sleeping giant.   (*Agamemnon*)

He that is proud eats up himself: pride is his own glass,   164
his own trumpet, his own chronicle.   (*Agamemnon*)

Light boats sail swift, though greater hulks draw deep.   277
                                    (*Agamemnon*)

In love, i' faith, to the very tip of the nose.   (*Helen*)   III. i. 138

I am giddy; expectation whirls me round.   III. ii. 19
The imaginary relish is so sweet
That it enchants my sense: what will it be,
When that the watery palate tastes indeed
Love's thrice repured nectar? death, I fear me,
Swooning destruction, or some joy too fine,
Too subtle-potent, tuned too sharp in sweetness,
For the capacity of my ruder powers:
I fear it much; and I do fear besides.
That I shall lose distinction in my joys;
As doth a battle, when they charge on heaps
The enemy flying.   (*Troilus*)

It is the prettiest villain: she fetches her breath as   34
short as a new-ta'en sparrow.   (*Pandarus*)

My heart beats thicker than a feverous pulse;   38
And all my powers do their bestowing lose,
Like vassalage at unawares encountering
The eye of majesty.   (*Troilus*)

Nay, you shall fight your hearts out ere I part you.   54
                                    (*Pandarus*)

My thoughts were like unbridled children, grown   130
Too headstrong for their mother.   (*Cressida*)

But, though I loved you well, I woo'd you not: 134
And yet, good faith, I wish'd myself a man,
Or that we women had men's privilege
Of speaking first.   (*Cressida*)

                        To be wise and love   163
Exceeds man's might.   (*Cressida*)

'Tis certain, greatness, once fall'n out with fortune,   III. iii. 75
Must fall out with men too: what the declined is
He shall as soon read in the eyes of others
As feel in his own fall; for men, like butterflies,
Show not their mealy wings but to the summer,
And not a man, for being simply man,
Hath any honour, but honour for those honours
That are without him, as place, riches, favour,
Prizes of accident as oft as merit:
Which when they fall, as being slippery standers,
The love that lean'd on them as slippery too,
Do one pluck down another and together
Die in the fall.   (*Achilles*)

Time hath, my lord, a wallet at his back,   145
Wherein he puts alms for oblivion,
A great-sized monster of ingratitudes:
Those scraps are good deeds past; which are devour'd
As fast as they are made, forgot as soon
As done: perseverance, dear my lord,
Keeps honour bright: to have done is to hang
Quite out of fashion, like a rusty mail
In monumental mockery.   Take the instant way;
For honour travels in a strait so narrow,
Where one but goes abreast.   (*Ulysses*)

For time is like a fashionable host   165
That slightly shakes his parting guest by the hand,
And with his arms outstretch'd, as he would fly,
Grasps in the comer: welcome ever smiles,
And farewell goes out sighing.   O, let not virtue seek
Remuneration for the thing it was:
For beauty, wit,
High birth, vigour of bone, desert in service,
Love, friendship, charity, are subjects all
To envious and calumniating time.
One touch of nature makes the whole world kin,
That all with one consent praise new-born gawds,
Though they are made and moulded of things past,
And give to dust that is a little gilt
More laud than gilt o'er-dusted.   (*Ulysses*)

A woman impudent and mannish grown   217
Is not more loathed than an effeminate man,
In time of action. (*Patroclus*)

And, like a dew-drop from the lion's mane,   224
Be shook to air. (*Patroclus*)

Those wounds heal ill that men do give themselves.   229
                         (*Patroclus*)

My mind is troubled, like a fountain stirr'd;   III. iii. 311
And I myself see not the bottom of it. (*Achilles*)

Aeneas. We know each other well.   IV. i. 30
Diomedes. We do; and long to know each other worse.

          You do as chapmen do,   75
Dispraise the thing that you desire to buy. (*Paris*)

Injurious time now with a robber's haste   IV. iv. 44
Crams his rich thievery up, he knows not how:
As many farewells as be stars in heaven,
With distinct breath and consign'd kisses to them,
He fumbles up into a loose adieu,
And scants us with a single famish'd kiss,
Distasted with the salt of broken tears. (*Troilus*)

And sometimes we are devils to ourselves,   97
When we will tempt the frailty of our powers,
Presuming on their changeful potency. (*Troilus*)

The kiss you take is better than you give. (*Cressida*)   IV. v. 38

There's language in her eye, her cheek, her lip,   55
Nay, her foot speaks; her wanton spirits look out
At every joint and motive of her body. (*Ulysses*)

Let me embrace thee, good old chronicle,   202
That hast so long walk'd hand in hand with time.
                              (*Hector*)

                The end crowns all,   224
And that old common arbitrator, Time,
Will one day end it. (*Hector*)

   To be a dog, a mule, a cat, a fitchew, a toad, a lizard, an   v. i. 67
owl, a puttock, or a herring without a roe, I would not
care; but to be Menelaus! I would conspire against
destiny. (*Thersites*)

Minds sway'd by eyes are full of turpitude. (*Cressida*)   v. ii. 112

If beauty have a soul, this is not she;   138
If souls guide vows, if vows be sanctimonies,
If sanctimony be the gods' delight,
If there be rule in unity itself,
This is not she. (*Troilus*)

The gods are deaf to hot and peevish vows. (*Cassandra*)   v. iii. 16

Words, words, mere words, no matter from the heart.   v. iii. 108
                    (*Troilus*)

Now they are clapper-clawing one another. (*Thersites*)   v. iv. 1

Dexterity so obeying appetite   v. v. 27
That what he will he does, and does so much
That proof is call'd impossibility.   (*Nestor*)

The dragon wing of night o'erspreads the earth.   v. viii. 17
                    (*Achilles*)

I'll haunt thee like a wicked conscience still,   v. x. 28
That mouldeth goblins swift as frenzy's thoughts.
                    (*Troilus*)

CORIOLANUS

For his valour in Rome's war against the Volscians of the city of Corioli, Caius Marcius is given the surname of Coriolanus. He is persuaded to stand for the consulship, but when canvassing votes cannot conceal his contempt for the common people. The tribunes Sicinius and Brutus then turn the mob against him, and though restraint is urged upon him by his old friend Menenius Agrippa, his mother Volumnia, and his wife Virgilia, he behaves with such pride and scorn that he is banished from Rome. To obtain revenge, he goes to the Volscians, offers his services to their general Tullus Aufidius, and joins in leading his former enemies against Rome. Cominius, the Roman general, and Menenius go out to him and plead for the city in vain, but the prayers of his mother, wife, and child melt Coriolanus's heart. He spares Rome, makes a treaty, and returns to the Volscians, who slay him as a traitor.

He's a very dog to the commonalty. (*Citizens*)   I. i. 28

They said they were an-hungry; sigh'd forth proverbs,   209
That hunger broke stone walls, that dogs must eat,
That meat was made for mouths, that the gods sent not
Corn for the rich men only. (*Marcius*)

                           They threw their caps   216
As they would hang them on the horns o' the moon,
Shouting their emulation. (*Marcius*)

I'll lean upon one crutch and fight with t'other,   246
Ere stay behind this business. (*Titus*)

   He did so set his teeth and tear it; O, I warrant, how he   I. iii. 70
mammocked it! (*Valeria*)

Like Romans, neither foolish in our stands,   I. vi. 2
Nor cowardly in retire. (*Cominius*)

The mouse ne'er shunn'd the cat as they did budge   44
From rascals worse than they. (*Marcius*)

Officious, and not valiant, you have shamed me   I. viii. 14
In your condemned seconds. (*Aufidius*)

   A letter for me! it gives me an estate of seven years'   II. i. 125
health. (*Menenius*)

My gracious silence, hail! (*Coriolanus*)   192

We call a nettle but a nettle and   207
The faults of fools but folly. (*Menenius*)

I had rather be their servant in my way   219
Than sway with them in theirs. (*Coriolanus*)

All tongues speak of him, and the bleared sights   221
Are spectacled to see him: your prattling nurse
Into a rapture lets her baby cry
While she chats him: the kitchen malkin pins
Her richest lockram 'bout her reechy neck,
Clambering the walls to eye him: stalls, bulks, windows,
Are smother'd up, leads fill'd, and ridges horsed
With variable complexions, all agreeing
In earnestness to see him. (*Brutus*)

I have seen the dumb men throng to see him and   278
The blind to hear him speak: matrons flung gloves,
Ladies and maids their scarfs and handkerchers,

Upon him as he pass'd: the nobles bended,   II. i. 281
As to Jove's statue, and the commons made
A shower and thunder with their caps and shouts.
                              (*Messenger*)

I had rather have my wounds to heal again   II. ii. 73
Than hear say how I got them.   (*Coriolanus*)

I had rather have one scratch my head i' the sun   79
When the alarum were struck than idly sit
To hear my nothings monster'd.   (*Coriolanus*)

                    What must I say?   II. iii. 55
'I pray, sir,'—Plague upon 't!   I cannot bring
My tongue to such a pace:—'Look, sir, my wounds!
I got them in my country's service, when
Some certain of your brethren roar'd and ran
From the noise of our own drums.'   (*Coriolanus*)

                    Bid them wash their faces   66
And keep their teeth clean.   (*Coriolanus*)

Coriolanus. I pray, your price o' the consulship?   79
First Citizen. The price is to ask it kindly.
Coriolanus. Kindly! Sir, I pray, let me ha't: I have
    wounds to show you, which shall be yours in private.

Most sweet voices!   119
Better it is to die, better to starve,
Than crave the hire which first we do deserve.
Why in this woolvish toge should I stand here,
To beg of Hob and Dick, that do appear,
Their needless vouches?   (*Coriolanus*)

What custom wills, in all things should we do't,   125
The dust on antique time would lie unswept,
And mountainous error be too highly heapt
For truth to o'er-peer.   (*Coriolanus*)

He said he had wounds, which he could show in private;   174
And with his hat, thus waving it in scorn,
'I would be consul,' says he: 'aged custom,
But by your voices, will not so permit me;
Your voices therefore.'   When we granted that,
Here was 'I thank you for your voices: thank you:
Your most sweet voices: now you have left your voices,
I have no further with you.'   Was not this mockery?
                              (*Third Citizen*)

For the mutable, rank-scented many, let them   III. i. 66
Regard me as I do not flatter, and
Therein behold themselves.   (*Coriolanus*)

                   You speak o' the people,   80
As if you were a god to punish, not
A man of their infirmity.   (*Brutus*)

Hear you this Triton of the minnows? mark you   88
His absolute 'shall'?   (*Coriolanus*)

His nature is too noble for the world: 255
He would not flatter Neptune for his trident,
Or Jove for's power to thunder.   His heart's his mouth:
What his breast forges, that his tongue must vent.
                           (*Menenius*)

He's a disease that must be cut away.   (*Sicinius*)   295

You might have been enough the man you are,   III. ii. 19
With striving less to be so.   (*Volumnia*)

                I'll mountebank their loves,   132
Cog their hearts from them, and come home beloved
Of all the trades in Rome.   (*Coriolanus*)

The fires i' the lowest hell fold-in the people!   III. iii. 68
                         (*Coriolanus*)

You common cry of curs! whose breath I hate   120
As reek o' the rotten fens, whose loves I prize
As the dead carcasses of unburied men
That do corrupt my air, I banish you.   (*Coriolanus*)

               A brief farewell: the beast   IV. i. 1
With many heads butts me away.   (*Coriolanus*)

'Tis fond to wail inevitable strokes,   26
As 'tis to laugh at 'em.   (*Coriolanus*)

To banish him that struck more blows for Rome   IV. ii. 19
Than thou hast spoken words.   (*Volumnia*)

Virgilia. He'ld make an end of thy posterity.   26
Volumnia. Bastards and all.

Third Servant. Where dwellest thou?   IV. v. 40
Coriolanus. Under the canopy.
Third Servant. Under the canopy!

Coriolanus. Ay.   IV. v. 43
Third Servant. Where's that?
Coriolanus. I' the city of kites and crows!

                           They follow him   IV. vi. 92
Against us brats, with no less confidence
Than boys pursuing summer butterflies,
Or butchers killing flies.   (*Cominius*)

                     Would half my wealth   160
Would buy this for a lie!   (*Brutus*)

I minded him how royal 'twas to pardon   v. i. 18
When it was less expected.   (*Cominius*)

He was not taken well; he had not dined: 50
The veins unfill'd, our blood is cold, and then
We pout upon the morning, are unapt
To give or to forgive; but when we have stuff'd
These pipes and these conveyances of our blood
With wine and feeding, we have suppler souls
Than in our priest-like fasts: therefore I'll watch him
Till he be dieted to my request,
And then I'll set upon him.   (*Menenius*)

You know the very road into his kindness,   59
And cannot lose your way.   (*Brutus*)

               Like a dull actor now,   v. iii. 40
I have forgot my part, and I am out,
Even to a full disgrace.   (*Coriolanus*)

                        O, a kiss   44
Long as my exile, sweet as my revenge!
Now, by the jealous queen of heaven, that kiss
I carried from thee, dear; and my true lip
Hath virgin'd it e'er since.   (*Coriolanus*)

                 Chaste as the icicle   65
That's curdied by the frost from purest snow
And hangs on Dian's temple.   (*Coriolanus*)

              A' shall not tread on me;   127
I'll run away till I am bigger, but then I'll fight.
                         (*Young Marcius*)

              Thou hast never in thy life   160
Show'd thy dear mother any courtesy,
When she, poor hen, fond of no second brood,
Has cluck'd thee to the wars and safely home,
Loaden with honour.   (*Volumnia*)

At a few drops of women's rheum, which are   v. vi. 46
As cheap as lies, he sold the blood and labour
Of our great action.   (*Aufidius*)

Breaking his oath and resolution like   95
A twist of rotten silk.   (*Aufidius*)

If you have writ your annals true, 'tis there,   114
That, like an eagle in a dove-cote, I
Flutter'd your Volscians in Corioli:
Alone I did it.   (*Coriolanus*)

TITUS ANDRONICUS

Leading characters in this crude tragedy are, on one side, Titus Andronicus, a Roman general, his brother Marcus, and his son Lucius; on the other Tamora, queen of the Goths, her son Demetrius, and her paramour Aaron. Each side vies with the other in ferocious and inhuman revenge, Titus beginning the horrible series by sacrificing one of Tamora's sons in his official triumph. Then the captured Tamora, taken by Saturninus, Emperor of Rome, to be his wife, contrives to have two of Titus's sons beheaded and his daughter mutilated. Titus retaliates by slaying Tamora's sons and serving them up to her at a banquet, where he kills Tamora and is himself killed by Saturninus, who is killed in turn by Lucius. This farrago of horror has been reckoned unworthy of Shakespeare, but the external evidence of his authorship is strong, and as it was a popular play it may have served as an effective 'pot-boiler' in his early days.

Sweet mercy is nobility's true badge. (*Tamora*)　　　　I. i. 119

As when the golden sun salutes the morn,　　　　　　　II. i. 5
And, having gilt the ocean with his beams,
Gallops the zodiac in his glistering coach,
And overlooks the highest-peering hills. (*Aaron*)

She is a woman, therefore may be woo'd;　　　　　　　82
She is a woman, therefore may be won;
She is Lavinia, therefore must be loved.
What, man! more water glideth by the mill
Than wots the miller of; and easy it is
Of a cut loaf to steal a shive, we know. (*Demetrius*)

A barren detested vale, you see it is;　　　　　　　　II. iii. 93
The trees, thou summer, yet forlorn and lean,
O'ercome with moss and baleful mistletoe;
Here never shines the sun; here nothing breeds,
Unless the nightly owl or fatal raven. (*Tamora*)

Sorrow concealed, like an oven stopp'd,　　　　　　　II. iv. 36
Doth burn the heart to cinders where it is. (*Marcus*)

When will this fearful slumber have an end? (*Titus*)　III. i. 253

Marcus. Alas, my lord, I have but kill'd a fly.　　　III. ii. 59
Titus. But how, if that fly had a father and mother?
How would he hang his slender gilded wings,
And buzz lamenting doings in the air!
Poor harmless fly,
That with his pretty buzzing melody,
Came here to make us merry! and thou hast kill'd him.

Come, and take choice of all my library,　　　　　　IV. i. 34
And so beguile thy sorrow. (*Titus*)

I'll broach the tadpole on my rapier's point. (*Demetrius*)　IV. ii. 85

Two may keep counsel when the third's away. (*Aaron*)　　144

Clown. God and Saint Stephen give you good den: I have　IV. iv. 42
brought you a letter and a couple of pigeons here.
Saturninus. Go, take him away, and hang him presently.
Clown. How much money must I have?
Tamora. Come, sirrah, you must be hanged.
Clown. Hanged! by'r lady, then I have brought up a neck
to a fair end.

King, be thy thoughts imperious, like thy name.   iv. iv. 81
Is the sun dimm'd, that gnats do fly in it?
The eagle suffers little birds to sing,
And is not careful what they mean thereby,
Knowing that with the shadow of his wings
He can at pleasure stint their melody.   (*Tamora*)

Even now I curse the day—and yet, I think,   v. i. 125
Few come within the compass of my curse—
Wherein I did not some notorious ill.   (*Aaron*)

Tut, I have done a thousand dreadful things   141
As willingly as one would kill a fly,
And nothing grieves me heartily indeed
But that I cannot do ten thousand more.   (*Aaron*)

If there be devils, would I were a devil,   147
To live and burn in everlasting fire,
So I might have your company in hell,
But to torment you with my bitter tongue!   (*Aaron*)

Revenge, which makes the foul offender quake. (*Tamora*)   v. ii. 40

I am no baby, I, that with base prayers   v. iii. 185
I should repent the evils I have done.   (*Aaron*)

If one good deed in all my life I did,   189
I do repent it from my very soul.   (*Aaron*)

ROMEO AND JULIET

Between two noble families of Verona, the Montagues and
the Capulets, there is rivalry and hatred. Old Capulet gives
a party at which his daughter Juliet is present; Romeo, a
Montague, attends it, and though he has lately been professing a romantic passion for Rosaline, falls violently in
love with Juliet and she with him. That night he climbs
into her garden and hears her soliloquizing on the balcony
of her room. They exchange vows, and with the connivance
of Juliet's old nurse are secretly married next day by Friar
Laurence. Later the Montagues Mercutio and Benvolio
have an encounter with a party of Capulets headed by Tybalt;
Romeo tries to part them, but Tybalt kills Mercutio, and
Romeo then kills Tybalt. For this he is banished, and after
one night with his bride flees to Mantua. Meanwhile old
Capulet, knowing nothing of the marriage, commands his
daughter to marry Paris, a nobleman. To get her out of this
fix, Friar Laurence gives her a drug which brings about a
death-like trance, and sends to Romeo to come and carry
her off while she is mourned as dead. But the message
miscarries, and Romeo, hearing of her supposed death, comes
to the Capulet tomb, kills Paris, who tries to stop him, and
takes poison, dying by Juliet's side. Juliet wakes, finds his
dead body beside her, and fatally stabs herself. Among
minor characters are Sampson and Gregory, servants to
Capulet, and Peter, servant to Juliet's nurse.

A pair of star-cross'd lovers take their life.   (*Chorus*)   *Prologue* 6

The two hours' traffic of our stage.   (*Chorus*)   12

    I do not bite my thumb at you, sir, but I bite my thumb,   I. i. 56
sir.   (*Sampson*)

Gregory, remember thy swashing blow.   (*Sampson*)   69

Capulet. What noise is this?   Give me my long sword,   82
    ho!
Lady Capulet. A crutch, a crutch! why call you for a
    sword?
Capulet. My sword, I say!   Old Montague is come,
And flourishes his blade in spite of me.

Who set this ancient quarrel new abroach?   (*Montague*)   111

Madam, an hour before the worshipp'd sun   125
Peer'd forth the golden window of the east,
A troubled mind drave me to walk abroad.   (*Benvolio*)

Many a morning hath he there been seen,   137
With tears augmenting the fresh morning's dew,
Adding to clouds more clouds with his deep sighs;
But all so soon as the all-cheering sun
Should in the furthest east begin to draw
The shady curtains from Aurora's bed,
Away from light steals home my heavy son,
And private in his chamber pens himself,
Shuts up his windows, locks fair daylight out
And makes himself an artificial night.   (*Montague*)

So far from sounding and discovery,   156
As is the bud bit with an envious worm,
Ere he can spread his sweet leaves to the air,
Or dedicate his beauty to the sun.   (*Montague*)

Alas, that love, so gentle in his view,   175
Should be so tyrannous and rough in proof!   (*Benvolio*)

O heavy lightness! serious vanity!   184
Mis-shapen chaos of well-seeming forms!
Feather of lead, bright smoke, cold fire, sick health!
Still-waking sleep, that is not what it is!   (*Romeo*)

Griefs of mine own lie heavy in my breast.   (*Romeo*)   192

Love is a smoke raised with the fume of sighs;   196
Being purged, a fire sparkling in lovers' eyes;

Being vex'd, a sea nourish'd with lovers' tears: I. i. 198
What is it else? a madness most discreet,
A choking gall and a preserving sweet. (*Romeo*)

She will not stay the siege of loving terms,   218
Nor bide the encounter of assailing eyes,
Nor ope her lap to saint-seducing gold:
O, she is rich in beauty, only poor,
That when she dies with beauty dies her store. (*Romeo*)

He that is strucken blind cannot forget   238
The precious treasure of his eyesight lost. (*Romeo*)

My child is yet a stranger in the world;   I. ii. 8
She hath not seen the change of fourteen years;
Let two more summers wither in their pride,
Ere we may think her ripe to be a bride. (*Capulet*)

The earth hath swallow'd all my hopes but she,   14
She is the hopeful lady of my earth. (*Capulet*)

At my poor house look to behold this night   24
Earth-treading stars that make dark heaven light:
Such comfort as do lusty young men feel
When well-apparell'd April on the heel
Of limping winter treads, even such delight
Among fresh female buds shall you this night
Inherit at my house. (*Capulet*)

Tut, man, one fire burns out another's burning,   46
　One pain is lessen'd by another's anguish;
Turn giddy, and be holp by backward turning;
　One desperate grief cures with another's languish.
                                          (*Benvolio*)

Compare her face with some that I shall show,   91
And I will make thee think thy swan a crow. (*Benvolio*)

One fairer than my love! the all-seeing sun   97
Ne'er saw her match since first the world begun. (*Romeo*)

Come Lammas-eve at night shall she be fourteen.   I. iii. 17
Susan and she—God rest all Christian souls!—
Were of an age: well, Susan is with God;
She was too good for me: but, as I said,
On Lammas-eve at night shall she be fourteen;
That shall she, marry; I remember it well.
'Tis since the earthquake now eleven years. (*Nurse*)

For even the day before, she broke her brow: 38
And then my husband—God be with his soul!

A' was a merry man—took up the child: I. iii. 40
'Yea,' quoth he, 'dost thou fall upon thy face?
Thou wilt fall backward when thou hast more wit;
Wilt thou not, Jule?' and, by my holidame,
The pretty wretch left crying and said 'Ay.'   (*Nurse*)

Thou wast the prettiest babe that e'er I nursed: 60
An I might live to see thee married once,
I have my wish.   (*Nurse*)

Lady Capulet. How stands your disposition to be   65
     married?
Juliet. It is an honour that I dream not of.

Why, he's a man of wax.   (*Nurse*)   76

What say you? can you love the gentleman?   79
                              (*Lady Capulet*)

That book in many's eyes doth share the glory,   91
That in gold clasps locks in the golden story.
                              (*Lady Capulet*)

A torch for me: let wantons light of heart   I. iv. 35
Tickle the senseless rushes with their heels,
For I am proverb'd with a grandsire phrase;
I'll be a candle-holder, and look on.   (*Romeo*)

Tut, dun's the mouse, the constable's own word: 40
If thou art dun, we'll draw thee from the mire
Of this sir-reverence love, wherein thou stick'st
Up to the ears.   Come, we burn daylight, ho!
                              (*Mercutio*)

O, then, I see Queen Mab hath been with you.   53
She is the fairies' midwife, and she comes
In shape no bigger than an agate-stone
On the fore-finger of an alderman,
Drawn with a team of little atomies
Athwart men's noses as they lie asleep;
Her waggon-spokes made of long spinners' legs,
The cover of the wings of grasshoppers,
The traces of the smallest spider's web,
The collars of the moonshine's watery beams,
Her whip of cricket's bone, the lash of film,
Her waggoner a small grey-coated gnat,
Not half so big as a round little worm
Prick'd from the lazy finger of a maid;
Her chariot is an empty hazel-nut
Made by the joiner squirrel, or old grub,

Time out o' mind the fairies' coachmakers.   I. iv. 69
And in this state she gallops night by night
Through lovers' brains, and then they dream of love;
O'er courtiers' knees, that dream on court'sies straight,
O'er lawyers' fingers, who straight dream on fees,
O'er ladies' lips, who straight on kisses dream,
Which oft the angry Mab with blisters plagues,
Because their breaths with sweetmeats tainted are:
Sometime she gallops o'er a courtier's nose,
And then dreams he of smelling out a suit;
And sometime comes she with a tithe-pig's tail
Tickling a parson's nose as a' lies asleep,
Then dreams he of another benefice:
Sometime she driveth o'er a soldier's neck,
And then dreams he of cutting foreign throats,
Of breaches, ambuscadoes, Spanish blades,
Of healths five-fathom deep; and then anon
Drums in his ear, at which he starts and wakes,
And being thus frighted swears a prayer or two
And sleeps again.   (*Mercutio*)

                        True, I talk of dreams,   96
Which are the children of an idle brain,
Begot of nothing but vain fantasy. (*Mercutio*)

First Servant. You are looked for and called for, asked   I. v. 13
   for and sought for, in the great chamber.
Second Servant. We cannot be here and there too.

Welcome, gentlemen! ladies that have their toes   18
Unplagued with corns will have a bout with you.
Ah ha, my mistresses! which of you all
Will now deny to dance? she that makes dainty,
She, I'll swear, hath corns; am I come near ye now?
Welcome, gentlemen! I have seen the day
That I have worn a visor and could tell
A whispering tale in a fair lady's ear,
Such as would please: 'tis gone, 'tis gone, 'tis gone.
                                        (*Capulet*)

For you and I are past our dancing days. (*Capulet*)   33

What lady is that, which doth enrich the hand   43
Of yonder knight? (*Romeo*)

O, she doth teach the torches to burn bright!   46
It seems she hangs upon the cheek of night
Like a rich jewel in an Ethiope's ear;
Beauty too rich for use, for earth too dear! (*Romeo*)

Did my heart love till now? forswear it, sight!   I. v. 54
For I ne'er saw true beauty till this night.   (*Romeo*)

Content thee, gentle coz, let him alone;   67
He bears him like a portly gentleman;
And, to say truth, Verona brags of him
To be a virtuous and well-govern'd youth:
I would not for the wealth of all the town
Here in my house do him disparagement:
Therefore be patient, take no note of him.   (*Capulet*)

Am I the master here, or you? go to.   80
You'll not endure him!   God shall mend my soul!
You'll make a mutiny among my guests!
You will set cock-a-hoop! you'll be the man!   (*Capulet*)

Romeo. If I profane with my unworthiest hand   95
   This holy shrine, the gentle fine is this:
My lips, two blushing pilgrims, ready stand
   To smooth that rough touch with a tender kiss.
Juliet. Good pilgrim, you do wrong your hand too much,
   Which mannerly devotion shows in this;
For saints have hands that pilgrims' hands do touch,
   And palm to palm is holy palmers' kiss.

Nurse. Her mother is the lady of the house,   115
And a good lady, and a wise and virtuous:
I nursed her daughter, that you talk'd withal;
I tell you, he that can lay hold of her
Shall have the chinks.
Romeo.   Is she a Capulet?
O dear account! my life is my foe's debt.

Nay, gentlemen, prepare not to be gone;   123
We have a trifling foolish banquet towards.   (*Capulet*)

My only love sprung from my only hate!   140
Too early seen unknown, and known too late!   (*Juliet*)

Now old desire doth in his death-bed lie,   II. *Prologue* 1
   And young affection gapes to be his heir.   (*Chorus*)

Turn back, dull earth, and find thy centre out.   (*Romeo*)   II. i. 2

                   Nay, I'll conjure too.   6
Romeo! humours! madman! passion! lover!
Appear thou in the likeness of a sigh:
Speak but one rhyme, and I am satisfied;
Cry but 'Ay me!' pronounce but 'love' and 'dove';
Speak to my gossip Venus one fair word,

One nick-name for her purblind son and heir,   II. i. 12
Young Adam Cupid, he that shot so trim,
When King Cophetua loved the beggar-maid! (*Mercutio*)

Now will he sit under a medlar-tree,   34
And wish his mistress were that kind of fruit
As maids call medlars when they laugh alone. (*Mercutio*)

He jests at scars that never felt a wound. (*Romeo*)   II. ii. 1

But, soft! what light through yonder window breaks?   2
It is the east, and Juliet is the sun.
Arise, fair sun, and kill the envious moon,
Who is already sick and pale with grief,
That thou her maid art far more fair than she·
Be not her maid, since she is envious;
Her vestal livery is but sick and green
And none but fools do wear it; cast it off.
It is my lady, O, it is my love!
O, that she knew she were!
She speaks, yet she says nothing: what of that?
Her eye discourses; I will answer it.
I am too bold, 'tis not to me she speaks:
Two of the fairest stars in all the heaven,
Having some business, do entreat her eyes
To twinkle in their spheres till they return.
What if her eyes were there, they in her head?
The brightness of her cheek would shame those stars,
As daylight doth a lamp; her eyes in heaven
Would through the airy region stream so bright
That birds would sing and think it were not night.
See, how she leans her cheek upon her hand!
O, that I were a glove upon that hand,
That I might touch that cheek! (*Romeo*)

O, speak again, bright angel! for thou art   26
As glorious to this night, being o'er my head,
As is a winged messenger of heaven
Unto the white-upturned wondering eyes
Of mortals that fall back to gaze on him
When he bestrides the lazy-pacing clouds
And sails upon the bosom of the air. (*Romeo*)

O, Romeo, Romeo! wherefore art thou Romeo?   33
Deny thy father and refuse thy name;
Or, if thou wilt not, be but sworn my love,
And I'll no longer be a Capulet. (*Juliet*)

What's in a name? that which we call a rose   43
By any other name would smell as sweet;

So Romeo would, were he not Romeo call'd,   II. ii. 45
Retain that dear perfection which he owes
Without that title.   Romeo, doff thy name,
And for that name which is no part of thee
Take all myself.   (*Juliet*)

What man art thou that thus bescreen'd in night   52
So stumblest on my counsel?   (*Juliet*)

With love's light wings did I o'erperch these walls;   66
For stony limits cannot hold love out.   (*Romeo*)

Alack, there lies more peril in thine eye   71
Than twenty of their swords.   (*Romeo*)

I have night's cloak to hide me from their sight.   (*Romeo*)   75

I am no pilot; yet, wert thou as far   82
As that vast shore wash'd with the farthest sea,
I would adventure for such merchandise.   (*Romeo*)

Thou know'st the mask of night is on my face,   85
Else would a maiden blush bepaint my cheek
For that which thou hast heard me speak to-night.
Fain would I dwell on form, fain, fain deny
What I have spoke: but farewell compliment!
Dost thou love me?   I know thou wilt say 'Ay,'
And I will take thy word: yet, if thou swear'st,
Thou mayst prove false; at lovers' perjuries,
They say, Jove laughs.   O gentle Romeo,
If thou dost love, pronounce it faithfully:
Or if thou think'st I am too quickly won,
I'll frown and be perverse and say thee nay,
So thou wilt woo; but else, not for the world.
In truth, fair Montague, I am too fond,
And therefore thou mayst think my 'haviour light:
But trust me, gentleman, I'll prove more true
Than those that have more cunning to be strange.   (*Juliet*)

Romeo. Lady, by yonder blessed moon I swear   107
That tips with silver all these fruit-tree tops—
Juliet. O, swear not by the moon, the inconstant moon,
That monthly changes in her circled orb,
Lest that thy love prove likewise variable.
Romeo. What shall I swear by?
Juliet.   Do not swear at all;
Or, if thou wilt, swear by thy gracious self,
Which is the god of my idolatry,
And I'll believe thee.

     Although I joy in thee, II. ii. 116
I have no joy of this contract to-night:
It is too rash, too unadvised, too sudden;
Too like the lightning, which doth cease to be
Ere one can say 'It lightens.' Sweet, good night!
This bud of love, by summer's ripening breath,
May prove a beauteous flower when next we meet.
Good night, good night! as sweet repose and rest
Come to thy heart as that within my breast! (*Juliet*)

My bounty is as boundless as the sea, 133
My love as deep; the more I give to thee,
The more I have, for both are infinite. (*Juliet*)

And all my fortunes at thy foot I'll lay 147
And follow thee my lord throughout the world. (*Juliet*)

A thousand times good night! (*Juliet*) 155

Love goes toward love, as schoolboys from their books, 157
But love from love, toward school with heavy looks.
       (*Romeo*)

Hist! Romeo, hist! O, for a falconer's voice, 159
To lure this tassel-gentle back again!
Bondage is hoarse, and may not speak aloud;
Else would I tear the cave where Echo lies,
And make her airy tongue more hoarse than mine,
With repetition of my Romeo's name. (*Juliet*)

How silver-sweet sound lovers' tongues by night, 166
Like softest music to attending ears! (*Romeo*)

Juliet. 'Tis almost morning; I would have thee gone: 177
And yet no further than a wanton's bird;
Who lets it hop a little from her hand,
Like a poor prisoner in his twisted gyves,
And with a silk thread plucks it back again,
So loving-jealous of his liberty.
Romeo. I would I were thy bird.
Juliet.   Sweet, so would I:
Yet I should kill thee with much cherishing.
Good night, good night! parting is such sweet sorrow,
That I shall say good night till it be morrow.

The grey-eyed morn smiles on the frowning night, II. iii. 1
Chequering the eastern clouds with streaks of light,
And flecked darkness like a drunkard reels
From forth day's path and Titan's fiery wheels:
Now, ere the sun advance his burning eye,

K   273

The day to cheer and night's dank dew to dry,   II. iii. 6
I must up-fill this osier cage of ours
With baleful weeds and precious-juiced flowers.
                                        (*Friar Laurence*)

O, mickle is the powerful grace that lies   15
In herbs, plants, stones, and their true qualities:
For nought so vile that on the earth doth live
But to the earth some special good doth give,
Nor aught so good but strain'd from that fair use
Revolts from true birth, stumbling on abuse:
Virtue itself turns vice, being misapplied;
And vice sometimes by action dignified.
                                        (*Friar Laurence*)

What early tongue so sweet saluteth me?   32
Young son, it argues a distemper'd head
So soon to bid good morrow to thy bed:
Care keeps his watch in every old man's eye,
And where care lodges, sleep will never lie;
But where unbruised youth with unstuff'd brain
Doth couch his limbs, there golden sleep doth reign:
Therefore thy earliness doth me assure
Thou art up-roused by some distemperature.
                                        (*Friar Laurence*)

Be plain, good son, and homely in thy drift;   55
Riddling confession finds but riddling shrift.
                                        (*Friar Laurence*)

Jesu Maria, what a deal of brine   69
Hath wash'd thy sallow cheeks for Rosaline!
How much salt water thrown away in waste,
To season love, that of it doth not taste!
The sun not yet thy sighs from heaven clears,
Thy old groans ring yet in my ancient ears;
Lo, here upon thy cheek the stain doth sit
Of an old tear that is not wash'd off yet:
If e'er thou wast thyself and these woes thine,
Thou and these woes were all for Rosaline:
And art thou changed? pronounce this sentence then,
Women may fall, when there's no strength in men.
                                        (*Friar Laurence*)

Wisely and slow; they stumble that run fast.   94
                                        (*Friar Laurence*)

    Alas, poor Romeo! he is already dead: stabbed with a   II. iv. 13
white wench's black eye.   (*Mercutio*)

O, he is the courageous captain of compliments. He   II. iv. 19
fights as you sing prick-song, keeps time, distance, and
proportion; rests me his minim rest, one, two, and the
third in your bosom: the very butcher of a silk button, a
duellist, a duellist; a gentleman of the very first house, of
the first and second cause: ah, the immortal passado! the
punto reverso! the hai!   (*Mercutio*)

O flesh, flesh, how art thou fishified!   (*Mercutio*)   39

Signior Romeo, bon jour! there's a French salutation   45
to your French slop.   (*Mercutio*)

Nay, I am the very pink of courtesy.   (*Mercutio*)   61

If thy wits run the wild-goose chase, I have done.   75
                                            (*Mercutio*)

I will bite thee by the ear for that jest.   (*Mercutio*)   82

Why, is not this better now than groaning for love?   92
now art thou sociable, now art thou Romeo; now art thou
what thou art, by art as well as by nature.   (*Mercutio*)

The bawdy hand of the dial is now upon the prick of   118
noon.   (*Mercutio*)

> An old hare hoar,
> And an old hare hoar,
> Is very good meat in lent:
> But a hare that is hoar
> Is too much for a score,
> When it hoars ere it be spent.
>   (*Mercutio, sings*)

A gentleman, nurse, that loves to hear himself talk, and   155
will speak more in a minute than he will stand to in a
month.   (*Romeo*)

Scurvy knave! I am none of his flirt-gills; I am none   161
of his skains-mates.   (*Nurse*)

If ye should lead her into a fool's paradise.   (*Nurse*)   175

Romeo. Nurse, commend me to thy lady and mistress. I   182
protest unto thee—
Nurse. Good heart, and, i' faith, I will tell her as much:
Lord, Lord, she will be a joyful woman.
Romeo. What wilt thou tell her, nurse? thou dost not
mark me.

Nurse. I will tell her, sir, that you do protest; which, as I   ii. iv. 188
take it, is a gentlemanlike offer.

Within this hour my man shall be with thee,   200
And bring thee cords made like a tackled stair;
Which to the high top-gallant of my joy
Must be my convoy in the secret night.   *(Romeo)*

Nurse. Is your man secret? Did you ne'er hear say,   208
Two may keep counsel, putting one away?
Romeo. I warrant thee, my man's as true as steel.

Nurse. Doth not rosemary and Romeo begin both with a   218
letter?
Romeo. Ay, nurse; what of that? both with an R.
Nurse. Ah, mocker! that's the dog's name; R is for the—
No: I know it begins with some other letter:—and she
hath the prettiest sententious of it, of you and rosemary, that it would do you good to hear it.

              Love's heralds should be thoughts,   ii. v. 4
Which ten times faster glide than the sun's beams,
Driving back shadows over louring hills:
Therefore do nimble-pinion'd doves draw love,
And therefore hath the wind-swift Cupid wings.   *(Juliet)*

Though news be sad, yet tell them merrily;   22
If good, thou shamest the music of sweet news
By playing it to me with so sour a face.   *(Juliet)*

Nurse. Fie, how my bones ache! what a jaunt have I had!   26
Juliet. I would thou hadst my bones, and I thy news.

How art thou out of breath, when thou hast breath   31
To say to me that thou art out of breath?   *(Juliet)*

Beshrew your heart for sending me about,   52
To catch my death with jaunting up and down! *(Nurse)*

  Your love says, like an honest gentleman, and a cour-   56
teous, and a kind, and a handsome, and, I warrant, a
virtuous,—Where is your mother? *(Nurse)*

These violent delights have violent ends   ii. vi. 9
And in their triumph die, like fire and powder,
Which as they kiss consume: the sweetest honey
Is loathsome in his own deliciousness
And in the taste confounds the appetite:
Therefore love moderately; long love doth so;
Too swift arrives as tardy as too slow.   *(Friar Laurence)*

Here comes the lady: O, so light a foot   II. vi. 16
Will ne'er wear out the everlasting flint:
A lover may bestride the gossamer
That idles in the wanton summer air,
And yet not fall; so light is vanity.   (*Friar Laurence*)

They are but beggars that can count their worth;   32
But my true love is grown to such excess
I cannot sum up sum of half my wealth.   (*Juliet*)

    Thou wilt quarrel with a man for cracking nuts, having   III. i. 20
no other reason but because thou hast hazel eyes.
                                        (*Mercutio*)

Thy head is as full of quarrels as an egg is full of meat.   24
                                        (*Mercutio*)

Tybalt. Mercutio, thou consort'st with Romeo,—   49
Mercutio. Consort! what, dost thou make us minstrels? an
thou make minstrels of us, look to hear nothing but
discords.

Benvolio. Here all eyes gaze on us.   56
Mercutio. Men's eyes were made to look, and let them
    gaze;
I will not budge for no man's pleasure, I.

Mercutio. O calm, dishonourable, vile submission!   76
Alla stoccata carries it away.   [*Draws.*]
Tybalt, you rat-catcher, will you walk?
Tybalt. What wouldst thou have with me?
Mercutio. Good king of cats, nothing but one of your nine
lives.

                    I am hurt.   94
A plague o' both your houses!   I am sped.
Is he gone, and hath nothing?   (*Mercutio*)

Romeo. Courage, man; the hurt cannot be much.   98
Mercutio. No, 'tis not so deep as a well, nor so wide as a
church-door; but 'tis enough, 'twill serve: ask for me
to-morrow, and you shall find me a grave man.

Gallop apace, you fiery-footed steeds,   III. ii. 1
Towards Phoebus' lodging: such a waggoner
As Phaethon would whip you to the west,
And bring in cloudy night immediately.
Spread thy close curtain, love-performing night,
That runaways' eyes may wink, and Romeo
Leap to these arms, untalk'd of and unseen.

Lovers can see to do their amorous rites   III. ii. 8
By their own beauties; or, if love be blind,
It best agrees with night.   Come, civil night,
Thou sober-suited matron, all in black,
And learn me how to lose a winning match,
Play'd for a pair of stainless maidenhoods:
Hood my unmann'd blood, bating in my cheeks,
With thy black mantle; till strange love, grown bold,
Think true love acted simple modesty.
Come, night; come, Romeo; come, thou day in night;
For thou wilt lie upon the wings of night
Whiter than new snow on a raven's back.
Come, gentle night, come, loving, black-brow'd night,
Give me my Romeo; and, when he shall die,
Take him and cut him out in little stars,
And he will make the face of heaven so fine
That all the world will be in love with night
And pay no worship to the garish sun.
O, I have bought the mansion of a love,
But not possess'd it, and, though I am sold,
Not yet enjoy'd: so tedious is this day
As is the night before some festival
To an impatient child that hath new robes
And may not wear them.   (*Juliet*)

I saw the wound, I saw it with mine eyes,—   52
God save the mark!—here on his manly breast:
A piteous corse, a bloody piteous corse;
Pale, pale as ashes, all bedaub'd in blood,
All in gore blood; I swounded at the sight.   (*Nurse*)

O serpent heart, hid with a flowering face!   73
Did ever dragon keep so fair a cave?
Beautiful tyrant! fiend angelical!
Dove-feather'd raven! wolvish-ravening lamb!
Despised substance of divinest show!
Just opposite to what thou justly seem'st,
A damned saint, an honourable villain!
O nature, what hadst thou to do in hell,
When thou didst bower the spirit of a fiend
In mortal paradise of such sweet flesh?
Was ever book containing such vile matter
So fairly bound?   O, that deceit should dwell
In such a gorgeous palace!   (*Juliet*)

Nurse. Shame come to Romeo!   90
Juliet.   Blister'd be thy tongue
For such a wish! he was not born to shame:
Upon his brow shame is ashamed to sit;
For 'tis a throne where honour may be crown'd
Sole monarch of the universal earth.

Affliction is enamour'd of thy parts,   III. iii. 2
And thou art wedded to calamity.   (*Friar Laurence*)

Thou cutt'st my head off with a golden axe,   22
And smilest upon the stroke that murders me.   (*Romeo*)

'Tis torture, and not mercy: heaven is here,   29
Where Juliet lives; and every cat and dog
And little mouse, every unworthy thing,
Live here in heaven and may look on her;
But Romeo may not: more validity,
More honourable state, more courtship lives
In carrion-flies than Romeo: they may seize
On the white wonder of dear Juliet's hand
And steal immortal blessing from her lips,
Who, even in pure and vestal modesty,
Still blush, as thinking their own kisses sin.   (*Romeo*)

Hadst thou no poison mix'd, no sharp-ground knife,   44
No sudden mean of death, though ne'er so mean,
But 'banished' to kill me?   (*Romeo*)

Adversity's sweet milk, philosophy.   (*Friar Laurence*)   55

                    Hold thy desperate hand: 108
Art thou a man? thy form cries out thou art:
Thy tears are womanish; thy wild acts denote
The unreasonable fury of a beast:
Unseemly woman in a seeming man!
Or ill-beseeming beast in seeming both!
                                    (*Friar Laurence*)

Thy wit, that ornament to shape and love,   130
Mis-shapen in the conduct of them both,
Like powder in a skilless soldier's flask,
Is set a-fire by thine own ignorance,
And thou dismember'd with thine own defence.
                                    (*Friar Laurence*)

Happiness courts thee in her best array;   142
But, like a misbehaved and sullen wench,
Thou pout'st upon thy fortune and thy love:
Take heed, take heed, for such die miserable.
                                    (*Friar Laurence*)

O Lord, I could have stay'd here all the night   159
To hear good counsel: O, what learning is!   (*Nurse*)

Juliet. Wilt thou be gone? it is not yet near day: III. v. 1
It was the nightingale, and not the lark,

That pierced the fearful hollow of thine ear;   III. v. 3
Nightly she sings on yond pomegranate-tree:
Believe me, love, it was the nightingale.
Romeo. It was the lark, the herald of the morn,
No nightingale: look, love, what envious streaks
Do lace the severing clouds in yonder east:
Night's candles are burnt out, and jocund day
Stands tiptoe on the misty mountain tops.
I must be gone and live, or stay and die.

It is the lark that sings so out of tune,   27
Straining harsh discords and unpleasing sharps. (*Juliet*)

            All these woes shall serve   52
For sweet discourses in our time to come. (*Romeo*)

Villain and he be many miles asunder. (*Juliet*)   82

How now! a conduit, girl? what, still in tears?   130
Evermore showering? In one little body
Thou counterfeit'st a bark, a sea, a wind;
For still thy eyes, which I may call the sea,
Do ebb and flow with tears; the bark thy body is,
Sailing in this salt flood; the winds, thy sighs;
Who, raging with thy tears, and they with them,
Without a sudden calm, will overset
Thy tempest-tossed body. (*Capulet*)

Thank me no thankings, nor proud me no prouds. (*Capulet*) 153

Out, you green-sickness carrion! out, you baggage!   157
You tallow-face! (*Capulet*)

You are to blame, my lord, to rate her so. (*Nurse*)   170

A gentleman of noble parentage,   181
Of fair demesnes, youthful, and nobly train'd,
Stuff'd, as they say, with honourable parts,
Proportion'd as one's thought would wish a man.

                         (*Capulet*)

Alack, alack, that heaven should practise stratagems   211
Upon so soft a subject as myself! (*Juliet*)

O, he's a lovely gentleman!   220
Romeo's a dishclout to him. (*Nurse*)

Ancient damnation! O most wicked fiend!   235
Is it more sin to wish me thus forsworn,
Or to dispraise my lord with that same tongue

Which she hath praised him with above compare   III. v. 238
So many thousand times?   (*Juliet*)

Come weep with me; past hope, past cure, past help!   IV. i. 45
                           (*Juliet*)

O, bid me leap, rather than marry Paris,   76
From off the battlements of yonder tower;
Or walk in thievish ways; or bid me lurk
Where serpents are; chain me with roaring bears;
Or shut me nightly in a charnel-house,
O'er-cover'd quite with dead men's rattling bones,
With reeky shanks and yellow chapless skulls;
Or bid me go into a new-made grave
And hide me with a dead man in his shroud;
Things that, to hear them told, have made me tremble;
And I will do it without fear or doubt,
To live an unstain'd wife to my sweet love.   (*Juliet*)

How now, my headstrong! where have you been gadding?   IV. ii. 16
                           (*Capulet*)

My dismal scene I needs must act alone.   (*Juliet*)   IV. iii. 19

Nurse.   Go, you cot-quean, go,   IV. iv. 6
Get you to bed; faith, you'll be sick to-morrow
For this night's watching.
Capulet. No, not a whit: what! I have watch'd ere now
All night for lesser cause, and ne'er been sick.
Lady Capulet. Ay, you have been a mouse-hunt in your
    time;
But I will watch you from such watching now.

Death lies on her like an untimely frost   IV. v. 28
Upon the sweetest flower of all the field.   (*Capulet*)

Friar Laurence. Come, is the bride ready to go to church?   33
Capulet. Ready to go, but never to return.

She's not well married that lives married long;   77
But she's best married that dies married young.
                           (*Friar Laurence*)

All things that we ordained festival,   84
Turn from their office to black funeral;
Our instruments to melancholy bells,
Our wedding cheer to a sad burial feast,
Our solemn hymns to sullen dirges change,
Our bridal flowers serve for a buried corse,
And all things change them to the contrary.   (*Capulet*)

'When griping grief the heart doth wound,   IV. v. 128
    And doleful dumps the mind oppress,
Then music with her silver sound—
    With speedy help doth lend redress.'   (*Peter*)   146

If I may trust the flattering truth of sleep,   v. i. 1
My dreams presage some joyful news at hand:
My bosom's lord sits lightly in his throne;
And all this day an unaccustom'd spirit
Lifts me above the ground with cheerful thoughts.

                                 (*Romeo*)

Her body sleeps in Capels' monument,   18
And her immortal part with angels lives.   (*Balthasar*)

I do remember an apothecary,—   37
And hereabouts he dwells,—which late I noted
In tatter'd weeds, with overwhelming brows,
Culling of simples; meagre were his looks,
Sharp misery had worn him to the bones:
And in his needy shop a tortoise hung,
An alligator stuff'd, and other skins
Of ill-shaped fishes; and about his shelves
A beggarly account of empty boxes,
Green earthen pots, bladders and musty seeds,
Remnants of packthread and old cakes of roses,
Were thinly scatter'd, to make up a show.
Noting his penury, to myself I said
'An if a man did need a poison now,
Whose sale is present death in Mantua,
Here lives a caitiff wretch would sell it him.'   (*Romeo*)

Being holiday, the beggar's shop is shut.   (*Romeo*)   56

Hold, there is forty ducats: let me have   59
A dram of poison, such soon-speeding gear
As will disperse itself through all the veins
That the life-weary taker may fall dead,
And that the trunk may be discharged of breath
As violently as hasty powder fired
Doth hurry from the fatal cannon's womb.   (*Romeo*)

Romeo.   Famine is in thy cheeks,   69
Need and oppression starveth in thine eyes,
Contempt and beggary hangs upon thy back;
The world is not thy friend nor the world's law;
The world affords no law to make thee rich;
Then be not poor, but break it, and take this.
Apothecary. My poverty, but not my will, consents.

There is thy gold, worse poison to men's souls,   v. i. 80
Doing more murders in this loathsome world,
Than these poor compounds that thou mayst not sell.
                                        (*Romeo*)

Sweet flower, with flowers thy bridal bed I strew,—   v. iii. 12
  O woe! thy canopy is dust and stones;—
Which with sweet water nightly I will dew,
  Or, wanting that, with tears distill'd by moans:
The obsequies that I for thee will keep
Nightly shall be to strew thy grave and weep. (*Paris*)

What cursed foot wanders this way to-night,   19
To cross my obsequies and true love's rite? (*Paris*)

Good gentle youth, tempt not a desperate man. (*Romeo*)   59

One writ with me in sour misfortune's book. (*Romeo*)   82

For here lies Juliet, and her beauty makes   85
This vault a feasting presence full of light. (*Romeo*)

How oft when men are at the point of death   88
Have they been merry! which their keepers call
A lightning before death: O, how may I
Call this a lightning? O my love! my wife!
Death, that hath suck'd the honey of thy breath,
Hath had no power yet upon thy beauty:
Thou art not conquer'd; beauty's ensign yet
Is crimson in thy lips and in thy cheeks,
And death's pale flag is not advanced there. (*Romeo*)

Romeo.   O, here   109
Will I set up my everlasting rest,
And shake the yoke of inauspicious stars
From this world-wearied flesh. Eyes, look your last!
Arms, take your last embrace! and, lips, O you
The doors of breath, seal with a righteous kiss
A dateless bargain to engrossing death!
Come bitter conduct, come, unsavoury guide!
Thou desperate pilot, now at once run on
The dashing rocks thy sea-sick weary bark!
Here's to my love! [*Drinks.*] O true apothecary!
Thy drugs are quick. Thus with a kiss I die. [*Dies.*]

What's here? a cup, closed in my true love's hand?   161
Poison, I see, hath been his timeless end:
O churl! drunk all, and left no friendly drop
To help me after? (*Juliet*)

TIMON OF ATHENS

Timon, a man of free and open nature, lets his generosity outrun his resources, in spite of the warnings of his steward Flavius. Finding himself in difficulties, he applies to Lucullus, Lucius, and other friends on whom he formerly lavished gifts, but now receives only rebuffs. Disillusioned and soured, he first invites his false friends to a banquet, at which nothing is served but warm water, which he throws in their faces, and then withdraws from Athens to live as a hermit in the woods. There he is seen by the general Alcibiades, who also has found Athens a thankless city, and who then goes on to take and rule it, afterwards finding Timon dead. Apemantus, a cynical philosopher, provides a foil to Timon's nobler misanthropy.

My free drift   I. i. 45
Halts not particularly, but moves itself
In a wide sea of wax: no levell'd malice
Infects one comma in the course I hold;
But flies an eagle flight, bold and forth on,
Leaving no tract behind.   (*Poet*)

'Tis not enough to help the feeble up,   107
But to support him after.   (*Timon*)

He that loves to be flattered is worthy o' the flatterer.   232
                         (*Apemantus*)

Aches contract and starve your supple joints!   257
That there should be small love 'mongst these sweet
   knaves,
And all this courtesy!   The strain of man's bred out
Into baboon and monkey.   (*Apemantus*)

            Ceremony was but devised at first   I. ii. 15
To set a gloss on faint deeds, hollow welcomes,
Recanting goodness, sorry ere 'tis shown;
But where there is true friendship, there needs none.
                          (*Timon*)

I wonder men dare trust themselves with men.
                       (*Apemantus*)   43

Here's that which is too weak to be a sinner, honest   58
water, which ne'er left man i' the mire.   (*Apemantus*)

         Immortal gods, I crave no pelf;   63
         I pray for no man but myself:
         Grant I may never prove so fond,
         To trust man on his oath or bond.
                    (*Apemantus's grace*)

I should fear those that dance before me now   148
Would one day stamp upon me: 't has been done;
Men shut their doors against a setting sun.   (*Apemantus*)

I weigh my friend's affection with mine own.   (*Timon*)   222

And so, intending other serious matters,   II. ii. 219
After distasteful looks and these hard fractions,
With certain half-caps and cold-moving nods
They froze me into silence.   (*Flavius*)

    Every man has his fault, and honesty is his: I ha' told   III. i. 29
him on 't, but I could ne'er get him from 't.   (*Lucullus*)

Men must learn now with pity to dispense;   III. ii. 93
For policy sits above conscience.   (*First Stranger*)

Many do keep their chambers are not sick.   III. iv. 74
                                        (*Lucius's servant*)

Nothing emboldens sin so much as mercy.   III. v. 3
                                        (*First Senator*)

   For these my present friends, as they are to me nothing,   III. vi. 93
so in nothing bless them, and to nothing are they welcome.
Uncover, dogs, and lap.   (*Timon*)

                         Live loathed and long,   103
Most smiling, smooth, detested parasites,
Courteous destroyers, affable wolves, meek bears,
You fools of fortune, trencher-friends, time's flies,
Cap and knee slaves, vapours, and minute-jacks!   (*Timon*)

Timon will to the woods; where he shall find   IV. i. 35
The unkindest beast more kinder than mankind.   (*Timon*)

O, the fierce wretchedness that glory brings us!   IV. ii. 30
                                        (*Flavius*)

                         All is oblique;   IV. iii. 18
There's nothing level in our cursed natures,
But direct villany.   Therefore, be abhorr'd
All feasts, societies, and throngs of men!   (*Timon*)

I am Misanthropos, and hate mankind.   53
For thy part, I do wish thou wert a dog,
That I might love thee something.   (*Timon*)

                         His wits   88
Are drown'd and lost in his calamities.   (*Alcibiades*)

                         What, think'st   221
That the bleak air, thy boisterous chamberlain,
Will put thy shirt on warm? will these moss'd trees,
That have outlived the eagle, page thy heels,
And skip where thou point'st out? will the cold brook,
Candied with ice, caudle thy morning taste,
To cure thy o'ernight's surfeit?   (*Apemantus*)

                         But myself,   259
Who had the world as my confectionary,
The mouths, the tongues, the eyes and hearts of men
At duty, more than I could frame employment,
That numberless upon me stuck as leaves
                         286

Do on the oak, have with one winter's brush   IV. iii. 264
Fell from their boughs and left me open, bare
For every storm that blows: I, to bear this,
That never knew but better, is some burden.   (*Timon*)

Timon. Would thou wert clean enough to spit upon!   364
Apemantus. A plague on thee! thou art too bad to curse.

Why should you want?   Behold, the earth hath roots;   420
Within this mile break forth a hundred springs;
The oaks bear mast, the briers scarlet hips;
The bounteous housewife, nature, on each bush
Lays her full mess before you.   (*Timon*)

        I'll example you with thievery: 438
The sun's a thief, and with his great attraction
Robs the vast sea: the moon's an arrant thief,
And her pale fire she snatches from the sun:
The sea's a thief, whose liquid surge resolves
The moon into salt tears: the earth's a thief,
That feeds and breeds by a composture stolen
From general excrement: each thing's a thief:
The laws, your curb and whip, in their rough power,
Have uncheck'd theft.   (*Timon*)

    Has almost charmed me from my profession, by per-   454
suading me to it.   (*Third Bandit*)

Life's uncertain voyage.   (*Timon*)   v. i. 205

Timon hath made his everlasting mansion   218
Upon the beached verge of the salt flood;
Who once a day with his embossed froth
The turbulent surge shall cover: thither come,
And let my grave-stone be your oracle.   (*Timon*)

Here lie I, Timon; who, alive, all living men did hate: v. iv. 72
Pass by and curse thy fill, but pass and stay not here thy
    gait.   (*Timon's epitaph*)

JULIUS CAESAR

This play covers the period shortly before and after Julius Caesar's assassination. In the opening scene the tribunes Flavius and Marullus are rebuking a crowd of Roman tradesmen for so readily turning their admiration from the defeated Pompey to Caesar. In the next we hear that Caesar has been offered a crown and has refused it, and of the arguments by which Cassius persuades the noble-minded Brutus that Caesar must be checked from gaining despotic power. Brutus finally agrees, and with Cassius, Casca, Ligarius, Decius, Metellus, and other conspirators assassinates Caesar in the senate-house, where he has gone in spite of the warnings of a soothsayer and the foreboding dreams of his wife Calpurnia. Brutus then allays public misgivings by a speech which vindicates the motives of the conspirators, but they make the fatal mistake of allowing Mark Antony to deliver a funeral oration after that. He skilfully inflames the mob so that the conspirators have to fly and Antony, Octavius (Caesar's heir), and Lepidus assume charge of affairs. After arranging a cold-blooded proscription of Caesar's enemies they take the field against Brutus and Cassius, who die by their own hands when defeated at Philippi. Notable minor characters are Brutus's wife Portia and his friends Lucilius and Messala.

Flavius. Hence! home, you idle creatures, get you home: I. i. 1
Is this a holiday? what! know you not,
Being mechanical, you ought not walk
Upon a labouring day without the sign
Of your profession?   Speak, what trade art thou?
First Commoner. Why, sir, a carpenter.
Marullus. Where is thy leather apron and thy rule?
What dost thou with thy best apparel on?

A mender of bad soles.   (*Second Commoner*)   15

   Truly, sir, all that I live by is with the awl: I meddle   24
with no tradesman's matters, nor women's matters, but
with awl. I am, indeed, sir, a surgeon to old shoes; when
they are in great danger, I recover them. As proper men
as ever trod upon neat's leather have gone upon my
handiwork. (*Second Commoner*)

Wherefore rejoice? What conquest brings he home?   37
What tributaries follow him to Rome,
To grace in captive bonds his chariot-wheels?
You blocks, you stones, you worse than senseless things!
O you hard hearts, you cruel men of Rome,
Knew you not Pompey? Many a time and oft
Have you climb'd up to walls and battlements,
To towers and windows, yea, to chimney tops,
Your infants in your arms, and there have sat
The live-long day, with patient expectation,
To see great Pompey pass the streets of Rome:
And when you saw his chariot but appear,
Have you not made an universal shout,
That Tiber trembled underneath her banks,
To hear the replication of your sounds
Made in her concave shores?
And do you now put on your best attire?
And do you now cull out a holiday?
And do you now strew flowers in his way
That comes in triumph over Pompey's blood?   (*Marullus*)

They vanish tongue-tied in their guiltiness. (*Flavius*)   67

Peace, ho! Caesar speaks. (*Casca*)   I. ii. 1

When Caesar says 'do this,' it is perform'd. (*Antony*)   10

Soothsayer. Beware the ides of March.   23
Caesar. He is a dreamer; let us leave him: pass.

I am not gamesome: I do lack some part   I. ii. 28
Of that quick spirit that is in Antony.   (*Brutus*)

I have not from your eyes that gentleness   32
And show of love as I was wont to have:
You bear too stubborn and too strange a hand
Over your friend that loves you.   (*Cassius*)

                        I have heard,   58
Where many of the best respect in Rome,
Except immortal Caesar, speaking of Brutus,
And groaning underneath this age's yoke,
Have wish'd that noble Brutus had his eyes.   (*Cassius*)

And since you know you cannot see yourself   67
So well as by reflection, I, your glass,
Will modestly discover to yourself
That of yourself which you yet know not of.   (*Cassius*)

Brutus. What means this shouting?   I do fear, the people   79
Choose Caesar for their king.
Cassius.   Ay, do you fear it?
Then must I think you would not have it so.

What is it that you would impart to me?   84
If it be aught toward the general good,
Set honour in one eye and death i' the other,
And I will look on both indifferently:
For let the gods so speed me as I love
The name of honour more than I fear death.   (*Brutus*)

Well, honour is the subject of my story.   92
I cannot tell what you and other men
Think of this life; but, for my single self,
I had as lief not be as live to be
In awe of such a thing as I myself.
I was born free as Caesar; so were you:
We both have fed as well, and we can both
Endure the winter's cold as well as he:
For once, upon a raw and gusty day,
The troubled Tiber chafing with her shores,
Caesar said to me 'Darest thou, Cassius, now
Leap in with me into this angry flood,
And swim to yonder point?'   Upon the word,
Accoutred as I was, I plunged in
And bade him follow; so indeed he did.
The torrent roar'd, and we did buffet it
With lusty sinews, throwing it aside
And stemming it with hearts of controversy;
But ere we could arrive the point proposed,
Caesar cried 'Help me, Cassius, or I sink!'   (*Cassius*)

                 And this man   I. ii. 115
Is now become a god, and Cassius is
A wretched creature and must bend his body,
If Caesar carelessly but nod on him.
He had a fever when he was in Spain,
And when the fit was on him, I did mark
How he did shake: 'tis true, this god did shake:
His coward lips did from their colour fly,
And that same eye whose bend doth awe the world
Did lose his lustre: I did hear him groan:
Ay, and that tongue of his that bade the Romans
Mark him and write his speeches in their books,
Alas, it cried 'Give me some drink, Titinius,'
As a sick girl. Ye gods, it doth amaze me
A man of such a feeble temper should
So get the start of the majestic world
And bear the palm alone. *(Cassius)*

Why, man, he doth bestride the narrow world   135
Like a Colossus, and we petty men
Walk under his huge legs and peep about
To find ourselves dishonourable graves.
Men at some time are masters of their fates:
The fault, dear Brutus, is not in our stars,
But in ourselves, that we are underlings.
Brutus and Caesar: what should be in that 'Caesar'?
Why should that name be sounded more than yours?
Write then together, yours is as fair a name;
Sound them, it doth become the mouth as well;
Weigh them, it is as heavy; conjure with 'em,
Brutus will start a spirit as soon as Caesar.
Now, in the name of all the gods at once,
Upon what meat doth this our Caesar feed,
That he is grown so great? Age, thou art shamed!
Rome, thou hast lost the breed of noble bloods!
When went there by an age, since the great flood,
But it was famed with more than with one man?
When could they say till now, that talk'd of Rome,
That her wide walls encompass'd but one man?
Now is it Rome indeed and room enough,
When there is in it but one only man.
O, you and I have heard our fathers say,
There was a Brutus once that would have brook'd
The eternal devil to keep his state in Rome
As easily as a king. *(Cassius)*

Till then, my noble friend, chew upon this·   171
Brutus had rather be a villager
Than to repute himself a son of Rome

Under these hard conditions as this time   I. ii. 174
Is like to lay upon us. (*Brutus*)

As they pass by, pluck Casca by the sleeve;   179
And he will, after his sour fashion, tell you
What hath proceeded worthy note to-day. (*Cassius*)

                But, look you, Cassius,   182
The angry spot doth glow on Caesar's brow,
And all the rest look like a chidden train:
Calpurnia's cheek is pale; and Cicero
Looks with such ferret and such fiery eyes
As we have seen him in the Capitol,
Being cross'd in conference by some senators. (*Brutus*)

Caesar. Let me have men about me that are fat;   192
Sleek-headed men and such as sleep o' nights:
Yond Cassius has a lean and hungry look;
He thinks too much: such men are dangerous.
Antony. Fear him not, Caesar; he's not dangerous;
He is a noble Roman and well given.

Yet if my name were liable to fear,   199
I do not know the man I should avoid
So soon as that spare Cassius.   He reads much;
He is a great observer and he looks
Quite through the deeds of men; he loves no plays,
As thou dost, Antony; he hears no music;
Seldom he smiles, and smiles in such a sort
As if he mock'd himself and scorn'd his spirit
That could be moved to smile at any thing.
Such men as he be never at heart's ease
Whiles they behold a greater than themselves,
And therefore are they very dangerous.
I rather tell thee what is to be fear'd
Than what I fear; for always I am Caesar.
Come on my right hand, for this ear is deaf,
And tell me truly what thou think'st of him. (*Cæsar*)

    Still as he refused it the rabblement hooted and clapped   245
their chopped hands and threw up their sweaty night-caps
and uttered such a deal of stinking breath because Caesar
refused the crown that it had almost choked Caesar; for he
swounded and fell down at it: and for mine own part, I
durst not laugh, for fear of opening my lips andreceiving
the bad air. (*Casca*)

Brutus. He hath the falling sickness.   257
Cassius. No, Caesar hath it not; but you and I
And honest Casca, we have the falling sickness.

When he perceived the common herd was glad he   I. ii. 268
refused the crown, he plucked me ope his doublet and
offered them his throat to cut.   (*Casca*)

Cassius. Did Cicero say any thing?   281
Casca. Ay, he spoke Greek.
Cassius. To what effect?
Casca. Nay, an I tell you that, I'll ne'er look you in the
face again: but those that understood him smiled at one
another and shook their heads; but for mine own part,
it was Greek to me.

Cassius. Will you dine with me to-morrow?   294
Casca. Ay, if I be alive and your mind hold and your
dinner worth the eating.

Brutus. What a blunt fellow is this grown to be!   299
He was quick mettle when he went to school.
Cassius. So is he now in execution
Of any bold or noble enterprise,
However he puts on this tardy form.
This rudeness is a sauce to his good wit,
Which gives men stomach to digest his words
With better appetite.

Well, Brutus, thou art noble; yet, I see,   312
Thy honourable metal may be wrought
From that it is disposed: therefore it is meet
That noble minds keep ever with their likes;
For who so firm that cannot be seduced?   (*Cassius*)

Are not you moved, when all the sway of earth   I. iii. 3
Shakes like a thing unfirm?   O Cicero,
I have seen tempests, when the scolding winds
Have rived the knotty oaks, and I have seen
The ambitious ocean swell and rage and foam,
To be exalted with the threatening clouds:
But never till to-night, never till now,
Did I go through a tempest dropping fire.   (*Casca*)

A common slave—you know him well by sight—   15
Held up his left hand, which did flame and burn
Like twenty torches join'd, and yet his hand,
Not sensible of fire, remain'd unscorch'd.
Besides—I ha' not since put up my sword—
Against the Capitol I met a lion,
Who glaz'd upon me, and went surly by,
Without annoying me: and there were drawn
Upon a heap a hundred ghastly women,
Transformed with their fear; who swore they saw

Men all in fire walk up and down the streets.   I. iii. 25
And yesterday the bird of night did sit
Even at noon-day upon the market-place,
Hooting and shrieking.   (*Casca*)

Casca. Cassius, what night is this!   42
Cassius. A very pleasing night to honest men.
Casca. Who ever knew the heavens menace so?
Cassius. Those that have known the earth so full of faults.
For my part, I have walk'd about the streets,
Submitting me unto the perilous night,
And, thus unbraced, Casca, as you see,
Have bared my bosom to the thunder-stone;
And when the cross blue lightning seem'd to open
The breast of heaven, I did present myself
Even in the aim and very flash of it.

Now could I, Casca, name to thee a man,   72
Most like this dreadful night,
That thunders, lightens, opens graves, and roars
As doth the lion in the Capitol,
A man no mightier than thyself or me
In personal action, yet prodigious grown
And fearful, as these strange eruptions are.   (*Cassius*)

But, woe the while! our fathers' minds are dead,   82
And we are govern'd with our mothers' spirits;
Our yoke and sufferance show us womanish.   (*Cassius*)

I know where I will wear this dagger then;   89
Cassius from bondage will deliver Cassius:
Therein, ye gods, you make the weak most strong;
Therein, ye gods, you tyrants do defeat:
Nor stony tower, nor walls of beaten brass,
Nor airless dungeon, nor strong links of iron,
Can be retentive to the strength of spirit;
But life, being weary of these worldly bars,
Never lacks power to dismiss itself.   (*Cassius*)

Poor man! I know he would not be a wolf,   104
But that he sees the Romans are but sheep:
He were no lion, were not Romans hinds.   (*Cassius*)

Those that with haste will make a mighty fire   107
Begin it with weak straws.   (*Cassius*)

You speak to Casca, and to such a man   116
That is no fleering tell-tale.   (*Casca*)

'Tis Cinna; I do know him by his gait.   (*Cassius*)   132

O, he sits high in all the people's hearts: I. iii. 157
And that which would appear offence is us,
His countenance, like richest alchemy,
Will change to virtue and to worthiness.   (*Casca*)

It must be by his death: and for my part,   II. i. 10
I know no personal cause to spurn at him,
But for the general.   He would be crown'd:
How that might change his nature, there's the question.
It is the bright day that brings forth the adder;
And that craves wary walking.   (*Brutus*)

                    But 'tis a common proof,   21
That lowliness is young ambition's ladder,
Whereto the climber-upward turns his face;
But when he once attains the upmost round,
He then unto the ladder turns his back,
Looks in the clouds, scorning the base degrees
By which he did ascend.   (*Brutus*)

And therefore think him as a serpent's egg   32
Which, hatch'd, would, as his kind, grow mischievous,
And kill him in the shell.   (*Brutus*)

Between the acting of a dreadful thing   62
And the first motion, all the interim is
Like a phantasma, or a hideous dream:
The Genius and the mortal instruments
Are then in council; and the state of man,
Like to a little kingdom, suffers then
The nature of an insurrection.   (*Brutus*)

                    O conspiracy,   77
Shamest thou to show thy dangerous brow by night,
When evils are most free?   O, then by day
Where wilt thou find a cavern dark enough
To mask thy monstrous visage?   Seek none, conspiracy;
Hide it in smiles and affability:
For if thou path, thy native semblance on,
Not Erebus itself were dim enough
To hide thee from prevention.   (*Brutus*)

Brutus. Give me your hands all over, one by one.   112
Cassius. And let us swear our resolution.
Brutus. No, not an oath: if not the face of men,
The sufferance of our souls, the time's abuse,—
If these be motives weak, break off betimes,
And every man hence to his idle bed;
So let high-sighted tyranny range on,
Till each man drop by lottery.   But if these,

As I am sure they do, bear fire enough,   II. i. 120
To kindle cowards and to steel with valour
The melting spirits of women, then, countrymen,
What need we any spur but our own cause
To prick us to redress? what other bond
Than secret Romans, that have spoke the word,
And will not palter? and what other oath
Than honesty to honesty engaged,
That this shall be, or we will fall for it?

O, let us have him, for his silver hairs   144
Will purchase us a good opinion
And buy men's voices to commend our deeds. (*Metellus*)

O, name him not: let us not break with him;   150
For he will never follow any thing
That other men begin. (*Brutus*)

Let us be sacrificers, but not butchers, Caius.   166
We all stand up against the spirit of Caesar;
And in the spirit of men there is no blood:
O, that we then could come by Caesar's spirit,
And not dismember Caesar! But, alas,
Caesar must bleed for it! And, gentle friends,
Let's kill him boldly, but not wrathfully;
Let's carve him as a dish fit for the gods,
Not hew him as a carcass fit for hounds. (*Brutus*)

For he is superstitious grown of late,   195
Quite from the main opinion he held once
Of fantasy, of dreams and ceremonies. (*Cassius*)

I can o'ersway him; for he loves to hear   203
That unicorns may be betray'd with trees,
And bears with glasses, elephants with holes,
Lions with toils and men with flatterers;
But when I tell him he hates flatterers,
He says he does, being then most flattered. (*Decius*)

Boy! Lucius! Fast asleep? It is no matter;   229
Enjoy the honey-heavy dew of slumber:
Thou hast no figures nor no fantasies,
Which busy care draws in the brains of men;
Therefore thou sleep'st so sound. (*Brutus*)

                              Wherefore rise you now?   234
It is not for your health thus to commit
Your weak condition to the raw cold morning. (*Brutus*)

You suddenly arose, and walk'd about,   II. i. 239
Musing and sighing, with your arms across,
And when I ask'd you what the matter was,
You stared upon me with ungentle looks;
I urged you further; then you scratch'd your head,
And too impatiently stamp'd with your foot;
Yet I insisted, yet you answer'd not,
But, with an angry wafture of your hand,
Gave sign for me to leave you.   (*Portia*)

Portia.   Dwell I but in the suburbs   285
Of your good pleasure?   If it be no more,
Portia is Brutus' harlot, not his wife.
Brutus. You are my true and honourable wife,
As dear to me as are the ruddy drops
That visit my sad heart.

I grant I am a woman; but withal   292
A woman that Lord Brutus took to wife:
I grant I am a woman; but withal
A woman well reputed, Cato's daughter.
Think you I am no stronger than my sex,
Being so father'd and so husbanded?   (*Portia*)

                  O ye gods,   302
Render me worthy of this noble wife!   (*Brutus*)

Vouchsafe good morrow from a feeble tongue. (*Ligarius*)   313

Ligarius.   What's to do?   326
Brutus. A piece of work that will make sick men whole.
Ligarius. But are not some whole that we must make sick?

Caesar shall forth: the things that threaten'd me   II. ii. 10
Ne'er look'd but on my back; when they shall see
The face of Caesar, they are vanished.   (*Caesar*)

A lioness hath whelped in the streets;   17
And graves have yawn'd, and yielded up their dead;
Fierce fiery warriors fought upon the clouds,
In ranks and squadrons and right form of war,
Which drizzled blood upon the Capitol;
The noise of battle hurtled in the air,
Horses did neigh, and dying men did groan,
And ghosts did shriek and squeal about the streets.
                         (*Calpurnia*)

When beggars die, there are no comets seen;   30
The heavens themselves blaze forth the death of princes.
                         (*Calpurnia*)

Cowards die many times before their deaths;   II. ii. 32
The valiant never taste of death but once.
Of all the wonders that I yet have heard,
It seems to me most strange that men should fear:
Seeing that death, a necessary end,
Will come when it will come.   (*Caesar*)

Plucking the entrails of an offering forth,   39
They could not find a heart within the beast.   (*Servant*)

      Danger knows full well   44
That Caesar is more dangerous than he:
We are two lions litter'd in one day,
And I the elder and more terrible.   (*Caesar*)

She dreamt to-night she saw my statua,   76
Which, like a fountain with an hundred spouts,
Did run pure blood; and many lusty Romans
Came smiling, and did bathe their hands in it.   (*Caesar*)

See! Antony, that revels long o' nights,   116
Is notwithstanding up.   (*Caesar*)

My heart laments that virtue cannot live   II. iii. 13
Out of the teeth of emulation.   (*Artemidorus*)

I would have had thee there, and here again,   II. iv. 4
Ere I can tell thee what thou shouldst do there. (*Portia*)

I have a man's mind, but a woman's might.   8
How hard it is for women to keep counsel!   (*Portia*)

Caesar. The ides of March are come.   III. i. 1
Soothsayer. Ay, Caesar; but not gone.

Artemidorus. Hail, Caesar! read this schedule.   3
Decius. Trebonius doth desire you to o'er-read
At your best leisure, this his humble suit.

What touches us ourself shall be last served.   (*Caesar*)   8

These couchings and these lowly courtesies   36
Might fire the blood of ordinary men,
And turn pre-ordinance and first decree
Into the law of children.   Be not fond,
To think that Caesar bears such rebel blood
That will be thaw'd from the true quality
With that which melteth fools; I mean, sweet words,
Low-crooked court'sies and base spaniel-fawning.
            (*Caesar*)

Know, Caesar doth not wrong, nor without cause   III. i. 47
Will he be satisfied.   (*Caesar*)

If I could pray to move, prayers would move me: 59
But I am constant as the northern star,
Of whose true-fix'd and resting quality
There is no fellow in the firmament.
The skies are painted with unnumber'd sparks,
They are all fire and every one doth shine,
But there's but one in all doth hold his place:
So in the world; 'tis furnish'd well with men,
And men are flesh and blood, and apprehensive;
Yet in the number I do know but one
That unassailable holds on his rank,
Unshaked of motion.   (*Caesar*)

Cinna. O Caesar,—   74
Caesar.   Hence! wilt thou lift up Olympus?
Decius. Great Caesar,—
Caesar.   Doth not Brutus bootless kneel?
Casca. Speak, hands, for me!
    [*Casca first, then the other conspirators and Marcus
            Brutus stab Caesar.*]
Caesar. Et tu, Brute!   Then fall, Caesar!   [*Dies.*]
Cinna. Liberty!   Freedom!   Tyranny is dead!
Run hence, proclaim, cry it about the streets.

People and senators, be not affrighted;   82
Fly not; stand still: ambition's debt is paid.   (*Brutus*)

Brutus. That we shall die, we know; 'tis but the time   99
And drawing days out, that men stand upon.
Cassius. Why, he that cuts off twenty years of life
Cuts off so many years of fearing death.
Brutus. Grant that, and then is death a benefit.

Cassius.   How many ages hence   111
Shall this our lofty scene be acted over
In states unborn and accents yet unknown!
Brutus. How many times shall Caesar bleed in sport,
That now on Pompey's basis lies along
No worthier than the dust!

Brutus is noble, wise, valiant, and honest;   126
Caesar was mighty, bold, royal, and loving:
Say I love Brutus, and I honour him;
Say I fear'd Caesar, honour'd him and loved him.
                (*Servant, giving Antony's message*)

O mighty Caesar! dost thou lie so low?   III. i. 148
Are all thy conquests, glories, triumphs, spoils,
Shrunk to this little measure?   (*Antony*)

                        Live a thousand years,   159
I shall not find myself so apt to die:
No place will please me so, no mean of death,
As here by Caesar, and by you cut off,
The choice and master spirits of this age.   (*Antony*)

As fire drives out fire, so pity pity.   (*Brutus*)   171

To you our swords have leaden points, Mark Antony.   173
                        (*Brutus*)

Let each man render me his bloody hand.   (*Antony*)   184

Though last, not least in love.   (*Antony*)   189

My credit now stands on such slippery ground,   191
That one of two bad ways you must conceit me,
Either a coward or a flatterer.   (*Antony*)

O, pardon me, thou bleeding piece of earth,   254
That I am meek and gentle with these butchers!
Thou art the ruins of the noblest man
That ever lived in the tide of times.
Woe to the hand that shed this costly blood!   (*Antony*)

Domestic fury and fierce civil strife   263
Shall cumber all the parts of Italy;
Blood and destruction shall be so in use
And dreadful objects so familiar
That mothers shall but smile when they behold
Their infants quarter'd with the hands of war;
All pity choked with custom of fell deeds:
And Caesar's spirit, ranging for revenge,
With Ate by his side come hot from hell,
Shall in these confines with a monarch's voice
Cry 'Havoc,' and let slip the dogs of war.   (*Antony*)

We will be satisfied; let us be satisfied.   (*Citizens*)   III. ii. 1

Not that I loved Caesar less, but that I loved Rome more.   23
                        (*Brutus*)

300

As Caesar loved me, I weep for him; as he was fortunate,
I rejoice at it; as he was valiant, I honour him: but as he
was ambitious, I slew him.   There is tears for his love;
joy for his fortune; honour for his valour; and death for
his ambition.   Who is here so base that would be a bondman?   If any, speak; for him have I offended.   Who is
here so rude that would not be a Roman?   If any, speak;
for him have I offended.   Who is here so vile that will not
love his country?   If any, speak; for him have I offended.
I pause for a reply.   (*Brutus*)

III. ii. 26

Friends, Romans, countrymen, lend me your ears;
I come to bury Caesar, not to praise him.
The evil that men do lives after them;
The good is oft interred with their bones;
So let it be with Caesar.   The noble Brutus
Hath told you Caesar was ambitious:
If it were so, it was a grievous fault,
And grievously hath Caesar answer'd it.
Here, under leave of Brutus and the rest—
For Brutus is an honourable man;
So are they all, all honourable men—
Come I to speak in Caesar's funeral.
He was my friend, faithful and just to me:
But Brutus says he was ambitious;
And Brutus is an honourable man.
He hath brought many captives home to Rome,
Whose ransoms did the general coffers fill:
Did this in Caesar seem ambitious?
When that the poor have cried, Caesar hath wept:
Ambition should be made of sterner stuff:
Yet Brutus says he was ambitious;
And Brutus is an honourable man.
You all did see that on the Lupercal
I thrice presented him a kingly crown,
Which he did thrice refuse: was this ambition?
Yet Brutus says he was ambitious;
And, sure, he is an honourable man.
I speak not to disprove what Brutus spoke,
But here I am to speak what I do know.
You all did love him once, not without cause:
What cause withholds you then, to mourn for him?
O judgment! thou art fled to brutish beasts,
And men have lost their reason.   Bear with me;
My heart is in the coffin there with Caesar,
And I must pause till it come back to me.   (*Antony*)

78

If thou consider rightly of the matter,
Caesar has had great wrong.   (*Second Citizen*)

114

301

Poor soul! his eyes are red as fire with weeping.   III. ii. 120
                                    (*Second Citizen*)

But yesterday the word of Caesar might   123
Have stood against the world; now lies he there,
And none so poor to do him reverence.   (*Antony*)

But here's a parchment with the seal of Caesar;   133
I found it in his closet, 'tis his will:
Let but the commons hear this testament—
Which, pardon me, I do not mean to read—
And they would go and kiss dead Caesar's wounds
And dip their napkins in his sacred blood,
Yea, beg a hair of him for memory,
And, dying, mention it within their wills,
Bequeathing it as a rich legacy
Unto their issue.   (*Antony*)

It is not meet you know how Caesar loved you.   146
You are not wood, you are not stones, but men;
And, being men, hearing the will of Caesar,
It will inflame you, it will make you mad:
'Tis good you know not that you are his heirs;
For, if you should, O, what would come of it!   (*Antony*)

Antony. I fear I wrong the honourable men   156
Whose daggers have stabb'd Caesar; I do fear it.
Fourth Citizen. They were traitors: honourable men!

If you have tears, prepare to shed them now.   173
You all do know this mantle: I remember
The first time ever Caesar put it on;
'Twas on a summer's evening, in his tent,
That day he overcame the Nervii:
Look, in this place ran Cassius' dagger through:
See what a rent the envious Casca made:
Through this the well-beloved Brutus stabb'd;
And, as he pluck'd his cursed steel away,
Mark how the blood of Caesar follow'd it,
As rushing out of doors, to be resolved
If Brutus so unkindly knock'd, or no;
For Brutus, as you know, was Caesar's angel:
Judge, O you gods, how dearly Caesar loved him!
This was the most unkindest cut of all;
For when the noble Caesar saw him stab,
Ingratitude, more strong than traitors' arms,
Quite vanquish'd him: then burst his mighty heart;
And, in his mantle muffling up his face,
Even at the base of Pompey's statua,
Which all the while ran blood, great Caesar fell.

O, what a fall was there, my countrymen!   III. ii. 194
Then I, and you, and all of us fell down,
Whilst bloody treason flourish'd over us.   (*Antony*)

I come not, friends, to steal away your hearts: 220
I am no orator, as Brutus is;
But, as you know me all, a plain blunt man,
That love my friend; and that they know full well
That gave me public leave to speak of him:
For I have neither wit, nor words, nor worth,
Action, nor utterance, nor the power of speech,
To stir men's blood: I only speak right on;
To tell you that which you yourselves do know;
Show you sweet Caesar's wounds, poor poor dumb mouths,
And bid them speak for me: but were I Brutus,
And Brutus Antony, there were an Antony
Would ruffle up your spirits and put a tongue
In every wound of Caesar that should move
The stones of Rome to rise and mutiny.   (*Antony*)

Moreover, he hath left you all his walks,   252
His private arbours and new-planted orchards,
On this side Tiber; he hath left them you,
And to your heirs for ever, common pleasures,
To walk abroad, and recreate yourselves.
Here was a Caesar! when comes such another?   (*Antony*)

Now let it work.   Mischief, thou art afoot,   265
Take thou what course thou wilt!   (*Antony*)

Third Citizen. Your name, sir, truly.   III. iii. 28
Cinna. Truly, my name is Cinna.
First Citizen. Tear him to pieces; he's a conspirator.
Cinna. I am Cinna the poet, I am Cinna the poet.
Fourth Citizen. Tear him for his bad verses, tear him for
his bad verses.
Cinna. I am not Cinna the conspirator.
Fourth Citizen. It is no matter, his name's Cinna; pluck
but his name out of his heart, and turn him going.

Octavius. Your brother too must die; consent you,   IV. i. 2
    Lepidus?
Lepidus. I do consent,—
Octavius.   Prick him down, Antony.
Lepidus. Upon condition Publius shall not live,
Who is your sister's son, Mark Antony.
Antony. He shall not live; look, with a spot I damn him.

This is a slight unmeritable man,   12
Meet to be sent on errands.   (*Antony*)

And though we lay these honours on this man,   IV. i. 19
To ease ourselves of divers slanderous loads,
He shall but bear them as the ass bears gold,
To groan and sweat under the business,
Either led or driven, as we point the way;
And having brought our treasure where we will,
Then take we down his load, and turn him off,
Like to the empty ass, to shake his ears,
And graze in commons. (*Antony*)

Octavius. He's a tried and valiant soldier.   28
Antony. So is my horse, Octavius; and for that
I do appoint him store of provender:
It is a creature that I teach to fight,
To wind, to stop, to run directly on,
His corporal motion govern'd by my spirit.
And, in some taste, is Lepidus but so;
He must be taught and train'd and bid go forth;
A barren-spirited fellow; one that feeds
On abjects, orts, and imitations,
Which, out of use and staled by other men,
Begin his fashion: do not talk of him
But as a property.

And some that smile have in their hearts, I fear,   50
Millions of mischiefs. (*Octavius*)

Brutus. How he received you, let me be resolved.   IV. ii. 14
Lucilius. With courtesy and with respect enough;
But not with such familiar instances,
Nor with such free and friendly conference,
As he hath used of old.

When love begins to sicken and decay,   20
It useth an enforced ceremony.
There are no tricks in plain and simple faith. (*Brutus*)

That you have wrong'd me doth appear in this. (*Cassius*) IV. iii. 1

Let me tell you, Cassius, you yourself   9
Are much condemn'd to have an itching palm;
To sell and mart your offices for gold
To undeservers. (*Brutus*)

Did not great Julius bleed for justice' sake?   19
What villain touch'd his body, that did stab,
And not for justice? What, shall one of us,
That struck the foremost man of all this world
But for supporting robbers, shall we now
Contaminate our fingers with base bribes,

And sell the mighty space of our large honours   IV. iii, 25
For so much trash as may be grasped thus?
I had rather be a dog, and bay the moon,
Than such a Roman.   (*Brutus*)

Cassius. Urge me no more, I shall forget myself: 35
Have mind upon your health, tempt me no farther.
Brutus. Away, slight man!

Must I give way and room to your rash choler?   39
Shall I be frighted when a madman stares?   (*Brutus*)

                    Fret till your proud heart break;   42
Go show your slaves how choleric you are,
And make your bondmen tremble.   Must I budge?
Must I observe you? must I stand and crouch
Under your testy humour?   By the gods,
You shall digest the venom of your spleen,
Though it do split you; for, from this day forth,
I'll use you for my mirth, yea, for my laughter,
When you are waspish.   (*Brutus*)

Cassius. When Caesar lived, he durst not thus have moved   58
    me.
Brutus. Peace, peace! you durst not so have tempted him.

Cassius. Do not presume too much upon my love;   63
I may do that I shall be sorry for.
Brutus. You have done that you should be sorry for.
There is no terror, Cassius, in your threats,
For I am arm'd so strong in honesty
That they pass by me as the idle wind,
Which I respect not.

By heaven, I had rather coin my heart,   72
And drop my blood for drachmas, than to wring
From the hard hands of peasants their vile trash
By any indirection: I did send
To you for gold to pay my legions,
Which you denied me: was that done like Cassius?
Should I have answer'd Caius Cassius so?
When Marcus Brutus grows so covetous,
To lock such rascal counters from his friends,
Be ready, gods, with all your thunderbolts;
Dash him to pieces.   (*Brutus*)

A friend should bear his friend's infirmities,   86
But Brutus makes mine greater than they are. (*Cassius*)
L   305

Cassius. You love me not.   IV. iii. 89
Brutus.   I do not like your faults.
Cassius. A friendly eye could never see such faults.

For Cassius is aweary of the world;   95
Hated by one he loves; braved by his brother;
Check'd like a bondman; all his faults observed,
Set in a note-book, learn'd, and conn'd by rote,
To cast into my teeth.   (*Cassius*)

O Cassius, you are yoked with a lamb   110
That carries anger as the flint bears fire;
Who, much enforced, shows a hasty spark,
And straight is cold again.   (*Brutus*)

Have you not love enough to bear with me,   119
When that rash humour which my mother gave me
Makes me forgetful?   (*Cassius*)

Poet. Love, and be friends, as two such men should be;   131
For I have seen more years, I'm sure, than ye.
Cassius. Ha, ha! how vilely doth this cynic rhyme!

What should the wars do with these jigging fools?   137
Companion, hence!   (*Brutus*)

Brutus. O Cassius, I am sick of many griefs.   144
Cassius. Of your philosophy you make no use,
If you give place to accidental evils.

How 'scaped I killing when I cross'd you so?   (*Cassius*)   150

                           She fell distract,   155
And, her attendants absent, swallow'd fire.   (*Brutus*)

Brutus. With meditating that she must die once,   191
I have the patience to endure it now.
Messala. Even so great men great losses should endure.

Good reasons must, of force, give place to better.   203
                                        (*Brutus*)

There is a tide in the affairs of men,   218
Which, taken at the flood, leads on to fortune;
Omitted, all the voyage of their life
Is bound in shallows and in miseries.
On such a full sea are we now afloat;
And we must take the current when it serves,
Or lose our ventures.   (*Brutus*)

The deep of night is crept upon our talk,   IV. iii. 226
And nature must obey necessity.   (*Brutus*)

Let me see, let me see; is not the leaf turn'd down   273
Where I left reading?   Here it is, I think. (*Brutus*)

Brutus. Speak to me what thou art.   281
Ghost of Caesar. Thy evil spirit, Brutus.
Brutus. Why comest thou?
Ghost. To tell thee thou shalt see me at Philippi.
Brutus. Well; then I shall see thee again?
Ghost. Ay, at Philippi.
Brutus. Why, I will see thee at Philippi, then.
                      [*Exit Ghost.*]

Antony. Octavius, lead your battle softly on,   v. i. 16
Upon the left hand of the even field.
Octavius. Upon the right hand I; keep thou the left.
Antony. Why do you cross me in this exigent?
Octavius. I do not cross you; but I will do so.

Good words are better than bad strokes, Octavius.   29
                            (*Brutus*)

But for your words, they rob the Hybla bees,   34
And leave them honeyless.   (*Cassius*)

Octavius. I was not born to die on Brutus' sword.   58
Brutus. O, if thou wert the noblest of thy strain,
Young man, thou couldst not die more honourable.
Cassius. A peevish schoolboy, worthless of such honour,
Join'd with a masker and a reveller!
Antony. Old Cassius still!

Why now, blow wind, swell billow and swim bark!   67
The storm is up, and all is on the hazard.   (*Cassius*)

For I am fresh of spirit and resolved   91
To meet all perils very constantly.   (*Cassius*)

But since the affairs of men rest still incertain,   96
Let's reason with the worst that may befall.   (*Cassius*)

No, Cassius, no: think not, thou noble Roman,   111
That ever Brutus will go bound to Rome;
He bears too great a mind.   But this same day
Must end that work the ides of March begun;
And whether we shall meet again I know not.
Therefore our everlasting farewell take:
For ever, and for ever, farewell, Cassius!

If we do meet again, why, we shall smile;   v. i. 118
If not, why then, this parting was well made.   (*Brutus*)

                    O, that a man might know   123
The end of this day's business ere it come!
But it sufficeth that the day will end,
And then the end is known.   (*Brutus*)

Fly further off, my lord, fly further off;   v. iii. 9
Mark Antony is in your tents, my lord.   (*Pindarus*)

O, coward that I am, to live so long,   34
To see my best friend ta'en before my face!

Cassius.   Caesar, thou art revenged,   45
Even with the sword that kill'd thee.   [*Dies.*]

                    O setting sun,   60
As in thy red rays thou dost sink to night,
So in his red blood Cassius' day is set;
The sun of Rome is set!   Our day is gone;
Clouds, dews, and dangers come; our deeds are done!
                                        (*Titinius*)

O hateful error, melancholy's child,   67
Why dost thou show to the apt thoughts of men
The things that are not?   (*Messala*)

O Julius Caesar, thou art mighty yet!   94
Thy spirit walks abroad, and turns our swords
In our own proper entrails.   (*Brutus*)

The last of all the Romans, fare thee well!   99
It is impossible that ever Rome
Should breed thy fellow.   Friends, I owe more tears
To this dead man than you shall see me pay.
I shall find time, Cassius, I shall find time.   (*Brutus*)

Brutus. Yet, countrymen, O, yet hold up your heads!   v. iv. 1
Cato. What bastard doth not?   Who will go with me?
I will proclaim my name about the field:
I am the son of Marcus Cato, ho!
A foe to tyrants, and my country's friend;
I am the son of Marcus Cato, ho!

Safe, Antony; Brutus is safe enough: 20
I dare assure thee that no enemy
Shall ever take alive the noble Brutus:
The gods defend him from so great a shame!
When you do find him, or alive or dead,
He will be found like Brutus, like himself.   (*Lucilius*)

Our enemies have beat us to the pit:
It is more worthy to leap in ourselves,
Than tarry till they push us.   (*Brutus*)

My heart doth joy that yet in all my life   34
I found no man but he was true to me.   (*Brutus*)

Brutus. [*Running on his sword.*] Caesar, now be still: 50
I kill'd not thee with half so good a will.   [*Dies.*]

This was the noblest Roman of them all: 68
All the conspirators save only he
Did what they did in envy of great Caesar;
He only, in a general honest thought
And common good to all, made one of them.
His life was gentle, and the elements
So mix'd in him that Nature might stand up
And say to all the world 'This was a man!'   (*Antony*)

MACBETH

Riding back after a victorious battle against rebels, the Scottish generals Macbeth and Banquo are met by three witches, who prophesy that Macbeth shall be king and Banquo the ancestor of kings. Influenced by this prediction, and egged on by his wife, Macbeth murders King Duncan while the king is a guest at his castle, and usurps the throne. Suspicion and insecurity drive him to further murders, first of Banquo, whose ghost later appears to haunt him, and then of the wife and children of Macduff, against whom he had been warned in a second interview with the witches, who nevertheless encourage him with the assurance that 'none of woman born' can harm him and that he will be undefeated 'till Birnam wood come to Dunsinane.' Lady Macbeth, tortured by her guilty conscience, walks in her sleep, babbling out thoughts of the crime, and soon afterwards dies. Meanwhile Duncan's son Malcolm marches with English support against Macbeth, who realizes that his case is desperate. Courageous to the last, even when he finds that the witches' prophecies have betrayed him, he is slain in hand-to-hand combat with Macduff, who with Lennox, Ross, Angus, and other Scottish lords has come to support Malcolm.

First Witch. When shall we three meet again   I. i. 1
In thunder, lightning, or in rain?
Second Witch. When the hurlyburly's done,
When the battle's lost and won.
Third Witch. That will be ere the set of sun.
First Witch. Where the place?
Second Witch.   Upon the heath.
Third Witch. There to meet with Macbeth.

Fair is foul and foul is fair: 11
Hover through the fog and filthy air. (*All Witches*)

      The merciless Macdonwald— I. ii. 9
Worthy to be a rebel, for to that
The multiplying villanies of nature
Do swarm upon him—from the western isles
Of kerns and gallowglasses is supplied;
And fortune, on his damned quarrel smiling,
Show'd like a rebel's whore: but all's too weak:
For brave Macbeth—well he deserves that name—
Disdaining fortune, with his brandish'd steel,
Which smoked with bloody execution,
Like valour's minion carved out his passage
Till he faced the slave;
Which ne'er shook hands, nor bade farewell to him,
Till he unseam'd him from the nave to the chaps,
And fix'd his head upon our battlements. (*Sergeant*)

As cannon overcharged with double cracks, so they 37
Doubly redoubled strokes upon the foe. (*Sergeant*)

What a haste looks through his eyes! So should he look 46
That seems to speak things strange. (*Lennox*)

Where the Norweyan banners flout the sky   49
And fan our people cold. (*Ross*)

Till that Bellona's bridegroom, lapp'd in proof,   54
Confronted him with self-comparisons,
Point against point rebellious, arm 'gainst arm,
Curbing his lavish spirit. (*Ross*)

Nor would we deign him burial of his men   60
Till he disbursed at Saint Colme's inch
Ten thousand dollars to our general use. (*Ross*)

A sailor's wife had chestnuts in her lap,   I. iii. 4
And munch'd, and munch'd, and munch'd:—'Give me,'
  quoth I:

'Aroint thee, witch!' the rump-fed ronyon cries.   I. iii. 6
Her husband's to Aleppo gone, master o' the Tiger:
But in a sieve I'll thither sail,
And, like a rat without a tail,
I'll do, I'll do, and I'll do.   (*First Witch*)

I will drain him dry as hay: 18
Sleep shall neither night nor day
Hang upon his pent-house lid;
He shall live a man forbid:
Weary se'nnights nine times nine
Shall he dwindle, peak and pine:
Though his bark cannot be lost,
Yet it shall be tempest-tost.   (*First Witch*)

The weird sisters, hand in hand,   32
Posters of the sea and land,
Thus do go about, about:
Thrice to thine and thrice to mine
And thrice again, to make up nine.
Peace! the charm's wound up.   (*All Witches*)

So foul and fair a day I have not seen.   (*Macbeth*)   38

How far is't call'd to Forres?   What are these   39
So wither'd and so wild in their attire,
That look not like the inhabitants o' the earth,
And yet are on't?   (*Banquo*)

If you can look into the seeds of time,   58
And say which grain will grow and which will not,
Speak then to me, who neither beg nor fear
Your favours nor your hate.   (*Banquo*)

The earth hath bubbles, as the water has,   79
And these are of them.   (*Banquo*)

Were such things here as we do speak about?   83
Or have we eaten on the insane root
That takes the reason prisoner?   (*Banquo*)

                                    As thick as hail   97
Came post with post.   (*Ross*)

What, can the devil speak true?   (*Banquo*)   107

And oftentimes, to win us to our harm,   123
The instruments of darkness tell us truths,
Win us with honest trifles, to betray's
In deepest consequence.   (*Banquo*)
                              312

Two truths are told,   I. iii. 127
As happy prologues to the swelling act
Of the imperial theme.   (*Macbeth*)

Why do I yield to that suggestion   134
Whose horrid image doth unfix my hair
And make my seated heart knock at my ribs,
Against the use of nature? Present fears
Are less than horrible imaginings.   (*Macbeth*)

Look, how our partner's rapt.   (*Banquo*)
                                                      142

If chance will have me king, why, chance may crown me,   143
Without my stir.   (*Macbeth*)

New honours come upon him,   144
Like our strange garments, cleave not to their mould
But with the aid of use.   (*Banquo*)

Come what come may,   146
Time and the hour runs through the roughest day.
                                              (*Macbeth*)

Nothing in his life   I. iv. 7
Became him like the leaving it; he died
As one that had been studied in his death
To throw away the dearest thing he owed,
As 'twere a careless trifle.   (*Malcolm*)

There's no art   11
To find the mind's construction in the face:
He was a gentleman on whom I built
An absolute trust.   (*Duncan*)

Would thou hadst less deserved,   18
That the proportion both of thanks and payment
Might have been mine!   (*Duncan*)

Stars, hide your fires;   50
Let not light see my black and deep desires.   (*Macbeth*)

Yet do I fear thy nature;   I. v. 17
It is too full o' the milk of human kindness
To catch the nearest way: thou wouldst be great;
Art not without ambition, but without
The illness should attend it: what thou wouldst highly,
That wouldst thou holily; wouldst not play false,
And yet wouldst wrongly win.   (*Lady Macbeth*)

*L   313

The raven himself is hoarse   I. v. 39
That croaks the fatal entrance of Duncan
Under my battlements.   Come, you spirits
That tend on mortal thoughts, unsex me here,
And fill me from the crown to the toe top-full
Of direst cruelty! make thick my blood;
Stop up the access and passage to remorse,
That no compunctious visitings of nature
Shake my fell purpose, nor keep peace between
The effect and it!   Come to my woman's breasts,
And take my milk for gall, you murdering ministers,
Wherever in your sightless substances
You wait on nature's mischief!   Come, thick night,
And pall thee in the dunnest smoke of hell,
That my keen knife see not the wound it makes,
Nor heaven peep through the blanket of the dark,
To cry 'Hold, hold!'   (*Lady Macbeth*)

Your face, my thane, is as a book where men   63
May read strange matters.   To beguile the time,
Look like the time; bear welcome in your eye,
Your hand, your tongue: look like the innocent flower,
But be the serpent under 't.   (*Lady Macbeth*)

Duncan. This castle hath a pleasant seat; the air   I. vi. 1
Nimbly and sweetly recommends itself
Unto our gentle senses.
Banquo.   This guest of summer,
The temple-haunting martlet, does approve,
By his loved mansionry, that the heaven's breath
Smells wooingly here: no jutty, frieze,
Buttress, nor coign of vantage, but this bird
Hath made his pendent bed and procreant cradle:
Where they most breed and haunt, I have observed
The air is delicate.

If it were done when 'tis done, then 'twere well   I. vii. 1
It were done quickly: if the assassination
Could trammel up the consequence, and catch
With his surcease success; that but this blow
Might be the be-all and the end-all here,
But here, upon this bank and shoal of time,
We'ld jump the life to come.   But in these cases
We still have judgment here; that we but teach
Bloody instructions, which, being taught, return
To plague the inventor: this even-handed justice
Commends the ingredients of our poison'd chalice
To our own lips.   (*Macbeth*)

He's here in double trust;   I. vii. 12
First, as I am his kinsman and his subject,
Strong both against the deed; then, as his host,
Who should against the murderer shut the door,
Not bear the knife myself.   Besides, this Duncan
Hath borne his faculties so meek, hath been
So clear in his great office, that his virtues
Will plead like angels, trumpet-tongued, against
The deep damnation of his taking-off;
And pity, like a naked new-born babe,
Striding the blast, or heaven's cherubin, horsed
Upon the sightless couriers of the air,
Shall blow the horrid deed in every eye,
That tears shall drown the wind.   I have no spur
To prick the sides of my intent, but only
Vaulting ambition, which o'erleaps itself
And falls on the other.   (*Macbeth*)

We will proceed no further in this business: 31
He hath honour'd me of late; and I have bought
Golden opinions from all sorts of people,
Which would be worn now in their newest gloss,
Not cast aside so soon.   (*Macbeth*)

                    Art thou afeard   39
To be the same in thine own act and valour
As thou art in desire?   Wouldst thou have that
Which thou esteem'st the ornament of life,
And live a coward in thine own esteem,
Letting 'I dare not' wait upon 'I would,'
Like the poor cat i' the adage?   (*Lady Macbeth*)

I dare do all that may become a man;   46
Who dares do more is none.   (*Macbeth*)

                    I have given suck, and I know   54
How tender 'tis to love the babe that milks me:
I would, while it was smiling in my face,
Have pluck'd my nipple from his boneless gums,
And dash'd the brains out, had I so sworn as you
Have done to this.   (*Lady Macbeth*)

Macbeth.   If we should fail?   59
Lady Macbeth.   We fail!
But screw your courage to the sticking-place,
And we'll not fail.

                    Bring forth men-children only;   72
For thy undaunted mettle should compose
Nothing but males.   (*Macbeth*)

I am settled, and bend up   I. vii. 79
Each corporal agent to this terrible feat.
Away, and mock the time with fairest show:
False face must hide what the false heart doth know.
                                                        (*Macbeth*)

                          There's husbandry in heaven;   II. i. 4
Their candles are all out.   (*Banquo*)

                          Merciful powers,   7
Restrain in me the cursed thoughts that nature
Gives way to in repose!   (*Banquo*)

                                        Shut up   16
In measureless content.   (*Banquo*)

Is this a dagger which I see before me,   33
The handle toward my hand? Come, let me clutch thee.
I have thee not, and yet I see thee still.
Art thou not, fatal vision, sensible
To feeling as to sight? or art thou but
A dagger of the mind, a false creation,
Proceeding from the heat-oppressed brain?
I see thee yet, in form as palpable
As this which now I draw.
Thou marshall'st me the way that I was going;
And such an instrument I was to use.
Mine eyes are made the fools o' the other senses,
Or else worth all the rest; I see thee still,
And on thy blade and dudgeon gouts of blood,
Which was not so before. There's no such thing:
It is the bloody business which informs
Thus to mine eyes. Now o'er the one half-world
Nature seems dead, and wicked dreams abuse
The curtain'd sleep; witchcraft celebrates
Pale Hecate's offerings, and wither'd murder,
Alarum'd by his sentinel, the wolf,
Whose howl's his watch, thus with his stealthy pace,
With Tarquin's ravishing strides, towards his design
Moves like a ghost. Thou sure and firm-set earth,
Hear not my steps, which way they walk, for fear
Thy very stones prate of my whereabout,
And take the present horror from the time,
Which now suits with it. Whiles I threat, he lives:
Words to the heat of deeds too cold breath gives.
                                        [*A bell rings*]
I go, and it is done; the bell invites me.
Hear it not, Duncan; for it is a knell
That summons thee to heaven or to hell. (*Macbeth*)
                          316

It was the owl that shriek'd, the fatal bellman,   II. ii. 3
Which gives the stern'st good-night.   (*Lady Macbeth*)

                        The attempt and not the deed   11
Confounds us.   (*Lady Macbeth*)

                         Had he not resembled   13
My father as he slept, I had done 't.   (*Lady Macbeth*)

Macbeth. This is a sorry sight.   [*Looking on his hands.*]   21
Lady Macbeth. A foolish thought, to say a sorry sight.

There's one did laugh in 's sleep, and one cried 'Murder!'   23
That they did wake each other: I stood and heard them:
But they did say their prayers, and address'd them
Again to sleep.   (*Macbeth*)

Macbeth. One cried 'God bless us!' and 'Amen' the   27
    other;
As they had seen me with these hangman's hands.
Listening their fear, I could not say 'Amen,'
When they did say 'God bless us!'
Lady Macbeth.   Consider it not so deeply.
Macbeth. But wherefore could not I pronounce 'Amen'?
I had most need of blessing, and 'Amen'
Stuck in my throat.
Lady Macbeth.   These deeds must not be thought
After these ways; so, it will make us mad.

Methought I heard a voice cry 'Sleep no more!   35
Macbeth does murder sleep,' the innocent sleep,
Sleep that knits up the ravell'd sleave of care,
The death of each day's life, sore labour's bath,
Balm of hurt minds, great nature's second course,
Chief nourisher in life's feast.   (*Macbeth*)

Still it cried 'Sleep no more!' to all the house: 41
'Glamis hath murder'd sleep, and therefore Cawdor
Shall sleep no more; Macbeth shall sleep no more.'
                                 (*Macbeth*)

You do unbend your noble strength, to think   45
So brainsickly of things.   (*Lady Macbeth*)

Macbeth. I am afraid to think what I have done;   51
Look on 't again I dare not.
Lady Macbeth.   Infirm of purpose!
Give me the daggers: the sleeping and the dead
Are but as pictures: 'tis the eye of childhood
That fears a painted devil.

Will all great Neptune's ocean wash this blood   II. ii. 60
Clean from my hand? No, this my hand will rather
The multitudinous seas incarnadine,
Making the green one red. (*Macbeth*)

My hands are of your colour; but I shame   64
To wear a heart so white. I hear a knocking
At the south entry: retire we to our chamber:
A little water clears us of this deed:
How easy is it, then! (*Lady Macbeth*)

Wake Duncan with thy knocking! I would thou   74
couldst! (*Macbeth*)

Here's a knocking indeed! If a man were porter of   II. iii. 1
hell-gate, he should have old turning the key. (*Porter*)

Knock, knock, knock! Who's there? Faith, here's   15
an English tailor come hither, for stealing out of a
French hose: come in, tailor; here you may roast your
goose. (*Porter*)

But this place is too cold for hell. I'll devil-porter   20
it no further: I had thought to have let in some of all
professions that go the primrose way to the everlasting
bonfire. [*Knocking within.*] Anon, anon! I pray you,
remember the porter. (*Porter*)

The labour we delight in physics pain. (*Macbeth*)   54

The night has been unruly: where we lay,   59
Our chimneys were blown down; and, as they say,
Lamentings heard i' the air; strange screams of death,
And prophesying with accents terrible
Of dire combustion and confused events
New hatch'd to the woeful time: the obscure bird
Clamour'd the livelong night: some say, the earth
Was feverous and did shake. (*Lennox*)

O horror, horror, horror! Tongue nor heart   69
Cannot conceive nor name thee! (*Macduff*)

Confusion now hath made his masterpiece!   71
Most sacrilegious murder hath broke ope
The Lord's anointed temple, and stole thence
The life o' the building! (*Macduff*)

Shake off this downy sleep, death's counterfeit.   81
And look on death itself! up, up, and see
The great doom's image! (*Macduff*)

Had I but died an hour before this chance,   II. iii. 96
I had lived a blessed time; for, from this instant,
There's nothing serious in mortality:
All is but toys: renown and grace is dead;
The wine of life is drawn, and the mere lees
Is left this vault to brag of.   (*Macbeth*)

Who can be wise, amazed, temperate and furious,   114
Loyal and neutral, in a moment?   (*Macbeth*)

                 Here lay Duncan,   117
His silver skin laced with his golden blood;
And his gash'd stabs look'd like a breach in nature
For ruin's wasteful entrance.   (*Macbeth*)

In the great hand of God I stand; and thence   136
Against the undivulged pretence I fight
Of treasonous malice.   (*Banquo*)

                 Where we are,   145
There's daggers in men's smiles: the near in blood,
The nearer bloody.   (*Donalbain*)

Threescore and ten I can remember well: II. iv. 1
Within the volume of which time I have seen
Hours dreadful and things strange; but this sore night
Hath trifled former knowings.   (*Old Man*)

              By the clock 'tis day,   6
And yet dark night strangles the travelling lamp.   (*Ross*)

A falcon, towering in her pride of place,   12
Was by a mousing owl hawk'd at and kill'd.   (*Old Man*)

                 Adieu!   37
Lest our old robes sit easier than our new!   (*Macduff*)

God's benison go with you; and with those   40
That would make good of bad, and friends of foes!
                 (*Old Man*)

I must become a borrower of the night   III. i. 26
For a dark hour or twain.   (*Banquo*)

              'Tis much he dares;   51
And, to that dauntless temper of his mind,
He hath a wisdom that doth guide his valour
To act in safety.   There is none but he
Whose being I do fear: and, under him,
My Genius is rebuked; as, it is said,
Mark Antony's was by Caesar.   (*Macbeth*)

For Banquo's issue have I filed my mind;   iii. i. 65
For them the gracious Duncan have I murder'd;
Put rancours in the vessel of my peace
Only for them; and mine eternal jewel
Given to the common enemy of man,
To make them kings, the seed of Banquo kings!
                                        (*Macbeth*)

First Murderer.   We are men, my liege.   91
Macbeth. Ay, in the catalogue ye go for men;
As hounds and greyhounds, mongrels, spaniels, curs,
Shoughs, water-rugs and demi-wolves are clept
All by the name of dogs.

Second Murderer.   I am one, my liege,   108
Whom the vile blows and buffets of the world
Have so incensed that I am reckless what
I do to spite the world.
First Murderer.   And I another
So weary with disasters, tugg'd with fortune,
That I would set my life on any chance,
To mend it, or be rid on 't.

Acquaint you with the perfect spy o' the time,   130
The moment on 't. (*Macbeth*)

                    Nought's had, all's spent,   iii. ii. 4
Where our desire is got without content:
'Tis safer to be that which we destroy
Than by destruction dwell in doubtful joy.
                                        (*Lady Macbeth*)

                    Things without all remedy   11
Should be without regard: what's done is done.
                                        (*Lady Macbeth*)

We have scotch'd the snake, not kill'd it.   (*Macbeth*)   13

                    Duncan is in his grave;   22
After life's fitful fever he sleeps well;
Treason has done his worst: nor steel, nor poison,
Malice domestic, foreign levy, nothing,
Can touch him further.   (*Macbeth*)

And make our faces vizards to our hearts,   34
Disguising what they are.   (*Macbeth*)

But in them nature's copy's not eterne. (*Lady Macbeth*)   38

                    Ere the bat hath flown   III. ii. 40
His cloister'd flight, ere to black Hecate's summons
The shard-borne beetle with his drowsy hums
Hath rung night's yawning peal, there shall be done
A deed of dreadful note.   (*Macbeth*)

Be innocent of the knowledge, dearest chuck,   45
Till thou applaud the deed.   Come, seeling night,
Scarf up the tender eye of pitiful day;
And with thy bloody and invisible hand
Cancel and tear to pieces that great bond
Which keeps me pale!   Light thickens; and the crow
Makes wing to the rooky wood:
Good things of day begin to droop and drowse;
Whiles night's black agents to their preys do rouse.
Thou marvell'st at my words: but hold thee still:
Things bad begun make strong themselves by ill.
                                    (*Macbeth*)

The west yet glimmers with some streaks of day: III. iii. 5
Now spurs the lated traveller apace
To gain the timely inn.   (*First Murderer*)

Macbeth.   There's blood upon thy face.   III. iv. 12
Murderer. 'Tis Banquo's then.
Macbeth. 'Tis better thee without than he within.

Thou art the best o' the cut-throats.   (*Macbeth*)   17

Then comes my fit again: I had else been perfect,   21
Whole as the marble, founded as the rock,
As broad and general as the casing air:
But now I am cabin'd, cribb'd, confined, bound in
To saucy doubts and fears.   (*Macbeth*)

                    Safe in a ditch he bides,   26
With twenty trenched gashes on his head;
The least a death to nature.   (*Murderer*)

Now, good digestion wait on appetite,   38
And health on both!   (*Macbeth*)

Thou canst not say I did it: never shake   50
Thy gory locks at me.   (*Macbeth*)

This is the very painting of your fear: 61
This is the air-drawn dagger which, you said,
Led you to Duncan.   O, these flaws and starts,
Impostors to true fear, would well become
A woman's story at a winter's fire,

Authorized by her grandam.   Shame itself!   III. iv. 66
Why do you make such faces?   (*Lady Macbeth*)

What, quite unmann'd in folly?   (*Lady Macbeth*)   73

               The time has been,   78
That, when the brains were out, the man would die,
And there an end; but now they rise again,
With twenty mortal murders on their crowns,
And push us from our stools.   (*Macbeth*)

What man dare, I dare: 99
Approach thou like the rugged Russian bear,
The arm'd rhinoceros, or the Hyrcan tiger;
Take any shape but that, and my firm nerves
Shall never tremble: or be alive again,
And dare me to the desert with thy sword;
If trembling I inhabit then, protest me
The baby of a girl.   Hence, horrible shadow!
Unreal mockery, hence!   (*Macbeth*)

You have displaced the mirth, broke the good meeting,   109
With most admired disorder.   (*Lady Macbeth*)

               Can such things be,   110
And overcome us like a summer's cloud,
Without our special wonder?   You make me strange
Even to the disposition that I owe,
When now I think you can behold such sights,
And keep the natural ruby of your cheeks,
When mine is blanch'd with fear.   (*Macbeth*)

Stand not upon the order of your going,   119
But go at once.   (*Lady Macbeth*)

It will have blood, they say; blood will have blood: 122
Stones have been known to move and trees to speak;
Augurs and understood relations have
By magot-pies and choughs and rooks brought forth
The secret'st man of blood.   (*Macbeth*)

Macbeth.   What is the night?   126
Lady Macbeth. Almost at odds with morning, which is
  which.

There's not a one of them but in his house   131
I keep a servant fee'd.   (*Macbeth*)

               I am in blood   136
Stepp'd in so far that, should I wade no more,
Returning were as tedious as go o'er.   (*Macbeth*)

You lack the season of all natures, sleep. (*Lady Macbeth*) III. iv. 141

And you all know, security   III. v. 32
Is mortals' chiefest enemy. (*Hecate*)

Lennox.   Sent he to Macduff? III. vi. 39
Lord. He did: and with an absolute 'Sir, not I,'
The cloudy messenger turns me his back,
And hums, as who should say 'You'll rue the time
That clogs me with this answer.'

First Witch. Thrice the brinded cat hath mew'd.   IV. i. 1
Second Witch. Thrice and once the hedge-pig whined.

First Witch. Round about the cauldron go: 4
In the poison'd entrails throw.
Toad, that under cold stone
Days and nights has thirty one
Swelter'd venom sleeping got,
Boil thou first i' the charmed pot.
All. Double, double, toil and trouble;
Fire burn and cauldron bubble.
Second Witch. Fillet of a fenny snake,
In the cauldron boil and bake;
Eye of newt and toe of frog,
Wool of bat and tongue of dog,
Adder's fork and blind-worm's sting,
Lizard's leg and howlet's wing,
For a charm of powerful trouble,
Like a hell-broth boil and bubble.

Third Witch. Scale of dragon, tooth of wolf,   22
Witches' mummy, maw and gulf
Of the ravin'd salt-sea shark,
Root of hemlock digg'd i' the dark,
Liver of blaspheming Jew,
Gall of goat, and slips of yew
Sliver'd in the moon's eclipse,
Nose of Turk and Tartar's lips,
Finger of birth-strangled babe
Ditch-deliver'd by a drab,
Make the gruel thick and slab:
Add thereto a tiger's chaudron,
For the ingredients of our cauldron.
All. Double, double, toil and trouble;
Fire burn and cauldron bubble.
Second Witch. Cool it with a baboon's blood,
Then the charm is firm and good.

By the pricking of my thumbs,   44
Something wicked this way comes.

Open, locks,   IV. i. 46
Whoever knocks!   (*Second Witch*)

Macbeth.   How now, you secret, black, and midnight hags!   48
What is 't you do?
All Witches.   A deed without a name.

Macbeth! Macbeth! Macbeth! beware Macduff;   71
Beware the thane of Fife.   Dismiss me.   Enough.
                              (*First Apparition*)

Be bloody, bold, and resolute; laugh to scorn   79
The power of man, for none of woman born
Shall harm Macbeth.   (*Second Apparition*)

But yet I'll make assurance double sure,   83
And take a bond of fate.   (*Macbeth*)

                              What is this   86
That rises like the issue of a king,
And wears upon his baby-brow the round
And top of sovereignty?   (*Macbeth*)

Be lion-mettled, proud; and take no care   90
Who chafes, who frets, or where conspirers are:
Macbeth shall never vanquish'd be until
Great Birnam wood to high Dunsinane hill
Shall come against him.   (*Third Apparition*)

What, will the line stretch out to the crack of doom?   117
                              (*Macbeth*)

          Now, I see, 'tis true;   122
For the blood-bolter'd Banquo smiles upon me.
                              (*Macbeth*)

Infected be the air whereon they ride;   138
And damn'd all those that trust them.   (*Macbeth*)

The flighty purpose never is o'ertook   145
Unless the deed go with it: from this moment
The very firstlings of my heart shall be
The firstlings of my hand.   (*Macbeth*)

His flight was madness: when our actions do not,   IV. ii. 3
Our fears do make us traitors.   (*Lady Macduff*)

He wants the natural touch: for the poor wren,   9
The most diminutive of birds, will fight,
Her young ones in her nest, against the owl.
                              (*Lady Macduff*)

But cruel are the times, when we are traitors   IV. ii. 18
And do not know ourselves, when we hold rumour
From what we fear, yet know not what we fear. (*Ross*)

Poor bird! thou'ldst never fear the net nor lime,   34
The pitfall nor the gin. (*Lady Macduff*)

I have done no harm.   But I remember now   74
I am in this earthly world; where to do harm
Is often laudable, to do good sometime
Accounted dangerous folly. (*Lady Macduff*)

First Murderer. Where is your husband?   80
Lady Macduff. I hope, in no place so unsanctified
Where such as thou mayst find him.
First Murderer.   He's a traitor.
Son. Thou liest, thou shag-hair'd villain!
First Murderer.   What, you egg!
                                    [*Stabbing him.*]
Young fry of treachery!

Let us seek out some desolate shade, and there   IV. iii. 1
Weep our sad bosoms empty. (*Malcolm*)

                              Each new morn   4
New widows howl, new orphans cry, new sorrows
Strike heaven on the face. (*Macduff*)

Angels are bright still, though the brightest fell: 22
Though all things foul would wear the brows of grace,
Yet grace must still look so. (*Malcolm*)

Bleed, bleed, poor country! (*Macduff*)   31

                              Not in the legions   55
Of horrid hell can come a devil more damn'd
In evils to top Macbeth. (*Macduff*)

Malcolm.   Had I power, I should   97
Pour the sweet milk of concord into hell,
Uproar the universal peace, confound
All unity on earth.
Macduff.   O Scotland, Scotland!

Such welcome and unwelcome things at once   138
'Tis hard to reconcile. (*Macduff*)

Macduff. Stands Scotland where it did?
Ross.   Alas, poor country!   164
Almost afraid to know itself.   It cannot

Be call'd our mother, but our grave; where nothing,   iv. iii. 166
But who knows nothing, is once seen to smile;
Where sighs and groans and shrieks that rend the air
Are made, not mark'd; where violent sorrow seems
A modern ecstasy: the dead man's knell
Is there scarce ask'd for who; and good men's lives
Expire before the flowers in their caps,
Dying or ere they sicken.

Macduff.   How does my wife?   176
Ross. Why, well.
Macduff.   And all my children?
Ross.   Well too.
Macduff. The tyrant has not batter'd at their peace?
Ross. No; they were well at peace when I did leave 'em.

What, man! ne'er pull your hat upon your brows;   208
Give sorrow words: the grief that does not speak
Whispers the o'erfraught heart and bids it break.
                                        (*Malcolm*)

He has no children. All my pretty ones?   216
Did you say all? O hell-kite! All?
What, all my pretty chickens and their dam
At one fell swoop? (*Macduff*)

Malcolm. Dispute it like a man.   220
Macduff.   I shall do so;
But I must also feel it as a man:
I cannot but remember such things were,
That were most precious to me.

O, I could play the woman with mine eyes   230
And braggart with my tongue! (*Macduff*)

                    Receive what cheer you may: 239
The night is long that never finds the day. (*Malcolm*)

Doctor. You see, her eyes are open.   v. i. 28
Gentleman. Ay, but their sense is shut.

   Out, damned spot! out, I say!—One: two: why, then   39
'tis time to do 't.—Hell is murky!—Fie, my lord, fie! a
soldier, and afeard? What need we fear who knows it,
when none can call our power to account?—Yet who
would have thought the old man to have had so much
blood in him. (*Lady Macbeth*)

   The thane of Fife had a wife: where is she now?—What,   47
will these hands ne'er be clean?—No more o' that, my
lord, no more o' that: you mar all with this starting.
                              (*Lady Macbeth*)

Here's the smell of the blood still: all the perfumes of   v. i. 56
Arabia will not sweeten this little hand. (*Lady Macbeth*)

Foul whisperings are abroad: unnatural deeds   79
Do breed unnatural troubles: infected minds
To their deaf pillows will discharge their secrets:
More needs she the divine than the physician. (*Doctor*)

Those he commands move only in command,   v. ii. 19
Nothing in love: now does he feel his title
Hang loose about him, like a giant's robe
Upon a dwarfish thief. (*Angus*)

The mind I sway by and the heart I bear   v. iii. 9
Shall never sag with doubt nor shake with fear. (*Macbeth*)

Macbeth. The devil damn thee black, thou cream-faced   11
    loon!
Where got'st thou that goose look?
Servant. There is ten thousand—
Macbeth.   Geese, villain?
Servant.   Soldiers, sir.
Macbeth. Go, prick thy face, and over-red thy fear,
Thou lily-liver'd boy. What soldiers, patch?
Death of my soul! those linen cheeks of thine
Are counsellors to fear. What soldiers, whey-face?
Servant. The English force, so please you.
Macbeth. Take thy face hence.

                                        This push   20
Will cheer me ever, or disseat me now. (*Macbeth*)

I have lived long enough: my way of life   22
Is fall'n into the sear, the yellow leaf;
And that which should accompany old age,
As honour, love, obedience, troops of friends,
I must not look to have; but, in their stead,
Curses, not loud but deep, mouth-honour, breath,
Which the poor heart would fain deny, and dare not.
                                        (*Macbeth*)

Send out moe horses; skirr the country round;   35
Hang those that talk of fear. (*Macbeth*)

Macbeth. Canst thou not minister to a mind diseased,   40
Pluck from the memory a rooted sorrow,
Raze out the written troubles of the brain
And with some sweet oblivious antidote

Cleanse the stuff'd bosom of that perilous stuff   v. iii. 44
Which weighs upon the heart?
Doctor.   Therein the patient
Must minister to himself.

Throw physic to the dogs; I'll none of it.   (*Macbeth*)   47

I would applaud thee to the very echo,   53
That should applaud again.   (*Macbeth*)

What rhubarb, senna, or what purgative drug,   55
Would scour these English hence?   (*Macbeth*)

Hang out our banners on the outward walls: v. v. 1
The cry is still 'They come.'   (*Macbeth*)

I have almost forgot the taste of fears: 9
The time has been, my senses would have cool'd
To hear a night-shriek; and my fell of hair
Would at a dismal treatise rouse and stir
As life were in't: I have supp'd full with horrors;
Direness, familiar to my slaughterous thoughts,
Cannot once start me.   (*Macbeth*)

To-morrow, and to-morrow, and to-morrow,   19
Creeps in this petty pace from day to day
To the last syllable of recorded time,
And all our yesterdays have lighted fools
The way to dusty death.   Out, out, brief candle!
Life's but a walking shadow, a poor player
That struts and frets his hour upon the stage
And then is heard no more: it is a tale
Told by an idiot, full of sound and fury,
Signifying nothing.   (*Macbeth*)

Messenger. I look'd toward Birnam, and anon, methought,   34
The wood began to move.
Macbeth.   Liar and slave!

I 'gin to be aweary of the sun,   49
And wish the estate o' the world were now undone.
Ring the alarum-bell!   Blow, wind! come, wrack!
At least we'll die with harness on our back.   (*Macbeth*)

Make all our trumpets speak; give them all breath,   v. vi. 9
Those clamorous harbingers of blood and death.
                                        (*Macduff*)

They have tied me to a stake; I cannot fly,   v. vii. 1
But, bear-like, I must fight the course.   (*Macbeth*)

But swords I smile at, weapons laugh to scorn,   v. vii. 12
Brandish'd by man that's of a woman born.   (*Macbeth*)

Macduff.   Turn, hell-hound, turn!   viii. 3
Macbeth. Of all men else I have avoided thee:
But get thee back; my soul is too much charged
With blood of thine already.

And be these juggling fiends no more believed,   19
That palter with us in a double sense;
That keep the word of promise to our ear,
And break it to our hope.   (*Macbeth*)

Then yield thee, coward,   23
And live to be the show and gaze o' the time. (*Macduff*)

                    Lay on, Macduff,   33
And damn'd be him that first cries 'Hold, enough!'
                                        (*Macbeth*)

Your son, my lord, has paid a soldier's debt: 39
He only lived but till he was a man;
The which no sooner had his prowess confirm'd
In the unshrinking station where he fought,
But like a man he died.   (*Ross*)

HAMLET, PRINCE OF DENMARK

The play opens with the changing of the guard at midnight before the Castle of Elsinore, Francisco being relieved by the officers Bernardo and Marcellus, accompanied by Horatio. To them appears the ghost of the king of Denmark, who had died a few weeks previously and had been supplanted on the throne by his brother Claudius, who had with unseemly haste married the widowed queen. Hamlet, son of the dead king, is told of the apparition, and keeps watch next night. On questioning the ghost, he is told that his father was murdered by his uncle. The rest of the play is taken up with Hamlet's plans for revenge, and the delay caused by his scrupulous anxiety to follow the right course. To corroborate the ghost's story he has a play acted before the king, reproducing the circumstances of the murder, and so causes him to betray his guilt. Meanwhile, to disarm suspicion, Hamlet feigns madness, and his eccentric behaviour is put down to his love for Ophelia, daughter of Polonius, the worldly-wise lord chamberlain. While upbraiding his mother he detects Polonius eavesdropping, and fatally stabs him through a curtain, thinking him to be the king. The king now determines to get rid of Hamlet, and sends him to England, accompanied by two courtiers, Rosencrantz and Guildenstern, with secret orders for his execution. But Hamlet discovers the plot, and returns to Denmark, to find himself witnessing the funeral of Ophelia, who has gone mad with grief at the death of her father and been drowned. Her brother Laertes demands revenge, and the king makes him the tool of a further plot. A fencing bout is arranged between Hamlet and Laertes, the latter being given a poisoned rapier; poisoned wine is also provided for Hamlet in case he survives the bout. The plot miscarries, for the queen drinks the poison by mistake, and dies, and when there is a scuffle between the duellists the foils are exchanged, so that both are wounded with the poisoned point. Laertes dies revealing the king's treachery, and Hamlet has only time to slay the king before he himself dies. Light relief is given in the final scene by the affected language of Osric, a young court exquisite.

Bernardo. Who's there?　　　　　　　　　　　　　　　　　　　　I. i. I
Francisco. Nay, answer me: stand, and unfold yourself.

You come most carefully upon your hour.　　(*Francisco*)　　6

For this relief much thanks: 'tis bitter cold,　　　　　　　　8
And I am sick at heart.　(*Francisco*)

Bernardo. Have you had quiet guard?　　　　　　　　　　　10
Francisco.　　　　　　　　　　　Not a mouse stirring.

Bernardo. What, is Horatio there?　　　　　　　　　　　　19
Horatio.　　　　　　　　　　　　　A piece of him.

What, has this thing appear'd again to-night?　(*Marcellus*)　21

Horatio says 'tis but our fantasy,　　　　　　　　　　　　23
And will not let belief take hold of him
Touching this dreaded sight, twice seen of us.　(*Marcellus*)

　　　　Let us once again assail your ears,　　　　　　　　31
That are so fortified against our story
What we have two nights seen.　(*Bernardo*)

Bernardo. Last night of all,　　　　　　　　　　　　　　34
When yond same star that's westward from the pole
Had made his course to illume that part of heaven
Where now it burns, Marcellus and myself,
The bell then beating one,—　　　　　　　[*Enter Ghost.*]
Marcellus. Peace, break thee off; look, where it comes
　again!
Bernardo. In the same figure, like the king that's dead.

Thou art a scholar; speak to it, Horatio.　(*Marcellus*)　42

What art thou that usurp'st this time of night,　　　　　46
Together with that fair and warlike form
In which the majesty of buried Denmark
Did sometimes march? by heaven I charge thee, speak!
　　　　　　　　　　　　　　　　(*Horatio*)

How now, Horatio! you tremble and look pale:　　　　　53
Is not this something more than fantasy?　(*Bernardo*)

Before my God, I might not this believe　　　　　　　　56
Without the sensible and true avouch
Of mine own eyes.　(*Horatio*)

331

Such was the very armour he had on   I. i. 60
When he the ambitious Norway combated;
So frown'd he once, when, in an angry parle,
He smote the sledded Polacks on the ice.   (*Horatio*)

Thus twice before, and jump at this dead hour,   65
With martial stalk hath he gone by our watch.
                                          (*Marcellus*)

But in the gross and scope of my opinion,   68
This bodes some strange eruption to our state.   (*Horatio*)

                              Tell me, he that knows,   70
Why this same strict and most observant watch
So nightly toils the subject of the land,
And why such daily cast of brazen cannon,
And foreign mart for implements of war;
Why such impress of shipwrights, whose sore task
Does not divide the Sunday from the week;
What might be toward, that this sweaty haste
Doth make the night joint-labourer with the day.
                                          (*Marcellus*)

Shark'd up a list of lawless resolutes.   (*Horatio*)   98

The source of this our watch and the chief head   106
Of this post-haste and romage in the land.   (*Horatio*)

In the most high and palmy state of Rome,   113
A little ere the mightiest Julius fell,
The graves stood tenantless and the sheeted dead
Did squeak and gibber in the Roman streets:
As stars with trains of fire and dews of blood,
Disasters in the sun; and the moist star
Upon whose influence Neptune's empire stands
Was sick almost to doomsday with eclipse.   (*Horatio*)

I'll cross it, though it blast me.   Stay, illusion!   127
If thou hast any sound, or use of voice,
Speak to me:
If there be any good thing to be done,
That may to thee do ease and grace to me,
Speak to me:
If thou art privy to thy country's fate,
Which, happily, foreknowing may avoid,
O, speak!
Or if thou hast uphoarded in thy life
Extorted treasure in the womb of earth,
For which, they say, you spirits oft walk in death,
Speak of it: stay, and speak!   (*Horatio*)

Marcellus. Shall I strike at it with my partisan?   I. i. 140
Horatio. Do, if it will not stand.
Bernardo.   'Tis here!
Horatio.   'Tis here!
Marcellus. 'Tis gone!   [*Exit Ghost.*]
We do it wrong, being so majestical,
To offer it the show of violence;
For it is, as the air, invulnerable,
And our vain blows malicious mockery.

Bernardo. It was about to speak, when the cock crew.   147
Horatio. And then it started like a guilty thing
Upon a fearful summons.   I have heard,
The cock, that is the trumpet to the morn,
Doth with his lofty and shrill-sounding throat
Awake the god of day; and, at his warning,
Whether in sea or fire, in earth or air,
The extravagant and erring spirit hies
To his confine: and of the truth herein
This present object made probation.

Some say that ever 'gainst that season comes   158
Wherein our Saviour's birth is celebrated,
The bird of dawning singeth all night long:
And then, they say, no spirit dare stir abroad;
The nights are wholesome; then no planets strike,
No fairy takes, nor witch hath power to charm,
So hallow'd and so gracious is the time.   (*Marcellus*)

But, look, the morn, in russet mantle clad,   166
Walks o'er the dew of yon high eastward hill.   (*Horatio*)

With an auspicious and a dropping eye,
With mirth in funeral and with dirge in marriage,   I. ii. 11
In equal scale weighing delight and dole.   (*King*)

The head is not more native to the heart,
The hand more instrumental to the mouth,   47
Than is the throne of Denmark to thy father.   (*King*)

He hath, my lord, wrung from me my slow leave
By laboursome petition, and at last   58
Upon his will I seal'd my hard consent.   (*Polonius*)

King. But now, my cousin Hamlet, and my son,—   64
Hamlet. [*Aside.*] A little more than kin, and less than
     kind.

King. How is it that the clouds still hang on you?   66
Hamlet. Not so, my lord; I am too much i' the sun.

Queen. Do not for ever with thy vailed lids   I. ii. 70
Seek for thy noble father in the dust:
Thou know'st 'tis common; all that lives must die,
Passing through nature to eternity.
Hamlet. Ay, madam, it is common.

Queen. Why seems it so particular with thee?   75
Hamlet. 'Seems,' madam! nay, it is; I know not 'seems.'
'Tis not alone my inky cloak, good mother,
Nor customary suits of solemn black,
Nor windy suspiration of forced breath,
No, nor the fruitful river in the eye,
Nor the dejected 'haviour of the visage,
Together with all forms, moods, shapes of grief,
That can denote me truly: these indeed seem,
For they are actions that a man might play:
But I have that within which passeth show;
These but the trappings and the suits of woe.

'Tis sweet and commendable in your nature, Hamlet,   87
To give these mourning duties to your father:
But, you must know, your father lost a father;
That father lost, lost his, and the survivor bound
In filial obligation for some term
To do obsequious sorrow: but to persever
In obstinate condolement is a course
Of impious stubbornness; 'tis unmanly grief;
It shows a will most incorrect to heaven,
A heart unfortified, a mind impatient,
An understanding simple and unschool'd:
For what we know must be and is as common
As any the most vulgar thing to sense,
Why should we in our peevish opposition
Take it to heart? Fie! 'tis a fault to heaven,
A fault against the dead, a fault to nature,
To reason most absurd; whose common theme
Is death of fathers, and who still hath cried,
From the first corse till he that died to-day,
'This must be so.' (*King*)

O, that this too too solid flesh would melt,   129
Thaw and resolve itself into a dew!
Or that the Everlasting had not fix'd
His canon 'gainst self-slaughter! O God! God!
How weary, stale, flat and unprofitable,
Seem to me all the uses of this world!
Fie on 't! ah fie! 'tis an unweeded garden,
That grows to seed; things rank and gross in nature
Possess it merely. That it should come to this!
But two months dead: nay, not so much, not two:

So excellent a king; that was, to this,   I. ii. 139
Hyperion to a satyr; so loving to my mother
That he might not beteem the winds of heaven
Visit her face too roughly.   Heaven and earth!
Must I remember? why, she would hang on him,
As if increase of appetite had grown
By what it fed on: and yet, within a month—
Let me not think on 't—Frailty, thy name is woman!—
A little month, or ere those shoes were old
With which she follow'd my poor father's body,
Like Niobe, all tears:—why she, even she—
O God! a beast, that wants discourse of reason,
Would have mourn'd longer—married with my uncle,
My father's brother, but no more like my father
Than I to Hercules.   (*Hamlet*)

It is not nor it cannot come to good: 158
But break, my heart; for I must hold my tongue.
                                    (*Hamlet*)

Hamlet. But what, in faith, make you from Wittenberg?   168
Horatio. A truant disposition, good my lord.

We 'll teach you to drink deep ere you depart.   (*Hamlet*) 175

Thrift, thrift, Horatio! the funeral baked meats   180
Did coldly furnish forth the marriage tables.   (*Hamlet*)

Hamlet.   Methinks I see my father.   184
Horatio. Where, my lord?
Hamlet.   In my mind's eye, Horatio.
Horatio. I saw him once; he was a goodly king.
Hamlet. He was a man, take him for all in all,
I shall not look upon his like again.

In the dead vast and middle of the night.   (*Horatio*)   198

                      A figure like your father,   199
Armed at point exactly, cap-a-pe,
Appears before them, and with solemn march
Goes slow and stately by them: thrice he walk'd
By their oppress'd and fear-surprised eyes,
Within his truncheon's length; whilst they, distill'd
Almost to jelly with the act of fear,
Stand dumb and speak not to him.   (*Horatio*)

Hamlet. Did you not speak to it?
Horatio.   My lord, I did: 214
But answer made it none.

Hamlet. Arm'd, say you?   I. ii. 226
Marcellus. }
Bernard.   }   Arm'd, my lord.
Hamlet.   From top to toe?
Marcellus. } My lord, from head to foot.
Bernard.   }

Hamlet. What, look'd he frowningly?   231
Horatio. A countenance more in sorrow than in anger.

Hamlet.   I would I had been there.   235
Horatio. It would have much amazed you.

Hamlet.   Stay'd it long?   237
Horatio. While one with moderate haste might tell a
    hundred.

Hamlet.   His beard was grizzled,—no?   240
Horatio. It was, as I have seen it in his life,
A sable silver'd.

I 'll speak to it, though hell itself should gape   245
And bid me hold my peace.   (*Hamlet*)

Give it an understanding, but no tongue.   (*Hamlet*)   250

I doubt some foul play.   (*Hamlet*)   256

                    Foul deeds will rise,   257
Though all the earth o'erwhelm them, to men's eyes.
                                (*Hamlet*)

For Hamlet and the trifling of his favour,   I. iii. 5
Hold it a fashion and a toy in blood,
A violet in the youth of primy nature,
Forward, not permanent, sweet, not lasting,
The perfume and suppliance of a minute;
No more.   (*Laertes*)

His greatness weigh'd, his will is not his own;   17
For he himself is subject to his birth:
He may not, as unvalued persons do,
Carve for himself; for on his choice depends
The safety and health of this whole state;
And therefore must his choice be circumscribed
Unto the voice and yielding of that body
Whereof he is the head.   (*Laertes*)

The chariest maid is prodigal enough,   36
If she unmask her beauty to the moon:

Virtue itself 'scapes not calumnious strokes: I. iii. 38
The canker galls the infants of the spring,
Too oft before their buttons be disclosed,
And in the morn and liquid dew of youth
Contagious blastments are most imminent.   (*Laertes*)

I shall the effect of this good lesson keep,   45
As watchman to my heart.   But, good my brother,
Do not, as some ungracious pastors do,
Show me the steep and thorny way to heaven;
Whiles, like a puff'd and reckless libertine,
Himself the primrose path of dalliance treads,
And recks not his own rede.   (*Ophelia*)

The wind sits in the shoulder of your sail,   56
And you are stay'd for.   (*Polonius*)

            My blessing with thee!   57
And these few precepts in thy memory
See thou character.   Give thy thoughts no tongue,
Nor any unproportion'd thought his act.
Be thou familiar, but by no means vulgar.
Those friends thou hast, and their adoption tried,
Grapple them to thy soul with hoops of steel;
But do not dull thy palm with entertainment
Of each new-hatch'd, unfledged comrade.   Beware
Of entrance to a quarrel, but being in,
Bear 't that the opposed may beware of thee.
Give every man thy ear, but few thy voice;
Take each man's censure, but reserve thy judgment.
Costly thy habit as thy purse can buy,
But not express'd in fancy; rich, not gaudy;
For the apparel oft proclaims the man,
And they in France of the best rank and station
Are of a most select and generous chief in that.
Neither a borrower nor a lender be;
For loan oft loses both itself and friend,
And borrowing dulls the edge of husbandry.
This above all: to thine own self be true,
And it must follow, as the night the day,
Thou canst not then be false to any man.   (*Polonius*)

Ophelia. He hath, my lord, of late made many tenders   99
Of his affection to me.
Polonius. Affection! pooh! you speak like a green girl,
Unsifted in such perilous circumstance.
Do you believe his tenders, as you call them?

My lord, he hath importuned me with love   110
In honourable fashion.   (*Ophelia*)
M   337

Ophelia. And hath given countenance to his speech, my   I. iii. 113
  lord,
With almost all the holy vows of heaven.
Polonius. Ay, springes to catch woodcocks. I do know,
When the blood burns, how prodigal the soul
Lends the tongue vows.

Be somewhat scanter of your maiden presence;   121
Set your entreatments at a higher rate
Than a command to parley.   (*Polonius*)

Hamlet. The air bites shrewdly; it is very cold.   I. iv. 1
Horatio. It is a nipping and an eager air.

The king doth wake to-night and takes his rouse,   8
Keeps wassail, and the swaggering up-spring reels;
And, as he drains his draughts of Rhenish down,
The kettle-drum and trumpet thus bray out
The triumph of his pledge.   (*Hamlet*)

Horatio.   Is it a custom?   12
Hamlet. Ay, marry, is 't:
But to my mind, though I am native here
And to the manner born, it is a custom
More honour'd in the breach than the observance.

This heavy-headed revel east and west   17
Makes us traduced and tax'd of other nations:
They clepe us drunkards, and with swinish phrase
Soil our addition.   (*Hamlet*)

                              These men,   30
Carrying, I say, the stamp of one defect,
Being nature's livery, or fortune's star,—
Their virtues else—be they as pure as grace,
As infinite as man may undergo—
Shall in the general censure take corruption
From that particular fault: the dram of eale
Doth all the noble substance of a doubt
To his own scandal.   (*Hamlet*)

Angels and ministers of grace defend us!   39
Be thou a spirit of health or goblin damn'd,
Bring with thee airs from heaven or blasts from hell,
Be thy intents wicked or charitable,
Thou comest in such a questionable shape
That I will speak to thee: I'll call thee Hamlet,
King, father, royal Dane: O, answer me!
Let me not burst in ignorance; but tell
Why thy canonized bones, hearsed in death,

Have burst their cerements; why the sepulchre,   I. iv. 48
Wherein we saw thee quietly inurn'd,
Hath oped his ponderous and marble jaws,
To cast thee up again.   What may this mean,
That thou, dead corse, again in complete steel
Revisit'st thus the glimpses of the moon,
Making night hideous?   (*Hamlet*)

Horatio. It beckons you to go away with it,   58
As if it some impartment did desire
To you alone.
Marcellus.   Look, with what courteous action
It waves you to a more removed ground:
But do not go with it.

I do not set my life at a pin's fee;   65
And for my soul, what can it do to that,
Being a thing immortal as itself?   (*Hamlet*)

What if it tempt you toward the flood, my lord,   69
Or to the dreadful summit of the cliff
That beetles o'er his base into the sea,
And there assume some other horrible form,
Which might deprive your sovereignty of reason
And draw you into madness? think of it:
The very place puts toys of desperation,
Without more motive, into every brain
That looks so many fathoms to the sea
And hears it roar beneath.   (*Horatio*)

                    Unhand me, gentlemen,   84
By heaven, I'll make a ghost of him that lets me!
                                        (*Hamlet*)

He waxes desperate with imagination.   (*Horatio*)   87

Something is rotten in the state of Denmark.   (*Marcellus*)   90

Ghost.   My hour is almost come,   I. v. 2
When I to sulphurous and tormenting flames
Must render up myself.
Hamlet.   Alas, poor ghost!

I am thy father's spirit,   9
Doom'd for a certain term to walk the night,
And for the day confined to fast in fires,
Till the foul crimes done in my days of nature
Are burnt and purged away.   But that I am forbid
To tell the secrets of my prison-house,
I could a tale unfold whose lightest word

Would harrow up thy soul, freeze thy young blood,   I. v. 16
Make thy two eyes, like stars, start from their spheres,
Thy knotted and combined locks to part
And each particular hair to stand an end,
Like quills upon the fretful porpentine:
But this eternal blazon must not be
To ears of flesh and blood. List, list, O, list!   (Ghost)

Ghost. Revenge his foul and most unnatural murder.   25
Hamlet. Murder!
Ghost. Murder most foul, as in the best it is;
But this most foul, strange and unnatural.

Ghost. The serpent that did sting thy father's life   39
Now wears his crown.
Hamlet.   O my prophetic soul!
My uncle!

But virtue, as it never will be moved,   53
Though lewdness court it in a shape of heaven,
So lust, though to a radiant angel link'd,
Will sate itself in a celestial bed,
And prey on garbage.   (Ghost)

But, soft! methinks I scent the morning air.   (Ghost)   58

                              Sleeping within my orchard,   59
My custom always of the afternoon.   (Ghost)

Thus was I, sleeping, by a brother's hand   74
Of life, of crown, of queen, at once dispatch'd:
Cut off even in the blossoms of my sin,
Unhousel'd, disappointed, unaneled,
No reckoning made, but sent to my account
With all my imperfections on my head.   (Ghost)

Taint not thy mind, nor let thy soul contrive   85
Against thy mother aught: leave her to heaven
And to those thorns that in her bosom lodge,
To prick and sting her.   (Ghost)

The glow-worm shows the matin to be near,   89
And 'gins to pale his uneffectual fire.   (Ghost)

Adieu, adieu! Hamlet, remember me.   (Ghost)   91

                              Remember thee!   95
Ay, thou poor ghost, while memory holds a seat
In this distracted globe.   Remember thee!
Yea, from the table of my memory

I 'll wipe away all trivial fond records,   I. V. 99
All saws of books, all forms, all pressures past,
That youth and observation copied there;
And thy commandment all alone shall live
Within the book and volume of my brain,
Unmix'd with baser matter: yes, by heaven!
O most pernicious woman!
O villain, villain, smiling, damned villain!
My tables,—meet it is I set it down,
That one may smile, and smile, and be a villain;
At least I 'm sure it may be so in Denmark.   (*Hamlet*)

Hamlet. There 's ne'er a villain dwelling in all Denmark   123
But he 's an arrant knave.
Horatio. There needs no ghost, my lord, come from the
    grave
To tell us this.

These are but wild and whirling words, my lord.   133

                                 (*Horatio*)

                        Touching this vision here,   137
It is an honest ghost, that let me tell you.   (*Hamlet*)

Ghost. [*Beneath.*] Swear.   149
Hamlet. Ah, ha, boy! say'st thou so? art thou there,
    truepenny?
Come on—you hear this fellow in the cellerage—
Consent to swear.

Hamlet. Swear by my sword.   154
Ghost. [*Beneath.*] Swear.
Hamlet. Hic et ubique? then we 'll shift our ground.
Come hither, gentlemen.

Hamlet. Swear by my sword.   160
Ghost. [*Beneath.*] Swear.
Hamlet. Well said, old mole! canst work i' the earth so
    fast?
A worthy pioner! Once more remove, good friends.
Horatio. O day and night, but this is wondrous strange!

There are more things in heaven and earth, Horatio,   166
Than are dreamt of in your philosophy.   (*Hamlet*)

Hamlet. How strange or odd soe'er I bear myself,   170
As I perchance hereafter shall think meet
To put an antic disposition on,
That you, at such times seeing me, never shall,
With arms encumber'd thus, or this head-shake,
Or by pronouncing of some doubtful phrase,

As 'Well, well, we know,' or 'We could, an if we would,'   I. v. 176
Or 'If we list to speak,' or 'There be, an if they might,'
Or such ambiguous giving out, to note
That you know aught of me: this not to do,
So grace and mercy at your most need help you,
Swear.
Ghost. [*Beneath.*] Swear.
Hamlet. Rest, rest, perturbed spirit!   [*They swear.*]

The time is out of joint: O cursed spite,   189
That ever I was born to set it right!   (*Hamlet*)

Take you, as 'twere, some distant knowledge of him;   II. i. 13
As thus, 'I know his father and his friends,
And in part him.'   (*Polonius*)

Your bait of falsehood takes this carp of truth: 63
And thus do we of wisdom and of reach,
With windlasses and with assays of bias,
By indirections find directions out.   (*Polonius*)

My lord, as I was sewing in my closet,   77
Lord Hamlet, with his doublet all unbraced;
No hat upon his head; his stockings foul'd,
Ungarter'd, and down-gyved to his ancle;
Pale as his shirt; his knees knocking each other;
And with a look so piteous in purport
As if he had been loosed out of hell
To speak of horrors,—he comes before me.   (*Ophelia*)

He took me by the wrist and held me hard;   87
Then goes he to the length of all his arm;
And, with his other hand thus o'er his brow,
He falls to such perusal of my face
As he would draw it.   (*Ophelia*)

And, with his head over his shoulder turn'd,   97
He seem'd to find his way without his eyes;
For out o' doors he went without their helps,
And, to the last, bended their light on me.   (*Ophelia*)

This is the very ecstasy of love,   102
Whose violent property fordoes itself
And leads the will to desperate undertakings
As oft as any passion under heaven
That does afflict our natures.   (*Polonius*)

By heaven, it is as proper to our age   114
To cast beyond ourselves in our opinions
As it is common for the younger sort
To lack discretion.   (*Polonius*)

Your visitation shall receive such thanks   II. ii. 25
As fits a king's remembrance.   (*Queen*)

Thou still hast been the father of good news.   (*King*)   42

I hold my duty, as I hold my soul,   44
Both to my God and to my gracious king.   (*Polonius*)

Polonius. My liege, and madam, to expostulate   86
What majesty should be, what duty is,
Why day is day, night night, and time is time,
Were nothing but to waste night, day and time.
Therefore, since brevity is the soul of wit,
And tediousness the limbs and outward flourishes,
I will be brief: your noble son is mad:
Mad call I it; for, to define true madness,
What is 't but to be nothing else but mad?
But let that go.
Queen.   More matter, with less art.

That he is mad, 'tis true: 'tis true 'tis pity;   97
And pity 'tis 'tis true: a foolish figure;
But farewell it, for I will use no art.   (*Polonius*)

'To the celestial, and my soul's idol, the most beautified   109
Ophelia,'—
That's an ill phrase, a vile phrase; 'beautified' is a vile
phrase.   (*Polonius*)

        'Doubt thou the stars are fire;   116
            Doubt that the sun doth move;
        Doubt truth to be a liar;
            But never doubt I love.'   (*Polonius, reads*)

Lord Hamlet is a prince, out of thy star.   (*Polonius*)   141

And he, repulsed—a short tale to make—   146
Fell into a sadness, then into a fast,
Thence to a watch, thence into a weakness,
Thence to a lightness, and, by this declension,
Into the madness wherein now he raves,
And all we mourn for.   (*Polonius*)

Hath there been such a time—I'd fain know that—   153
That I have positively said ''Tis so,'
When it proved otherwise?   (*Polonius*)

Polonius. [*Pointing to his head and shoulder.*] Take this   156
    from this, if this be otherwise:
If circumstances lead me, I will find
Where truth is hid, though it were hid indeed
Within the centre.

                    If he love her not   II. ii. 164
And be not from his reason fall'n thereon,
Let me be no assistant for a state,
But keep a farm and carters.   (*Polonius*)

Polonius. Do you know me, my lord?   173
Hamlet. Excellent well; you are a fishmonger.
Polonius. Not I, my lord.
Hamlet. Then I would you were so honest a man.

    To be honest, as this world goes, is to be one man   177
picked out of ten thousand.   (*Hamlet*)

    If the sun breed maggots in a dead dog, being a good   181
kissing carrion.   (*Hamlet*)

    Still harping on my daughter: yet he knew me not at   188
first; he said I was a fishmonger: he is far gone, far gone:
and truly in my youth I suffered much extremity for love;
very near this.   (*Polonius*)

Polonius. What do you read, my lord?   193
Hamlet. Words, words, words.

    The satirical rogue says here that old men have grey   197
beards, that their faces are wrinkled, their eyes purging
thick amber and plum-tree gum and that they have a
plentiful lack of wit, together with most weak hams: all
which, sir, though I most powerfully and potently believe,
yet I hold it not honesty to have it thus set down, for
yourself, sir, should be old as I am, if like a crab you
could go backward. (*Hamlet*)

Polonius. Will you walk out of the air, my lord?   208
Hamlet. Into my grave.
Polonius. Indeed, that is out o' the air. [*Aside.*] How
pregnant sometimes his replies are!

Polonius. My honourable lord, I will most humbly take   217
my leave of you.
Hamlet. You cannot, sir, take from me any thing that I
will more willingly part withal: except my life, except
my life, except my life.
Polonius. Fare you well, my lord.
Hamlet. These tedious old fools!

Guildenstern. On fortune's cap we are not the very   233
button.
Hamlet. Nor the soles of her shoe?
Rosencrantz. Neither, my lord.

Hamlet. Then you live about her waist, or in the middle of   II. ii. 237
her favours?
Guildenstern. 'Faith, her privates we.
Hamlet. In the secret parts of fortune? O, most true;
she is a strumpet.

Hamlet. What's the news?   240
Rosencrantz. None, my lord, but that the world's grown
honest.
Hamlet. Then is doomsday near: but your news is not
true.

There is nothing either good or bad, but thinking   255
makes it so. (*Hamlet*)

O God, I could be bounded in a nutshell and count   260
myself a king of infinite space, were it not that I have bad
dreams. (*Hamlet*)

Guildenstern. The very substance of the ambitious is   264
merely the shadow of a dream.
Hamlet. A dream itself is but a shadow.
Rosencrantz. Truly, and I hold ambition of so airy and
light a quality that it is but a shadow's shadow.

I have of late—but wherefore I know not—lost all my   307
mirth, forgone all custom of exercises; and indeed it goes
so heavily with my disposition that this goodly frame, the
earth, seems to me a sterile promontory, this most excellent canopy, the air, look you, this brave o'erhanging
firmament, this majestical roof fretted with golden fire,
why, it appears no other thing to me than a foul and
pestilent congregation of vapours. What a piece of work
is a man! how noble in reason! how infinite in faculty! in
form and moving how express and admirable! in action
how like an angel! in apprehension how like a god! the
beauty of the world! the paragon of animals! And yet, to
me, what is this quintessence of dust? man delights not
me: no, nor woman neither, though by your smiling you
seem to say so. (*Hamlet*)

He that plays the king shall be welcome; his majesty   332
shall have tribute of me; the adventurous knight shall use
his foil and target; the lover shall not sigh gratis; the
humorous man shall end his part in peace; the clown
shall make those laugh whose lungs are tickle o' the sere;
and the lady shall say her mind freely or the blank verse
shall halt for 't. (*Hamlet*)

*M

There is, sir, an aery of children, little eyases, that cry   II. ii. 354
out on the top of question, and are most tyrannically
clapped for't: these are now the fashion, and so berattle
the common stages—so they call them—that many
wearing rapiers are afraid of goose-quills and dare scarce
come thither.   (*Rosencrantz*)

There is something in this more than natural, if   384
philosophy could find it out.   (*Hamlet*)

I am but mad north-north-west: when the wind is   397
southerly I know a hawk from a handsaw.   (*Hamlet*)

Hamlet. That great baby you see there is not yet out of   401
his swaddling-clouts.
Rosencrantz. Happily he's the second time come to them;
for they say an old man is twice a child.

The best actors in the world, either for tragedy, comedy,   415
history, pastoral, pastoral-comical, historical-pastoral,
tragical-historical, tragical-comical-historical-pastoral,
scene individable, or poem unlimited: Seneca cannot be
too heavy, nor Plautus too light.   For the law of writ and
the liberty, these are the only men.   (*Polonius*)

Hamlet. O Jephthah, judge of Israel, what a treasure   422
hadst thou!
Polonius. What a treasure had he, my lord?
Hamlet. Why,
   'One fair daughter, and no more,
   The which he loved passing well.'
Polonius. [*Aside.*] Still on my daughter.

Welcome, good friends.   O, my old friend! thy face is   441
valanced since I saw thee last: comest thou to beard me in
Denmark?   What, my young lady and mistress!   By'r
lady, your ladyship is nearer to heaven than when I saw
you last, by the altitude of a chopine.   Pray God, your
voice, like a piece of uncurrent gold, be not cracked
within the ring.   (*Hamlet*)

Come, give us a taste of your quality; come, a passionate   451
speech.   (*Hamlet*)

The play, I remember, pleased not the million; 'twas   456
caviare to the general.   (*Hamlet*)

One said there were no sallets in the lines to make the   462
matter savoury, nor no matter in the phrase that might
indict the author of affectation; but called it an honest
method, as wholesome as sweet, and by very much more
handsome than fine.   (*Hamlet*)

346

'The rugged Pyrrhus, he whose sable arms,   II. ii. 474
Black as his purpose, did the night resemble
When he lay couched in the ominous horse,
Hath now this dread and black complexion smear'd
With heraldry more dismal; head to foot
Now is he total gules; horridly trick'd
With blood of fathers, mothers, daughters, sons,
Baked and impasted with the parching streets,
That lend a tyrannous and damned light
To their lord's murder: roasted in wrath and fire,
And thus o'er-sized with coagulate gore,
With eyes like carbuncles, the hellish Pyrrhus
Old grandsire Priam seeks.'   (*Hamlet*)

   'Fore God, my lord, well spoken, with good accent and   488
good discretion.   (*Polonius*)

               'Anon he finds him   490
Striking too short at Greeks; his antique sword,
Rebellious to his arm, lies where it falls,
Repugnant to command: unequal match'd,
Pyrrhus at Priam drives; in rage strikes wide;
But with the whiff and wind of his fell sword
The unnerved father falls.   Then senseless Ilium,
Seeming to feel this blow, with flaming top
Stoops to his base, and with a hideous crash
Takes prisoner Pyrrhus' ear: for, lo! his sword,
Which was declining on the milky head
Of reverend Priam, seem'd i' the air to stick:
So, as a painted tyrant, Pyrrhus stood,
And like a neutral to his will and matter,
Did nothing.
But, as we often see, against some storm,
A silence in the heavens, the rack stand still,
The bold winds speechless and the orb below
As hush as death, anon the dreadful thunder
Doth rend the region, so, after Pyrrhus' pause,
Aroused vengeance sets him new a-work;
And never did the Cyclops' hammers fall
On Mars's armour forged for proof eterne
With less remorse than Pyrrhus' bleeding sword
Now falls on Priam.
Out, out, thou strumpet, Fortune! All you gods,
In general synod, take away her power;
Break all the spokes and fellies from her wheel,
And bowl the round nave down the hill of heaven,
As low as to the fiends!'   (*First Player*)

Polonius. This is too long.
Hamlet. It shall to the barber's, with your beard.   520

First Player. 'But who, O, who had seen the mobled   II. ii. 525
    queen—'
Hamlet. 'The mobled queen?'
Polonius. That's good; 'mobled queen' is good.
First Player. 'Run barefoot up and down, threatening the
    flames
With bisson rheum; a clout upon that head
Where late the diadem stood, and for a robe,
About her lank and all o'er-teemed loins,
A blanket, in the alarm of fear caught up;
Who this had seen, with tongue in venom steep'd,
'Gainst Fortune's state would treason have pronounced:
But if the gods themselves did see her then
When she saw Pyrrhus make malicious sport
In mincing with his sword her husband's limbs,
The instant burst of clamour that she made,
Unless things mortal move them not at all,
Would have made milch the burning eyes of heaven,
And passion in the gods.'

    Good my lord, will you see the players well bestowed?   546
Do you hear, let them be well used; for they are the
abstract and brief chronicles of the time: after your death
you were better have a bad epitaph than their ill report
while you live.   (*Hamlet*)

Polonius. My lord, I will use them according to their deserts.   552
Hamlet. God's bodykins, man, much better: use every
man after his desert, and who should 'scape whipping?
Use them after your own honour and dignity: the less
they deserve, the more merit is in your bounty.

O, what a rogue and peasant slave am I!   576
Is it not monstrous that this player here,
But in a fiction, in a dream of passion,
Could force his soul so to his own conceit
That from her working all his visage wann'd,
Tears in his eyes, distraction in 's aspect,
A broken voice, and his whole function suiting
With forms to his conceit? and all for nothing!
For Hecuba!
What's Hecuba to him, or he to Hecuba,
That he should weep for her? What would he do,
Had he the motive and the cue for passion
That I have? He would drown the stage with tears
And cleave the general ear with horrid speech,
Make mad the guilty and appal the free,
Confound the ignorant, and amaze indeed
The very faculties of eyes and ears.
Yet I,

A dull and muddy-mettled rascal, peak,   II. ii. 594
Like John-a-dreams, unpregnant of my cause,
And can say nothing; no, not for a king,
Upon whose property and most dear life
A damn'd defeat was made.   Am I a coward?
Who calls me villain? breaks my pate across?
Plucks off my beard and blows it in my face?
Tweaks me by the nose? gives me the lie i' the throat
As deep as to the lungs? who does me this?
Ha!
'Swounds, I should take it: for it cannot be
But I am pigeon-liver'd and lack gall
To make oppression bitter, or ere this
I should have fatted all the region kites
With this slave's offal: bloody, bawdy villain!
Remorseless, treacherous, lecherous, kindless villain!
O, vengeance!
Why, what an ass am I!   This is most brave,
That I, the son of a dear father murder'd,
Prompted to my revenge by heaven and hell,
Must, like a whore, unpack my heart with words,
And fall a-cursing, like a very drab,
A scullion!
Fie upon 't! foh!   About, my brain!   I have heard
That guilty creatures sitting at a play
Have by the very cunning of the scene
Been struck so to the soul that presently
They have proclaim'd their malefactions;
For murder, though it have no tongue, will speak
With most miraculous organ.   (*Hamlet*)

                    The play's the thing   633
Wherein I'll catch the conscience of the king.   (*Hamlet*)

Niggard of question; but, of our demands,
Most free in his reply.   (*Rosencrantz*)   III. i. 13

                 We are oft to blame in this,—   46
'Tis too much proved—that with devotion's visage
And pious action we do sugar o'er
The devil himself.   (*Polonius*)

How smart a lash that speech doth give my conscience!   (*King*) 50

To be, or not to be: that is the question: 56
Whether 'tis nobler in the mind to suffer
The slings and arrows of outrageous fortune,
Or to take arms against a sea of troubles,
And by opposing end them?   To die: to sleep;
No more; and by a sleep to say we end

The heart-ache and the thousand natural shocks   III. i 62
That flesh is heir to, 'tis a consummation
Devoutly to be wish'd.   To die, to sleep;
To sleep: perchance to dream; ay, there's the rub;
For in that sleep of death what dreams may come
When we have shuffled off this mortal coil,
Must give us pause: there's the respect
That makes calamity of so long life;
For who would bear the whips and scorns of time,
The oppressor's wrong, the proud man's contumely,
The pangs of despised love, the law's delay,
The insolence of office and the spurns
That patient merit of the unworthy takes,
When he himself might his quietus make
With a bare bodkin? who would fardels bear,
To grunt and sweat under a weary life,
But that the dread of something after death,
The undiscover'd country from whose bourn
No traveller returns, puzzles the will
And makes us rather bear those ills we have
Than fly to others that we know not of?
Thus conscience does make cowards of us all;
And thus the native hue of resolution
Is sicklied o'er with the pale cast of thought,
And enterprises of great pitch and moment
With this regard their currents turn awry,
And lose the name of action.   (*Hamlet*)

Nymph, in thy orisons   89
Be all my sins remember'd.   (*Hamlet*)

Take these again; for to the noble mind   100
Rich gifts wax poor when givers prove unkind. (*Ophelia*)

Get thee to a nunnery: why wouldst thou be a breeder of   122
sinners?   I am myself indifferent honest; but yet I could
accuse me of such things that it were better my mother had
not borne me: I am very proud, revengeful, ambitious,
with more offences at my beck than I have thoughts to put
them in, imagination to give them shape, or time to act
them in.   What should such fellows as I do crawling
between earth and heaven?   We are arrant knaves, all;
believe none of us.   Go thy ways to a nunnery.   (*Hamlet*)

Let the doors be shut upon him, that he may play the   135
fool no where but in's own house.   (*Hamlet*)

If thou dost marry, I'll give thee this plague for thy   139
dowry: be thou as chaste as ice, as pure as snow, thou
shalt not escape calumny.   Get thee to a nunnery, go:

farewell. Or, if thou wilt needs marry, marry a fool; for   III. i. 142
wise men know well enough what monsters you make of
them. To a nunnery, go, and quickly too. (*Hamlet*)

I have heard of your paintings too, well enough; God   148
has given you one face, and you make yourselves another:
you jig, you amble, and you lisp, and nickname God's
creatures, and make your wantonness your ignorance.
(*Hamlet*)

O, what a noble mind is here o'erthrown!   158
The courtier's, soldier's, scholar's, eye, tongue, sword;
The expectancy and rose of the fair state,
The glass of fashion and the mould of form,
The observed of all observers, quite, quite down!
And I, of ladies most deject and wretched,
That suck'd the honey of his music vows,
Now see that noble and most sovereign reason,
Like sweet bells jangled, out of tune and harsh;
That unmatch'd form and feature of blown youth
Blasted with ecstasy. (*Ophelia*)

Madness in great ones must not unwatch'd go. (*King*)   196

Speak the speech, I pray you, as I pronounced it to you,   III. ii. 1
trippingly on the tongue: but if you mouth it, as many of
your players do, I had as lief the town-crier spoke my lines.
Nor do not saw the air too much with your hand, thus, but
use all gently; for in the very torrent, tempest, and, as I
may say, the whirlwind of passion, you must acquire and
beget a temperance that may give it smoothness. O, it
offends me to the soul to hear a robustious periwig-pated
fellow tear a passion to tatters, to very rags, to split the
ears of the groundlings, who for the most part are capable
of nothing but inexplicable dumb-shows and noise: I
would have such a fellow whipped for o'erdoing Terma-
gant; it out-herods Herod: pray you, avoid it. (*Hamlet*)

Be not too tame neither, but let your own discretion be   19
your tutor: suit the action to the word, the word to the
action; with this special observance, that you o'erstep not
the modesty of nature: for any thing so overdone is from
the purpose of playing, whose end, both at the first and
now, was and is, to hold, as 'twere, the mirror up to
nature; to show virtue her own feature, scorn her own
image, and the very age and body of the time his form and
pressure. Now this overdone, or come tardy off, though
it make the unskilful laugh, cannot but make the judicious
grieve; the censure of the which one must in your allowance o'erweigh a whole theatre of others. (*Hamlet*)

Hamlet. O, there be players that I have seen play, and   III. ii 34
heard others praise, and that highly, not to speak it pro-
fanely, that neither having the accent of Christians nor
the gait of Christian, pagan, nor man, have so strutted
and bellowed that I have thought some of nature's
journeymen had made men and not made them well,
they imitated humanity so abominably.
First Player. I hope we have reformed that indifferently
with us, sir.
Hamlet. O, reform it altogether.

Let those that play your clowns speak no more than is   42
set down for them; for there be of them that will themselves laugh, to set on some quantity of barren spectators
to laugh too; though, in the mean time, some necessary
question of the play be then to be considered: that's
villanous, and shows a most pitiful ambition in the fool
that uses it.   (*Hamlet*)

Horatio, thou art e'en as just a man   59
As e'er my conversation coped withal.   (*Hamlet*)

                    Nay, do not think I flatter;   61
For what advancement may I hope from thee
That no revenue hast but thy good spirits,
To feed and clothe thee?   Why should the poor be
    flatter'd?
No, let the candied tongue lick absurd pomp,
And crook the pregnant hinges of the knee
Where thrift may follow fawning.   (*Hamlet*)

A man that fortune's buffets and rewards   72
Hast ta'en with equal thanks: and blest are those
Whose blood and judgment are so well commingled,
That they are not a pipe for fortune's finger
To sound what stop she please.   Give me that man
That is not passion's slave, and I will wear him
In my heart's core, ay, in my heart of heart,
As I do thee.   (*Hamlet*)

Observe mine uncle: if his occulted guilt   85
Do not itself unkennel in one speech,
It is a damned ghost that we have seen,
And my imaginations are as foul
As Vulcan's stithy.   (*Hamlet*)

King. How fares our cousin Hamlet?   97
Hamlet. Excellent, i' faith; of the chameleon's dish: I eat
the air, promise-crammed: you cannot feed capons so.

Hamlet. My lord, you played once i' the university, you   III. ii. 104
say ?
Polonius. That did I, my lord; and was accounted a good
actor.
Hamlet. What did you enact?
Polonius. I did enact Julius Caesar: I was killed i' the
Capitol; Brutus killed me.
Hamlet. It was a brute part of him to kill so capital a calf
there.

Queen. Come hither, my dear Hamlet, sit by me.   114
Hamlet. No, good mother, here's metal more attractive.

What should a man do but be merry ? for, look you, how   132
cheerfully my mother looks, and my father died within
these two hours.   (*Hamlet*)

O heavens! die two months ago, and not forgotten yet ?   138
Then there's hope a great man's memory may outlive his
life half a year: but, by 'r lady, he must build churches,
then; or else shall he suffer not thinking on, with the
hobby-horse, whose epitaph is 'For, O, for, O, the hobby-
horse is forgot.'   (*Hamlet*)

Marry, this is miching mallecho; it means mischief.   147
                                                       (*Hamlet*)

You are naught, you are naught: I'll mark the play.   157
                                                    (*Ophelia*)
Prologue.   For us, and for our tragedy,   159
            Here stooping to your clemency,
            We beg your hearing patiently.

Hamlet. Is this a prologue, or the posy of a ring?
Ophelia. 'Tis brief, my lord.
Hamlet. As woman's love.

Full thirty times hath Phoebus' cart gone round   165
Neptune's salt wash and Tellus' orbed ground,
And thirty dozen moons with borrow'd sheen
About the world have times twelve thirties been,
Since love our hearts and Hymen did our hands
Unite commutual in most sacred bands.   (*Player King*)

Where love is great, the littlest doubts are fear;   181
Where little fears grow great, great love grows there.
                                                  (*Player Queen*)

Player Queen. In second husband let me be accurst!   189
None wed the second but who kill'd the first.
Hamlet. [*Aside.*] Wormwood, wormwood.

What to ourselves in passion we propose,   III. ii. 204
The passion ending, doth the purpose lose.
                          (*Player King*)

This world is not for aye, nor 'tis not strange   210
That even our loves should with our fortunes change;
For 'tis a question left us yet to prove,
Whether love lead fortune, or else fortune love.
                          (*Player King*)

Our wills and fates do so contrary run   221
That our devices still are overthrown;
Our thoughts are ours, their ends none of our own.
                          (*Player King*)

                Sleep rock thy brain;   237
And never come mischance between us twain!
                          (*Player Queen*)

Hamlet. Madam, how like you this play?   239
Queen. The lady doth protest too much, methinks.

King. Have you heard the argument? Is there no   242
offence in't?
Hamlet. No, no, they do but jest, poison in jest; no offence
i' the world.

   'Tis a knavish piece of work: but what o' that? your   250
majesty and we that have free souls, it touches us not:
let the galled jade wince, our withers are unwrung.
                          (*Hamlet*)

Hamlet. This is one Lucianus, nephew to the king.   254
Ophelia. You are as good as a chorus, my lord.

Come: 'the croaking raven doth bellow for revenge.'   264
                          (*Hamlet*)

   He poisons him i' the garden for 's estate.   His name's   272
Gonzago: the story is extant, and writ in choice Italian.
                          (*Hamlet*)

Ophelia. The king rises.   277
Hamlet. What, frighted with false fire!

Why, let the stricken deer go weep,   282
   The hart ungalled play;
For some must watch, while some must sleep:
   So runs the world away. (*Hamlet*)

Hamlet. For thou dost know, O Damon dear,   III. ii. 292
      This realm dismantled was
    Of Jove himself; and now reigns here
      A very, very—pajock.

Horatio. You might have rhymed.

O good Horatio, I 'll take the ghost's word for a thou-   297
sand pound. (*Hamlet*)

    For if the king like not the comedy,   304
    Why then, belike, he likes it not, perdy. (*Hamlet*)

Guildenstern. The king, sir,—   310
Hamlet. Ay, sir, what of him?
Guildenstern. Is in his retirement marvellous dis-
tempered.
Hamlet. With drink, sir?
Guildenstern. No, my lord, rather with choler.

Hamlet. O wonderful son, that can so astonish a mother! 340
But is there no sequel at the heels of this mother's ad-
miration? Impart.
Rosencrantz. She desires to speak with you in her closet,
ere you go to bed.
Hamlet. We shall obey, were she ten times our mother.

Rosencrantz. My lord, you once did love me.   348
Hamlet. So I do still, by these pickers and stealers.

'While the grass grows,'—the proverb is something   358
musty. (*Hamlet*)

Hamlet. 'Tis as easy as lying: govern these ventages with 372
your fingers and thumb, give it breath with your mouth,
and it will discourse most eloquent music. Look you,
these are the stops.
Guildenstern. But these cannot I command to any utterance of harmony; I have not the skill.
Hamlet. Why, look you now, how unworthy a thing you
make of me! You would play upon me; you would
seem to know my stops; you would pluck out the heart
of my mystery; you would sound me from my lowest
note to the top of my compass: and there is much music,
excellent voice, in this little organ; yet cannot you make
it speak. 'Sblood, do you think I am easier to be played
on than a pipe?

Hamlet. Do you see yonder cloud that 's almost in shape 393
of a camel?
Polonius. By the mass, and 'tis like a camel, indeed.
Hamlet. Methinks it is like a weasel.

Polonius. It is backed like a weasel.   III. ii. 397
Hamlet. Or like a whale?
Polonius. Very like a whale.

They fool me to the top of my bent.   (*Hamlet*)   401

By and by is easily said.   (*Hamlet*)   404

'Tis now the very witching time of night,   406
When churchyards yawn and hell itself breathes out
Contagion to the world: now could I drink hot blood,
And do such bitter business as the day
Would quake to look on.   (*Hamlet*)

Let me be cruel, not unnatural: 413
I will speak daggers to her, but use none.   (*Hamlet*)

O, my offence is rank, it smells to heaven;   III. iii. 36
It hath the primal eldest curse upon 't,
A brother's murder. Pray can I not,
Though inclination be as sharp as will:
My stronger guilt defeats my strong intent;
And, like a man to double business bound,
I stand in pause where I shall first begin,
And both neglect. What if this cursed hand
Were thicker than itself with brother's blood,
Is there not rain enough in the sweet heavens
To wash it white as snow?   Whereto serves mercy
But to confront the visage of offence?
And what's in prayer but this two-fold force,
To be forestalled ere we come to fall,
Or pardon'd being down?   (*King*)

May one be pardon'd and retain the offence?   56
In the corrupted currents of this world
Offence's gilded hand may shove by justice,
And oft 'tis seen the wicked prize itself
Buys out the law: but 'tis not so above;
There is no shuffling, there the action lies
In his true nature; and we ourselves compell'd,
Even to the teeth and forehead of our faults,
To give in evidence. What then? what rests?
Try what repentance can: what can it not?
Yet what can it when one can not repent?
O wretched state!   O bosom black as death!
O limed soul, that, struggling to be free,
Art more engaged!   Help, angels!   Make assay!
Bow, stubborn knees; and, heart with strings of steel,
Be soft as sinews of the new-born babe!
All may be well.   (*King*)

Now might I do it pat, now he is praying;   III. iii. 73
And now I'll do't. And so he goes to heaven;
And so am I revenged. That would be scann'd:
A villain kills my father; and for that,
I, his sole son, do this same villain send
To heaven.
O, this is hire and salary, not revenge.
He took my father grossly, full of bread;
With all his crimes broad blown, as flush as May;
And how his audit stands who knows save heaven?
But in our circumstance and course of thought,
'Tis heavy with him: and am I then revenged,
To take him in the purging of his soul,
When he is fit and season'd for his passage?
No!
Up, sword; and know thou a more horrid hent:
When he is drunk asleep, or in his rage,
Or in the incestuous pleasure of his bed;
At gaming, swearing, or about some act
That has no relish of salvation in 't;
Then trip him, that his heels may kick at heaven,
And that his soul may be as damn'd and black
As hell, whereto it goes.   (*Hamlet*)

My words fly up, my thoughts remain below: 97
Words without thoughts never to heaven go.   (*King*)

Hamlet. Now, mother, what's the matter?   III. iv. 8
Queen. Hamlet, thou hast thy father much offended.
Hamlet. Mother, you have my father much offended.
Queen. Come, come, you answer with an idle tongue.
Hamlet. Go, go, you question with a wicked tongue.

You are the queen, your husband's brother's wife;   15
And—would it were not so!—you are my mother.
                     (*Hamlet*)

You go not till I set you up a glass   19
Where you may see the inmost part of you.   (*Hamlet*)

Polonius. [*Behind.*] What, ho! help, help, help!   22
Hamlet. [*Drawing.*] How now! a rat? Dead, for a ducat,
   dead!   [*Makes a pass through the arras.*]

Queen. O, what a rash and bloody deed is this!   27
Hamlet. A bloody deed! almost as bad, good mother,
As kill a king, and marry with his brother.

Thou wretched, rash, intruding fool, farewell!   31
I took thee for thy better: take thy fortune;
Thou find'st to be too busy is some danger.   (*Hamlet*)

Hamlet. Leave wringing of your hands: peace! sit you   III. iv. 34
    down,
And let me wring your heart; for so I shall,
If it be made of penetrable stuff,
If damned custom have not brass'd it so
That it be proof and bulwark against sense.
Queen. What have I done, that thou darest wag thy
    tongue
In noise so rude against me?
Hamlet.   Such an act
That blurs the grace and blush of modesty,
Calls virtue hypocrite, takes off the rose
From the fair forehead of an innocent love
And sets a blister there, makes marriage vows
As false as dicers' oaths.

Look here, upon this picture, and on this,   53
The counterfeit presentment of two brothers.
See, what a grace was seated on this brow;
Hyperion's curls; the front of Jove himself;
An eye like Mars, to threaten and command;
A station like the herald Mercury
New-lighted on a heaven-kissing hill;
A combination and a form indeed,
Where every god did seem to set his seal,
To give the world assurance of a man:
This was your husband.   Look you now, what follows:
Here is your husband; like a mildew'd ear,
Blasting his wholesome brother.   Have you eyes?
Could you on this fair mountain leave to feed,
And batten on this moor?   Ha! have you eyes?
You cannot call it love; for at your age
The hey-day in the blood is tame, it's humble,
And waits upon the judgment: and what judgment
Would step from this to this?   Sense, sure, you have,
Else could you not have motion; but sure, that sense
Is apoplex'd; for madness would not err,
Nor sense to ecstasy was ne'er so thrall'd
But it reserved some quantity of choice,
To serve in such a difference.   What devil was 't
That thus hath cozen'd you at hoodman-blind?
Eyes without feeling, feeling without sight,
Ears without hands or eyes, smelling sans all,
Or but a sickly part of one true sense
Could not so mope.
O shame! where is thy blush?   Rebellious hell,
If thou canst mutine in a matron's bones,
To flaming youth let virtue be as wax,
And melt in her own fire: proclaim no shame
When the compulsive ardour gives the charge,

Since frost itself as actively doth burn   III. iv. 87
And reason pandars will.   (*Hamlet*)

Thou turn'st mine eyes into my very soul;   89
And there I see such black and grained spots
As will not leave their tinct.   (*Queen*)

                A murderer and a villain;   96
A slave that is not twentieth part the tithe
Of your precedent lord; a vice of kings;
A cutpurse of the empire and the rule,
That from a shelf the precious diadem stole,
And put it in his pocket!   (*Hamlet*)

A king of shreds and patches.   (*Hamlet*)   102

Do you not come your tardy son to chide,   107
That, lapsed in time and passion, lets go by
The important acting of your dread command?   (*Hamlet*)

Alas, how is 't with you,   116
That you do bend your eye on vacancy
And with the incorporal air do hold discourse?
Forth at your eyes your spirits wildly peep;
And, as the sleeping soldiers in the alarm,
Your bedded hair, like life in excrements.
Start up, and stand an end.   (*Queen*)

This is the very coinage of your brain: 137
This bodiless creation ecstasy
Is very cunning in.   (*Queen*)

My pulse, as yours, doth temperately keep time,   140
And makes as healthful music: it is not madness
That I have utter'd: bring me to the test,
And I the matter will re-word; which madness
Would gambol from.   Mother, for love of grace,
Lay not that flattering unction to your soul,
That not your trespass, but my madness speaks:
It will but skin and film the ulcerous place,
Whiles rank corruption, mining all within,
Infects unseen.   Confess yourself to heaven;
Repent what's past; avoid what is to come;
And do not spread the compost on the weeds,
To make them ranker.   (*Hamlet*)

Queen. O Hamlet, thou hast cleft my heart in twain.   156
Hamlet. O, throw away the worser part of it,
And live the purer with the other half.

Assume a virtue, if you have it not.   (*Hamlet*)   III. iv. 160

I must be cruel, only to be kind.   (*Hamlet*)   178

Queen.   What shall I do?   180
Hamlet. Not this, by no means, that I bid you do:
Let the bloat king tempt you again to bed;
Pinch wanton on your cheek; call you his mouse;
And let him, for a pair of reechy kisses,
Or paddling in your neck with his damn'd fingers,
Make you to ravel all this matter out,
That I essentially am not in madness,
But mad in craft.

                              My two schoolfellows,   202
Whom I will trust as I will adders fang'd.   (*Hamlet*)

For 'tis the sport to have the enginer   206
Hoist with his own petar: and 't shall go hard
But I will delve one yard below their mines,
And blow them at the moon.   (*Hamlet*)

I 'll lug the guts into the neighbour room.   (*Hamlet*)   212

                              Indeed this counsellor   213
Is now most still, most secret and most grave,
Who was in life a foolish prating knave.   (*Hamlet*)

King.   How does Hamlet?   IV. i. 5
Queen. Mad as the sea and wind, when both contend
Which is the mightier: in his lawless fit,
Behind the arras hearing something stir,
Whips out his rapier, cries, 'A rat, a rat!'
And, in this brainish apprehension, kills
The unseen good old man.

The sun no sooner shall the mountains touch,   29
But we will ship him hence.   (*King*)

Safely stowed.   (*Hamlet*)   IV. ii. 1

Rosencrantz. What have you done, my lord, with the   5
dead body?
Hamlet. Compounded it with dust, whereto 'tis kin.

Rosencrantz. Take you me for a sponge, my lord?   15
Hamlet. Ay, sir, that soaks up the king's countenance, his
rewards, his authorities.   But such officers do the king
best service in the end: he keeps them, like an ape, in the
corner of his jaw; first mouthed, to be last swallowed:

when he needs what you have gleaned, it is but squeez-   IV. ii. 20
ing you, and, sponge, you shall be dry again.

A knavish speech sleeps in a foolish ear. (*Hamlet*)   25

Hamlet. The king is a thing—   30
Guildenstern. A thing, my lord!
Hamlet. Of nothing: bring me to him.   Hide fox, and all
after.

How dangerous is it that this man goes loose!   IV. iii. 2
Yet must not we put the strong law on him:
He's loved of the distracted multitude,
Who like not in their judgment, but their eyes;
And where 'tis so, the offender's scourge is weigh'd,
But never the offence. (*King*)

                         Diseases desperate grown   9
By desperate appliance are relieved,
Or not at all. (*King*)

King. Now, Hamlet, where's Polonius?   17
Hamlet. At supper.
King. At supper! where?
Hamlet. Not where he eats, but where he is eaten; a
certain convocation of politic worms are e'en at him.

Hamlet. A man may fish with the worm that hath eat of a   28
king, and eat of the fish that hath fed of that worm.
King. What dost thou mean by this?
Hamlet. Nothing but to show you how a king may go a
progress through the guts of a beggar.

King. Where is Polonius?   34
Hamlet. In heaven; send thither to see: if your messenger
find him not there, seek him i' the other place yourself.
But indeed, if you find him not within this month, you
shall nose him as you go up the stairs into the lobby.

Truly to speak, and with no addition,   IV. iv. 17
We go to gain a little patch of ground
That hath in it no profit but the name.
To pay five ducats, five, I would not farm it. (*Captain*)

How all occasions do inform against me,   32
And spur my dull revenge!   What is a man,
If his chief good and market of his time
Be but to sleep and feed? a beast, no more.
Sure, he that made us with such large discourse,
Looking before and after, gave us not

That capability and god-like reason   IV. iv. 38
To fust in us unused.   Now, whether it be
Bestial oblivion, or some craven scruple
Of thinking too precisely on the event,
A thought which, quarter'd, hath but one part wisdom
And ever three parts coward, I do not know
Why yet I live to say 'This thing's to do';
Sith I have cause and will and strength and means
To do 't.   Examples gross as earth exhort me:
Witness this army of such mass and charge
Led by a delicate and tender prince,
Whose spirit with divine ambition puff'd
Makes mouths at the invisible event,
Exposing what is mortal and unsure
To all that fortune, death and danger dare,
Even for an egg-shell.   Rightly to be great
Is not to stir without great argument,
But greatly to find quarrel in a straw
When honour's at the stake.   (*Hamlet*)

           O, from this time forth,   65
My thoughts be bloody, or be nothing worth!   (*Hamlet*)

To my sick soul, as sin's true nature is,   IV. v. 17
Each toy seems prologue to some great amiss:
So full of artless jealousy is guilt,
It spills itself in fearing to be spilt.   (*Queen*)

    How should I your true love know   23
      From another one?
    By his cockle hat and staff,
      And his sandal shoon.   (*Ophelia, sings*)

    He is dead and gone, lady,   29
      He is dead and gone;
    At his head a grass-green turf,
      At his heels a stone.   (*Ophelia, sings*)

    White his shroud as the mountain snow,   35
      Larded with sweet flowers;   37
    Which bewept to the grave did go
      With true-love showers.   (*Ophelia, sings*)

  Well, God 'ild you!   They say the owl was a baker's   41
daughter.   Lord, we know what we are, but know not
what we may be.   (*Ophelia*)

    To-morrow is Saint Valentine's day,   48
      All in the morning betime,
    And I a maid at your window,
      To be your Valentine.

Then up he rose, and donn'd his clothes,   IV. V. 52
And dupp'd the chamber door;
Let in the maid, that out a maid
Never departed more.   (*Ophelia, sings*)

I hope all will be well. We must be patient: but I   68
cannot choose but weep, to think they should lay him i'
the cold ground. My brother shall know of it: and so I
thank you for your good counsel. Come, my coach!
Good night, ladies; good night, sweet ladies; good night,
good night.   (*Ophelia*)

When sorrows come, they come not single spies,   78
But in battalions.   (*King*)

                        We have done but greenly,   83
In hugger-mugger to inter him.   (*King*)

The ocean, overpeering of his list,   99
Eats not the flats with more impetuous haste
Than young Laertes, in a riotous head,
O'erbears your officers.   (*Gentleman*)

There's such divinity doth hedge a king,   123
That treason can but peep to what it would,
Acts little of his will.   (*King*)

To hell, allegiance! vows, to the blackest devil!   131
Conscience and grace, to the profoundest pit!
I dare damnation. To this point I stand,
That both the worlds I give to negligence,
Let come what comes.   (*Laertes*)

O heat, dry up my brains! tears seven times salt,   154
Burn out the sense and virtue of mine eye!
By heaven, thy madness shall be paid with weight,
Till our scale turn the beam. O rose of May!
Dear maid, kind sister, sweet Ophelia!
O heavens! is 't possible, a young maid's wits
Should be as mortal as an old man's life?
Nature is fine in love, and where 'tis fine,
It sends some precious instance of itself
After the thing it loves.   (*Laertes*)

They bore him barefaced on the bier;   164
Hey non nonny, nonny, hey nonny;
And in his grave rain'd many a tear.
               (*Ophelia, sings*)

Hadst thou thy wits, and didst persuade revenge,   168
It could not move thus.   (*Laertes*)

There's rosemary, that's for remembrance; pray, love, IV. v. 175
remember: and there is pansies, that's for thoughts.

               (*Ophelia*)

There's fennel for you, and columbines: there's rue 180
for you; and here's some for me: we may call it herb-
grace o' Sundays: O, you must wear your rue with a
difference. There's a daisy: I would give you some
violets, but they withered all when my father died: they
say he made a good end,—
[*Sings.*] For bonny sweet Robin is all my joy. (*Ophelia*)

Thought and affliction, passion, hell itself,   188
She turns to favour and to prettiness. (*Laertes*)

  And will he not come again?   190
  And will he not come again?
    No, no, he is dead:
    Go to thy death-bed:
  He never will come again.

  His beard was as white as snow,
  All flaxen was his poll:
    He is gone, he is gone,
    And we cast away moan:
  God ha' mercy on his soul! (*Ophelia, sings*)

Make choice of whom your wisest friends you will, 204
And they shall hear and judge 'twixt you and me. (*King*)

His means of death, his obscure funeral—   213
No trophy, sword, nor hatchment o'er his bones,
No noble rite nor formal ostentation—
Cry to be heard, as 'twere from heaven to earth,
That I must call 't in question. (*Laertes*)

And where the offence is let the great axe fall. (*King*) 218

Now must your conscience my acquittance seal, IV. vii. 1
And you must put me in your heart for friend. (*King*)

          You must not think 30
That we are made of stuff so flat and dull
That we can let our beard be shook with danger
And think it pastime. (*King*)

It warms the very sickness in my heart,   56
That I shall live and tell him to his teeth,
'Thus didest thou.' (*Laertes*)

A very riband in the cap of youth,   IV. vii. 78
Yet needful too; for youth no less becomes
The light and careless livery that it wears
Than settled age his sables and his weeds,
Importing health and graveness.   (*King*)

Here was a gentleman of Normandy:—   83
I've seen myself, and served against, the French,
And they can well on horseback: but this gallant
Had witchcraft in 't; he grew unto his seat;
And to such wondrous doing brought his horse,
As had he been incorpsed and demi-natured
With the brave beast.   (*King*)

                    He is the brooch indeed   94
And gem of all the nation.   (*Laertes*)

Laertes, was your father dear to you?   108
Or are you like the painting of a sorrow,
A face without a heart?   (*King*)

There lives within the very flame of love   115
A kind of wick or snuff that will abate it.   (*King*)

                    That we would do   119
We should do when we would; for this 'would' changes
And hath abatements and delays as many
As there are tongues, are hands, are accidents;
And then this 'should' is like a spendthrift sigh,
That hurts by easing.   (*King*)

King. Hamlet comes back: what would you undertake,   125
To show yourself your father's son in deed
More than in words?
Laertes.   To cut his throat i' the church.
King. No place, indeed, should murder sanctuarize;
Revenge should have no bounds.

I bought an unction of a mountebank,   142
So mortal that, but dip a knife in it,
Where it draws blood no cataplasm so rare,
Collected from all simples that have virtue
Under the moon, can save the thing from death
That is but scratch'd withal.   (*Laertes*)

One woe doth tread upon another's heel,   164
So fast they follow.   (*Queen*)

There is a willow grows aslant a brook,   167
That shows his hoar leaves in the glassy stream;
There with fantastic garlands did she come

Of crow-flowers, nettles, daisies, and long purples   IV. vii. 170
That liberal shepherds give a grosser name,
But our cold maids do dead men's fingers call them:
There, on the pendent boughs her coronet weeds
Clambering to hang, an envious sliver broke;
When down her weedy trophies and herself
Fell in the weeping brook.   Her clothes spread wide;
And, mermaid-like, awhile they bore her up:
Which time she chanted snatches of old tunes;
As one incapable of her own distress,
Or like a creature native and indued
Unto that element: but long it could not be
Till that her garments, heavy with their drink,
Pull'd the poor wretch from her melodious lay
To muddy death.   (Queen)

Laertes.   Alas, then, she is drown'd?   184
Queen. Drown'd, drown'd.
Laertes. Too much of water hast thou, poor Ophelia,
And therefore I forbid my tears.

First Clown. Is she to be buried in Christian burial that   V. i. 1
wilfully seeks her own salvation?
Second Clown. I tell thee she is; and therefore make her
grave straight.

First Clown. Give me leave.   Here lies the water; good: 17
here stands the man; good: if the man go to this water,
and drown himself, it is, will he, nill he, he goes,—
mark you that; but if the water come to him and drown
him, he drowns not himself: argal, he that is not guilty
of his own death shortens not his own life.
Second Clown. But is this law?
First Clown. Ay, marry, is 't; crowner's quest law.

Second Clown. Will you ha' the truth on 't?   If this had   27
not been a gentlewoman, she should have been buried
out o' Christian burial.
First Clown. Why, there thou say'st: and the more pity
that great folk should have countenance in this world
to drown or hang themselves, more than their even
Christian.

There is no ancient gentlemen but gardeners, ditchers   34
and grave-makers: they hold up Adam's profession.
                                             (*First Clown*)

First Clown. What is he that builds stronger than either   46
the mason, the shipwright, or the carpenter?
Second Clown. The gallows-maker; for that frame outlives
a thousand tenants.

Cudgel thy brains no more about it, for your dull ass will   v. i. 63
not mend his pace with beating; and, when you are asked
this question next, say 'a grave-maker': the houses that
he makes last till doomsday. (*First Clown*)

Hamlet. Has this fellow no feeling of his business, that he   73
sings at grave-making?
Horatio. Custom hath made it in him a property of
easiness.
Hamlet. 'Tis e'en so: the hand of little employment hath
the daintier sense.

> But age, with his stealing steps,   79
>   Hath claw'd me in his clutch,
> And hath shipped me intil the land,
>   As if I had never been such.
>   (*First Clown, sings*)

Did these bones cost no more the breeding, but to play   99
at loggats with 'em? (*Hamlet*)

> A pick-axe, and a spade, a spade,   102
>   For and a shrouding sheet:
> O, a pit of clay for to be made
>   For such a guest is meet. (*First Clown, sings*)

Why may not that be the skull of a lawyer?   Where be   105
his quiddities now, his quillets, his cases, his tenures, and
his tricks? why does he suffer this rude knave now to
knock him about the sconce with a dirty shovel, and will
not tell him of his action of battery. (*Hamlet*)

Hamlet. What man dost thou dig it for?   141
First Clown. For no man, sir.
Hamlet. What woman, then?
First Clown. For none, neither.
Hamlet. Who is to be buried in 't?
First Clown. One that was a woman, sir; but, rest her
soul, she's dead.
Hamlet. How absolute the knave is! we must speak by the
card, or equivocation will undo us.

The age is grown so picked that the toe of the peasant   151
comes so near the heel of the courtier, he galls his kibe.
                                   (*Hamlet*)

Hamlet. Why was he sent into England?   163
First Clown. Why, because he was mad: he shall recover
his wits there; or, if he do not, it's no great matter
there.

Hamlet. Why?   v. i. 167
First Clown. 'Twill not be seen in   there; there the
men are as mad as he.

Hamlet. How came he mad?   171
First Clown. Very strangely, they say.
Hamlet. How strangely?
First Clown. Faith, e'en with losing his wits.

    Alas, poor Yorick! I knew him, Horatio: a fellow of   202
infinite jest, of most excellent fancy: he hath borne me on
his back a thousand times; and now, how abhorred in my
imagination it is! my gorge rises at it. Here hung those
lips that I have kissed I know not how oft. Where be
your gibes now? your gambols? your songs? your flashes
of merriment, that were wont to set the table on a roar?
Not one now, to mock your own grinning? quite chap-
fallen? Now get you to my lady's chamber, and tell her,
let her paint an inch thick, to this favour she must come;
make her laugh at that. (*Hamlet*)

Hamlet. Dost thou think Alexander looked o' this   218
fashion i' the earth?
Horatio. E'en so.
Hamlet. And smelt so? pah!

Hamlet. To what base uses we may return, Horatio!   223
Why may not imagination trace the noble dust of
Alexander, till he find it stopping a bung-hole?
Horatio. 'Twere to consider too curiously, to consider so.

Imperious Caesar, dead and turn'd to clay,   236
Might stop a hole to keep the wind away:
O, that that earth, which kept the world in awe,
Should patch a wall to expel the winter's flaw! (*Hamlet*)

First Priest. We should profane the service of the dead   259
To sing a requiem and such rest to her
As to peace-parted souls.
Laertes.   Lay her i' the earth:
And from her fair and unpolluted flesh
May violets spring! I tell thee, churlish priest,
A ministering angel shall my sister be,
When thou liest howling.

Sweets to the sweet: farewell! (*Queen*)   266

I thought thy bride-bed to have deck'd, sweet maid,   268
And not have strew'd thy grave. (*Queen*)

What is he whose grief   v. i. 277
Bears such an emphasis? whose phrase of sorrow
Conjures the wandering stars, and makes them stand
Like wonder-wounded hearers?   (*Hamlet*)

I prithee, take thy fingers from my throat;   283
For, though I am not splenetive and rash,
Yet have I something in me dangerous,
Which let thy wiseness fear.   (*Hamlet*)

I loved Ophelia: forty thousand brothers
Could not with all their quantity of love,
Make up my sum.   (*Hamlet*)

'Swounds, show me what thou'lt do: 297
Woo 't weep? woo 't fight? woo 't fast? woo 't tear thyself?
Woo 't drink up eisel? eat a crocodile?
I 'll do 't.   Dost thou come here to whine?
To outface me with leaping in her grave?
Be buried quick with her and so will I:
And, if thou prate of mountains, let them throw
Millions of acres on us, till our ground,
Singeing his pate against the burning zone,
Make Ossa like a wart!   Nay, an thou'lt mouth,
I 'll rant as well as thou.   (*Hamlet*)

                     This is mere madness: 307
And thus awhile the fit will work on him;
Anon, as patient as the female dove,
When that her golden couplets are disclosed,
His silence will sit drooping.   (*Queen*)

Let Hercules himself do what he may,   314
The cat will mew and dog will have his day.   (*Hamlet*)

Our indiscretion sometimes serves us well,   v. ii. 8
When our deep plots do pall: and that should teach us
There 's a divinity that shapes our ends,
Rough-hew them how we will.   (*Hamlet*)

Being thus be-netted round with villanies.   (*Hamlet*)   29

I once did hold it, as our statists do,   33
A baseness to write fair and labour'd much
How to forget that learning, but, sir, now
It did me yeoman's service.   (*Hamlet*)

'Tis dangerous when the baser nature comes   60
Between the pass and fell incensed points
Of mighty opposites.   (*Hamlet*)
N   369

And a man's life's no more than to say 'One.' (*Hamlet*)   v. ii. 74

Hamlet. Dost know this water-fly?   83
Horatio. No, my good lord.
Hamlet. Thy state is the more gracious; for 'tis a vice to
know him.

Hamlet. Put your bonnet to his right use; 'tis for the head.   95
Osric. I thank your lordship, it is very hot.
Hamlet. No, believe me, 'tis very cold; the wind is
northerly.
Osric. It is indifferent cold, my lord, indeed.
Hamlet. But yet methinks it is very sultry and hot for my
complexion.
Osric. Exceedingly, my lord; it is very sultry,—as 'twere,
—I cannot tell how.

Osric. An absolute gentleman, full of most excellent   111
differences, of very soft society and great showing:
indeed, to speak feelingly of him, he is the card or
calendar of gentry, for you shall find in him the continent of what part a gentleman would see.
Hamlet. Sir, his definement suffers no perdition in you;
though, I know, to divide him inventorially would
dizzy the arithmetic of memory, and yet but yaw
neither, in respect of his quick sail. But, in the verity
of extolment, I take him to be a soul of great article;
and his infusion of such dearth and rareness, as, to make
true diction of him, his semblable is his mirror; and
who else would trace him, his umbrage, nothing more.

The concernancy, sir? why do we wrap the gentleman   128
in our more rawer breath? (*Hamlet*)

Hamlet. What imports the nomination of this gentleman?   133
Osric. Of Laertes?
Horatio. His purse is empty already; all's golden words
are spent.

Hamlet. What's his weapon?   151
Osric. Rapier and dagger.
Hamlet. That's two of his weapons.

Osric. Three of the carriages, in faith, are very dear   158
to fancy, very responsive to the hilts, most delicate carriages, and of very liberal conceit.
Hamlet. What call you the carriages?
Horatio. I knew you must be edified by the margent ere
you had done.
Osric. The carriages, sir, are the hangers.

Hamlet. The phrase would be more german to the matter   v. ii. 165
if we could carry cannon by our sides: I would it might
be hangers till then.

He did comply with his dug before he sucked it. Thus   195
has he—and many more of the same breed that I know the
drossy age dotes on—only got the tune of the time and
outward habit of encounter.   (*Hamlet*)

Not a whit, we defy augury: there's a special providence   230
in the fall of a sparrow.   If it be now, 'tis not to come; if it
be not to come, it will be now; if it be not now, yet it will
come: the readiness is all: since no man has aught of what
he leaves, what is 't to leave betimes?   (*Hamlet*)

Let my disclaiming from a purposed evil   252
Free me so far in your most generous thoughts,
That I have shot mine arrow o'er the house,
And hurt my brother.   (*Hamlet*)

I 'll be your foil, Laertes: in mine ignorance   266
Your skill shall, like a star i' the darkest night,
Stick fiery off indeed.   (*Hamlet*)

Set me the stoups of wine upon that table.   (*King*)   278

The king shall drink to Hamlet's better breath;   282
And in the cup an union shall he throw,
Richer than that which four successive kings
In Denmark's crown have worn.   Give me the cups;
And let the kettle to the trumpet speak,
The trumpet to the cannoneer without,
The cannons to the heavens, the heavens to earth,
'Now the king drinks to Hamlet.'   (*King*)

A hit, a very palpable hit.   (*Osric*)   292

A touch, a touch, I do confess.   (*Laertes*)   297

He's fat, and scant of breath.   298
Here, Hamlet, take my napkin, rub thy brows.   (*Queen*)

Part them; they are incensed.   (*King*)   313

Why, as a woodcock to mine own springe, Osric;   317
I am justly kill'd with mine own treachery.   (*Laertes*)

No medicine in the world can do thee good;   325
In thee there is not half an hour of life;
The treacherous instrument is in thy hand,
Unbated and envenom'd.   (*Laertes*)

Hamlet. The point envenom'd too!   v. ii. 332
Then, venom, to thy work.   [*Stabs the King.*]

Had I but time—as this fell sergeant, death,   347
Is strict in his arrest—O, I could tell you—
But let it be. Horatio, I am dead;
Thou livest; report me and my cause aright
To the unsatisfied. (*Hamlet*)

I am more an antique Roman than a Dane: 352
Here's yet some liquor left. (*Horatio*)

If thou didst ever hold me in thy heart,   357
Absent thee from felicity awhile,
And in this harsh world draw thy breath in pain,
To tell my story. (*Hamlet*)

The potent poison quite o'ercrows my spirit. (*Hamlet*)   364

Hamlet. The rest is silence.   [*Dies.*]   369
Horatio. Now cracks a noble heart. Good night, sweet
     prince;
And flights of angels sing thee to thy rest!

                        O proud death,   375
What feast is toward in thine eternal cell? (*Fortinbras*)

And let me speak to the yet unknowing world   390
How these things came about: so shall you hear
Of carnal, bloody, and unnatural acts,
Of accidental judgments, casual slaughters,
Of deaths put on by cunning and forced cause,
And, in this upshot, purposes mistook
Fall'n on the inventors' heads: all this can I
Truly deliver. (*Horatio*)

                        Let four captains   406
Bear Hamlet, like a soldier, to the stage;
For he was likely, had he been put on,
To have proved most royally. (*Fortinbras*)

KING LEAR

Lear, king of ancient Britain, has three daughters—Goneril, who is married to the Duke of Albany; Regan, wife of the Duke of Cornwall; and Cordelia, whose hand is sought by the King of France and the Duke of Burgundy. Being over eighty, he has decided to abdicate, dividing up his realm among his children in proportion to the affection they profess for him. Goneril and Regan make flowery speeches and receive their portions, but Cordelia will not stoop to this, and is dismissed dowerless to become queen of France. The Earl of Kent, who protests at the king's action, is banished, but returns disguised to be his servant. Succeeding scenes show Lear's disillusionment and fury when his elder daughters treat him as an old fool whose wishes may now be disregarded, so that he is left without even a roof over his head. A sub-plot is provided by the villainy of Edmund, the bastard son of the Earl of Gloucester; he contrives to discredit the legitimate son Edgar, who is driven from home and wanders about disguised as a mad beggar. The scenes where Lear, Lear's fool, Edgar, and Kent seek refuge together from the storm are among the most harrowing in Shakespeare. When Cordelia comes with French forces to rescue the king, Gloucester, suspected of aiding them, is blinded by Cornwall, wanders away guided by his disguised son Edgar and tries unsuccessfully to kill himself. Lear and Cordelia, defeated and taken captive, comfort each other in prison, but Cordelia is hanged and Lear dies of grief while trying to revive her, his other daughters having already fallen victims to their mutual hatred.

'Tis our fast intent   I. i. 39
To shake all cares and business from our age;
Conferring them on younger strengths, while we
Unburthen'd crawl toward death.   *(Lear)*

Sir, I love you more than words can wield the matter;   56
Dearer than eye-sight, space, and liberty;
Beyond what can be valued, rich or rare;
No less than life, with grace, health, beauty, honour;
As much as child e'er loved, or father found;
A love that makes breath poor, and speech unable;
Beyond all manner of so much I love you.   *(Goneril)*

In my true heart   72
I find she names my very deed of love;
Only she comes too short: that I profess
Myself an enemy to all other joys,
Which the most precious square of sense possesses;
And find I am alone felicitate
In your dear highness' love.   *(Regan)*

My love's   79
More richer than my tongue.   *(Cordelia)*

Although the last, not least.   *(Lear)*   85

Nothing will come of nothing.   *(Lear)*   92

Unhappy that I am, I cannot heave   93
My heart into my mouth; I love your majesty
According to my bond; nor more, nor less.   *(Cordelia)*

Mend your speech a little,   96
Lest it may mar your fortunes.   *(Lear)*

Lear. So young, and so untender?   108
Cordelia. So young, my lord, and true.

Come not between the dragon and his wrath.   *(Lear)*   124

Hence, and avoid my sight!   *(Lear)*   126

The bow is bent and drawn, make from the shaft.   *(Lear)*   145

Be Kent unmannerly,   147
When Lear is mad.   *(Kent)*

Thus Kent, O princes, bids you all adieu;   189
He'll shape his old course in a country new.   *(Kent)*

If for I want that glib and oily art,
To speak and purpose not; since what I well intend,
I'll do't before I speak.   (*Cordelia*)   I. i. 227

A still-soliciting eye, and such a tongue
As I am glad I have not.   (*Cordelia*)   234

Fairest Cordelia, that art most rich, being poor;
Most choice, forsaken; and most loved, despised!   253
                              (*King of France*)

Not all the dukes of waterish Burgundy
Can buy this unprized precious maid of me.   261
                              (*King of France*)

                  Therefore be gone
Without our grace, our love, our benison.   (*Lear*)   267

                  I know you what you are;
And like a sister am most loath to call   272
Your faults as they are named.   (*Cordelia*)

Prescribe not us our duties.   (*Regan*)
                                                           279
Time shall unfold what plaited cunning hides:
Who cover faults, at last shame them derides.   (*Cordelia*) 283

                  Why bastard? wherefore base?   I. ii. 6
When my dimensions are as well compact,
My mind as generous, and my shape as true,
As honest madam's issue?   Why brand they us
With base? with baseness? bastardy? base, base?
Who, in the lusty stealth of nature, take
More composition and fierce quality
Than doth, within a dull, stale, tired bed,
Go to the creating a whole tribe of fops,
Got 'tween asleep and wake?   (*Edmund*)

Legitimate Edgar, I must have your land:
Our father's love is to the bastard Edmund   16
As to the legitimate: fine word,—legitimate!   (*Edmund*)

Now, gods, stand up for bastards!   (*Edmund*)   22

                  All this done   25
Upon the gad!   (*Gloucester*)

Gloucester. What paper were you reading?
Edmund. Nothing, my lord.   30
Gloucester. No?   What needed, then, that terrible dis-
patch of it into your pocket? the quality of nothing

hath not such need to hide itself. Let's see: come, if it   I. ii. 34
be nothing, I shall not need spectacles. (*Gloucester*)

These late eclipses in the sun and moon portend no   112
good to us: though the wisdom of nature can reason it thus
and thus, yet nature finds itself scourged by the sequent
effects: love cools, friendship falls off, brothers divide:
in cities, mutinies; in countries, discord; in palaces,
treason; and the bond cracked 'twixt son and father.

                                                 (*Gloucester*)

This is the excellent foppery of the world, that, when   129
we are sick in fortune,—often the surfeit of our own
behaviour,—we make guilty of our disasters the sun, the
moon, and the stars: as if we were villains by necessity;
fools by heavenly compulsion; knaves, thieves, and
treachers, by spherical predominance; drunkards, liars,
and adulterers, by an enforced obedience of planetary
influence; and all that we are evil in, by a divine thrusting
on. (*Edmund*)

Edgar—[*Enter Edgar*]—and pat he comes like the   145
catastrophe of the old comedy: my cue is villainous
melancholy, with a sigh like Tom o' Bedlam. (*Edmund*)

Some villain hath done me wrong. (*Edgar*)   180

Let me, if not by birth, have lands by wit: 199
All with me's meet that I can fashion fit. (*Edmund*)

Put on what weary negligence you please. (*Goneril*)   I. iii. 12

Old fools are babes again: and must be used   19
With checks as flatteries. (*Goneril*)

I do profess to be no less than I seem; to serve him truly I. iv. 14
that will put me in trust; to love him that is honest; to
converse with him that is wise, and says little; to fear
judgment; to fight when I cannot choose; and to eat no
fish. (*Kent*)

Kent. You have that in your countenance which I would   29
    fain call master.
Lear. What's that?
Kent. Authority.

I can keep honest counsel, ride, run, mar a curious tale   34
in telling it, and deliver a plain message bluntly: that
which ordinary men are fit for, I am qualified in; and the
best of me is diligence. (*Kent*)

Lear. How old art thou?   I. iv. 39
Kent. Not so young, sir, to love a woman for singing, nor
so old to dote on her for any thing: I have years on my
back forty eight.

Lear. Do you bandy looks with me, you rascal?   92
                        [Striking him.]
Oswald. I'll not be struck, my lord.
Kent. Nor tripped neither, you base foot-ball player.
                   [Tripping up his heels.]

An thou canst not smile as the wind sits, thou'lt catch   112
cold shortly.   *(Fool)*

Truth's a dog must to kennel; he must be whipped out,   124
when Lady the brach may stand by the fire and stink.
                            (Fool)

      Have more than thou showest,   131
      Speak less than thou knowest,
      Lend less than thou owest,
      Ride more than thou goest,
      Learn more than thou trowest,
      Set less than thou throwest;
      Leave thy drink and thy whore,
      And keep in-a-door,
      And thou shalt have more
      Than two tens to a score.   *(Fool)*

Lear. Dost thou call me fool, boy?   162
Fool. All thy other titles thou hast given away; that thou
wast born with.
Kent. This is not altogether fool, my lord.

I marvel what kin thou and thy daughters are: they'll   199
have me whipped for speaking true, thou'lt have me
whipped for lying; and sometimes I am whipped for
holding my peace.   *(Fool)*

Methinks you are too much of late i' the frown.   *(Lear)*   208

The hedge-sparrow fed the cuckoo so long,   235
That it had it head bit off by it young.   *(Fool)*

Here do you keep a hundred knights and squires;   262
Men so disorder'd, so debosh'd and bold,
That this our court, infected with their manners,
Shows like a riotous inn.   *(Goneril)*

A little to disquantity your train.   *(Goneril)*   270

Ingratitude, thou marble-hearted fiend,   I. iv. 281
More hideous when thou show'st thee in a child
Than the sea-monster! (*Lear*)

            Detested kite! thou liest: 284
My train are men of choice and rarest parts,
That all particulars of duty know,
And in the most exact regard support
The worships of their name. (*Lear*)

Hear, nature, hear; dear goddess, hear!   297
Suspend thy purpose, if thou didst intend
To make this creature fruitful!
Into her womb convey sterility!
Dry up in her the organs of increase;
And from her derogate body never spring
A babe to honour her!   If she must teem,
Create her child of spleen; that it may live,
And be a thwart disnatured torment to her!
Let it stamp wrinkles in her brow of youth;
With cadent tears fret channels in her cheeks;
Turn all her mother's pains and benefits
To laughter and contempt; that she may feel
How sharper than a serpent's tooth it is
To have a thankless child! (*Lear*)

         Let his disposition have that scope   314
That dotage gives it.   (*Goneril*)

            I am ashamed   318
That thou hast power to shake my manhood thus;
That these hot tears, which break from me perforce,
Should make thee worth them.   (*Lear*)

Albany. Well, you may fear too far.   351
Goneril.   Safer than trust too far.

Striving to better, oft we mar what's well. (*Albany*)   369

Fool. If a man's brains were in's heels, were 't not in   I. v. 8
danger of kibes?
Lear. Ay, boy.
Fool. Then, I prithee, be merry; thy wit shall ne'er go
slip-shod.

Fool. The reason why the seven stars are no more than   37
seven is a pretty reason.
Lear. Because they are not eight?
Fool. Yes, indeed: thou wouldst make a good fool.

Thou shouldst not have been old till thou hadst been   I. v. 47
wise. (*Fool*)

O, let me not be mad, not mad, sweet heaven!   50
Keep me in temper: I would not be mad. (*Lear*)

Here stood he in the dark, his sharp sword out,   II. i. 40
Mumbling of wicked charms, conjuring the moon
To stand auspicious mistress. (*Edmund*)

But that I told him, the revenging gods   47
'Gainst parricides did all their thunders bend. (*Edmund*)

All ports I'll bar; the villain shall not 'scape;   82
The duke must grant me that: besides, his picture
I will send far and near, that all the kingdom
May have due note of him. (*Gloucester*)

O, madam, my old heart is crack'd, is crack'd!   92
(*Gloucester*)

O, lady, lady, shame would have it hid! (*Gloucester*)   95

Natures of such deep trust we shall much need.   117
(*Cornwall*)

Oswald. What dost thou know me for?   II. ii. 14
Kent. A knave; a rascal; an eater of broken meats; a base,
proud, shallow, beggarly, three-suited, hundred-pound,
filthy, worsted-stocking knave; a lily-livered, action-
taking knave, a whoreson, glass-gazing, superservice-
able, finical rogue; one-trunk-inheriting slave; one that
wouldst be a bawd, in way of good service, and art
nothing but the composition of a knave, beggar, coward,
pandar, and the son and heir of a mongrel bitch: one
whom I will beat into clamorous whining, if thou deniest
the least syllable of thy addition.

I'll make a sop o' the moonshine of you. (*Kent*)   34

Thou whoreson zed! thou unnecessary letter! My   69
lord, if you will give me leave, I will tread this unbolted
villain into mortar, and daub the walls of a jakes with
him. (*Kent*)

You beastly knave, know you no reverence? (*Cornwall*)   75

               Such smiling rogues as these,   79
Like rats, oft bite the holy cords a-twain
Which are too intrinse t'unloose; smooth every passion

That in the natures of their lords rebel;   II. ii. 82
Bring oil to fire, snow to their colder moods;
Renege, affirm, and turn their halcyon beaks
With every gale and vary of their masters,
Knowing nought, like dogs, but following. (*Kent*)

A plague upon your epileptic visage!   87
Smile you my speeches, as I were a fool?
Goose, if I had you upon Sarum plain,
I'ld drive ye cackling home to Camelot. (*Kent*)

Cornwall. Why dost thou call him knave? What's his   95
   offence?
Kent. His countenance likes me not.
Cornwall. No more, perchance, does mine, nor his, nor
   hers.
Kent. Sir, 'tis my occupation to be plain:
I have seen better faces in my time
Than stands on any shoulder that I see
Before me at this instant.

                           This is some fellow,   101
Who, having been praised for bluntness, doth affect
A saucy roughness, and constrains the garb
Quite from his nature: he cannot flatter, he,
An honest mind and plain, he must speak truth!
An they will take it, so; if not, he's plain.
These kind of knaves I know, which in this plainness
Harbour more craft and more corrupter ends
Than twenty silly ducking observants
That stretch their duties nicely. (*Cornwall*)

Kent. Sir, in good sooth, in sincere verity,   111
Under the allowance of your great aspect,
Whose influence, like the wreath of radiant fire
On flickering Phoebus' front,—
Cornwall.   What mean'st by this?
Kent. To go out of my dialect, which you discommend so
much.

                           None of these rogues and cowards 131
But Ajax is their fool. (*Kent*)

Kent. Call not your stocks for me: I serve the king;   135
On whose employment I was sent to you:
You shall do small respect, show too bold malice
Against the grace and person of my master,
Stocking his messenger.
Cornwall. Fetch forth the stocks! As I have life and
   honour,

                              380

There shall he sit till noon.   II. ii. 141
Regan. Till noon! till night, my lord; and all night too.

              Your purposed low correction   149
Is such as basest and contemned'st wretches
For pilferings and most common trespasses
Are punish'd with.   (*Gloucester*)

Some time I shall sleep out, the rest I'll whistle.   163
A good man's fortune may grow out at heels.   (*Kent*)

           All weary and o'erwatch'd,   177
Take vantage, heavy eyes, not to behold
This shameful lodging.
Fortune, good night: smile once more; turn thy wheel!
                  (*Kent*)

I will preserve myself: and am bethought   II. iii. 6
To take the basest and most poorest shape
That ever penury, in contempt of man,
Brought near to beast: my face I'll grime with filth;
Blanket my loins; elf all my hair in knots;
And with presented nakedness out-face
The winds and persecutions of the sky.
The country gives me proof and precedent
Of Bedlam beggars, who, with roaring voices,
Strike in their numb'd and mortified bare arms
Pins, wooden pricks, nails, sprigs of rosemary;
And with this horrible object, from low farms,
Poor pelting villages, sheep-cotes, and mills,
Sometime with lunatic bans, sometime with prayers,
Enforce their charity.   Poor Turlygod! poor Tom!
That's something yet: Edgar I nothing am.   (*Edgar*)

            They durst not do't;   II. iv. 22
They could not, would not do't; 'tis worse than murder,
To do upon respect such violent outrage.   (*Lear*)

He raised the house with loud and coward cries.   (*Kent*)   43

Winter's not gone yet, if the wild-geese fly that way.   46
                  (*Fool*)

       Fathers that wear rags   48
         Do make their children blind;
       But fathers that bear bags
         Shall see their children kind.   (*Fool*)

O, how this mother swells up toward my heart!   56
Hysterica passio, down, thou climbing sorrow,
Thy element's below!   (*Lear*)

Let go thy hold when a great wheel runs down a hill,   II. iv. 71
lest it break thy neck with following it; but the great one
that goes up the hill, let him draw thee after.   (*Fool*)

> That sir which serves and seeks for gain,   79
>   And follows but for form,
> Will pack when it begins to rain,
>   And leave thee in the storm.
> But I will tarry; the fool will stay,
>   And let the wise man fly:
> The knave turns fool that runs away;
>   The fool no knave, perdy.   (*Fool*)

Fiery? the fiery duke?   Tell the hot duke that—   105
No, but not yet: may be he is not well:
Infirmity doth still neglect all office
Whereto our health is bound; we are not ourselves
When nature, being oppress'd, commands the mind
To suffer with the body.   (*Lear*)

Lear. O me, my heart, my rising heart! but, down!   122
Fool. Cry to it, nuncle, as the cockney did to the eels
when she put 'em i' the paste alive; she knapped 'em o'
the coxcombs with a stick, and cried 'Down, wantons,
down!' 'Twas her brother that, in pure kindness to his
horse, buttered his hay.

                        I have hope   140
You less know how to value her desert
Than she to scant her duty.   (*Regan*)

                   O, sir, you are old;   148
Nature in you stands on the very verge
Of her confine: you should be ruled and led
By some discretion, that discerns your state
Better than you yourself.   (*Regan*)

Do you but mark how this becomes the house: 155
'Dear daughter, I confess that I am old;
Age is unnecessary: on my knees I beg
That you'll vouchsafe me raiment, bed, and food.'   (*Lear*)

All the stored vengeances of heaven fall   164
On her ingrateful top!   Strike her young bones,
You taking airs, with lameness!   (*Lear*)

You nimble lightnings, dart your blinding flames   167
Into her scornful eyes!   Infect her beauty,
You fen-suck'd fogs, drawn by the powerful sun,
To fall and blast her pride!   (*Lear*)

Thy tender-hefted nature shall not give II. iv. 174
Thee o'er to harshness: her eyes are fierce; but thine
Do comfort and not burn. (*Lear*)

All's not offence that indiscretion finds 199
And dotage terms so. (*Goneril*)

I pray you, father, being weak, seem so. (*Regan*) 204

Return to her, and fifty men dismiss'd? 210
No, rather I abjure all roofs, and choose
To wage against the enmity o' the air;
To be a comrade with the wolf and owl,—
Necessity's sharp pinch! (*Lear*)

How, in one house, 243
Should many people, under two commands,
Hold amity? 'Tis hard; almost impossible. (*Regan*)

O, reason not the need: our basest beggars 267
Are in the poorest thing superfluous:
Allow not nature more than nature needs,
Man's life's as cheap as beast's: thou art a lady;
If only to go warm were gorgeous,
Why, nature needs not what thou gorgeous wear'st,
Which scarcely keeps thee warm. But, for true need,—
You heavens, give me that patience, patience I need!
You see me here, you gods, a poor old man,
As full of grief as age; wretched in both!
If it be you that stir these daughters' hearts
Against their father, fool me not so much
To bear it tamely; touch me with noble anger,
And let not women's weapons, water-drops,
Stain my man's cheeks! No, you unnatural hags,
I will have such revenges on you both,
That all the world shall—I will do such things,—
What they are, yet I know not; but they shall be
The terrors of the earth. You think I'll weep:
No, I'll not weep:
I have full cause of weeping; but this heart
Shall break into a hundred thousand flaws,
Or ere I'll weep. O fool, I shall go mad! (*Lear*)

To wilful men, 305
The injuries that they themselves procure
Must be their schoolmasters. (*Regan*)

Kent. Who's there, besides foul weather? III. i. 1
Gentleman. One minded like the weather, most unquietly.

Kent.   Where's the king?   III. i. 3
Gentleman. Contending with the fretful element;
Bids the wind blow the earth into the sea,
Or swell the curled waters 'bove the main,
That things might change or cease; tears his white hair,
Which the impetuous blasts, with eyeless rage,
Catch in their fury, and make nothing of;
Strives in his little world of man to out-scorn
The to-and-fro conflicting wind and rain.
This night, wherein the cub-drawn bear would couch,
The lion and the belly-pinched wolf
Keep their fur dry, unbonneted he runs,
And bids what will take all.

Kent.   But who is with him?   15
Gentleman. None but the fool; who labours to out-jest
His heart-struck injuries.

Blow, winds, and crack your cheeks! rage! blow!   III. ii. 1
You cataracts and hurricanoes, spout
Till you have drench'd our steeples, drown'd the cocks!
You sulphurous and thought-executing fires,
Vaunt-couriers to oak-cleaving thunderbolts,
Singe my white head!   And thou, all-shaking thunder,
Smite flat the thick rotundity o' the world!
Crack nature's moulds, all germens spill at once,
That make ingrateful man!   (*Lear*)

    O nuncle, court holy-water in a dry house is better than   10
this rain-water out o' door.   (*Fool*)

Rumble thy bellyful!   Spit, fire! spout, rain!   14
Nor rain, wind, thunder, fire, are my daughters:
I tax not you, you elements, with unkindness;
I never gave you kingdom, call'd you children,
You owe me no subscription: then let fall
Your horrible pleasure; here I stand, your slave,
A poor, infirm, weak, and despised old man:
But yet I call you servile ministers,
That have with two pernicious daughters join'd
Your high engender'd battles 'gainst a head
So old and white as this.   O! O! 'tis foul!   (*Lear*)

            The man that makes his toe   31
                What he his heart should make
            Shall of a corn cry woe,
                And turn his sleep to wake.

For there was never yet fair woman but she made mouths
in a glass.   (*Fool*)

Things that love night   III. ii. 42
Love not such nights as these; the wrathful skies
Gallow the very wanderers of the dark,
And make them keep their caves: since I was man,
Such sheets of fire, such bursts of horrid thunder,
Such groans of roaring wind and rain, I never
Remember to have heard.   (*Kent*)

Let the great gods,   49
That keep this dreadful pother o'er our heads,
Find out their enemies now.   Tremble, thou wretch,
That hast within thee undivulged crimes,
Unwhipp'd of justice: hide thee, thou bloody hand;
Thou perjured, and thou simular man of virtue
That art incestuous: caitiff, to pieces shake,
That under covert and convenient seeming
Hast practised on man's life: close pent-up guilts,
Rive your concealing continents, and cry
These dreadful summoners grace. I am a man
More sinn'd against than sinning.   (*Lear*)

The art of our necessities is strange,
That can make vile things precious.   (*Lear*)   70

He that has and a little tiny wit,—
With hey, ho, the wind and the rain,—   74
Must make content with his fortunes fit,
For the rain it raineth every day.   (*Fool, sings*)

When priests are more in word than matter;   81
When brewers mar their malt with water;
When nobles are their tailors' tutors;
No heretics burn'd, but wenches' suitors;
When every case in law is right;
No squire in debt, nor no poor knight;
When slanders do not live in tongues;
Nor cutpurses come not to throngs;
When usurers tell their gold i' the field;
And bawds and whores do churches build;
Then shall the realm of Albion
Come to great confusion:
Then comes the time, who lives to see 't,
That going shall be used with feet.   (*Fool*)

The younger rises when the old doth fall.   (*Edmund*)   III. iii. 28

The tyranny of the open night's too rough   III. iv. 2
For nature to endure.   (*Kent*)

Thou think'st 'tis much that this contentious storm   III. iv. 6
Invades us to the skin: so 'tis to thee;
But where the greater malady is fix'd,
The lesser is scarce felt.   Thou'ldst shun a bear;
But if thy flight lay toward the raging sea,
Thou'ldst meet the bear i' the mouth.   When the mind's
   free,
The body's delicate: the tempest in my mind
Doth from my senses take all feeling else
Save what beats there.   Filial ingratitude!
Is it not as this mouth should tear this hand
For lifting food to 't?   But I will punish home:
No, I will weep no more.   In such a night
To shut me out!   Pour on; I will endure.
In such a night as this!   O Regan, Goneril!
Your kind old father, whose frank heart gave all,—
O, that way madness lies; let me shun that;
No more of that.   (*Lear*)

Poor naked wretches, wheresoe'er you are,   28
That bide the pelting of this pitiless storm,
How shall your houseless heads and unfed sides,
Your loop'd and window'd raggedness, defend you
From seasons such as these?   O, I have ta'en
Too little care of this!   Take physic, pomp;
Expose thyself to feel what wretches feel,
That thou mayst shake the superflux to them,
And show the heavens more just.   (*Lear*)

Fathom and half, fathom and half!   Poor Tom!   37
                                        (*Edgar*)

Through the sharp hawthorn blows the cold wind,   47
Hum! go to thy cold bed, and warm thee.   (*Edgar*)

   Who gives any thing to poor Tom? whom the foul fiend   51
hath led through fire and through flame, through ford and
whirlpool, o'er bog and quagmire; that hath laid knives
under his pillow, and halters in his pew; set ratsbane by
his porridge; made him proud of heart, to ride on a bay
trotting-horse over four-inched bridges, to course his own
shadow for a traitor.   Bless thy five wits!   Tom's a-cold.
                                        (*Edgar*)

            Pillicock sat on Pillicock-hill: 78
            Halloo, halloo, loo, loo!   (*Edgar*)

This cold night will turn us all to fools and madmen.   80
                                        (*Fool*)

Lear. What hast thou been?   III. iv. 86
Edgar. A serving-man, proud in heart and mind; that
curled my hair; wore gloves in my cap; served the lust
of my mistress' heart, and did the act of darkness with
her; swore as many oaths as I spake words, and broke
them in the sweet face of heaven: one that slept in the
contriving of lust, and waked to do it: wine loved I
deeply, dice dearly; and in woman out-paramoured the
Turk: false of heart, light of ear, bloody of hand; hog in
sloth, fox in stealth, wolf in greediness, dog in madness,
lion in prey.

Is man no more than this? Consider him well. Thou   107
owest the worm no silk, the beast no hide, the sheep no
wool, the cat no perfume. Ha! here's three on's are
sophisticated! Thou art the thing itself: unaccommo-
dated man is no more but such a poor, bare, forked animal
as thou art. Off, off, you lendings! come, unbutton here.
                                                    (*Lear*)

'Tis a naughty night to swim in.   (*Fool*)   115

    Saint Withold footed thrice the old;   127
    He met the night-mare, and her nine-fold;
        Bid her alight,
        And her troth plight,
    And aroint thee, witch, aroint thee!   (*Edgar*)

Poor Tom; that eats the swimming frog, the toad, the   134
tadpole, the wall-newt and the water; that in the fury of
his heart, when the foul fiend rages, eats cow-dung for
sallets; swallows the old rat and the ditch-dog; drinks the
green mantle of the standing pool; who is whipped from
tithing to tithing, and stock-punished, and imprisoned;
who hath had three suits to his back, six shirts to his body,
horse to ride, and weapon to wear;

    But mice and rats, and such small deer,
    Have been Tom's food for seven long year.   (*Edgar*)

The prince of darkness is a gentleman: 148
Modo he's call'd, and Mahu.   (*Edgar*)

First let me talk with this philosopher.   159
What is the cause of thunder?   (*Lear*)

I'll talk a word with this same learned Theban.   (*Lear*) 162

His wits begin to unsettle.   (*Kent*)   166

Child Rowland to the dark tower came,   III. iv. 188
His word was still, Fie, foh, and fum,
 I smell the blood of a British man. (*Edgar*)

Frateretto calls me; and tells me Nero is an angler in the III. vi. 9
lake of darkness. Pray, innocent, and beware the foul
fiend. (*Edgar*)

To have a thousand with red burning spits   16
Come hissing in upon 'em. (*Lear*)

He's mad that trusts in the tameness of a wolf, a horse's 19
health, a boy's love, or a whore's oath. (*Fool*)

Wantest thou eyes at trial, madam?   26
  Come o'er the bourn, Bessy, to me. (*Edgar*)

Sleepest or wakest thou, jolly shepherd?   43
 Thy sheep be in the corn;
And for one blast of thy minikin mouth,
 Thy sheep shall take no harm. (*Edgar*)

Cry you mercy, I took you for a joint-stool. (*Fool*) 54

My tears begin to take his part so much,   63
They'll mar my counterfeiting. (*Edgar*)

The little dogs and all,   65
Tray, Blanch, and Sweet-heart, see, they bark at me.
        (*Lear*)

Be thy mouth or black or white,   69
Tooth that poisons if it bite;
Mastiff, greyhound, mongrel grim,
Hound or spaniel, brach or lym,
Or bobtail tike or trundle-tail,
Tom will make them weep and wail:
For, with throwing thus my head,
Dogs leap the hatch, and all are fled. (*Edgar*)

You, sir, I entertain for one of my hundred; only I do 83
not like the fashion of your garments: you will say they
are Persian attire; but let them be changed. (*Lear*)

Lear. Make no noise, make no noise; draw the curtains: 90
so, so, so. We'll go to supper i' the morning. So, so,
so.
Fool. And I'll go to bed at noon.

Oppressed nature sleeps: III. vi. 104
This rest might yet have balm'd thy broken sinews,
Which, if convenience will not allow,
Stand in hard cure.   (*Kent*)

When we our betters see bearing our woes,   109
We scarcely think our miseries our foes.
Who alone suffers suffers most i' the mind,
Leaving free things and happy shows behind:
But then the mind much sufferance doth o'erskip,
When grief hath mates, and bearing fellowship.
How light and portable my pain seems now,
When that which makes me bend makes the king bow,
He childed as I father'd!   (*Edgar*)

Bind fast his corky arms.   (*Cornwall*)   III. vii. 29

By the kind gods, 'tis most ignobly done   35
To pluck me by the beard.   (*Gloucester*)

I am tied to the stake, and I must stand the course.   54
(*Gloucester*)

The sea, with such a storm as his bare head   59
In hell-black night endured, would have buoy'd up,
And quench'd the stelled fires:
Yet, poor old heart, he holp the heavens to rain.
If wolves had at thy gate howl'd that stern time,
Thou shouldst have said 'Good porter, turn the key,'
All cruels else subscribed.   (*Gloucester*)

Out, vile jelly!   (*Cornwall*)   83

Go thrust him out at gates, and let him smell   93
His way to Dover.   (*Regan*)

If she live long,   100
And in the end meet the old course of death,
Women will all turn monsters.   (*Third Servant*)

Yet better thus, and known to be contemn'd,   IV. i. 1
Than still contemn'd and flatter'd.   To be worst,
The lowest and most dejected thing of fortune,
Stands still in esperance, lives not in fear:
The lamentable change is from the best;
The worst returns to laughter.   (*Edgar*)

Thy comforts can do me no good at all;   17
Thee they may hurt.   (*Gloucester*)

I have no way, and therefore want no eyes;   IV. i. 20
I stumbled when I saw: full oft 'tis seen,
Our means secure us, and our mere defects
Prove our commodities.   (*Gloucester*)

                        The worst is not   29
So long as we can say 'This is the worst.'   (*Edgar*)

As flies to wanton boys, are we to the gods,   38
They kill us for their sport.   (*Gloucester*)

'Tis the times' plague, when madmen lead the blind.   48
                                     (*Gloucester*)

Gloucester. Know'st thou the way to Dover?   57
Edgar. Both stile and gate, horse-way and foot-path.

                That I am wretched   68
Makes thee the happier: heavens, deal so still!
Let the superfluous and lust-dieted man,
That slaves your ordinance, that will not see
Because he doth not feel, feel your power quickly;
So distribution should undo excess,
And each man have enough.   (*Gloucester*)

There is a cliff, whose high and bending head   76
Looks fearfully in the confined deep:
Bring me but to the very brim of it,
And I'll repair the misery thou dost bear
With something rich about me: from that place
I shall no leading need.   (*Gloucester*)

What most he should dislike seems pleasant to him;   IV. ii. 10
What like, offensive.   (*Oswald*)

I must change arms at home, and give the distaff   17
Into my husband's hands.   (*Goneril*)

Yours in the ranks of death.   (*Edmund*)   25

O, the difference of man and man!   26
To thee a woman's services are due:
My fool usurps my body.   (*Goneril*)

You are not worth the dust which the rude wind   30
Blows in your face.   I fear your disposition:
That nature, which contemns it origin,
Cannot be border'd certain in itself;
She that herself will sliver and disbranch
From her material sap, perforce must wither
And come to deadly use.   (*Albany*)

Wisdom and goodness to the vile seem vile: IV. ii. 38
Filths savour but themselves.   (*Albany*)

Proper deformity seems not in the fiend   60
So horrid as in woman.   (*Albany*)

Thou changed and self-cover'd thing, for shame,   62
Be-monster not thy feature.   (*Albany*)

     Patience and sorrow strove   IV. iii. 18
Who should express her goodliest.   You have seen
Sunshine and rain at once: her smiles and tears
Were like a better way: those happy smilets
That play'd on her ripe lip, seem'd not to know
What guests were in her eyes; which parted thence
As pearls from diamonds dropp'd.   In brief,
Sorrow would be a rarity most beloved,
If all could so become it.   (*Gentleman*)

      It is the stars,
The stars above us, govern our conditions.   (*Kent*)   34

As mad as the vex'd sea; singing aloud;   IV. iv. 2
Crown'd with rank fumiter and furrow-weeds,
With bur-docks, hemlock, nettles, cuckoo-flowers,
Darnel, and all the idle weeds that grow
In our sustaining corn.   (*Cordelia*)

She gave strange oeillades and most speaking looks   IV. v. 25
To noble Edmund.   (*Regan*)

       How fearful   IV. vi. 11
And dizzy 'tis to cast one's eyes so low!
The crows and choughs that wing the midway air
Show scarce so gross as beetles: half way down
Hangs one that gathers samphire, dreadful trade!
Methinks he seems no bigger than his head:
The fishermen that walk upon the beach
Appear like mice; and yond tall anchoring bark,
Diminish'd to her cock; her cock, a buoy
Almost too small for sight: the murmuring surge,
That on the unnumber'd idle pebbles chafes,
Cannot be heard so high.   (*Edgar*)

Hadst thou been aught but gossamer, feathers, air,   49
So many fathom down precipitating,
Thou'dst shiver'd like an egg: but thou dost breathe;
Hast heavy substance; bleed'st not; speak'st; art sound.
Ten masts at each make not the altitude
Which thou hast perpendicularly fell:
Thy life's a miracle.   (*Edgar*)

From the dread summit of this chalky bourn.   IV. vi. 57
Look up a-height; the shrill-gorged lark so far
Cannot be seen or heard.   (*Edgar*)

Is wretchedness deprived that benefit,   61
To end itself by death?   'Twas yet some comfort,
When misery could beguile the tyrant's rage,
And frustrate his proud will.   (*Gloucester*)

As I stood here below, methought his eyes   69
Were two full moons; he had a thousand noses,
Horns whelk'd and waved like the enridged sea:
It was some fiend.   (*Edgar*)

                              Henceforth I'll bear   75
Affliction till it do cry out itself
'Enough, enough,' and die.   (*Gloucester*)

O thou side-piercing sight!   (*Edgar*)   85

    There's your press-money.   That fellow handles his   87
bow like a crow-keeper: draw me a clothier's yard.
Look, look, a mouse!   Peace, peace; this piece of toasted
cheese will do't.   There's my gauntlet; I'll prove it on a
giant.   (*Lear*)

Lear. Give the word.   93
Edgar. Sweet marjoram.

    To say 'ay' and 'no' to every thing that I said!   'Ay'   100
and 'no' too was no good divinity.   (*Lear*)

    Go to, they are not men o' their words: they told me   105
I was every thing; 'tis a lie, I am not ague-proof. (*Lear*)

Gloucester. The trick of that voice I do well remember: 108
Is't not the king?
Lear.   Ay, every inch a king:
When I do stare, see how the subject quakes.

Thou shalt not die: die for adultery!   No: 113
The wren goes to't, and the small gilded fly
Does lecher in my sight.
Let copulation thrive; for Gloucester's bastard son
Was kinder to his father than my daughters
Got 'tween the lawful sheets.
To't, luxury, pell-mell! for I lack soldiers.
Behold yond simpering dame,
Whose face between her forks presages snow;

That minces virtue, and does shake the head   IV. vi. 122
To hear of pleasure's name;
The fitchew, nor the soiled horse, goes to 't
With a more riotous appetite.   (*Lear*)

Give me an ounce of civet, good apothecary, to sweeten   132
my imagination.   (*Lear*)

Gloucester. O, let me kiss that hand!   135
Lear. Let me wipe it first; it smells of mortality.

Dost thou squiny at me?   No, do thy worst, blind   140
Cupid; I'll not love.   (*Lear*)

A man may see how this world goes with no eyes.   Look   153
with thine ears: see how yond justice rails upon yond
simple thief.   Hark, in thine ear: change places; and,
handy-dandy, which is the justice, which is the thief?
                                                    (*Lear*)

Through tatter'd clothes small vices do appear;   168
Robes and furr'd gowns hide all.   Plate sin with gold,
And the strong lance of justice hurtless breaks;
Arm it in rags, a pigmy's straw does pierce it.   (*Lear*)

                    Get thee glass eyes;   174
And, like a scurvy politician, seem
To see the things thou dost not.   (*Lear*)

Thou must be patient: we came crying hither: 182
Thou know'st, the first time that we smell the air,
We wawl and cry.   (*Lear*)

When we are born, we cry that we are come   186
To this great stage of fools.   (*Lear*)

                    A serviceable villain;   257
As duteous to the vices of thy mistress
As badness could desire.   (*Edgar*)

Had you not been their father, these white flakes   IV. vii. 30
Had challenged pity of them.   Was this a face
To be opposed against the warring winds?
To stand against the deep dread-bolted thunder?
In the most terrible and nimble stroke
Of quick cross lightning? to watch—poor perdu!—
With this thin helm?   Mine enemy's dog,
Though he had bit me, should have stood that night
Against my fire.   (*Cordelia*)

Thou art a soul in bliss; but I am bound   IV. vii. 46
Upon a wheel of fire, that mine own tears
Do scald like molten lead.   (*Lear*)

Lear. You are a spirit, I know: when did you die?   49
Cordelia. Still, still, far wide!

I am mightily abused.   I should e'en die with pity,   53
To see another thus.   (*Lear*)

                              Pray, do not mock me: 59
I am a very foolish fond old man,
Fourscore and upward, not an hour more nor less;
And, to deal plainly,
I fear I am not in my perfect mind.   (*Lear*)

Pray you now, forget and forgive: I am old and foolish.   85
                                                    (*Lear*)

To both these sisters have I sworn my love;   v. i. 55
Each jealous of the other, as the stung
Are of the adder.   (*Edmund*)

Edgar. Give me thy hand; come on.   v. ii. 7
Gloucester. No farther, sir; a man may rot even here.
Edgar. What, in ill thoughts again?   Men must endure
Their going hence, even as their coming hither:
Ripeness is all: come on.
Gloucester.   And that's true too.

                        We are not the first   v. iii. 3
Who, with best meaning, have incurr'd the worst.
For thee, oppressed king, am I cast down;
Myself could else out-frown false fortune's frown.
                                                (*Cordelia*)

No, no, no, no!   Come, let's away to prison: 8
We two alone will sing like birds i' the cage:
When thou dost ask me blessing, I'll kneel down,
And ask of thee forgiveness: so we'll live,
And pray, and sing, and tell old tales, and laugh
At gilded butterflies, and hear poor rogues
Talk of court news; and we'll talk with them too,
Who loses and who wins; who's in, who's out;
And take upon's the mystery of things,
As if we were God's spies: and we'll wear out,
In a wall'd prison, packs and sects of great ones
That ebb and flow by the moon.   (*Lear*)

Upon such sacrifices, my Cordelia,
The gods themselves throw incense. (*Lear*)   v. iii. 20

I cannot draw a cart, nor eat dried oats;
If it be man's work, I'll do it. (*Captain*)   38

The let-alone lies not in your good will. (*Albany*)   79

The gods are just, and of our pleasant vices
Make instruments to plague us. (*Edgar*)   170

The wheel is come full circle. (*Edmund*)   174

             His flaw'd heart,   196
Alack, too weak the conflict to support!
'Twixt two extremes of passion, joy and grief,
Burst smilingly. (*Edgar*)

           Some good I mean to do,   243
Despite of mine own nature. (*Edmund*)

Kent. Is this the promised end?   263
Edgar. Or image of that horror?

A plague upon you, murderers, traitors all!   269
I might have saved her; now she's gone for ever!
Cordelia, Cordelia! stay a little. Ha!
What is't thou say'st? Her voice was ever soft,
Gentle and low, an excellent thing in woman. (*Lear*)

Lear. I kill'd the slave that was a-hanging thee.   274
Captain. 'Tis true, my lords, he did.
Lear.   Did I not, fellow?
I have seen the day, with my good biting falchion
I would have made them skip: I am old now,
And these same crosses spoil me.

If fortune brag of two she loved and hated,   280
One of them we behold. (*Kent*)

           All's cheerless, dark, and deadly.   290
Your eldest daughters have fordone themselves,
And desperately are dead. (*Kent*)

Lear. And my poor fool is hang'd! No, no, no life!   305
Why should a dog, a horse, a rat, have life,
And thou no breath at all? Thou'lt come no more,
Never, never, never, never, never!
Pray you, undo this button: thank you, sir.
Do you see this? Look on her, look, her lips,
Look there, look there!   [*Dies.*]

Edgar. He faints! My lord, my lord!   v. iii. 312
Kent. Break, heart; I prithee, break!

Vex not his ghost: O, let him pass! he hates him much   313
That would upon the rack of this tough world
Stretch him out longer. (*Kent*)

I have a journey, sir, shortly to go;   321
My master calls me, I must not say no. (*Kent*)

The oldest hath borne most: we that are young   325
Shall never see so much, nor live so long. (*Albany*)

OTHELLO, THE MOOR OF VENICE

Othello, a Moorish general in the service of the Venetians, has married Desdemona secretly and against the wishes of her father, the senator Brabantio. Iago, an army officer, hates Othello for having given to Cassio the promotion which he himself wanted, and determines to be revenged on them both. Cassio has no head for liquor, and Iago contrives to get him drunk, so that Othello has to dismiss him from his post. Iago then advises Cassio to ask Desdemona to use her influence with her husband to get him reinstated. Meanwhile, by sly hints and insinuations, while making a great show of honesty and reluctance, he persuades Othello into the belief that his wife has been unfaithful with Cassio. As proof, he refers to a missing handkerchief of Desdemona's which has in fact been purloined at his request by her maid Emilia, who is Iago's wife. Convinced of Desdemona's infidelity, Othello smothers her, but immediately afterwards the plot is revealed by Emilia, who is promptly stabbed by her husband. Othello, overcome by remorse, commits suicide, and Iago is led off to pay the penalty for his crimes.

One Michael Cassio, a Florentine,   I. i. 20
A fellow almost damn'd in a fair wife;
That never set a squadron in the field,
Nor the division of a battle knows
More than a spinster; unless the bookish theoric,
Wherein the toged consuls can propose
As masterly as he: mere prattle, without practice,
Is all his soldiership. (*Iago*)

                  'Tis the curse of service,   35
Preferment goes by letter and affection,
And not by old gradation, where each second
Stood heir to the first. (*Iago*)

We cannot all be masters, nor all masters   43
Cannot be truly follow'd. You shall mark
Many a duteous and knee-crooking knave
That, doting on his own obsequious bondage,
Wears out his time, much like his master's ass,
For nought but provender, and when he's old, cashier'd:
Whip me such honest knaves. (*Iago*)

In following him, I follow but myself. (*Iago*)   58

But I will wear my heart upon my sleeve   64
For daws to peck at: I am not what I am. (*Iago*)

What a full fortune does the thick-lips owe,   66
If he can carry 't thus! (*Roderigo*)

Even now, now, very now, an old black ram   88
Is tupping your white ewe. (*Iago*)

Being full of supper and distempering draughts,   99
Upon malicious bravery, dost thou come
To start my quiet. (*Brabantio*)

   'Zounds, sir, you are one of those that will not serve   107
God, if the devil bid you. (*Iago*)

   Your daughter and the Moor are now making the beast   117
with two backs. (*Iago*)

   An extravagant and wheeling stranger   137
Of here and every where. (*Roderigo*)

Though I do hate him as I do hell-pains,   155
Yet, for necessity of present life,
I must show out a flag and sign of love,
Which is indeed but sign. (*Iago*)

Though in the trade of war I have slain men,   I. ii. I
Yet do I hold it very stuff o' the conscience
To do no contrived murder: I lack iniquity
Sometimes to do me service.   *(Iago)*

My parts, my title and my perfect soul   31
Shall manifest me rightly.   *(Othello)*

Keep up your bright swords, for the dew will rust them.   59
Good signior, you shall more command with years
Than with your weapons.   *(Othello)*

Whether a maid so tender, fair and happy,   66
So opposite to marriage that she shunn'd
The wealthy curled darlings of our nation,
Would ever have, to incur a general mock,
Run from her guardage to the sooty bosom
Of such a thing as thou, to fear, not to delight.
                                 (Brabantio)

           My particular grief   I. iii. 55
Is of so flood-gate and o'erbearing nature
That it engluts and swallows other sorrows
And it is still itself.   *(Brabantio)*

Most potent, grave, and reverend signiors,   76
My very noble and approved good masters,
That I have ta'en away this old man's daughter,
It is most true; true, I have married her:
The very head and front of my offending
Hath this extent, no more.   Rude am I in my speech,
And little bless'd with the soft phrase of peace;
For since these arms of mine had seven years' pith,
Till now some nine moons wasted, they have used
Their dearest action in the tented field,
And little of this great world can I speak,
More than pertains to feats of broil and battle,
And therefore little shall I grace my cause
In speaking for myself.   Yet, by your gracious patience,
I will a round unvarnish'd tale deliver
Of my whole course of love; what drugs, what charms,
What conjuration and what mighty magic,
For such proceeding I am charged withal,
I won his daughter.   *(Othello)*

           A maiden never bold;   94
Of spirit so still and quiet, that her motion
Blush'd at herself.   *(Brabantio)*

Her father loved me; oft invited me;
Still question'd me the story of my life,
From year to year, the battles, sieges, fortunes,
That I have pass'd.
I ran it through, even from my boyish days,
To the very moment that he bade me tell it;
Wherein I spake of most disastrous chances,
Of moving accidents by flood and field,
Of hair-breadth 'scapes i' the imminent deadly breach,
Of being taken by the insolent foe
And sold to slavery, of my redemption thence
And portance in my travels' history:
Wherein of antres vast and deserts idle,
Rough quarries, rocks and hills whose heads touch heaven,
It was my hint to speak,—such was the process;
And of the Cannibals that each other eat,
The Anthropophagi and men whose heads
Do grow beneath their shoulders.   This to hear
Would Desdemona seriously incline.   (*Othello*)

              I did consent,   155
And often did beguile her of her tears,
When I did speak of some distressful stroke
That my youth suffer'd.   My story being done,
She gave me for my pains a world of sighs:
She swore, in faith, 'twas strange, 'twas passing strange,
'Twas pitiful, 'twas wondrous pitiful:
She wish'd she had not heard it, yet she wish'd
That heaven had made her such a man: she thank'd me,
And bade me, if I had a friend that loved her,
I should but teach him how to tell my story,
And that would woo her.   Upon this hint I spake:
She loved me for the dangers I had pass'd,
And I loved her that she did pity them.   (*Othello*)

              My noble father,   180
I do perceive here a divided duty:
To you I am bound for life and education;
My life and education both do learn me
How to respect you; you are the lord of duty;
I am hitherto your daughter: but here's my husband,
And so much duty as my mother show'd
To you, preferring you before her father,
So much I challenge that I may profess
Due to the Moor my lord.   (*Desdemona*)

When remedies are past, the griefs are ended   202
By seeing the worst, which late on hopes depended.
To mourn a mischief that is past and gone
Is the next way to draw new mischief on.

What cannot be preserved when fortune takes
Patience her injury a mockery makes.
The robb'd that smiles steals something from the thief;
He robs himself that spends a bootless grief.   (*Duke*)

The tyrant custom, most grave senators,   230
Hath made the flinty and steel couch of war
My thrice-driven bed of down: I do agnize
A natural and prompt alacrity
I find in hardness, and do undertake
These present wars against the Ottomites.   (*Othello*)

           My heart's subdued   251
Even to the very quality of my lord:
I saw Othello's visage in his mind,
And to his honours and his valiant parts
Did I my soul and fortunes consecrate.   (*Desdemona*)

Let housewives make a skillet of my helm.   (*Othello*)   273

Look to her, Moor, if thou hast eyes to see: 293
She has deceived her father, and may thee.   (*Brabantio*)

Roderigo. I will incontinently drown myself.   306
Iago. If thou dost, I shall never love thee after.   Why,
thou silly gentleman!

    I have looked upon the world for four times seven   312
years; and since I could distinguish betwixt a benefit and
an injury, I never found man that knew how to love himself.   Ere I would say, I would drown myself for the love
of a guinea-hen, I would change my humanity with a
baboon.   (*Iago*)

    Virtue! a fig! 'tis in ourselves that we are thus or thus.   322
Our bodies are our gardens, to the which our wills are
gardeners; so that if we will plant nettles or sow lettuce,
set hyssop and weed up thyme, supply it with one gender
of herbs or distract it with many, either to have it sterile
with idleness or manured with industry, why, the power
and corrigible authority of this lies in our wills.   (*Iago*)

    Put money in thy purse; follow thou the wars; defeat   345
thy favour with an usurped beard; I say, put money in thy
purse.   It cannot be that Desdemona should long continue her love to the Moor,—put money in thy purse,—
nor he his to her: it was a violent commencement, and thou
shalt see an answerable sequestration; put but money
in thy purse.   These Moors are changeable in their wills:
—fill thy purse with money:—the food that to him now is
as luscious as locusts, shall be to him shortly as bitter as
coloquintida.   (*Iago*)

Thus do I ever make my fool my purse;   I. iii. 389
For I mine own gain'd knowledge should profane,
If I would time expend with such a snipe,
But for my sport and profit. (*Iago*)

The Moor is of a free and open nature,   405
That thinks men honest that but seem to be so,
And will as tenderly be led by the nose
As asses are. (*Iago*)

I have 't.   It is engender'd.   Hell and night   409
Must bring this monstrous birth to the world's light.
                                              (*Iago*)

For do but stand upon the foaming shore,   II. i. 11
The chidden billow seems to pelt the clouds;
The wind-shaked surge, with high and monstrous mane,
Seems to cast water on the burning bear,
And quench the guards of the ever-fixed pole.
                                    (*Second Gentleman*)

                              A maid   61
That paragons description and wild fame;
One that excels the quirks of blazoning pens,
And in the essential vesture of creation
Does tire the ingener. (*Cassio*)

Tempests themselves, high seas and howling winds,   68
The gutter'd rocks and congregated sands,—
Traitors ensteep'd to clog the guiltless keel,—
As having sense of beauty, do omit
Their mortal natures, letting go safely by
The divine Desdemona. (*Cassio*)

                    You are pictures out of doors,   110
Bells in your parlours, wild-cats in your kitchens,
Saints in your injuries, devils being offended,
Players in your housewifery, and housewives in your beds.
                                              (*Iago*)

                    Do not put me to 't;   119
For I am nothing, if not critical. (*Iago*)

I am not merry; but I do beguile   123
The thing I am, by seeming otherwise. (*Desdemona*)

If she be fair and wise, fairness and wit,   130
The one's for use, the other useth it. (*Iago*)

If she be black, and thereto have a wit,   II. i. 133
She'll find a white that shall her blackness fit.   (*Iago*)

Iago. She never yet was foolish that was fair;   137
For even her folly help'd her to an heir.
Desdemona. These are old fond paradoxes to make fools
laugh i' the alehouse.

Iago. She that was ever fair and never proud,   149
Had tongue at will and yet was never loud,
Never lack'd gold and yet went never gay,
Fled from her wish and yet said 'Now I may,'
She that being anger'd, her revenge being nigh,
Bade her wrong stay and her displeasure fly,
She that in wisdom never was so frail
To change the cod's head for the salmon's tail,
She that could think and ne'er disclose her mind,
See suitors following and not look behind,
She was a wight, if ever such wight were,—
Desdemona. To do what?
Iago. To suckle fools and chronicle small beer.
Desdemona. O most lame and impotent conclusion!

                    If it were now to die,   191
'Twere now to be most happy; for, I fear,
My soul hath her content so absolute
That not another comfort like to this
Succeeds in unknown fate.   (*Othello*)

Honey, you shall be well desired in Cyprus.   (*Othello*)   206

    A slipper and subtle knave, a finder out of occasions; that   247
has an eye can stamp and counterfeit advantages, though
true advantage never present itself: a devilish knave.
Besides, the knave is handsome, young, and hath all
those requisites in him that folly and green minds look
after: a pestilent complete knave; and the woman hath
found him already.   (*Iago*)

This poor trash of Venice.   (*Iago*)   312

Make the Moor thank me, love me and reward me   317
For making him egregiously an ass.   (*Iago*)

    Not to-night, good Iago: I have very poor and unhappy   II. iii. 34
brains for drinking: I could well wish courtesy would
invent some other custom of entertainment.   (*Cassio*)

Potations pottle-deep.   (*Iago*)   56

If consequence do but approve my dream,   II. iii. 64
My boat sails freely, both with wind and stream.   (*Iago*)

    And let me the canakin clink, clink;   71
    And let me the canakin clink:
      A soldier's a man;
      A life's but a span;
    Why, then, let a soldier drink.   (*Iago, sings*)

    I learned it in England, where, indeed, they are most   78
potent in potting: your Dane, your German, and your
swag-bellied Hollander—Drink, ho!—are nothing to
your English.   (*Iago*)

    King Stephen was a worthy peer,   92
      His breeches cost him but a crown;
    He held them sixpence all too dear,
      With that he call'd the tailor lown.
    He was a wight of high renown,
      And thou art but of low degree:
    'Tis pride that pulls the country down;
      Then take thine auld cloak about thee.
                                (*Iago, sings*)

    Well, God's above all; and there be souls must be saved,   105
and there be souls must not be saved.   (*Cassio*)

Cassio. For mine own part,—no offence to the general,   109
nor any man of quality,—I hope to be saved.
Iago. And so do I too, lieutenant.
Cassio. Ay, but, by your leave, not before me; the lieutenant is to be saved before the ancient.

Cassio. Do not think, gentlemen, I am drunk: this is my   116
ancient; this is my right hand, and this is my left: I am
not drunk now; I can stand well enough, and speak
well enough.
All. Excellent well.

He is a soldier fit to stand by Caesar   127
And give direction.   (*Iago*)

For Christian shame, put by this barbarous brawl: 172
He that stirs next to carve for his own rage
Holds his soul light; he dies upon his motion.
Silence that dreadful bell: it frights the isle
From her propriety.   (*Othello*)

But men are men; the best sometimes forget.   (*Iago*)   241

As men in rage strike those that wish them best.   (*Iago*)   243

    Cassio, I love thee;   II. iii. 248
But never more be officer of mine. (*Othello*)

     'Tis the soldier's life   257
To have their balmy slumbers waked with strife.
        (*Othello*)

Reputation, reputation, reputation! O, I have lost my 262
reputation! I have lost the immortal part of myself, and
what remains is bestial. (*Cassio*)

Reputation is an idle and most false imposition; oft got 268
without merit, and lost without deserving. (*Iago*)

Drunk? and speak parrot? and squabble? swagger? 280
swear? and discourse fustian with one's own shadow? O
thou invisible spirit of wine, if thou hast no name to be
known by, let us call thee devil! (*Cassio*)

O God, that men should put an enemy in their mouths 290
to steal away their brains! that we should with joy, pleasance, revel and applause, transform ourselves into beasts!
        (*Cassio*)

Cassio. To be now a sensible man, by and by a fool, and 309
presently a beast! O strange! Every inordinate cup is
unblessed and the ingredient is a devil.
Iago. Come, come, good wine is a good familiar creature,
if it be well used: exclaim no more against it.

She is of so free, so kind, so apt, so blessed a disposition, 324
she holds it a vice in her goodness not to do more than
she is requested. (*Iago*)

And what's he then that says I play the villain? 342
When this advice is free I give and honest? (*Iago*)

When devils will the blackest sins put on, 357
They do suggest at first with heavenly shows. (*Iago*)

So will I turn her virtue into pitch, 366
And out of her own goodness make the net
That shall enmesh them all. (*Iago*)

How poor are they that have not patience! 376
What wound did ever heal but by degrees?
Thou know'st we work by wit, and not by witchcraft;
And wit depends on dilatory time. (*Iago*)

Pleasure and action make the hours seem short. (*Iago*) 385

Clown. Masters, here's money for you: and the general III. i. 11
so likes your music, that he desires you, for love's sake,
to make no more noise with it.
First Musician. Well, sir, we will not.
Clown. If you have any music that may not be heard, to't
again: but, as they say, to hear music the general does not
greatly care.

Cassio. Dost thou hear, my honest friend? 22
Clown. No, I hear not your honest friend; I hear you.

If I do vow a friendship, I'll perform it III. iii. 21
To the last article: my lord shall never rest;
I'll watch him tame and talk him out of patience;
His bed shall seem a school, his board a shrift;
I'll intermingle every thing he does
With Cassio's suit. (*Desdemona*)

Desdemona.   Good love, call him back. 54
Othello. Not now, sweet Desdemona; some other time.
Desdemona. But shall't be shortly?
Othello.   The sooner, sweet, for you.
Desdemona. Shall't be to-night at supper?
Othello.   No, not to-night.
Desdemona. To-morrow dinner, then?
Othello.   I shall not dine at home;
I meet the captains at the citadel.
Desdemona. Why, then, to-morrow night; or Tuesday
    morn;
On Tuesday noon, or night; on Wednesday morn;
I prithee name the time, but let it not
Exceed three days.

                Why, this is not a boon; 76
'Tis as I should entreat you wear your gloves,
Or feed on nourishing dishes, or keep you warm,
Or sue to you to do a peculiar profit
To your own person: nay, when I have a suit
Wherein I mean to touch your love indeed,
It shall be full of poise and difficult weight
And fearful to be granted. (*Desdemona*)

Excellent wretch! Perdition catch my soul, 90
But I do love thee! and when I love thee not,
Chaos is come again. (*Othello*)

                By heaven, he echoes me, 106
As if there were some monster in his thought
Too hideous to be shown. (*Othello*)

And, for I know thou 'rt full of love and honesty,　　iii. iii. 118
And weigh'st thy words before thou givest them breath,
Therefore these stops of thine fright me the more.
　　　　　　　　　　　　　　　　　(Othello)

　　　　　　　Men should be what they seem;　　126
Or those that be not, would they might seem none!
　　　　　　　　　　　　　　　　　(Iago)

Utter my thoughts?　Why, say they are vile and false;　136
As where 's that palace whereinto foul things
Sometimes intrude not? who has a breast so pure
But some uncleanly apprehensions
Keep leets and law-days, and in session sit
With meditations lawful?　(Iago)

Good name in man and woman, dear my lord,　　155
Is the immediate jewel of their souls:
Who steals my purse steals trash; 'tis something, nothing;
'Twas mine, 'tis his, and has been slave to thousands;
But he that filches from me my good name
Robs me of that which not enriches him
And makes me poor indeed.　(Iago)

　　　　　O, beware, my lord, of jealousy;　　165
It is the green-eyed monster which doth mock
The meat it feeds on.　(Iago)

But, O, what damned minutes tells he o'er　　169
Who dotes, yet doubts, suspects, yet strongly loves!
　　　　　　　　　　　　　　　　　(Iago)

Poor and content is rich and rich enough,　　172
But riches fineless is as poor as winter
To him that ever fears he shall be poor.　(Iago)

Iago. I see this hath a little dash'd your spirits.　　214
Othello. Not a jot, not a jot.

　　　　　　　Haply, for I am black　　263
And have not those soft parts of conversation
That chamberers have, or for I am declined
Into the vale of years,—yet that 's not much—
She 's gone.　I am abused; and my relief
Must be to loathe her.　O curse of marriage,
That we can call these delicate creatures ours,
And not their appetites!　I had rather be a toad,
And live upon the vapour of a dungeon,
Than keep a corner in the thing I love
For others' uses.　(Othello)

If she be false, O, then heaven mocks itself!
I'll not believe't. (*Othello*)

     Trifles light as air   322
Are to the jealous confirmations strong
As proofs of holy writ. (*Iago*)

     Not poppy, nor mandragora,   330
Nor all the drowsy syrups of the world,
Shall ever medicine thee to that sweet sleep
Which thou owedst yesterday. (*Iago*)

I swear 'tis better to be much abused   336
Than but to know't a little. (*Othello*)

He that is robb'd, not wanting what is stol'n,   342
Let him not know't, and he's not robb'd at all.
          (*Othello*)

     O, now, for ever   347
Farewell the tranquil mind! farewell content!
Farewell the plumed troop, and the big wars,
That make ambition virtue! O, farewell!
Farewell the neighing steed, and the shrill trump,
The spirit-stirring drum, the ear-piercing fife,
The royal banner, and all quality,
Pride, pomp and circumstance of glorious war!
And, O you mortal engines, whose rude throats
The immortal Jove's dread clamours counterfeit,
Farewell! Othello's occupation's gone! (*Othello*)

Be sure of it; give me the ocular proof. (*Othello*)   360

     So prove it,   364
That the probation bear no hinge nor loop
To hang a doubt on. (*Othello*)

If thou dost slander her and torture me,   368
Never pray more; abandon all remorse;
On horror's head horrors accumulate;
Do deeds to make heaven weep, all earth amazed;
For nothing canst thou to damnation add
Greater than that. (*Othello*)

O monstrous world! Take note, take note, O world, 377
To be direct and honest is not safe. (*Iago*)

     Her name, that was as fresh   386
As Dian's visage, is now begrimed and black
As mine own face. (*Othello*)
     408

There are a kind of men so loose of soul,   III. iii. 416
That in their sleeps will mutter their affairs.   (*Iago*)

But this denoted a foregone conclusion.   (*Othello*)   428

O, that the slave had forty thousand lives!   442
One is too poor, too weak for my revenge.   (*Othello*)

            Like to the Pontic sea,   453
Whose icy current and compulsive course
Ne'er feels retiring ebb, but keeps due on
To the Propontic and the Hellespont,
Even so my bloody thoughts, with violent pace,
Shall ne'er look back, ne'er ebb to humble love,
Till that a capable and wide revenge
Swallow them up.   (*Othello*)

Damn her, lewd minx!   O, damn her!   (*Othello*)   476

I know not where he lodges, and for me to devise a   III. iv. 11
lodging and say he lies here or he lies there, were to lie in
mine own throat.   (*Clown*)

Othello. Give me your hand: this hand is moist, my lady.   36
Desdemona. It yet hath felt no age nor known no sorrow.
Othello. This argues fruitfulness and liberal heart:
Hot, hot, and moist: this hand of yours requires
A sequester from liberty, fasting and prayer,
Much castigation, exercise devout;
For here's a young and sweating devil here,
That commonly rebels. 'Tis a good hand,
A frank one.
Desdemona.   You may, indeed, say so;
For 'twas that hand that gave away my heart.

            That handkerchief   55
Did an Egyptian to my mother give;
She was a charmer, and could almost read
The thoughts of people.   (*Othello*)

'Tis true: there's magic in the web of it: 69
A sibyl, that had number'd in the world
The sun to course two hundred compasses,
In her prophetic fury sew'd the work;
The worms were hallow'd that did breed the silk;
And it was dyed in mummy which the skilful
Conserved of maiden's hearts.   (*Othello*)

Men's natures wrangle with inferior things,   144
Though great ones are their object. 'Tis even so;

For let our finger ache, and it indues   III. iv. 146
Our other healthful members even to that sense
Of pain.   (*Desdemona*)

Desdemona. Alas the day! I never gave him cause.   158
Emilia. But jealous souls will not be answer'd so;
They are not ever jealous for the cause,
But jealous for they are jealous: 'tis a monster
Begot upon itself, born on itself.

What, keep a week away? seven days and nights?   173
Eight score eight hours? and lovers' absent hours,
More tedious than the dial eight score times?
O weary reckoning!   (*Bianca*)

            O, it comes o'er my memory,   IV. i. 20
As doth the raven o'er the infected house,
Boding to all.   (*Othello*)

My medicine, work! Thus credulous fools are caught.   46
                                   (*Iago*)

            Do but encave yourself,   82
And mark the fleers, the gibes and notable scorns,
That dwell in every region of his face.   (*Iago*)

I will be found most cunning in my patience;   91
But—dost thou hear?—most bloody.   (*Othello*)

Alas, poor rogue! I think, i' faith, she loves me.   112
                                   (*Cassio*)

O, I see that nose of yours, but not that dog I shall   146
throw it to.   (*Othello*)

I would have him nine years a-killing.   (*Othello*)   188

    My heart is turned to stone; I strike it, and it hurts my   193
hand.   (*Othello*)

    I do but say what she is: so delicate with her needle: 197
an admirable musician: O! she will sing the savageness out
of a bear: of so high and plenteous wit and invention.
                                   (*Othello*)

    But yet the pity of it, Iago! O Iago, the pity of it,   206
Iago!   (*Othello*)

If that the earth could teem with woman's tears,   256
Each drop she falls would prove a crocodile.   (*Othello*)

                    Is this the nature   IV. i. 276
Whom passion could not shake? whose solid virtue
The shot of accident nor dart of chance
Could neither graze nor pierce?   (*Lodovico*)

Heaven truly knows that thou art false as hell.   (*Othello*)   IV. ii. 39

                   Had it pleased heaven   47
To try me with affliction; had they rain'd
All kinds of sores and shames on my bare head,
Steep'd me in poverty to the very lips,
Given to captivity me and my utmost hopes,
I should have found in some place of my soul
A drop of patience: but, alas, to make me
A fixed figure for the time of scorn
To point his slow unmoving finger at!
Yet could I bear that too; well, very well:
But there, where I have garner'd up my heart,
Where either I must live, or bear no life;
The fountain from the which my current runs,
Or else dries up; to be discarded thence!
Or keep it as a cistern for foul toads
To knot and gender in!   Turn thy complexion there,
Patience, thou young and rose-lipp'd cherubin,—
Ay, there, look grim as hell! (*Othello*)

                  O thou weed,   67
Who art so lovely fair and smell'st so sweet
That the sense aches at thee, would thou hadst ne'er been
  born! (*Othello*)

I should make very forges of my cheeks,   74
That would to cinders burn up modesty,
Did I but speak thy deeds.   What committed!
Heaven stops the nose at it and the moon winks,
The bawdy wind that kisses all it meets
Is hush'd within the hollow mine of earth,
And will not hear it.   (*Othello*)

              Those that do teach young babes   111
Do it with gentle means and easy tasks:
He might have chid me so; for, in good faith,
I am a child to chiding. (*Desdemona*)

I will be hang'd, if some eternal villain,   130
Some busy and insinuating rogue,
Some cogging, cozening slave, to get some office,
Have not devised this slander. (*Emilia*)

A halter pardon him! and hell gnaw his bones! (*Emilia*)   IV. ii. 136

O heaven, that such companions thou'ldst unfold,   141
And put in every honest hand a whip
To lash the rascals naked through the world
Even from the east to the west! (*Emilia*)

                     Unkindness may do much;   159
And his unkindness may defeat my life,
But never taint my love. (*Desdemona*)

Emilia. I would you had never seen him!   IV. iii. 18
Desdemona. So would not I: my love doth so approve him,
That even his stubbornness, his checks, his frowns,—
Prithee, unpin me,—have grace and favour in them.

My mother had a maid call'd Barbara: 26
She was in love, and he she loved proved mad
And did forsake her: she had a song of 'willow';
An old thing 'twas, but it express'd her fortune,
And she died singing it: that song to-night
Will not go from my mind; I have much to do
But to go hang my head all at one side,
And sing it like poor Barbara. (*Desdemona*)

    I know a lady in Venice would have walked barefoot to   38
Palestine for a touch of his nether lip. (*Emilia*)

The poor soul sat sighing by a sycamore-tree,   41
    Sing all a green willow;
Her hand on her bosom, her head on her knee,
    Sing willow, willow, willow:
The fresh streams ran by her, and murmur'd her moans;
    Sing willow, willow, willow;
Her salt tears fell from her, and soften'd the stones;
    Sing willow, willow, willow. (*Desdemona, sings*)

Desdemona.   Mine eyes do itch;   58
Doth that bode weeping?
Emilia.   'Tis neither here nor there.

Desdemona.   O, these men, these men!   60
Dost thou in conscience think,—tell me, Emilia,—
That there be women do abuse their husbands
In such gross kind?
Emilia.   There be some such, no question.
Desdemona. Wouldst thou do such a deed for all the
    world?
Emilia. Why, would not you?
Desdemona.   No, by this heavenly light!

Emilia. Nor I neither by this heavenly light; I might do 't   IV. iii. 66
as well i' the dark.

But I do think it is their husbands' faults   87
If wives do fall: say that they slack their duties,
And pour our treasures into foreign laps,
Or else break out in peevish jealousies,
Throwing restraint upon us; or say they strike us,
Or scant our former having in despite;
Why, we have galls, and though we have some grace,
Yet have we some revenge.   Let husbands know
Their wives have sense like them: they see and smell
And have their palates both for sweet and sour,
As husbands have.   What is it that they do
When they change us for others?   Is it sport?
I think it is: and doth affection breed it?
I think it doth: is 't frailty that thus errs?
It is so too: and have not we affections,
Desires for sport, and frailty, as men have?
Then let them use us well: else let them know,
The ills we do, their ills instruct us so.   (*Emilia*)

It makes us, or it mars us; think on that,   v. i. 4
And fix most firm thy resolution.   (*Iago*)

He hath a daily beauty in his life   19
That makes me ugly.   (*Iago*)

                  This is the night   128
That either makes me or fordoes me quite.   (*Iago*)

It is the cause, it is the cause, my soul,—   v. ii. 1
Let me not name it to you, you chaste stars!—
It is the cause.   Yet I 'll not shed her blood;
Nor scar that whiter skin of hers than snow,
And smooth as monumental alabaster.
Yet she must die, else she 'll betray more men.
Put out the light, and then put out the light:
If I quench thee, thou flaming minister,
I can again thy former light restore,
Should I repent me: but once put out thy light,
Thou cunning'st pattern of excelling nature,
I know not where is that Promethean heat
That can thy light relume.   When I have pluck'd the
     rose,
I cannot give it vital growth again,
It must needs wither: I 'll smell it on the tree.
                         [*Kissing her.*]
Ah, balmy breath, that dost almost persuade
Justice to break her sword!   One more, one more.

Be thus when thou art dead, and I will kill thee,   v. ii. 18
And love thee after.   One more, and this the last:
So sweet was ne'er so fatal.   I must weep,
But they are cruel tears: this sorrow's heavenly;
It strikes where it doth love.   (*Othello*)

If you bethink yourself of any crime   26
Unreconciled as yet to heaven and grace,
Solicit for it straight.   (*Othello*)

I would not kill thy unprepared spirit: 31
No; heaven forfend! I would not kill thy soul.   (*Othello*)

And yet I fear you; for you are fatal then   37
When your eyes roll so.   (*Desdemona*)

Othello. Think on thy sins.   40
Desdemona.   They are loves I bear to you.
Othello. Ay, and for that thou diest.
Desdemona. That death's unnatural that kills for loving.

Take heed of perjury; thou art on thy death-bed.   51
                                        (*Othello*)

Had all his hairs been lives, my great revenge   74
Had stomach for them all.   (*Othello*)

Desdemona. Kill me to-morrow: let me live to-night!   80
Othello. Nay, if you strive,—
Desdemona. But half an hour!
Othello.   Being done, there is no pause.
Desdemona. But while I say one prayer!
Othello.   It is too late.   [*He stifles her.*]

                    Not dead? not yet quite dead?   85
I that am cruel am yet merciful;
I would not have thee linger in thy pain.   (*Othello*)

My wife! my wife! what wife? I have no wife.   97
O, insupportable!   O heavy hour!
Methinks it should be now a huge eclipse
Of sun and moon, and that the affrighted globe
Should yawn at alteration.   (*Othello*)

It is the very error of the moon;   109
She comes more nearer earth than she was wont,
And makes men mad.   (*Othello*)

Not Cassio kill'd! then murder's out of tune,   115
And sweet revenge grows harsh.   (*Othello*)

O, falsely, falsely murder'd!   (*Desdemona*)   v. ii. 117

Desdemona. A guiltless death I die.   122
Emilia. O, who hath done this deed?
Desdemona. Nobody; I myself.   Farewell:
Commend me to my kind lord: O, farewell!   [*Dies.*]

Othello. You heard her say herself, it was not I.   127
Emilia. She said so: I must needs report the truth.
Othello. She's like a liar gone to burning hell:
'Twas I that kill'd her.

                    Nay, had she been true,   143
If heaven would make me such another world
Of one entire and perfect chrysolite,
I'ld not have sold her for it.   (*Othello*)

An honest man he is, and hates the slime   148
That sticks on filthy deeds.   (*Othello*)

If he say so, may his pernicious soul   155
Rot half a grain a day! he lies to the heart:
She was too fond of her most filthy bargain.   (*Emilia*)

Do thy worst: 159
This deed of thine is no more worthy heaven
Than thou wast worthy her.   (*Emilia*)

Thou hast not half that power to do me harm   162
As I have to be hurt.   O gull!   O dolt!
As ignorant as dirt! thou hast done a deed—
I care not for thy sword; I'll make thee known,
Though I lost twenty lives.   (*Emilia*)

You told a lie; an odious, damned lie;   180
Upon my soul, a lie, a wicked lie.   (*Emilia*)

                    Nay, lay thee down and roar;   198
For thou hast kill'd the sweetest innocent
That e'er did lift up eye.   (*Emilia*)

I know this act shows horrible and grim.   (*Othello*)   203

Poor Desdemona! I am glad thy father's dead: 204
Thy match was mortal to him, and pure grief
Shore his old thread in twain: did he live now,
This sight would make him do a desperate turn,
Yea, curse his better angel from his side,
And fall to reprobation.   (*Gratiano*)

O murderous coxcomb! what should such a fool   233
Do with so good a woman?   (*Emilia*)
                           415

                              Are there no stones in heaven   v. ii. 234
But what serve for the thunder?—Precious villain!
                                        (*Othello*)

'Tis a notorious villain.   Take you this weapon,   239
Which I have here recover'd from the Moor:
Come, guard the door without; let him not pass,
But kill him rather.   I'll after that same villain,
For 'tis a damned slave.   (*Montano*)

                     I am not valiant neither,   243
But every puny whipster gets my sword:
But why should honour outlive honesty?
Let it go all.   (*Othello*)

Emilia.   What did thy song bode, lady?   246
Hark, canst thou hear me?   I will play the swan,
And die in music.   [*Singing.*] Willow, willow, willow:—
Moor, she was chaste; she loved thee, cruel Moor;
So come my soul to bliss, as I speak true;
So speaking as I think, I die, I die.   [*Dies.*]

I have another weapon in this chamber;   252
It is a sword of Spain, the ice-brook's temper.   (*Othello*)

                  Behold, I have a weapon;   259
A better never did itself sustain
Upon a soldier's thigh: I have seen the day,
That, with this little arm and this good sword,
I have made my way through more impediments
Than twenty times your stop: but, O vain boast!
Who can control his fate? 'tis not so now.
Be not afraid, though you do see me weapon'd;
Here is my journey's end, here is my butt,
And very sea-mark of my utmost sail.
Do you go back dismay'd? 'tis a lost fear;
Man but a rush against Othello's breast,
And he retires.   Where should Othello go?
Now, how dost thou look now?   O ill-starr'd wench!
Pale as thy smock! when we shall meet at compt,
This look of thine will hurl my soul from heaven,
And fiends will snatch at it.   Cold, cold, my girl!
Even like thy chastity.   O cursed slave!
Whip me, ye devils,
From the possession of this heavenly sight!
Blow me about in winds! roast me in sulphur!
Wash me in steep-down gulfs of liquid fire!
O Desdemona! Desdemona! dead!   (*Othello*)

Lodovico. Where is this rash and most unfortunate man?   v. ii. 283
Othello. That's he that was Othello: here I am.

I look down towards his feet; but that's a fable.   286
If that thou be'st a devil, I cannot kill thee.   (*Othello*)

Iago. I bleed, sir; but not kill'd.   288
Othello. I am not sorry neither: I'ld have thee live;
For, in my sense, 'tis happiness to die.

An honourable murderer, if you will;   294
For nought I did in hate, but all in honour.   (*Othello*)

Othello. Will you, I pray, demand that demi-devil   301
Why he hath thus ensnared my soul and body?
Iago. Demand me nothing: what you know, you know:
From this time forth I never will speak word.

Torments will ope your lips.   (*Gratiano*)   305

Most heathenish and most gross!   (*Cassio*)   312

                              For this slave,   332
If there be any cunning cruelty
That can torment him much and hold him long,
It shall be his.   (*Lodovico*)

Othello. Soft you; a word or two before you go.   338
I have done the state some service, and they know 't.
No more of that.   I pray you, in your letters,
When you shall these unlucky deeds relate,
Speak of me as I am; nothing extenuate,
Nor set down aught in malice: then must you speak
Of one that loved not wisely but too well;
Of one not easily jealous, but being wrought
Perplex'd in the extreme; of one whose hand,
Like the base Indian, threw a pearl away
Richer than all his tribe; of one whose subdued eyes,
Albeit unused to the melting mood,
Drop tears as fast as the Arabian trees
Their medicinal gum.   Set you down this;
And say besides, that in Aleppo once,
Where a malignant and a turban'd Turk
Beat a Venetian and traduced the state,
I took by the throat the circumcised dog,
And smote him, thus.   [*Stabs himself.*]

Othello. I kiss'd thee ere I kill'd thee: no way but this; 358
Killing myself, to die upon a kiss.   [*Dies.*]

This did I fear, but thought he had no weapon;   360
For he was great of heart.   (*Cassio*)

ANTONY AND CLEOPATRA

From the historical point of view this is a sequel to *Julius Caesar*, describing the dissensions among the triumvirs Mark Antony, Lepidus, and Octavius (who is called Caesar in the later play, but is better known to history by his greater title of the Emperor Augustus). Antony, infatuated with Cleopatra, the sensual queen of Egypt, is wasting his time in dalliance and debauchery. On the death of his wife Fulvia he returns to Rome and renews the former threefold alliance, marrying Octavius Caesar's sister Octavia. But he is soon at war with Caesar, and is defeated at the naval battle of Actium, where Cleopatra's galley turns in flight and is followed by the rest. Caesar pursues the pair to Egypt, where Antony takes his life on hearing a report of Cleopatra's death, and Cleopatra dies with royal stoicism by the bite of an asp so that she may not grace a Roman triumph. Important minor characters are Antony's friends Enobarbus, Philo, Scarus, and Ventidius, and Cleopatra's attendants Charmian and Iras.

Nay, but this dotage of our general's I. i. I
O'erflows the measure: those his goodly eyes,
That o'er the files and musters of the war
Have glow'd like plated Mars, now bend, now turn,
The office and devotion of their view
Upon a tawny front: his captain's heart,
Which in the scuffles of great fights hath burst
The buckles on his breast, reneges all temper,
And is become the bellows and the fan
To cool a gipsy's lust. (*Philo*)

Take but good note, and you shall see in him 11
The triple pillar of the world transform'd
Into a strumpet's fool. (*Philo*)

Cleopatra. If it be love indeed, tell me how much. 14
Antony. There's beggary in the love that can be reckon'd.
Cleopatra. I'll set a bourn how far to be beloved.
Antony. Then must thou needs find out new heaven, new
earth.

Let Rome in Tiber melt, and the wide arch 33
Of the ranged empire fall! Here is my space.
Kingdoms are clay: our dungy earth alike
Feeds beast as man: the nobleness of life
Is to do this; when such a mutual pair
And such a twain can do 't, in which I bind,
On pain of punishment, the world to weet
We stand up peerless. (*Antony*)

To-night we 'll wander through the streets and note 53
The qualities of people. (*Antony*)

In nature's infinite book of secrecy I. ii. 9
A little I can read. (*Soothsayer*)

You shall be yet far fairer than you are. (*Soothsayer*) 16

You shall be more beloving than beloved. (*Soothsayer*) 22

Soothsayer. You shall outlive the lady whom you serve. 31
Charmian. O excellent! I love long life better than figs.

He was disposed to mirth; but on the sudden 86
A Roman thought hath struck him. (*Cleopatra*)

The nature of bad news infects the teller. (*Messenger*) 99

What our contempt doth often hurl from us,   I. ii. 127
We wish it ours again; the present pleasure,
By revolution lowering, does become
The opposite of itself.   (*Antony*)

Antony. Would I had never seen her!   158
Enobarbus. O, sir, you had then left unseen a wonderful
piece of work.

                        If you find him sad,   I. iii. 3
Say I am dancing; if in mirth, report
That I am sudden sick.   (*Cleopatra*)

Charmian. In each thing give him way, cross him in   9
   nothing.
Cleopatra. Thou teachest like a fool; the way to lose him.

In time we hate that which we often fear.   (*Charmian*)   11

                        This common body,   I. iv. 44
Like to a vagabond flag upon the stream,
Goes to and back, lackeying the varying tide,
To rot itself with motion.   (*Caesar*)

                        At thy heel   58
Did famine follow; whom thou fought'st against,
Though daintily brought up, with patience more
Than savages could suffer: thou didst drink
The stale of horses, and the gilded puddle
Which beasts would cough at: thy palate then did deign
The roughest berry on the rudest hedge;
Yea, like the stag, when snow the pasture sheets,
The barks of trees thou browsed'st; on the Alps
It is reported thou didst eat strange flesh,
Which some did die to look on: and all this—
It wounds thine honour that I speak it now—
Was borne so like a soldier, that thy cheek
So much as lank'd not.   (*Caesar*)

Where think'st thou he is now?   Stands he, or sits he?   I. v. 19
Or does he walk? or is he on his horse?
O happy horse, to bear the weight of Antony!
Do bravely, horse! for wot'st thou whom thou movest?
The demi-Atlas of this earth, the arm
And burgonet of men.   He's speaking now,
Or murmuring 'Where's my serpent of old Nile?'
For so he calls me.   (*Cleopatra*)

                        My salad days,   73
When I was green in judgment.   (*Cleopatra*)

We, ignorant of ourselves,   II. i. 5
Beg often our own harms, which the wise powers
Deny us for our good; so find we profit
By losing of our prayers.   (*Menecrates*)

Every time   II. ii. 9
Serves for the matter that is then born in 't.

(*Enobarbus*)

Thou art a soldier only: speak no more. (*Antony*)   109

The barge she sat in, like a burnish'd throne,   196
Burn'd on the water: the poop was beaten gold;
Purple the sails, and so perfumed that
The winds were love-sick with them; the oars were silver,
Which to the tune of flutes kept stroke, and made
The water which they beat to follow faster,
As amorous of their strokes.   For her own person,
It beggar'd all description: she did lie
In her pavilion—cloth-of-gold of tissue—
O'er-picturing that Venus where we see
The fancy outwork nature: on each side her
Stood pretty dimpled boys, like smiling Cupids,
With divers-colour'd fans, whose wind did seem
To glow the delicate cheeks which they did cool,
And what they undid did.   (*Enobarbus*)

Her gentlewomen, like the Nereides,   211
So many mermaids, tended her i' the eyes,
And made their bends adornings: at the helm
A seeming mermaid steers: the silken tackle
Swell with the touches of those flower-soft hands,
That yarely frame the office.   From the barge
A strange invisible perfume hits the sense
Of the adjacent wharfs.   The city cast
Her people out upon her; and Antony,
Enthroned i' the market-place, did sit alone,
Whistling to the air; which, but for vacancy,
Had gone to gaze on Cleopatra too
And made a gap in nature.   (*Enobarbus*)

I saw her once   233
Hop forty paces through the public street;
And having lost her breath, she spoke, and panted,
That she did make defect perfection,
And, breathless, power breathe forth.   (*Enobarbus*)

Age cannot wither her, nor custom stale   240
Her infinite variety: other women cloy
The appetites they feed; but she makes hungry

Where most she satisfies: for vilest things   II. ii. 243
Become themselves in her; that the holy priests
Bless her when she is riggish.   (*Enobarbus*)

Give me some music; music, moody food   II. v. 1
Of us that trade in love.   (*Cleopatra*)

Give me mine angle; we'll to the river: there   10
My music playing far off, I will betray
Tawny-finn'd fishes; my bended hook shall pierce
Their slimy jaws; and as I draw them up,
I'll think them every one an Antony,
And say 'Ah ha! you're caught.'   (*Cleopatra*)

                    That time,—O times!—   18
I laugh'd him out of patience; and that night
I laugh'd him into patience: and next morn,
Ere the ninth hour, I drunk him to his bed;
Then put my tires and mantles on him, whilst
I wore his sword Philippan.   (*Cleopatra*)

                    There is gold, and here   28
My bluest veins to kiss; a hand that kings
Have lipp'd, and trembled kissing.   (*Cleopatra*)

Messenger.   But yet, madam,—   49
Cleopatra. I do not like 'But yet,' it does allay
The good precedence; fie upon 'But yet'!
'But yet' is as a gaoler to bring forth
Some monstrous malefactor.   Prithee, friend,
Pour out the pack of matter to mine ear
The good and bad together.

These hands do lack nobility, that they strike   82
A meaner than myself.   (*Cleopatra*)

Though it be honest, it is never good   85
To bring bad news: give to a gracious message
An host of tongues; but let ill tidings tell
Themselves when they be felt.   (*Cleopatra*)

Lepidus. What manner o' thing is your crocodile?   II. vii. 46
Antony. It is shaped, sir, like itself; and it is as broad as
it hath breadth: it is just so high as it is, and moves with
it own organs: it lives by that which nourisheth it; and
the elements once out of it, it transmigrates.
Lepidus. What colour is it of?
Antony. Of it own colour too.
Lepidus. 'Tis a strange serpent.
Antony. 'Tis so.   And the tears of it are wet.

Ah, this thou shouldst have done,   II. vii. 79
And not have spoke on't!   In me 'tis villany;
In thee't had been good service.   (*Pompey*)

Come, thou monarch of the vine,   120
Plumpy Bacchus with pink eyne!
In thy fats our cares be drown'd,
With thy grapes our hairs be crown'd:
Cup us, till the world go round,
Cup us, till the world go round!   (*Song*)

Who does i' the wars more than his captain can   III. i. 21
Becomes his captain's captain: and ambition,
The soldier's virtue, rather makes choice of loss,
Than gain which darkens him.   (*Ventidius*)

Ho! hearts, tongues, figures, scribes, bards, poets, cannot   III. ii. 16
Think, speak, cast, write, sing, number, ho!
His love to Antony.   But as for Caesar,
Kneel down, kneel down, and wonder.   (*Enobarbus*)

The April's in her eyes: it is love's spring,   43
And these the showers to bring it on.   (*Antony*)

Her tongue will not obey her heart, nor can   47
Her heart inform her tongue,—the swan's down-feather,
That stands upon the swell at full of tide,
And neither way inclines.   (*Antony*)

Cleopatra. Is she as tall as me?   III. iii. 14
Messenger.   She is not, madam.
Cleopatra. Didst hear her speak? is she shrill-tongued or
   low?
Messenger. Madam, I heard her speak; she is low-voiced.
Cleopatra. That's not so good: he cannot like her long.

            Wars 'twixt you twain would be   III. iv. 30
As if the world should cleave, and that slain men
Should solder up the rift.   (*Octavia*)

Then, world, thou hast a pair of chaps, no more;   III. v. 14
And throw between them all the food thou hast,
They'll grind the one the other.   (*Enobarbus*)

Be you not troubled with the time, which drives   III. vi. 82
O'er your content these strong necessities;
But let determined things to destiny
Hold unbewail'd their way.   (*Caesar*)

Celerity is never more admired   III. vii. 25
Than by the negligent. (*Cleopatra*)

The greater cantle of the world is lost   III. x. 6
With very ignorance; we have kiss'd away
Kingdoms and provinces. (*Scarus*)

              Yon ribaudred nag of Egypt,—   10
Whom leprosy o'ertake!—i' the midst o' the fight,
When vantage like a pair of twins appear'd,
Both as the same, or rather ours the elder,
The breese upon her, like a cow in June,
Hoists sail and flies. (*Scarus*)

Hark! the land bids me tread no more upon't;   III. xi. 1
It is ashamed to bear me! (*Antony*)

My very hairs do mutiny; for the white   13
Reprove the brown for rashness, and they them
For fear and doting. (*Antony*)

He is unqualitied with very shame.   (*Iras*)   44

                    Women are not   III. xii. 29
In their best fortunes strong; but want will perjure
The ne'er-touch'd vestal. (*Caesar*)

                Tell him he wears the rose   III. xiii. 20
Of youth upon him. (*Antony*)

                I see men's judgments are   31
A parcel of their fortunes; and things outward
Do draw the inward quality after them,
To suffer all alike. (*Enobarbus*)

               Your Caesar's father oft,   82
When he hath mused of taking kingdoms in,
Bestow'd his lips on that unworthy place,
As it rain'd kisses. (*Cleopatra*)

Authority melts from me: of late, when I cried 'Ho!'   90
Like boys unto a muss, kings would start forth,
And cry 'Your will?' (*Antony*)

You have been a boggler ever: 110
But when we in our viciousness grow hard—
O misery on't!—the wise gods seel our eyes;
In our own filth drop our clear judgments; make us
Adore our errors; laugh at's, while we strut
To our confusion. (*Antony*)

I found you as a morsel cold upon   III. xiii. 116
Dead Caesar's trencher. (*Antony*)

Though you can guess what temperance should be,   121
You know not what it is. (*Antony*)

To let a fellow that will take rewards   123
And say 'God quit you!' be familiar with
My playfellow, your hand; this kingly seal
And plighter of high hearts! (*Antony*)

I will be treble-sinew'd, hearted, breathed,   178
And fight maliciously: for when mine hours
Were nice and lucky, men did ransom lives
Of me for jests; but now I'll set my teeth,
And send to darkness all that stop me. (*Antony*)

Let's have one other gaudy night. (*Antony*)   183

Now he'll outstare the lightning. To be furious   195
Is to be frighted out of fear; and in that mood
The dove will peck the estridge. (*Enobarbus*)

                    Give him no breath, but now   IV. i. 8
Make boot of his distraction: never anger
Made good guard for itself. (*Mecaenas*)

To-morrow the last of many battles   11
We mean to fight. (*Caesar*)

To business that we love we rise betime,   IV. iv. 20
And go to't with delight. (*Antony*)

                    I will go seek   IV. vi. 37
Some ditch wherein to die; the foul'st best fits
My latter part of life. (*Enobarbus*)

I had a wound here that was like a T,   IV. vii. 7
But now 'tis made an H. (*Scarus*)

                    I have yet   9
Room for six scotches more. (*Scarus*)

                    O thou day o' the world,   IV. viii. 13
Chain mine arm'd neck; leap thou, attire and all,
Through proof of harness to my heart, and there
Ride on the pants triumphing! (*Antony*)

What, girl! though grey   IV. viii. 19
Do something mingle with our younger brown, yet ha' we
A brain that nourishes our nerves, and can
Get goal for goal of youth.   (*Antony*)

Swallows have built   IV. xii. 3
In Cleopatra's sails their nests: the augurers
Say they know not, they cannot tell; look grimly,
And dare not speak their knowledge.   (*Scarus*)

O sun, thy uprise shall I see no more: 18
Fortune and Antony part here; even here
Do we shake hands.   All come to this?   The hearts
That spaniel'd me at heels, to whom I gave
Their wishes, do discandy, melt their sweets
On blossoming Caesar; and this pine is bark'd,
That overtopp'd them all.   Betray'd I am:
O this false soul of Egypt! this grave charm,
Whose eye beck'd forth my wars, and call'd them home;
Whose bosom was my crownet, my chief end,
Like a right gipsy, hath, at fast and loose,
Beguiled me to the very heart of loss.   (*Antony*)

The soul and body rive not more in parting   IV. xiii. 5
Than greatness going off.   (*Charmian*)

Sometime we see a cloud that's dragonish;   IV. xiv. 2
A vapour sometime like a bear or lion,
A tower'd citadel, a pendent rock,
A forked mountain, or blue promontory
With trees upon 't, that nod unto the world
And mock our eyes with air: thou hast seen these signs;
They are black vesper's pageants.   (*Antony*)

That which is now a horse, even with a thought   9
The rack dislimns, and makes it indistinct,
As water is in water.   (*Antony*)

Unarm, Eros; the long day's task is done,   35
And we must sleep.   (*Antony*)

Where souls do couch on flowers, we 'll hand in hand,   51
And with our sprightly port make the ghosts gaze:
Dido and her Aeneas shall want troops,
And all the haunt be ours.   (*Antony*)

I, that with my sword   57
Quarter'd the world, and o'er green Neptune's back
With ships made cities, condemn myself to lack
The courage of a woman.   (*Antony*)

          But I will be   IV. xiv. 99
A bridegroom in my death, and run into 't,
As to a lover's bed. (*Antony*)

I am dying, Egypt, dying; only   IV. xv. 18
I here importune death awhile, until
Of many thousand kisses the poor last
I lay upon thy lips. (*Antony*)

          Let me rail so high,   43
That the false housewife Fortune break her wheel,
Provoked by my offence. (*Cleopatra*)

         Noblest of men, woo 't die?   59
Hast thou no care of me? shall I abide
In this dull world, which in thy absence is
No better than a sty? (*Cleopatra*)

O, wither'd is the garland of the war,   64
The soldier's pole is fall'n: young boys and girls
Are level now with men; the odds is gone,
And there is nothing left remarkable
Beneath the visiting moon. (*Cleopatra*)

No more, but e'en a woman, and commanded   73
By such poor passion as the maid that milks
And does the meanest chares.   It were for me
To throw my sceptre at the injurious gods;
To tell them that this world did equal theirs
Till they had stol'n our jewel.   All's but naught;
Patience is sottish, and impatience does
Become a dog that's mad: then is it sin
To rush into the secret house of death,
Ere death dare come to us? (*Cleopatra*)

We'll bury him; and then, what's brave, what's noble,   86
Let's do it after the high Roman fashion,
And make death proud to take us. (*Cleopatra*)

         I must perforce   v. i. 37
Have shown to thee such a declining day,
Or look on thine; we could not stall together
In the whole world. (*Caesar*)

        Where art thou, death?   v. ii. 46
Come hither, come! come, come, and take a queen
Worth many babes and beggars! (*Cleopatra*)

Know, sir, that I   v. ii. 52
Will not wait pinion'd at your master's court;
Nor once be chastised with the sober eye
Of dull Octavia.   Shall they hoist me up
And show me to the shouting varletry
Of censuring Rome?   Rather a ditch in Egypt
Be gentle grave unto me! rather on Nilus' mud
Lay me stark naked, and let the water-flies
Blow me into abhorring! rather make
My country's high pyramides my gibbet,
And hang me up in chains!   (*Cleopatra*)

His face was as the heavens; and therein stuck   79
A sun and moon, which kept their course, and lighted
The little O, the earth.   (*Cleopatra*)

His legs bestrid the ocean: his rear'd arm   82
Crested the world: his voice was propertied
As all the tuned spheres, and that to friends;
But when he meant to quail and shake the orb,
He was as rattling thunder.   For his bounty,
There was no winter in't; an autumn 'twas
That grew the more by reaping: his delights
Were dolphin-like; they show'd his back above
The element they lived in: in his livery
Walk'd crowns and crownets; realms and islands were
As plates dropp'd from his pocket.   (*Cleopatra*)

He words me, girls, he words me, that I should not   191
Be noble to myself.   (*Cleopatra*)

Finish, good lady; the bright day is done,   193
And we are for the dark.   (*Iras*)

Thou, an Egyptian puppet, shalt be shown   208
In Rome, as well as I: mechanic slaves
With greasy aprons, rules, and hammers, shall
Uplift us to the view; in their thick breaths,
Rank of gross diet, shall we be enclouded,
And forced to drink their vapour.   (*Cleopatra*)

                    The quick comedians   216
Extemporally will stage us, and present
Our Alexandrian revels; Antony
Shall be brought drunken forth, and I shall see
Some squeaking Cleopatra boy my greatness
I' the posture of a whore.   (*Cleopatra*)

What poor an instrument   v. ii. 236
May do a noble deed! he brings me liberty.
My resolution's placed, and I have nothing
Of woman in me: now from head to foot
I am marble-constant; now the fleeting moon
No planet is of mine.   (*Cleopatra*)

Hast thou the pretty worm of Nilus there,
That kills and pains not?   (*Cleopatra*)   243

His biting is immortal; those that do die of it do seldom   247
or never recover.   (*Clown*)

A very honest woman, but something given to lie. (*Clown*)   252

Clown. You must think this, look you, that the worm will   263
do his kind.
Cleopatra. Ay, ay; farewell.
Clown. Look you, the worm is not to be trusted but in the
keeping of wise people; for, indeed, there is no goodness
in the worm.

Cleopatra. Will it eat me?   272
Clown. You must not think I am so simple but I know the
devil himself will not eat a woman: I know that a woman
is a dish for the gods, if the devil dress her not.

I wish you joy o' the worm.   (*Clown*)   281

Give me my robe, put on my crown; I have   283
Immortal longings in me: now no more
The juice of Egypt's grape shall moist this lip:
Yare, yare, good Iras; quick.   Methinks I hear
Antony call; I see him rouse himself
To praise my noble act; I hear him mock
The luck of Caesar, which the gods give men
To excuse their after wrath: husband, I come:
Now to that name my courage prove my title!
I am fire and air; my other elements
I give to baser life.   (*Cleopatra*)

If thou and nature can so gently part,   297
The stroke of death is as a lover's pinch,
Which hurts, and is desired.   (*Cleopatra*)

If she first meet the curled Antony,   304
He'll make demand of her, and spend that kiss
Which is my heaven to have. Come, thou mortal wretch,
With thy sharp teeth this knot intrinsicate
Of life at once untie: poor venomous fool,
Be angry, and dispatch.   (*Cleopatra*)

Charmian. O eastern star!   v. ii. 311
Cleopatra.   Peace, peace!
Dost thou not see my baby at my breast,
That sucks the nurse asleep?

Now boast thee, death, in thy possession lies   318
A lass unparallel'd.   Downy windows, close;
And golden Phoebus never be beheld
Of eyes again so royal!   Your crown's awry;
I'll mend it, and then play.   (*Charmian*)

First Guard. Where is the queen?   323
Charmian.   Speak softly, wake her not.
First Guard. Caesar hath sent—
Charmian.   Too slow a messenger.

First Guard. What work is here! Charmian, is this well   328
   done?
Charmian. It is well done, and fitting for a princess
Descended of so many royal kings.

                  Bravest at the last,   338
She levell'd at our purposes, and, being royal,
Took her own way.   (*Caesar*)

CYMBELINE

Cymbeline is a king of ancient Britain. His two sons, Guiderius and Arviragus, have been stolen away before the play opens by the banished lord Belarius, who has brought them up as his own in the Welsh mountains. Cymbeline's daughter Imogen is married to Posthumus Leonatus; her mother is dead, and the king's second wife wants to get her married to Cloten, her own son by an earlier marriage; as a first step to this she contrives that Posthumus should be banished, and he goes to Rome, where he lays a wager with Iachimo, an Italian gallant, about Imogen's chastity. Iachimo goes to Britain and is repulsed by Imogen, but surreptitiously enters her bedroom and obtains evidence which convinces Posthumus of her infidelity. Posthumus sends instructions to his servant Pisanio to kill Imogen, but instead he helps her to escape from the court dressed as a boy and take refuge, under the name Fidele, with her brothers in Wales, whom she does not know. Cloten, pursuing her, is killed by Guiderius. Through a mistake, Imogen drinks a potion which causes a death-like trance, is mourned by her brothers as dead, and revives only to be captured by Lucius, a Roman general who has come to demand tribute of Britain. The Romans are defeated through the valour of Belarius, Posthumus (who has come over with Lucius) and the two boys. Belarius is reinstated, the lost princes are restored to their father, and Imogen is reconciled to Posthumus.

A thing
Too bad for bad report.   (*First Gentleman*)

Dissembling courtesy!   How fine this tyrant   84
Can tickle where she wounds!   (*Imogen*)

For so long   I. iii. 8
As he could make me with this eye or ear
Distinguish him from others, he did keep
The deck, with glove, or hat, or handkerchief,
Still waving, as the fits and stirs of's mind
Could best express how slow his soul sail'd on,
How swift his ship.   (*Pisanio*)

Since doubting things go ill often hurts more   I. vi. 95
Than to be sure they do; for certainties
Either are past remedies, or, timely knowing,
The remedy then born.   (*Imogen*)

Had I this cheek   99
To bathe my lips upon; this hand, whose touch,
Whose every touch, would force the feeler's soul
To the oath of loyalty; this object, which
Takes prisoner the wild motion of mine eye,
Fixing it only here; should I, damn'd then,
Slaver with lips as common as the stairs
That mount the Capitol; join gripes with hands
Made hard with hourly falsehood—falsehood, as
With labour; then by-peeping in an eye
Base and unlustrous as the smoky light
That's fed with stinking tallow; it were fit
That all the plagues of hell should at one time
Encounter such revolt.   (*Iachimo*)

Thou wrong'st a gentleman, who is as far   145
From thy report as thou from honour, and
Solicit'st here a lady that disdains
Thee and the devil alike.   (*Imogen*)

   A whoreson jackanapes must take me up for swearing;   II. i. 4
as if I borrowed mine oaths of him and might not spend
them at my pleasure. (*Cloten*)

The crickets sing, and man's o'er-labour'd sense   II. ii. 11
Repairs itself by rest.   Our Tarquin thus
Did softly press the rushes, ere he waken'd
The chastity he wounded.   Cytherea,
How bravely thou becomest thy bed, fresh lily,

And whiter than the sheets!   That I might touch!   II. ii. 16
But kiss; one kiss!   Rubies unparagon'd,
How dearly they do 't!   'Tis her breathing that
Perfumes the chamber thus: the flame o' the taper
Bows toward her, and would under-peep her lids,
To see the enclosed lights, now canopied
Under these windows, white and azure laced
With blue of heaven's own tinct.   (*Iachimo*)

O sleep, thou ape of death.   (*Iachimo*)   31

                  On her left breast   37
A mole cinque-spotted, like the crimson drops
I' the bottom of a cowslip.   (*Iachimo*)

    Hark, hark! the lark at heaven's gate sings,   II. iii. 21
        And Phoebus 'gins arise,
      His steeds to water at those springs
        On chaliced flowers that lies;
    And winking Mary-buds begin
        To ope their golden eyes:
    With every thing that pretty is,
        My lady sweet, arise:
        Arise, arise.   (*Song*)

                    'Tis gold   75
Which makes the true man kill'd and saves the thief;
Nay, sometime hangs both thief and true man.   (*Cloten*)

               The thanks I give   93
Is telling you that I am poor of thanks
And scarce can spare them.   (*Imogen*)

             His meanest garment,   138
That ever hath but clipp'd his body, is dearer
In my respect than all the hairs above thee,
Were they all made such men.   (*Imogen*)

Quake in the present winter's state and wish   II. iv. 5
That warmer days would come.   (*Posthumus*)

             Our countrymen   20
Are men more order'd than when Julius Caesar
Smiled at their lack of skill, but found their courage
Worthy his frowning at: their discipline,
Now mingled with their courages, will make known
To their approvers they are people such
That mend upon the world.   (*Posthumus*)

She stripp'd it from her arm; I see her yet;   101
Her pretty action did outsell her gift,
And yet enrich'd it too.   (*Iachimo*)

Me of my lawful pleasure she restrain'd   II. v. 9
And pray'd me oft forbearance. (*Posthumus*)

As chaste as unsunn'd snow. (*Posthumus*)   13

               There's no motion   20
That tends to vice in man, but I affirm
It is the woman's part: be it lying, note it,
The woman's; flattering, hers; deceiving, hers;
Lust and rank thoughts, hers, hers; revenges, hers;
Ambitions, covetings, change of prides, disdain,
Nice longing, slanders, mutability,
All faults that may be named, nay, that hell knows,
Why, hers, in part or all; but rather, all;
For even to vice
They are not constant, but are changing still
One vice, but of a minute old, for one
Not half so old as that. (*Posthumus*)

           There be many Caesars   III. i. 11
Ere such another Julius. Britain is
A world by itself; and we will nothing pay
For wearing our own noses. (*Cloten*)

         Remember, sir, my liege,   16
The kings your ancestors, together with
The natural bravery of your isle, which stands
As Neptune's park, ribbed and paled in
With rocks unscaleable and roaring waters,
With sands that will not bear your enemies' boats,
But suck them up to the topmast. (*Queen*)

O, for a horse with wings! (*Imogen*)   III. ii. 50

Why, one that rode to's execution, man,   72
Could never go so slow. (*Imogen*)

And often, to our comfort, shall we find   III. iii. 19
The sharded beetle in a safer hold
Than is the full-wing'd eagle. O, this life
Is nobler than attending for a check,
Richer than doing nothing for a bauble,
Prouder than rustling in unpaid-for silk. (*Belarius*)

          What should we speak of   35
When we are old as you? when we shall hear
The rain and wind beat dark December, how,
In this our pinching cave, shall we discourse
The freezing hours away? (*Arviragus*)

How hard it is to hide the sparks of nature! (*Belarius*)   79

                      Slander,   III. iv. 35
Whose edge is sharper than the sword, whose tongue
Outvenoms all the worms of Nile, whose breath
Rides on the posting winds and doth belie
All corners of the world.   (*Pisanio*)

                   Some jay of Italy   51
Whose mother was her painting, hath betray'd him:
Poor I am stale, a garment out of fashion;
And, for I am richer than to hang by the walls,
I must be ripp'd:—to pieces with me!—O,
Men's vows are women's traitors!   (*Imogen*)

                 Against self-slaughter   78
There is a prohibition so divine
That cravens my weak hand.   (*Imogen*)

Pisanio. Since I received command to do this business   102
I have not slept one wink.
Imogen.   Do't, and to bed then.

Hath Britain all the sun that shines?   Day, night,   139
Are they not but in Britain?   (*Imogen*)

You must forget to be a woman; change   157
Command into obedience: fear and niceness—
The handmaids of all women, or, more truly,
Woman it pretty self—into a waggish courage;
Ready in gibes, quick-answer'd, saucy and
As quarrelous as the weasel.   (*Pisanio*)

               Our subjects, sir,   III. v. 4
Will not endure his yoke; and for ourself
To show less sovereignty than they, must needs
Appear unkinglike.   (*Cymbeline*)

A thing more made of malice than of duty.   (*Cymbeline*)   33

                  She's a lady   39
So tender of rebukes that words are strokes
And strokes death to her.   (*Queen*)

I love and hate her: for she's fair and royal,   70
And that she hath all courtly parts more exquisite
Than lady, ladies, woman; from every one
The best she hath, and she, of all compounded,
Outsells them all.   (*Cloten*)

I see a man's life is a tedious one.   (*Imogen*)   III. vi. 1

Best draw my sword; and if mine enemy   III. vi. 25
But fear the sword like me, he'll scarce look on't.
                              (*Imogen*)

                       Our stomachs   32
Will make what's homely savoury: weariness
Can snore upon the flint, when resty sloth
Finds the down pillow hard.   (*Belarius*)

All gold and silver rather turn to dirt!   54
As 'tis no better reckon'd, but of those
Who worship dirty gods.   (*Arviragus*)

Arviragus. Are we not brothers?   IV. ii. 3
Imogen.   So man and man should be;
But clay and clay differs in dignity,
Whose dust is both alike.

                 I am ill, but your being by me   11
Cannot amend me; society is no comfort
To one not sociable: I am not very sick,
Since I can reason of it.   (*Imogen*)

Cowards father cowards and base things sire base.   26
                           (*Belarius*)

Arviragus.   How angel-like he sings!   47
Guiderius. But his neat cookery! he cut our roots
In characters,
And sauced our broths, as Juno had been sick
And he her dieter.

Those that I reverence, those I fear, the wise: 95
At fools I laugh, not fear them.   (*Guiderius*)

                      Not Hercules   114
Could have knock'd out his brains, for he had none.
                          (*Guiderius*)

                   O thou goddess,   169
Thou divine Nature, how thyself thou blazon'st
In these two princely boys! They are as gentle
As zephyrs blowing below the violet,
Not wagging his sweet head; and yet as rough,
Their royal blood enchafed, as the rudest wind,
That by the top doth take the mountain pine,
And make him stoop to the vale.   (*Belarius*)

                  With fairest flowers   218
Whilst summer lasts and I live here, Fidele,
I'll sweeten thy sad grave: thou shalt not lack

The flower that's like thy face, pale primrose, nor   IV. ii. 221
The azured harebell, like thy veins, no, nor
The leaf of eglantine, whom not to slander,
Out-sweeten'd not thy breath: the ruddock would,
With charitable bill,—O bill, sore shaming
Those rich-left heirs that let their fathers lie
Without a monument!—bring thee all this;
Yea, and furr'd moss besides, when flowers are none,
To winter-ground thy corse.   (*Arviragus*)

Great griefs, I see, medicine the less.   (*Belarius*)   243

Thersites' body is as good as Ajax',   252
When neither are alive.   (*Guiderius*)

Guiderius.   Fear no more the heat o' the sun,   258
            Nor the furious winter's rages;
        Thou thy worldly task hast done,
            Home art gone, and ta'en thy wages:
        Golden lads and girls all must,
        As chimney-sweepers, come to dust.

Arviragus.   Fear no more the frown o' the great;
            Thou art past the tyrant's stroke;
        Care no more to clothe and eat;
            To thee the reed is as the oak:
        The sceptre, learning, physic, must
        All follow this, and come to dust.

Guiderius.   Fear no more the lightning-flash,
Arviragus.   Nor the all-dreaded thunder-stone;
Guiderius.   Fear not slander, censure rash;
Arviragus.   Thou hast finish'd joy and moan:
Both.   All lovers young, all lovers must
            Consign to thee, and come to dust.

Guiderius.   No exorciser harm thee!
Arviragus.   Nor no witchcraft charm thee!
Guiderius.   Ghost unlaid forbear thee!
Arviragus.   Nothing ill come near thee!
Both.   Quiet consummation have;
            And renowned be thy grave!   (*Song*)

Fortune brings in some boats that are not steer'd   IV. iii. 46
                              (*Pisanio*)

Every good servant does not all commands.   (*Posthumus*)   v. i. 6

Those that would die or ere resist are grown   v. iii. 50
The mortal bugs o' the field.   (*Posthumus*)

O, the charity of a penny cord! it sums up thousands in   v. iv. 170
a trice: you have no true debitor and creditor but it; of
what's past, is, and to come, the discharge: your neck, sir,
is pen, book and counters; so the acquittance follows.
                                              (*First Gaoler*)

Posthumus. I am merrier to die than thou art to live.   176
First Gaoler. Indeed, sir, he that sleeps feels not the
toothache.

                          I never saw   v. v. 7
Such noble fury in so poor a thing;
Such precious deeds in one that promised nought
But beggary and poor looks.   (*Belarius*)

By medicine life may be prolong'd, yet death   29
Will seize the doctor too.   (*Cymbeline*)

Who is't can read a woman?   (*Cymbeline*)   48

A Roman with a Roman's heart can suffer.   (*Lucius*)   81

                 A nobler sir ne'er lived   145
'Twixt sky and ground.   (*Iachimo*)

                 Let his arms alone;   305
They were not born for bondage.   (*Belarius*)

The benediction of these covering heavens   350
Fall on their heads like dew! for they are worthy
To inlay heaven with stars.   (*Belarius*)

Pardon's the word to all.   (*Cymbeline*)

PERICLES, PRINCE OF TYRE

The Pericles of this play is not the famous Athenian statesman, but a prince of Tyre, hero of a medieval romance related in the poems of Gower, who appears in the play as chorus. After a visit to Antioch, where he discovers an infamous secret attaching to its king Antiochus, Pericles knows that he will not be safe in Tyre, and puts to sea, leaving his realm to be governed by the lord Helicanus. The ship is wrecked on the shores of Pentapolis, where Pericles wins the hand of the king's daughter Thaisa. News comes of Antiochus's death, and Pericles sails for Tyre with his wife, who gives birth in a storm to a daughter Marina, and then falls into a death-like trance. The sailors insist that the supposed dead body must be jettisoned, and Thaisa, drifting in a chest to Ephesus, is there revived and becomes a priestess of Diana. On the way home Pericles leaves the infant Marina at Tarsus, to be brought up by its governor Cleon and his wife Dionyza. Jealous of Marina's accomplishments when she grows up, Dionyza plans to have her murdered, but it falls out that she is captured by pirates and sold to a brothel-keeper in Mytilene. From him her virtue wins her release, and she is held in such regard by the governor Lysimachus that when Pericles, prostrated with grief, visits the town, she is asked to tend him. Pericles then finds that she is his lost daughter, and a vision directs him to the temple at Ephesus, where he finds Thaisa, so that all three are again united. It is generally believed that a large part of this play is not by Shakespeare.

See where she comes, apparell'd like the spring! (*Pericles*)   I. i. 12

Few love to hear the sins they love to act.   (*Pericles*)   92

They do abuse the king that flatter him: I. ii. 38
For flattery is the bellows blows up sin.   (*Helicanus*)

'Tis time to fear when tyrants seem to kiss.   (*Pericles*)   79

Third Fisherman. Master, I marvel how the fishes live in   II. i. 29
the sea.
First Fisherman. Why, as men do a-land; the great ones
eat up the little ones.

    The cat, with eyne of burning coal,   III. Chorus,
    Now couches fore the mouse's hole.   5

Thou god of this great vast, rebuke these surges,   III. i. 1
Which wash both heaven and hell; and thou, that hast
Upon the winds command, bind them in brass,
Having call'd them from the deep!   O, still
Thy deafening, dreadful thunders; gently quench
Thy nimble, sulphurous flashes!   (*Pericles*)

        O you gods!   22
Why do you make us love your goodly gifts,
And snatch them straight away?   (*Pericles*)

Yet my good will is great, though the gift small. (*Thaisa*)   III. iv. 18

No, I will rob Tellus of her weed,   IV. i. 14
To strew thy green with flowers: the yellows, blues,
The purple violets, and marigolds,
Shall as a carpet hang upon thy grave,
While summer days do last.   Ay me! poor maid,
Born in a tempest, when my mother died,
This world to me is like a lasting storm,
Whirring me from my friends.   (*Marina*)

Walk, and be cheerful once again; reserve   40
That excellent complexion, which did steal
The eyes of young and old.   (*Dionyza*)

My father, as nurse said, did never fear,   53
But cried 'Good seamen!' to the sailors, galling
His kingly hands, haling ropes;
And, clasping to the mast, endured a sea
That almost burst the deck.   (*Marina*)

Never was waves nor wind more violent;   IV. i. 60
And from the ladder-tackle washes off
A canvas-climber. 'Ha!' says one, 'wilt out?'
And with a dropping industry they skip
From stem to stern: the boatswain whistles, and
The master calls, and trebles their confusion. (*Marina*)

Why would she have me kill'd?   73
Now, as I can remember, by my troth,
I never did her hurt in all my life:
I never spake bad word, nor did ill turn
To any living creature: believe me, la,
I never kill'd a mouse, nor hurt a fly:
I trod upon a worm against my will,
But I wept for it. (*Marina*)

      She would make a puritan of the devil, if he should   IV. vi. 8
cheapen a kiss of her. (*Bawd*)

                                          For me,   102
That am a maid, though most ungentle fortune
Have placed me in this sty, where, since I came,
Diseases have been sold dearer than physic,
O, that the gods
Would set me free from this unhallow'd place,
Though they did change me to the meanest bird
That flies i' the purer air! (*Marina*)

                    Thou art a piece of virtue, and   118
I doubt not but thy training hath been noble.
                              (*Lysimachus*)

      Will you not go the way of women-kind? Marry,   158
come up, my dish of chastity with rosemary and bays!
                              (*Bawd*)

Thou hold'st a place, for which the pained'st fiend   173
Of hell would not in reputation change:
Thou art the damned doorkeeper to every
Coistrel that comes inquiring for his Tib. (*Marina*)

Boult. What would you have me do? go to the wars, would   180
you? where a man may serve seven years for the loss of a
leg, and have not money enough in the end to buy him a
wooden one?
Marina. Do any thing but this thou doest. Empty
Old receptacles, or common shores, of filth;
Serve by indenture to the common hangman:
Any of these ways are yet better than this;

*P   441

For what thou professest, a baboon, could he speak,   iv. vi. 188
Would own a name too dear.

If I should tell my history, it would seem   v. i. 119
Like lies disdain'd in the reporting.   (*Marina*)

                              My heart   v. iii. 44
Leaps to be gone into my mother's bosom.   (*Marina*)

POEMS

VENUS AND ADONIS

Even as the sun with purple-colour'd face   1
Had ta'en his last leave of the weeping morn,
Rose-cheek'd Adonis hied him to the chase;
Hunting he loved, but love he laugh'd to scorn.

Ten kisses short as one, one long as twenty.   22

Pure shame and awed resistance made him fret,   69
Which bred more beauty in his angry eyes.

Upon this promise did he raise his chin,   85
Like a dive-dapper peering through a wave,
Who, being look'd on, ducks as quickly in.

Leading him prisoner in a red-rose chain.   110

Were I hard-favour'd, foul, or wrinkled-old,   133
Ill-nurtured, crooked, churlish, harsh in voice,
O'erworn, despised, rheumatic and cold,
Thick-sighted, barren, lean, and lacking juice,
    Then mightst thou pause, for then I were not for thee;
    But having no defects, why dost abhor me?

Bid me discourse, I will enchant thine ear,   145
Or, like a fairy, trip upon the green,
Or, like a nymph, with long dishevell'd hair,
Dance on the sands, and yet no footing seen:
    Love is a spirit all compact of fire,
    Not gross to sink, but light, and will aspire.

Round-hoof'd, short-jointed, fetlocks shag and long,   295
Broad breast, full eye, small head and nostril wide,
High crest, short ears, straight legs and passing strong,
Thin mane, thick tail, broad buttock, tender hide:
    Look, what a horse should have he did not lack,
    Save a proud rider on so proud a back.

O, what a war of looks was then between them!   355
Her eyes petitioners to his eyes suing.

The sea hath bounds, but deep desire hath none.   389

A thousand kisses buys my heart from me;   517
And pay them at thy leisure, one by one.
What is ten hundred touches unto thee?
Are they not quickly told and quickly gone?
    Say, for non-payment that the debt should double,
    Is twenty hundred kisses such a trouble?

445

'Good night,' quoth she, and, ere he says 'Adieu,'   537
The honey fee of parting tender'd is.

Foul words and frowns must not repel a lover;   573
What though the rose have prickles, yet 'tis pluck'd:
    Were beauty under twenty locks kept fast,
    Yet love breaks through and picks them all at last.

O, let him keep his loathsome cabin still;   637
Beauty hath nought to do with such foul fiends.

This sour informer, this bate-breeding spy,   655
This canker that eats up Love's tender spring,
This carry-tale, dissentious Jealousy,
That sometime true news, sometime false doth bring.

And when thou hast on foot the purblind hare,   679
Mark the poor wretch, to overshoot his troubles
How he outruns the wind and with what care
He cranks and crosses with a thousand doubles.

Danger deviseth shifts; wit waits on fear.   690

By this, poor Wat, far off upon a hill,   697
Stands on his hinder legs with listening ear,
To hearken if his foes pursue him still.

The path is smooth that leadeth on to danger.   788

Call it not love, for Love to heaven is fled,   793
Since sweating Lust on earth usurp'd his name;
Under whose simple semblance he hath fed
Upon fresh beauty, blotting it with blame;
    Which the hot tyrant stains and soon bereaves,
    As caterpillars do the tender leaves.

Love comforteth like sunshine after rain,   799
But Lust's effect is tempest after sun;
Love's gentle spring doth always fresh remain,
Lust's winter comes ere summer half be done;
    Love surfeits not, Lust like a glutton dies;
    Love is all truth, Lust full of forged lies.

Lo, here the gentle lark, weary of rest,   853
From his moist cabinet mounts up on high,
And wakes the morning, from whose silver breast
The sun ariseth in his majesty;
    Who doth the world so gloriously behold
    That cedar-tops and hills seem burnish'd gold.

For he being dead, with him is beauty slain,   1019
And, beauty dead, black chaos comes again.

The grass stoops not, she treads on it so light.   1028

Or, as the snail, whose tender horns being hit,   1033
Shrinks backward in his shelly cave with pain,
And there, all smother'd up, in shade doth sit,
Long after fearing to creep forth again.

It shall suspect where is no cause of fear: 1153
It shall not fear where it should most mistrust;
It shall be merciful and too severe,
And most deceiving when it seems most just;
    Perverse it shall be where it shows most toward,
    Put fear to valour, courage to the coward. [*Of love.*]

THE RAPE OF LUCRECE

Beauty itself doth of itself persuade   29
The eyes of men without an orator.

Here pale with fear he doth premeditate   183
The dangers of his loathsome enterprise.

Who buys a minute's mirth to wail a week?   213
Or sells eternity to get a toy?

For princes are the glass, the school, the book,   615
Where subjects' eyes do learn, do read, do look.

O comfort-killing Night, image of hell!   764
Dim register and notary of shame!
Black stage for tragedies and murders fell!
Vast sin-concealing chaos! nurse of blame!

Unruly blasts wait on the tender spring;   869
Unwholesome weeds take root with precious flowers;
The adder hisses where the sweet birds sing;
What virtue breeds iniquity devours.

O Opportunity, thy guilt is great!   876
'Tis thou that executest the traitor's treason:
Thou set'st the wolf where he the lamb may get;
Whoever plots the sin, thou 'point'st the season;
'Tis thou that spurn'st at right, at law, at reason.

Mis-shapen Time, copesmate of ugly Night,   925
Swift subtle post, carrier of grisly care,
Eater of youth, false slave to false delight,
Base watch of woes, sin's pack-horse, virtue's snare.

Time's glory is to calm contending kings,   939
To unmask falsehood and bring truth to light,
To stamp the seal of time in aged things,
To wake the morn and sentinel the night,
To wrong the wronger till he render right,
  To ruinate proud buildings with thy hours,
  And smear with dust their glittering golden towers.

The mightier man, the mightier is the thing   1004
That makes him honour'd, or begets him hate;
For greatest scandal waits on greatest state.

True grief is fond and testy as a child,   1094
Who wayward once, his mood with nought agrees.

A woeful hostess brooks not merry guests.   1125

For men have marble, women waxen, minds.   1240

To see sad sights moves more than hear them told.   1324

It easeth some, though none it ever cured,   1581
To think their dolour others have endured.

He with the Romans was esteemed so   1811
  As silly-jeering idiots are with kings,
  For sportive words and uttering foolish things.

Do wounds help wounds, or grief help grievous deeds?   1822

SONNETS

From fairest creatures we desire increase,　　　　　　I
That thereby beauty's rose might never die.

When forty winters shall besiege thy brow,　　　　　II
And dig deep trenches in thy beauty's field,
Thy youth's proud livery, so gazed on now,
Will be a tatter'd weed, of small worth held.

Thou art thy mother's glass, and she in thee　　　　III
Calls back the lovely April of her prime:
So thou through windows of thine age shalt see
Despite of wrinkles this thy golden time.

Lo! in the orient when the gracious light　　　　　VII
Lifts up his burning head, each under eye
Doth homage to his new-appearing sight,
Serving with looks his sacred majesty.

Music to hear, why hear'st thou music sadly?　　　VIII
Sweets with sweets war not, joy delights in joy.
Why lovest thou that which thou receivest not gladly,
Or else receivest with pleasure thine annoy?

When I do count the clock that tells the time,　　　XII
And see the brave day sunk in hideous night;
When I behold the violet past prime,
And sable curls all silver'd o'er with white;
When lofty trees I see barren of leaves
Which erst from heat did canopy the herd,
And summer's green all girded up in sheaves
Borne on the bier with white and bristly beard,
Then of thy beauty do I question make,
That thou among the wastes of time must go.

Against the stormy gusts of winter's day　　　　　XIII
And barren rage of death's eternal cold.

When I consider every thing that grows　　　　　　XV
Holds in perfection but a little moment,
That this huge stage presenteth nought but shows
Whereon the stars in secret influence comment.

Now stand you on the top of happy hours.　　　　　XVI

449

So should the lines of life that life repair,   XVI
Which this, Time's pencil, or my pupil pen,
Neither in inward worth nor outward fair,
Can make you live yourself in eyes of men.

If I could write the beauty of your eyes   XVII
And in fresh numbers number all your graces,
The age to come would say 'This poet lies;
Such heavenly touches ne'er touch'd earthly faces.'
So should my papers yellow'd with their age
Be scorn'd like old men of less truth than tongue,
And your true rights be term'd a poet's rage
And stretched metre of an antique song.

Shall I compare thee to a summer's day?   XVIII
Thou art more lovely and more temperate:
Rough winds do shake the darling buds of May,
And summer's lease hath all too short a date:
Sometime too hot the eye of heaven shines,
And often is his gold complexion dimm'd;
And every fair from fair sometime declines,
By chance or nature's changing course untrimm'd;
But thy eternal summer shall not fade
Nor lose possession of that fair thou owest;
Nor shall Death brag thou wander'st in his shade,
When in eternal lines to time thou growest:
    So long as men can breathe or eyes can see,
    So long lives this and this gives life to thee.

Yet, do thy worst, old Time: despite thy wrong,   XIX
My love shall in my verse ever live young.

A woman's face with Nature's own hand painted   XX
Hast thou, the master-mistress of my passion;
A woman's gentle heart, but not acquainted
With shifting change, as is false women's fashion.

My glass shall not persuade me I am old,   XXII
So long as youth and thou are of one date;
But when in thee time's furrows I behold,
Then look I death my days should expiate.

As an unperfect actor on the stage   XXIII
Who with his fear is put besides his part.

The painful warrior famoused for fight,   XXV
After a thousand victories once foil'd,
Is from the book of honour razed quite,
And all the rest forgot for which he toil'd.

Lord of my love, to whom in vassalage   XXVI
Thy merit hath my duty strongly knit.

Weary with toil, I haste me to my bed,   XXVII
The dear repose for limbs with travel tired;
But then begins a journey in my head,
To work my mind, when body's work's expired.

When, in disgrace with fortune and men's eyes,   XXIX
I all alone beweep my outcast state,
And trouble deaf heaven with my bootless cries,
And look upon myself, and curse my fate,
Wishing me like to one more rich in hope,
Featured like him, like him with friends possess'd,
Desiring this man's art and that man's scope,
With what I most enjoy contented least;
Yet in these thoughts myself almost despising,
Haply I think on thee, and then my state,
Like to the lark at break of day arising
From sullen earth, sings hymns at heaven's gate;
    For thy sweet love remember'd such wealth brings
    That then I scorn to change my state with kings.

When to the sessions of sweet silent thought   XXX
I summon up remembrance of things past,
I sigh the lack of many a thing I sought,
And with old woes new wail my dear time's waste:
Then can I drown an eye, unused to flow,
For precious friends hid in death's dateless night,
And weep afresh love's long since cancell'd woe,
And moan the expense of many a vanish'd sight:
Then can I grieve at grievances foregone,
And heavily from woe to woe tell o'er
The sad account of fore-bemoaned moan,
Which I new pay as if not paid before.
    But if the while I think on thee, dear friend,
    All losses are restored and sorrows end.

But since he died and poets better prove,   XXXII
Theirs for their style I'll read, his for his love.

Full many a glorious morning have I seen   XXXIII
Flatter the mountain-tops with sovereign eye,
Kissing with golden face the meadows green,
Gilding pale streams with heavenly alchemy.

Why didst thou promise such a beauteous day   XXXIV
And make me travel forth without my cloak?

No more be grieved at that which thou hast done: XXXV
Roses have thorns, and silver fountains mud;
Clouds and eclipses stain both moon and sun,
And loathsome canker lives in sweetest bud.

I love thee in such sort XXXVI and
As, thou being mine, mine is thy good report. XCVI

As a decrepit father takes delight XXXVII
To see his active child do deeds of youth.

Those pretty wrongs that liberty commits, XLI
When I am sometime absent from thy heart,
Thy beauty and thy years full well befits,
For still temptation follows where thou art.
Gentle thou art and therefore to be won,
Beauteous thou art, therefore to be assailed;
And when a woman woos, what woman's son
Will sourly leave her till she have prevailed?

All days are nights to see till I see thee, XLIII
And nights bright days when dreams do show thee me.

No matter then although my foot did stand XLIV
Upon the farthest earth removed from thee;
For nimble thought can jump both sea and land
As soon as think the place where he would be.

Against that time when thou shalt strangely pass XLIX
And scarcely greet me with that sun, thine eye,
When love, converted from the thing it was,
Shall reasons find of settled gravity.

So am I as the rich, whose blessed key LII
Can bring him to his sweet up-locked treasure,
The which he will not every hour survey,
For blunting the fine point of seldom pleasure.
Therefore are feasts so solemn and so rare,
Since, seldom coming, in the long year set,
Like stones of worth they thinly placed are,
Or captain jewels in the carcanet.

Describe Adonis, and the counterfeit LIII
Is poorly imitated after you;
On Helen's cheek all art of beauty set,
And you in Grecian tires are painted new.

O, how much more doth beauty beauteous seem LIV
By that sweet ornament which truth doth give!
The rose looks fair, but fairer we it deem
For that sweet odour which doth in it live.

Not marble, nor the gilded monuments LV
Of princes, shall outlive this powerful rhyme.

Being your slave, what should I do but tend   LVII
Upon the hours and times of your desire?
I have no precious time at all to spend,
Nor services to do, till you require.
Nor dare I chide the world-without-end hour
Whilst I, my sovereign, watch the clock for you,
Nor think the bitterness of absence sour
When you have bid your servant once adieu;
Nor dare I question with my jealous thought
Where you may be, or your affairs suppose,
But, like a sad slave, stay and think of nought
Save, where you are, how happy you make those.
    So true a fool is love that in your will,
    Though you do any thing, he thinks no ill.

O, that record could with a backward look,   LIX
Even of five hundred courses of the sun,
Show me your image in some antique book,
Since mind at first in character was done!
That I might see what the old world could say
To this composed wonder of your frame.

Like as the waves make towards the pebbled shore,   LX
So do our minutes hasten to their end.

And all those beauties whereof now he's king   LXIII
Are vanishing or vanish'd out of sight,
Stealing away the treasure of his spring.

When I have seen by Time's fell hand defaced   LXIV
The rich proud cost of outworn buried age.

When I have seen the hungry ocean gain   LXIV
Advantage on the kingdom of the shore.

Since brass, nor stone, nor earth, nor boundless sea,   LXV
But sad mortality o'er-sways their power,
How with this rage shall beauty hold a plea,
Whose action is no stronger than a flower?
O, how shall summer's honey breath hold out
Against the wreckful siege of battering days,
When rocks impregnable are not so stout,
Nor gates of steel so strong, but Time decays?

Tired with all these, for restful death I cry,   LXVI
As, to behold desert a beggar born,
And needy nothing trimm'd in jollity,
And purest faith unhappily forsworn,
And gilded honour shamefully misplaced,
And maiden virtue rudely strumpeted,
And right perfection wrongfully disgraced,

453

And strength by limping sway disabled,   LXVI
And art made tongue-tied by authority,
And folly doctor-like controlling skill,
And simple truth miscall'd simplicity,
And captive good attending captain ill:
   Tired with all these, from these would I be gone,
   Save that, to die, I leave my love alone.

No longer mourn for me when I am dead   LXXI
Than you shall hear the surly sullen bell
Give warning to the world that I am fled
From this vile world, with vilest worms to dwell:
Nay, if you read this line, remember not
The hand that writ it; for I love you so
That I in your sweet thoughts would be forgot
If thinking on me then should make you woe.

That time of year thou mayst in me behold   LXXIII
When yellow leaves, or none, or few, do hang
Upon those boughs which shake against the cold,
Bare ruin'd choirs, where late the sweet birds sang.
In me thou see'st the twilight of such day
As after sunset fadeth in the west,
Which by and by black night doth take away,
Death's second self, that seals up all in rest.

This thou perceivest, which makes thy love more strong,   LXXIII
To love that well which thou must leave ere long.

Sometime all full with feasting on your sight   LXXV
And by and by clean starved for a look.

O, know, sweet love, I always write of you,   LXXVI
And you and love are still my argument;
So all my best is dressing old words new,
Spending again what is already spent:
   For as the sun is daily new and old,
   So is my love still telling what is told.

Thy glass will show thee how thy beauties wear,   LXXVII
Thy dial how thy precious minutes waste.

Thou by thy dial's shady stealth mayst know   LXXVII
Time's thievish progress to eternity.

Your monument shall be my gentle verse,   LXXXI
Which eyes not yet created shall o'er-read,
And tongues to be your being shall rehearse
When all the breathers of this world are dead;
   You still shall live—such virtue hath my pen—
   Where breath most breathes, even in the mouths of men.

I think good thoughts whilst other write good words,   LXXXV
And like unletter'd clerk still cry 'Amen'
To every hymn that able spirit affords
In polish'd form of well-refined pen.

Was it the proud full sail of his great verse   LXXXVI
Bound for the prize of all too precious you,
That did my ripe thoughts in my brain inhearse,
Making their tomb the womb wherein they grew?

Farewell! thou art too dear for my possessing,   LXXXVII
And like enough thou know'st thy estimate:
The charter of thy worth gives thee releasing;
My bonds in thee are all determinate.
For how do I hold thee but by thy granting?
And for that riches where is my deserving?
The cause of this fair gift in me is wanting,
And so my patent back again is swerving.
Thyself thou gavest, thy own worth then not knowing,
Or me, to whom thou gavest it, else mistaking;
So thy great gift, upon misprision growing,
Comes home again, on better judgment making.
   Thus have I had thee, as a dream doth flatter,
   In sleep a king, but waking no such matter.

Ah, do not, when my heart hath 'scaped this sorrow,   XC
Come in the rearward of a conquer'd woe;
Give not a windy night a rainy morrow,
To linger out a purposed overthrow.

Some glory in their birth, some in their skill,   XCI
Some in their wealth, some in their bodies' force,
Some in their garments, though new-fangled ill,
Some in their hawks and hounds, some in their horse.

They that have power to hurt and will do none,   XCIV
That do not do the thing they most do show,
Who, moving others, are themselves as stone,
Unmoved, cold, and to temptation slow,
They rightly do inherit heaven's graces
And husband nature's riches from expense;
They are the lords and owners of their faces,
Others but stewards of their excellence.
The summer's flower is to the summer sweet,
Though to itself it only live and die,
But if that flower with base infection meet,
The basest weed outbraves his dignity:
   For sweetest things turn sourest by their deeds:
   Lilies that fester smell far worse than weeds.

O, what a mansion have those vices got   XCV
Which for their habitation chose out thee,
Where beauty's veil doth cover every blot,
And all things turn to fair that eyes can see!

Some say thy fault is youth, some wantonness;   XCVI
Some say thy grace is youth and gentle sport;
Both grace and faults are loved of more and less;
Thou makest faults graces that to thee resort.

How like a winter hath my absence been   XCVII
From thee, the pleasure of the fleeting year!
What freezings have I felt, what dark days seen!
What old December's bareness every where!

From you have I been absent in the spring,   XCVIII
When proud-pied April dress'd in all his trim
Hath put a spirit of youth in every thing.

The forward violet thus did I chide: XCIX
Sweet thief, whence didst thou steal thy sweet that smells,
If not from my love's breath? The purple pride
Which on thy soft cheek for complexion dwells
In my love's veins thou hast too grossly dyed.
The lily I condemned for thy hand,
And buds of marjoram had stol'n thy hair:
The roses fearfully on thorns did stand,
One blushing shame, another white despair.

That love is merchandized whose rich esteeming   CII
The owner's tongue doth publish every where.

And sweets grown common lose their dear delight.   CII

To me, fair friend, you never can be old,   CIV
For as you were when first your eye I eyed,
Such seems your beauty still. Three winters cold
Have from the forests shook three summers' pride,
Three beauteous springs to yellow autumn turn'd
In process of the seasons have I seen,
Three April perfumes in three hot Junes burn'd,
Since first I saw you fresh, which yet are green.
Ah! yet doth beauty, like a dial-hand,
Steal from his figure and no pace perceived;
So your sweet hue, which methinks still doth stand,
Hath motion and mine eye may be deceived:
    For fear of which, hear this, thou age unbred;
    Ere you were born was beauty's summer dead.

When in the chronicle of wasted time   CVI
I see descriptions of the fairest wights,
And beauty making beautiful old rhyme
In praise of ladies dead and lovely knights,
Then, in the blazon of sweet beauty's best,
Of hand, of foot, of lip, of eye, of brow,
I see their antique pen would have express'd
Even such a beauty as you master now.
So all their praises are but prophecies
Of this our time, all you prefiguring;
And, for they look'd but with divining eyes,
They had not skill enough your worth to sing:
    For we, which now behold these present days,
    Have eyes to wonder, but lack tongues to praise.

O, never say that I was false of heart,   CIX
Though absence seem'd my flame to qualify.
As easy might I from myself depart
As from my soul, which in thy breast doth lie.

Alas, 'tis true I have gone here and there   CX
And made myself a motley to the view,
Gored mine own thoughts, sold cheap what is most dear,
Made old offences of affections new.

O, for my sake, do you with Fortune chide,   CXI
The guilty goddess of my harmful deeds,
That did not better for my life provide
Than public means which public manners breeds.
Thence comes it that my name receives a brand,
And almost thence my nature is subdued
To what it works in, like the dyer's hand.

Let me not to the marriage of true minds   CXVI
Admit impediments.   Love is not love
Which alters when it alteration finds,
Or bends with the remover to remove:
O, no! it is an ever-fixed mark
That looks on tempests and is never shaken;
It is the star to every wandering bark,
Whose worth's unknown, although his height be taken.
Love's not Time's fool, though rosy lips and cheeks
Within his bending sickle's compass come;
Love alters not with his brief hours and weeks,
But bears it out even to the edge of doom.
    If this be error and upon me proved,
    I never writ, nor no man ever loved.

O benefit of ill! now I find true   CXIX
That better is by evil still made better;

457

And ruin'd love, when it is built anew, CXIX
Grows fairer than at first, more strong, far greater.

'Tis better to be vile than vile esteem'd, CXXI
When not to be receives reproach of being.

No, I am that I am, and they that level CXXI
At my abuses reckon up their own:
I may be straight, though they themselves be bevel;
By their rank thoughts my deeds must not be shown.

Our dates are brief, and therefore we admire CXXIII
What thou dost foist upon us that is old.

The expense of spirit in a waste of shame CXXIX
Is lust in action; and till action, lust
Is perjured, murderous, bloody, full of blame,
Savage, extreme, rude, cruel, not to trust,
Enjoy'd no sooner but despised straight,
Past reason hunted, and no sooner had
Past reason hated, as a swallow'd bait
On purpose laid to make the taker mad;
Mad in pursuit and in possession so;
Had, having, and in quest to have, extreme;
A bliss in proof, and proved, a very woe;
Before, a joy proposed; behind, a dream.
   All this the world well knows; yet none knows well
   To shun the heaven that leads men to this hell.

My mistress' eyes are nothing like the sun; CXXX
Coral is far more red than her lips' red;
If snow be white, why then her breasts are dun;
If hairs be wires, black wires grow on her head.
I have seen roses damask'd, red and white,
But no such roses see I in her cheeks;
And in some perfumes is there more delight
Than in the breath that from my mistress reeks.
I love to hear her speak, yet well I know
That music hath a far more pleasing sound;
I grant I never saw a goddess go;
My mistress, when she walks, treads on the ground:
   And yet, by heaven, I think my love as rare
   As any she belied with false compare.

And truly not the morning sun of heaven CXXXII
Better becomes the grey cheeks of the east,
Nor that full star that ushers in the even
Doth half that glory to the sober west,
As those two mourning eyes become thy face.

Whoever hath her wish, thou hast thy 'Will,'   CXXXV
And 'Will' to boot, and 'Will' in overplus;
More than enough am I that vex thee still,
To thy sweet will making addition thus.

When my love swears that she is made of truth   CXXXVIII
I do believe her, though I know she lies,
That she might think me some untutor'd youth,
Unlearned in the world's false subtleties.

Lo! as a careful housewife runs to catch   CXLIII
One of her feather'd creatures broke away,
Sets down her babe and makes all swift dispatch
In pursuit of the thing she would have stay,
Whilst her neglected child holds her in chase,
Cries to catch her whose busy care is bent
To follow that which flies before her face,
Not prizing her poor infant's discontent.

Two loves I have of comfort and despair,   CXLIV
Which like two spirits do suggest me still:
The better angel is a man right fair,
The worser spirit a woman colour'd ill.

Yet this shall I ne'er know, but live in doubt,   CXLIV
Till my bad angel fire my good one out.

So shalt thou feed on Death, that feeds on men,   CXLVI
And Death once dead, there's no more dying then.

Love is too young to know what conscience is;   CLI
Yet who knows not conscience is born of love?

THE PASSIONATE PILGRIM

(The authorship of this collection is doubtful)

If music and sweet poetry agree,   VIII
As they must needs, the sister and the brother,
Then must the love be great 'twixt thee and me,
Because thou lovest the one, and I the other.

Crabbed age and youth cannot live together: XII
Youth is full of pleasance, age is full of care;
Youth like summer morn, age like winter weather;
Youth like summer brave, age like winter bare.
Youth is full of sport, age's breath is short;
    Youth is nimble, age is lame;
Youth is hot and bold, age is weak and cold;
    Youth is wild, and age is tame.
Age, I do abhor thee; youth, I do adore thee;
    O, my love, my love is young!
Age, I do defy thee: O, sweet shepherd, hie thee,
    For methinks thou stay'st too long.

LIFE AND TRIBUTES

SHAKESPEARE AND CONTEMPORARY EVENTS

1558   Accession of Elizabeth I.
1561   Francis Bacon born.
1564   WILLIAM SHAKESPEARE CHRISTENED, 26 April.
      Christopher Marlowe born.
1572   Massacre of St Bartholomew.
1573   Ben Jonson born.
1576   The Theatre, London's first playhouse, built.
1577   Drake's voyage round the world (1577–80).
1579   John Fletcher born.
1582   SHAKESPEARE MARRIES ANNE HATHAWAY.
1583   SHAKESPEARE'S DAUGHTER SUSANNA CHRISTENED, 26 May.
1585   SHAKESPEARE'S TWINS HAMNET AND JUDITH CHRISTENED, 2
      February.
1586   Death of Sir Philip Sidney.
1587   Mary Queen of Scots executed.
1588   Marlowe's *Tamburlaine the Great* acted.
      Defeat of the Spanish Armada.
1589   Henri IV becomes King of France.
1590   Edmund Spenser's *Faery Queen*, first books.
1593   Death of Marlowe.
1596   SHAKESPEARE'S SON HAMNET BURIED, 11 August.
      COAT OF ARMS GRANTED TO SHAKESPEARE'S FATHER.
1597   SHAKESPEARE BUYS NEW PLACE IN STRATFORD.
      Bacon's *Essays* published.
1599   Globe Theatre opened.
      Death of Spenser.
1600   East India Company founded.
1601   SHAKESPEARE'S FATHER BURIED, 8 September.
      Revolt and execution of the Earl of Essex.
1603   Death of Queen Elizabeth. James VI of Scotland succeeds
      as James I of England.
1605   Gunpowder Plot.
1606   William D'Avenant born.
1607   SHAKESPEARE'S DAUGHTER SUSANNA MARRIES JOHN HALL, 5 June.
1608   THEIR DAUGHTER ELIZABETH CHRISTENED, 21 February.
      SHAKESPEARE'S MOTHER BURIED, 9 September.
      John Milton born.
1611   Authorized Version of the Bible.
1612   Death of Prince Henry.
1613   Globe Theatre burned.
      Marriage of Princess Elizabeth to Elector Palatine.
1616   JUDITH SHAKESPEARE MARRIES THOMAS QUINEY, 10 February.
      SHAKESPEARE'S WILL, 25 March. HIS DEATH, 23 April.
1618   Sir Walter Ralegh executed.
      Thirty Years War begins.
1620   Pilgrim Fathers land in America in *Mayflower*.
1623   DEATH OF SHAKESPEARE'S WIDOW, 6 August.
      SHAKESPEARE'S PLAYS, FIRST FOLIO, November.

APPROXIMATE DATES AND LENGTHS OF THE PLAYS
AND POEMS

	Date Written	First Printed	Number of Lines
Henry VI, Part I	1591	1623	2,677
Henry VI, Part II	1591	1594	3,162
Henry VI, Part III	1591	1595	2,904
The Comedy of Errors	1592	1623	1,777
Richard III	1593	1597	3,619
Titus Andronicus	1593	1600	2,523
The Taming of the Shrew	1594	1623	2,647
The Two Gentlemen of Verona	1594	1623	2,292
Love's Labour's Lost	1594	1598	2,785
Romeo and Juliet	1595	1597	3,050
Richard II	1595	1597	2,757
A Midsummer Night's Dream	1596	1600	2,174
King John	1596	1623	2,570
The Merchant of Venice	1596	1600	2,658
Henry IV, Part I	1597	1598	3,176
Henry IV, Part II	1598	1600	3,446
The Merry Wives of Windsor	1598	1602	3,018
Much Ado About Nothing	1598	1600	2,825
Henry V	1599	1600	3,381
Julius Caesar	1599	1623	2,477
As You Like It	1600	1623	2,856
Twelfth Night	1601	1623	2,690
Hamlet	1601	1603	3,929
Troilus and Cressida	1602	1609	3,496
All's Well That Ends Well	1603	1623	2,966
Measure for Measure	1604	1623	2,820
Othello	1604	1622	3,316
King Lear	1605	1608	3,328
Macbeth	1606	1623	2,106
Antony and Cleopatra	1607	1623	3,059
Pericles	1608	1609	2,393
Coriolanus	1609	1623	3,406
Timon of Athens	1609	1623	2,374
Cymbeline	1610	1623	3,339
The Winter's Tale	1611	1623	3,074
The Tempest	1611	1623	2,062
Henry VIII	1613	1623	2,819
Venus and Adonis	1592	1594	1,194
The Rape of Lucrece	1593	1594	1,855
The Sonnets		1609	2,156

LIFE OF SHAKESPEARE

THE authenticated facts of Shakespeare's life are scanty. He was baptized at Stratford-upon-Avon on 26th April 1564, but the exact date of his birth is uncertain. His father, John Shakespeare, is variously described as a glover, a butcher, and a dealer in wool, and may very possibly have been all three, in an age when trade was far less specialized than it is now; he was one of Stratford's leading citizens, and rose to hold the offices of alderman and high bailiff or mayor. His house in Henley Street is now shown as the poet's birth-place. William's mother, Mary Arden, was an heiress in a small way, and belonged to an old and distinguished Roman Catholic family. There were at least eight children, William being the third child and eldest son.

Of his boyhood nothing is known, but it is usually assumed that he attended the local grammar school. In 1582, at the age of 18, he married Anne Hathaway, a farmer's daughter eight years his senior; the little Hathaway farmhouse is still preserved in beautiful surroundings at Shottery, near Stratford. Six months later a daughter Susanna was born, and in 1585 twins, Hamnet and Judith.

Thenceforward, apart from untrustworthy traditions, there is a gap of about seven years in the record, until we find Shakespeare established in London at the age of 28 as a rising actor-dramatist whose success is already resented by the group of university men who were the leading lights of the theatre. In the next two years the poems *Venus and Adonis* and *Lucrece* were published, both dedicated to the young Earl of Southampton as patron. In 1594 the Lord Chamberlain's Company, which later became the King's Players, was formed, with Shakespeare as a regular member. Very little is known about his career as an actor, but his name

Q

appears in the cast of two of Ben Jonson's plays, and there is a tradition that he took the parts of the Ghost in *Hamlet* and of old Adam in *As You Like It*.

In 1596, a year saddened by the death of his son Hamnet at the age of eleven, Shakespeare attained full maturity and success as a playwright. He celebrated his prosperity by the purchase next year of New Place, the largest house in his native town, but still continued to lodge in London, where there are records of his having lived in Southwark, in Bishopsgate, on Bankside, and in Cripplegate. He is thought to have finally retired about 1610 to Stratford, where he died on 23rd April 1616.

His elder daughter Susanna was married in 1607 to Dr John Hall; they had a daughter Elizabeth, who was twice married, but died childless. A few weeks before his death his younger daughter Judith married Thomas Quiney, son of a Stratford friend. Shakespeare's widow survived till 1623, and shortly after her death there was published the collected edition of his plays commonly termed the First Folio.

Motto and Dedication to 'Venus and Adonis' (1593).

'Vilia miretur vulgus; mihi flavus Apollo
Pocula Castalia plena ministret aqua.' *

TO THE RIGHT HONOURABLE HENRY WRIOTHESLY
Earl of Southampton, and Baron of Tichfield

Right Honourable,
    I know not how I shall offend in dedicating my unpolished lines
to your lordship, nor how the world will censure me for choosing so
strong a prop to support so weak a burden: only if your honour seem
but pleased, I account myself highly praised, and vow to take advantage of all idle hours, till I have honoured you with some graver
labour.   But if the first heir of my invention prove deformed, I shall
be sorry it had so noble a god-father, and never after ear so barren a
land, for fear it yield me still so bad a harvest.   I leave it to your
honourable survey, and your honour to your heart's content; which
I wish may always answer your own wish and the world's hopeful
expectation.

Your honour's in all duty,

WILLIAM SHAKESPEARE.

   * Let the common herd admire things of little worth; to me may
golden-haired Apollo dispense cups filled with Castalian water.

Ovid, Amores, i. xv. 35.

Dedication to 'The Rape of Lucrece' (1594)

TO THE RIGHT HONOURABLE HENRY WRIOTHESLY
Earl of Southampton, and Baron of Tichfield

   The love I dedicate to your lordship is without end; whereof this
pamphlet, without beginning, is but a superfluous moiety.   The
warrant I have of your honourable disposition, not the worth of my
untutored lines, makes it assured of acceptance.   What I have done
is yours; what I have to do is yours; being part in all I have, devoted
yours.   Were my worth greater, my duty would show greater; meantime, as it is, it is bound to your lordship, to whom I wish long life,
still lengthened with all happiness.

Your lordship's in all duty,

WILLIAM SHAKESPEARE.

DEDICATION TO THE SONNETS (1609)

TO THE ONLIE BEGETTER OF
THESE INSUING SONNETS
MR W. H. ALL HAPPINESS
AND THAT ETERNITIE
PROMISED
BY
OUR EVER-LIVING POET
WISHETH
THE WELL-WISHING
ADVENTURER IN
SETTING
FORTH

T. T.

INSCRIPTION ON THE MONUMENT IN STRATFORD CHURCH

Iudicio Pylium, genio Socratem, arte Maronem:
Terra tegit, populus maeret, Olympus habet.*

Stay, passenger, why goest thou by so fast?
Read, if thou canst, whom envious Death hath placed
Within this monument, Shakespeare: with whom
Quick Nature died; whose name doth deck this tomb
Far more than cost: sith all that he hath writ
Leaves living art but page to serve his wit.

* A Pylian (Nestor) in wisdom, a Socrates in inspiration, a Maro
(Virgil) in art, the earth covers, the people mourn, Olympus possesses.

SHAKESPEARE'S WILL (25th March 1616)

*In the name of God, amen, I, William Shakespeare, of Stratford upon
Avon in the county of Warwick, gentleman, in perfect health and memory,
God be praised, do make and ordain this my last will and testament in
manner and form following.*

*That is to say, First, I commend my soul into the hands of God my
creator, hoping and assuredly believing, through the only merits of Jesus
Christ my Saviour, to be made partaker of life everlasting, and my body
to the earth whereof it is made.*

*Item, I give and bequeath unto my daughter Judith one hundred
and fifty pounds of lawful English money, to be paid unto her in manner
and form following; that is to say, one hundred pounds in discharge of
her marriage portion within one year after my decease, with consideration
after the rate of two shillings in the pound for so long time as the same*

shall be unpaid unto her after my decease, and the fifty pounds residue thereof upon her surrendering of, or giving of such sufficient security as the overseers of this my will shall like of to surrender or grant, all her estate and right that shall descend or come unto her after my decease or that she now hath of, in, or to one copyhold tenement with the appurtenances lying and being in Stratford upon Avon aforesaid in the said county of Warwick, being parcel or holden of the manor of Rowington, unto my daughter Susanna Hall and her heirs for ever.

Item, I give and bequeath unto my said daughter Judith one hundred and fifty pounds more, if she or any issue of her body be living at the end of three years next ensuing the day of the date of this my will, during which time my executors to pay her consideration from my decease according to the rate aforesaid. And if she die within the said term without issue of her body then my will is, and I do give and bequeath one hundred pounds thereof to my niece Elizabeth Hall, and the fifty pounds to be set forth by my executors during the life of my sister Joan Hart, and the use and profit thereof coming shall be paid to my said sister Joan, and after her decease the said £50 shall remain amongst the children of my said sister equally to be divided amongst them. But if my said daughter Judith be living at the end of the said three years, or any issue of her body, then my will is, and so I devise and bequeath the said hundred and fifty pounds to be set out by my executors and overseers for the best benefit of her and her issue, and the stock not to be paid unto her so long as she shall be married and covert baron; but my will is that she shall have the consideration yearly paid unto her during her life, and after her decease the said stock and consideration to be paid to her children if she have any, and if not, to her executors or assigns, she living the said term after my decease. Provided that if such husband as she shall at the end of the said three years be married unto or attain after do sufficiently assure unto her and the issue of her body lands answerable to the portion of this my will given unto her and to be adjudged so by my executors and overseers, then my will is that the said £150 shall be paid to such husband as shall make assurance to his own use.

Item, I give and bequeath unto my said sister Joan £20 and all my wearing apparel, to be paid and delivered within one year after my decease, and I do will and devise unto her the house with the appurtenances in Stratford wherein she dwelleth, for her natural life under the yearly rent of 12d.

Item, I give and bequeath unto her three sons, William Hart, —— Hart, and Michael Hart, five pounds apiece, to be paid within one year after my decease.

Item, I give and bequeath unto the said Elizabeth Hall all my plate (except my broad silver and gilt bowl) that I now have at the date of this my will.

Item I give and bequeath unto the poor of Stratford aforesaid ten pounds, to Mr Thomas Combe my sword, to Thomas Russell Esquire five pounds, and to Francis Collins, of the borough of Warwick, in the county of Warwick, gentleman, thirteen pounds six shillings and eightpence, to be paid within one year after my decease.

Item, I give and bequeath to Hamlet Sadler 26s. 8d. to buy him a ring; to William Reynolds, gentleman, 26s. 8d. to buy him a ring; to my godson William Walker 20s. in gold; to Anthony Nash, gentleman, 26s. 8d.; and to Mr John Nash 26s. 8d.; and to my fellows John Heminge, Richard Burbage, and Henry Condell 26s. 8d. apiece to buy them rings.

Item, I give, will, bequeath and devise unto my daughter Susanna Hall for better enabling of her to perform this my will, and towards the performance thereof, all that capital messuage or tenement, with the appurtenances, in Stratford aforesaid, called the New Place, wherein I now dwell, and two messuages or tenements, with the appurtenances, situate, lying, and being in Henley Street within the borough of Stratford aforesaid; and all my barns, stables, orchards, gardens, lands, tenements, and hereditaments whatsoever situate, lying, and being, or to be had, received, perceived, or taken within the towns, hamlets, villages, fields, and grounds of Stratford upon Avon, Old Stratford, Bishopton, and Welcombe, or in any of them in the said county of Warwick; and also all that messuage or tenement, with the appurtenances, wherein one John Robinson dwelleth, situate, lying, and being in the Blackfriars in London, near the Wardrobe; and all other my lands, tenements, and hereditaments whatsoever, to have and to hold all and singular the said premises, with their appurtenances, unto the said Susanna Hall for and during the term of her natural life, and after her decease to the first son of her body lawfully issuing, and to the heirs males of the body of the said first son lawfully issuing, and for default of such issue, to the second son of her body lawfully issuing, and to the heirs males of the body of the said second son lawfully issuing, and for default of such heirs to the third son of the body of the said Susanna lawfully issuing, and of the heirs males of the body of the said third son lawfully issuing; and for default of such issue the same so to be and remain to the fourth, fifth, sixth, and seventh sons of her body lawfully issuing one after another, and to the heirs males of the bodies of the said fourth, fifth, sixth, and seventh sons lawfully issuing, in such manner as it is before limited to be and remain to the first, second, and third sons of her body, and to their heirs males; and for default of such issue, the said premises to be and remain to my said niece Hall and the heirs males of her body lawfully issuing, and for default of issue to my daughter Judith and the heirs males of her body lawfully issuing, and for default of such issue, to the right heirs of me the said William Shakespeare for ever.

Item, I give unto my wife my second best bed with the furniture.

Item, I give and bequeath to my said daughter Judith my broad silver gilt bowl.

All the rest of my goods, chattels, leases, plate, jewels, and household stuff whatsoever, after my debts and legacies paid and my funeral expenses discharged, I give, devise, and bequeath to my son-in-law John Hall, gentleman, and my daughter Susanna his wife, whom I ordain and make executors of this my last will and testament.

And I do entreat and appoint the said Thomas Russell Esquire and Francis Collins, gentleman, to be overseers hereof; and do revoke all *former wills and publish this to be my last will and testament.   In witness whereof I have hereunto put my hand the day and year first above written.*

By me William Shakespeare.

Witness to the publishing hereof:

> *Francis Collins.*
> *Julius Shaw.*
> *John Robinson.*
> *Hamnet Sadler.*
> *Robert Whatcot.*

FROM THOMAS FULLER'S 'HISTORY OF THE WORTHIES OF ENGLAND' (1662)

William Shakespeare was born at Stratford on Avon in this county, in whom three eminent poets may seem in some sort to be compounded: 1. Martial in the warlike sound of his surname (whence some may conjecture him of a military extraction), *Hasti-vibrans* or *Shake-speare*; 2. Ovid, the most natural and witty of all poets, and hence it was that Queen Elizabeth coming into a grammar school made this extemporary verse—

Persius a crab-staff, bawdy Martial, Ovid a fine wag.

—3. Plautus, who was an exact comedian, yet never any scholar, as our Shakespeare (if alive) would confess himself.   Add to all these, that though his genius generally was jocular, and inclining him to festivity, yet he could (when so disposed) be solemn and serious, as appears by his tragedies, so that Heraclitus himself (I mean if secret and unseen) might afford to smile at his comedies, they were so merry, and Democritus scarce forbear to sigh at his tragedies, they were so mournful.

He was an eminent instance of the truth of that rule, *Poeta non fit, sed nascitur*—one is not made but born a poet.   Indeed his learning was very little, so that as Cornish diamonds are not polished by any lapidary, but are pointed and smoothed even as they are taken out of the earth, so nature itself was all the art which was used upon him.

Many were the wit-combats betwixt him and Ben Jonson, which two I behold like a Spanish great galleon, and an English man-of-war; Master Jonson (like the former) was built far higher in learning; solid, but slow in his performances.   Shakespeare with the English man-of-war, lesser in bulk, but lighter in sailing, could turn with all tides, tack about and take advantage of all winds, by the quickness of his wit and invention.   He died *Anno Domini* 16— and was buried at Stratford upon Avon, the town of his nativity.

FROM JOHN MANNINGHAM'S DIARY (1602)

Upon a time when Burbage played Richard III there was a citizen grew so far in liking with him that before she went from the play she appointed him to come that night unto her by the name of Richard the Third. Shakespeare, overhearing their conclusion, went before, was entertained and at his game ere Burbage came. Then message being brought that Richard the Third was at the door, Shakespeare caused return to be made that William the Conqueror was before Richard the Third.

FROM JOHN WARD'S DIARY (1661–3)

I have heard that Mr Shakespeare was a natural wit, without any art at all; he frequented the plays all his younger time, but in his elder days lived at Stratford: and supplied the stage with two plays every year, and for that had an allowance so large that he spent at the rate of £1,000 a year, as I have heard.

Shakespeare, Drayton, and Ben Jonson had a merry meeting, and it seems drank too hard, for Shakespeare died of a fever there contracted.

LIFE OF SHAKESPEARE BY JOHN AUBREY (1626–97)

Mr William Shakespeare was born at Stratford upon Avon in the county of Warwick. His father was a butcher, and I have been told heretofore by some of the neighbours that when he was a boy he exercised his father's trade, but when he killed a calf he would do it in a high style, and make a speech. There was at that time another butcher's son in this town that was held not at all inferior to him for a natural wit, his acquaintance and coetanean, but died young. This William being inclined naturally to poetry and acting, came to London, I guess about eighteen, and was an actor at one of the playhouses, and did act exceedingly well: now Ben Jonson was never a good actor, but an excellent instructor. He began early to make essays at dramatic poetry, which at that time was very low; and his plays took well. He was a handsome, well-shaped man: very good company, and of a very ready and pleasant smooth wit. The humour of the constable in *Midsummer Night's Dream* he happened to take at Grendon in Bucks—I think it was midsummer night that he happened to lie there—which is the road from London to Stratford, and there was living that constable about 1642, when I first came to Oxon: Mr Josias Howe is of that parish, and knew him. Ben Jonson and he did gather humours of men daily where ever they came. One time, as he was at the tavern at Stratford super Avon, one Combes, an old rich usurer, was to be buried, he makes there this extempory epitaph:

> Ten in the hundred the Devil allows,
> But Combes will have twelve, he swears and vows:
> If any one asks who lies in this tomb,
> 'Ho!' quoth the Devil, ''Tis my John o' Combe.'

He was wont to go to his native country once a year. I think I have been told that he left 2 or 300 *li. per annum* there and thereabout to a sister. I have heard Sir William Davenant and Mr Thomas Shadwell (who is counted the best comedian we have now) say that he had a most prodigious wit, and did admire his natural parts beyond all other dramatical writers. He was wont to say, That he never blotted out a line in his life: said Ben Jonson, I wish he had blotted out a thousand. His comedies will remain wit as long as the English tongue is understood, for that he handles *mores hominum*. Now our present writers reflect so much upon particular persons and coxcombeities, that twenty years hence they will not be understood. Though, as Ben Jonson says of him that he had but little Latin and less Greek, he understood Latin pretty well, for he had been in his younger years a schoolmaster in the country.

FROM NICHOLAS ROWE'S LIFE OF SHAKESPEARE (1709)

He was the son of Mr John Shakespeare, and was born at Stratford upon Avon, in Warwickshire, in April 1564. His family, as appears by the register and public writings relating to that town, were of good figure and fashion there, and are mentioned as gentlemen. His father, who was a considerable dealer in wool, had so large a family, ten children in all, that though he was his eldest son, he could give him no better education than his own employment. He had bred him, 'tis true, for some time at a free school, where 'tis probable he acquired that little Latin he was master of.

.   .   .   .

In order to settle in the world after a family manner, he thought fit to marry while he was yet very young. His wife was the daughter of one Hathaway, said to have been a substantial yeoman in the neighbourhood of Stratford. In this kind of settlement he continued for some time, till an extravagance that he was guilty of, forced him out of his country and that way of living which he had taken up; and though it seemed at first to be a blemish upon his good manners, and a misfortune to him, yet it afterwards happily proved the occasion of exerting one of the greatest geniuses that ever was known in dramatic poetry. He had, by a misfortune common enough to young fellows, fallen into ill company; and amongst them, some that made a frequent practice of deer-stealing, engaged him with them more than once in robbing a park that belonged to Sir Thomas Lucy of Charlecot, near Stratford. For this he was prosecuted by that gentleman, as he thought, somewhat too severely; and in order to revenge that ill usage, he made a ballad upon him. And though this, probably the first essay of his poetry, be lost, yet it is said to have been so very bitter, that it redoubled the prosecution against him to that degree, that he was obliged to leave his business and family in Warwickshire, for some time, and shelter himself in London.

It is at this time, and upon this accident, that he is said to have made his first acquaintance in the playhouse. He was received into the company then in being, at first in a very mean rank; but his admirable wit, and the natural turn of it to the stage, soon distinguished him, if not as an extraordinary actor, yet as an excellent writer. His name is printed, as the custom was in those times,

*Q

amongst those of the other players, before some old plays, but without any particular account of what sort of parts he used to play; and though I have inquired, I could never meet with any further account of him this way, than that the top of his performance was the Ghost in his own *Hamlet*.

.　　　　　.　　　　　.　　　　　.

The latter part of his life was spent, as all men of good sense will wish theirs may be, in ease, retirement, and the conversation of his friends. He had the good fortune to gather an estate equal to his occasion, and, in that, to his wish; and is said to have spent some years before his death at his native Stratford. His pleasurable wit, and good nature, engaged him in the acquaintance, and entitled him to the friendship of the gentlemen of the neighbourhood. Amongst them, it is a story almost still remembered in that country, that he had a particular intimacy with Mr Combe, an old gentleman noted thereabouts for his wealth and usury. It happened that in a pleasant conversation amongst their common friends Mr Combe told Shakespeare in a laughing manner that he fancied he intended to write his epitaph, if he happened to outlive him; and since he could not know what might be said of him when he was dead, he desired it might be done immediately: upon which Shakespeare gave him these four verses:

'Ten in the hundred lies here ingraved,
'Tis a hundred to ten, his soul is not saved:
If any man ask, Who lies in this tomb?
"Oh! ho!" quoth the Devil, "'tis my John-a-Combe."'

But the sharpness of the satire is said to have stung the man so severely that he never forgave it.

He died in the 53rd year of his age, and was buried in the north side of the chancel, in the Great Church at Stratford, where a monument, as engraved in the plate, is placed in the wall. On his gravestone underneath is:

'Good friend, for Jesus sake forbear
To dig the dust inclosed here.
Blest be the man that spares these stones,
And curst be he that moves my bones.'

He had three daughters, of which two lived to be married; Judith, the elder, to one Mr Thomas Quiney, by whom she had three sons, who all died without children; and Susannah, who was his favourite, to Dr John Hall, a physician of good reputation in that country. She left one child only, a daughter, who was married first to Thomas Nash, Esq.; and afterwards to Sir John Bernard of Abington, but died likewise without issue.

TRIBUTES TO SHAKESPEARE

Myself have seen his demeanour no less civil than he excellent in the quality he professes: Besides, divers of worship have reported his uprightness of dealing, which argues his honesty, and his facetious grace in writing, that approves his art.

HENRY CHETTLE, Kind Heart's Dream (1592).

As the soul of Euphorbus was thought to live in Pythagoras: so the sweet witty soul of Ovid lives in mellifluous and honey-tongued Shakespeare, witness his *Venus and Adonis*, his *Lucrece*, his sugared Sonnets among his private friends, etc.

As Plautus and Seneca are accounted the best for comedy and tragedy among the Latins: so Shakespeare among the English is the most excellent in both kinds for the stage; for comedy, witness his *Gentlemen of Verona*, his *Errors*, his *Love's Labour's Lost*, his *Love's Labour's Won*, his *Midsummer Night Dream*, and his *Merchant of Venice*: for tragedy, his *Richard the 2*, *Richard the 3*, *Henry the 4*, *King John*, *Titus Andronicus*, and his *Romeo and Juliet*.

As Epius Stolo said, that the Muses would speak with Plautus's tongue, if they would speak Latin: so I say that the Muses would speak with Shakespeare's fine filed phrase, if they would speak English.

FRANCIS MERES, Palladis Tamia (1598).

Live ever you, at least in fame live ever:
Well may the body die, but fame lives ever.

RICHARD BARNFIELD, A Remembrance of Some English Poets (1598).

Few of the university men pen plays well, they smell too much of that writer Ovid, and that writer Metamorphosis, and talk too much of Proserpina and Jupiter. Why, here's our fellow Shakespeare puts them all down.

ANON., Return from Parnassus, IV. iii. (1601).

ON MR. WM. SHAKESPEARE (c. 1620)

Renowned Spenser, lie a thought more nigh
To learned Chaucer, and rare Beaumont lie
A little nearer Spenser, to make room
For Shakespeare in your threefold, fourfold tomb.
To lodge all four in one bed make a shift
Until doomsday, for hardly will a fift
Betwixt this day and that by fate be slain
For whom your curtains may be drawn again.
If your precedency in death doth bar
A fourth place in your sacred sepulchre,

475

Under this carved marble of thine own
Sleep, rare tragedian Shakespeare, sleep alone,
Thy unmolested peace, unshared cave,
Possess as lord, not tenant, of thy grave,
   That unto us and others it may be
   Honour hereafter to be laid by thee.

WILLIAM BASSE.

FROM PREFACE TO THE FIRST FOLIO (1623)
To the great Variety of Readers

From the most able, to him that can but spell: there you are numbered. We had rather you were weighed. Especially when the fate of all books depends upon your capacities: and not of your heads alone, but of your purses. Well! it is now public, and you will stand for your privileges we know: to read, and censure. Do so, but buy it first. That doth best commend a book, the stationer says. Then, how odd soever your brains be, or your wisdoms, make your licence the same, and spare not. Judge your sixpennyworth, your shilling's worth, your five shillings' worth at a time, or higher, so you rise to the just rates, and welcome. But, whatever you do, buy. Censure will not drive a trade, or make the Jack go. And though you be a magistrate of wit, and sit on the stage at Blackfriars, or the Cockpit, to arraign plays daily, know, these plays have had their trial already, and stood out all appeals; and do now come forth quitted rather by a decree of court, than any purchased letters of commendation.

It had been a thing, we confess, worthy to have been wished, that the author himself had lived to have set forth and overseen his own writings; but since it hath been ordained otherwise, and he by death departed from that right, we pray you do not envy his friends the office of their care and pain to have collected and published them; and so to have published them, as where (before) you were abused with diverse stolen and surreptitious copies, maimed and deformed by the frauds and stealths of injurious impostors that exposed them: even those are now offered to your view cured, and perfect of their limbs; and all the rest, absolute in their numbers, as he conceived them. Who, as he was a happy imitator of Nature, was a most gentle expresser of it. His mind and hand went together: and what he thought, he uttered with that easiness that we have scarce received from him a blot in his papers. But it is not our province, who only gather his works and give them you, to praise him. It is yours that read him. And there we hope, to your divers capacities, you will find enough both to draw and hold you: for his wit can no more lie hid than it could be lost. Read him, therefore; and again, and again: and then if you do not like him, surely you are in some manifest danger not to understand him. And so we leave you to other of his friends, whom if you need, can be your guides: if you need them not, you can lead your selves and others. And such readers we wish him.

JOHN HEMINGE.
HENRY CONDELL.

TO THE MEMORY OF MY BELOVED
THE AUTHOR
MR. WILLIAM SHAKESPEARE
AND WHAT HE HATH LEFT US.

To draw no envy (Shakespeare) on thy name,
  Am I thus ample to thy book, and fame:
While I confess thy writings to be such,
  As neither man, nor Muse, can praise too much.
'Tis true, and all men's suffrage. But these ways
  Were not the paths I meant unto thy praise:
For seeliest Ignorance on these may light,
  Which, when it sounds at best, but echo's right;
Or blind Affection, which doth ne'er advance
  The truth, but gropes, and urgeth all by chance;
Or crafty Malice might pretend this praise,
  And think to ruin, where it seem'd to raise.
These are, as some infamous bawd or whore,
  Should praise a matron. What could hurt her more?
But thou art proof against them, and indeed
  Above th'ill fortune of them, or the need.
I, therefore will begin. Soul of the Age!
  The applause! delight! the wonder of our stage!
My Shakespeare, rise; I will not lodge thee by
  Chaucer, or Spenser, or bid Beaumont lie
A little further, to make thee a room:
  Thou art a monument, without a tomb,
And art alive still, while thy book doth live,
  And we have wits to read, and praise to give.
That I not mix thee so, my brain excuses;
  I mean with great, but disproportion'd Muses:
For, if I thought my judgment were of years,
  I should commit thee surely with thy peers,
And tell, how far thou didst our Lyly outshine,
  Or sporting Kyd, or Marlowe's mighty line.
And though thou hadst small Latin, and less Greek,
  From thence to honour thee, I would not seek
For names; but call forth thund'ring Aeschylus,
  Euripides, and Sophocles to us,
Pacuvius, Accius, him of Cordova dead,
  To life again, to hear thy buskin tread,
And shake a stage; or, when thy socks were on,
  Leave thee alone, for the comparison
Of all, that insolent Greece, or haughty Rome
  Sent forth, or since did from their ashes come
Triúmph, my Britain, thou hast one to show,
  To whom all scenes of Europe homage owe.
He was not of an age, but for all time!
  And all the Muses still were in their prime,

When like Apollo he came forth to warm
　　Our ears, or like a Mercury to charm!
Nature her self was proud of his designs,
　　And joy'd to wear the dressing of his lines!
Which were so richly spun, and woven so fit,
　　As, since, she will vouchsafe no other wit.
The merry Greek, tart Aristophanes,
　　Neat Terence, witty Plautus, now not please;
But antiquated, and deserted lie
　　As they were not of Nature's family.
Yet must I not give Nature all: thy art
　　My gentle Shakespeare, must enjoy a part.
For though the poet's matter, Nature be,
　　His art doth give the fashion. And, that he,
Who casts to write a living line, must sweat,
　　(Such as thine are) and strike the second heat
Upon the Muse's anvil: turn the same,
　　(And himself with it) that he thinks to frame;
Or for the laurel, he may gain a scorn,
　　For a good poet's made, as well as born.
And such wert thou. Look how the father's face
　　Lives in his issue, even so, the race
Of Shakespeare's mind and manners brightly shines
　　In his well-turned and true-filed lines:
In each of which he seems to shake a lance,
　　As brandish't at the eyes of Ignorance.
Sweet Swan of Avon! what a sight it were
　　To see thee in our waters yet appear,
And make those flights upon the banks of Thames,
　　That so did take Eliza, and our James!
But stay, I see thee in the Hemisphere
　　Advanc'd, and made a constellation there!
Shine forth, thou star of poets, and with rage,
　　Or influence, chide, or cheer the drooping stage;
Which, since thy flight from hence, hath mourn'd like night,
　　And despairs day, but for thy volume's light.

BEN JONSON, in the First Folio (1623)

　　This figure, that thou here seest put,
　　It was for gentle Shakespeare cut;
　　Wherein the graver had a strife
　　With Nature, to out-do the life:
　　O could he but have drawn his wit
　　As well in brass, as he hath hit
　　His face; the print would then surpass
　　All that was ever writ in brass.
　　But since he cannot, reader, look
　　Not on his picture, but his book.

BEN JONSON on the portrait of Shakespeare (1623).

DE SHAKESPEARE NOSTRATI (CONCERNING OUR SHAKESPEARE)

I remember, the players have often mentioned it as an honour to Shakespeare, that in his writing (whatsoever he penned) he never blotted out line. My answer hath been, would he had blotted a thousand. Which they thought a malevolent speech. I had not told posterity this, but for their ignorance, who choose that circumstance to commend their friend by, wherein he most faulted. And to justify mine own candour (for I loved the man, and do honour his memory (on this side idolatry) as much as any). He was (indeed) honest, and of an open, and free nature: had an excellent fancy; brave notions, and gentle expressions: wherein he flowed with that facility, that sometime it was necessary he should be stopped: *Sufflaminandus erat*; as Augustus said of Haterius. His wit was in his own power; would the rule of it had been so too. Many times he fell into those things, could not escape laughter: as when he said in the person of Caesar, one speaking to him; 'Caesar, thou dost me wrong.' He replied: 'Caesar did never wrong, but with just cause': and such like; which were ridiculous. But he redeemed his vices, with his virtues. There was ever more in him to be praised, than to be pardoned.

BEN JONSON, *Timber, or Discoveries made*
upon Men and Matters (1641).

What needs my Shakespeare for his honour'd bones,
The labour of an age in piled stones,
Or that his hallow'd relics should be hid
Under a star-y-pointing pyramid?
Dear son of memory, great heir of fame,
What need'st thou such weak witness of thy name?
Thou in our wonder and astonishment
Hast built thyself a live-long monument.
For whilst to th' shame of slow-endeavouring art,
Thy easy numbers flow, and that each heart
Hath from the leaves of thy unvalued book
Those Delphic lines with deep impression took,
Then thou our fancy of itself bereaving,
Dost make us marble with too much conceiving;
And so sepulchred in such pomp dost lie,
That kings for such a tomb would wish to die.

JOHN MILTON, *On Shakespeare* (1630).

Then to the well-trod stage anon,
If Jonson's learned sock be on,
Or sweetest Shakespeare, Fancy's child,
Warble his native wood-notes wild.

JOHN MILTON, *L'Allegro* (1632).

Shakespeare who (taught by none) did first impart
To Fletcher wit, to labouring Jonson art.
JOHN DRYDEN, *Prologue to the Tempest* (1667).

But Shakespeare's magic could not copied be;
Within that circle none durst walk but he.
Ibid.

To begin then with Shakespeare; he was the man who of all modern, and perhaps ancient poets, had the largest and most comprehensive soul. All the images of nature were still present to him, and he drew them not laboriously, but luckily: when he describes any thing, you more than see it, you feel it too. Those who accuse him to have wanted learning, give him the greater commendation: he was naturally learned; he needed not the spectacles of books to read nature; he looked inwards, and found her there. I cannot say he is every where alike; were he so, I should do him injury to compare him with the greatest of mankind. He is many times flat, insipid; his comick wit degenerating into clenches, his serious swelling into bombast. But he is always great when some great occasion is presented to him: no man can say he ever had a fit subject for his wit, and did not then raise himself as high above the rest of poets,

*Quantum lenta solent inter viburna cupressi.**

The consideration of this made Mr Hales of Eton say, That there was no subject of which any poet ever writ, but he would produce it much better treated of in Shakespeare.

JOHN DRYDEN, *Of Dramatic Poesy, an Essay* (1668).

* As cypresses are wont to do among the pliant osiers.

He seems to have known the world by intuition, to have looked through human nature at one glance.

ALEXANDER POPE, *Preface to the Works of Shakespeare* (1725).

With all his faults, and with all the irregularity of his drama, one may look upon his works, in comparison of those that are more finished and regular, as upon an ancient majestick piece of Gothick architecture, compared with a neat modern building: The latter is more elegant and glaring, but the former is more strong and more solemn. It must be allowed, that in one of these there are materials enough to make many of the other. It has much the greater variety, and much the nobler apartments; though we are often conducted to them by dark, odd, and uncouth passages. Nor does the whole fail to strike us with greater reverence, though many of the parts are childish, ill-placed, and unequal to its grandeur.

Ibid.

Shakespeare (whom you and every playhouse bill
Style the divine, the matchless, what you will)
For gain, not glory, winged his roving flight,
And grew immortal in his own despite.

ALEXANDER POPE, *Epistle to Augustus* (1737).

Far from the sun and summer-gale,
In thy green lap was Nature's darling laid,
What time, where lucid Avon strayed,
   To him the mighty mother did unveil
Her awful face: the dauntless child
Stretched forth his little arms and smiled.
This pencil take (she said), whose colours clear
Richly paint the vernal year:
Thine too these golden keys, immortal Boy!
This can unlock the gates of joy;
Of horror that, and thrilling fears,
Or ope the sacred source of sympathetic tears.

THOMAS GRAY, *The Progress of Poesy* (1757).

When Learning's triumph o'er her barb'rous foes
First rear'd the Stage, immortal Shakespeare rose;
Each change of many-colour'd life he drew,
Exhausted worlds, and then imagin'd new:
Existence saw him spurn her bounded reign,
And panting Time toil'd after him in vain.

SAMUEL JOHNSON, *Prologue at the opening
of the theatre in Drury Lane* (1747).

The stream of time, which is continually washing the dissoluble
fabricks of other poets, passes without injury by the adamant of
Shakespeare.

SAMUEL JOHNSON, *Preface to Shakespeare* (1765).

The work of a correct and regular writer is a garden accurately
formed and diligently planted, varied with shades, and scented with
flowers; the composition of Shakespeare is a forest, in which oaks
extend their branches, and pines tower in the air, interspersed sometimes with weeds and brambles, and sometimes giving shelter to
myrtles and to roses; filling the eye with awful pomp, and gratifying
the mind with endless diversity.   Other poets display cabinets of
precious rarities, minutely finished, wrought into shape, and polished
unto brightness.   Shakespeare opens a mine which contains gold and
diamonds in unexhaustible plenty, though clouded by incrustations,
debased by impurities, and mingled with a mass of meaner minerals.

Ibid.

And one wild Shakespeare, following Nature's lights,
Is worth whole planets filled with Stagyrites.

THOMAS MOORE, *The Sceptic* (1809).

Scorn not the Sonnet; Critic, you have frowned,
Mindless of its just honours; with this key
Shakespeare unlocked his heart.

WILLIAM WORDSWORTH, *Scorn not the Sonnet* (1811).

'With this same key
Shakespeare unlocked his heart' once more!
Did Shakespeare? If so, the less Shakespeare he!

ROBERT BROWNING, *House* (1876).

Our myriad-minded Shakespeare.

S. T. COLERIDGE, *Biographia Literaria* (1817).

If we wish to know the force of human genius we should read
Shakespeare. If we wish to see the insignificance of human learning
we may study his commentators.

WILLIAM HAZLITT, *On the Ignorance of the Learned* (1821).

Shakespeare is not *our* poet, but the world's.

W. S. LANDOR, *To Robert Browning* (1845).

Others abide our question. Thou art free.
We ask and ask: Thou smilest and art still,
Out-topping knowledge. For the loftiest hill
That to the stars uncrowns his majesty,
Planting his steadfast footsteps in the sea,
Making the Heaven of Heavens his dwelling-place,
Spares but the cloudy border of his base
To the foil'd searching of mortality:
And thou, who didst the stars and sunbeams know,
Self-school'd, self-scann'd, self-honour'd, self-secure,
Didst walk on Earth unguess'd at. Better so!
All pains the immortal spirit must endure,
All weakness that impairs, all griefs that bow,
Find their sole voice in that victorious brow.

MATTHEW ARNOLD, *Shakespeare* (1849).

If we could make his living acquaintance, we should expect to find in him one of those well-balanced and plastic tempers which enable men to attract something less than their due share of observation and remark as they pass to and fro among their fellows. Children, we feel sure, did not stop their talk when he came near them, but continued, in the happy assurance that it was only Master Shakespeare. The tradition of geniality clings to his name like a faded perfume. Every one was more himself for being in the company of Shakespeare.

WALTER A. RALEIGH, *Shakespeare* (1907).

SOME HOSTILE CRITICISMS

There is an upstart crow, beautified with our feathers, that with his *Tiger's heart wrapped in a player's hide*, supposes he is as well able to bombast out a blank verse as the best of you: and being an absolute *Johannes fac totum*, is in his own conceit the only Shake-scene in a country.

> ROBERT GREENE, *A Groatsworth of Wit bought with a Million of Repentance* (1592).

I saw Hamlet Prince of Denmark played; but now the old plays began to disgust this refined age.   JOHN EVELYN, *Diary* (1661).

To the King's Theatre, where we saw *Midsummer Night's Dream*, which I had never seen before, nor shall ever again, for it is the most insipid ridiculous play that ever I saw in my life.

> SAMUEL PEPYS, *Diary* (1662).

There is in this play (*Othello*) some burlesque, some humour and ramble of comical wit, some show, and some mimicry to divert the spectators: but the tragical part is plainly none other than a bloody farce, without salt or savour.

> THOMAS RYMER, *A Short View of Tragedy* (1692).

If Shakespeare's genius had been cultivated, those beauties which we so justly admire in him would have been undisgraced by those extravagancies, and that nonsense, with which they are so frequently accompanied.   EARL OF CHESTERFIELD, *Letters* (1748).

One of the greatest geniuses that ever existed, Shakespeare, undoubtedly wanted taste.   HORACE WALPOLE, *Letters* (1764).

Shakespeare est un sauvage avec des etincelles de génie qui brillent dans une nuit horrible.—Shakespeare is a savage with sparks of genius which shine in a dreadful darkness.

> VOLTAIRE, *Irène*, Preliminary Letter (1778).

Was there ever such stuff as great part of Shakespeare? only one must not say so! But what think you?—What?—Is there not sad stuff? What?—what?   GEORGE III to Fanny Burney (1785).

With the single exception of Homer, there is no eminent writer, not even Sir Walter Scott, whom I can despise so entirely as I despise Shakespeare when I measure my mind against his.

> G. BERNARD SHAW, *Dramatic Opinions and Essays* (1907).

INDEX

INDEX

*R

Makes me or fordoes me quite, 413
   us or it mars us, 413
Malady, lesser is scarce felt, 386
Males' subjects, winged fowls are, 33
Malice domestic, foreign levy, 320
   extenuate nor set down in, 417
   pretence of treasonous, 319
   than of duty, more made of, 435
Mammocked it, how he, 257
Man, defused infection of, 232
   delights not me, 345
   he died, like a, 329
   I dare do all that may become, 315
   I must also feel it as a, 326
   I wished myself, 252
   let him pass for, 84
   most like this dreadful night, 294
   no more than this, is, 387
   not old enough for, 135
   O that I were a, 44
   per se and stands alone, 250
   proud man, 27
   right fair, better angel is, 459
   say to the world This was a, 309
   suit me all points like, 98
   to give the world assurance of, 358
   what a piece of work is, 345
   you are, you might have been, 259
Manhood daring, bold, and venturous, 237
   melted into courtesies, 44
Manhoods cheap, hold their, 216
Mankind, I am Misanthropos and hate, 286
   is, how beauteous, 13
Manly enterprise, a trim exploit, 73
Manner born, native here and to, 338
Manners be your speed, good, 188
   blush to see nobleman want, 242
   ne'er were preach'd, where, 144
   never sawest good, 107
   says that I lack, 115
   we are the makers of, 219
Manningham, John, 471
Man's estate, when I came to, 146
   life is a tedious one, 435
   life's as cheap as beast's, 383
   mind but woman's might, 298
   work, I'll do it if it be, 395
Mansion, made his everlasting, 287
   of a love, I have bought, 278
Mantle, you all do know this, 302
Mantles on him, put my tires and, 422
Mantuan, good old, 55
Many, mutable rank-scented, 259
Maps for ports, peering in, 82
Mar what's well, striving to better, 378
Marble, when I sleep in dull cold, 243
Marching, besmirched with rainy, 217
Mare again, man shall have, 75
Margent, you must be edified by, 370

Mariana, resides this dejected, 30
Marigold that goes to bed wi' the sun, 152
Markets, you are not for all, 112
Marlowe's mighty line, 477
Marmoset, how to snare the nimble, 9
Maronem, arte, 468
Marriage crept too near his conscience, 241
   curse of, 407
   made a pair of stairs to, 116
   maid so opposite to, 399
   of true minds, 457
   railed so long against, 39
   seldom proveth well, hasty, 229
   to be conjoin'd in, 46
Marriages, God best maker of all, 219
Marriage-vows false as dicers' oaths, 358
Married, did not think I should live till, 40
   ear, word unpleasing to, 62
   in an afternoon, wench, 125
   is a man that's marred, man, 130
   man, Benedick the, 37, 47
   that dies married young, best, 281
   to me, not unto my clothes, 124
   your disposition to be, 268
Marry fool, if thou wilt needs marry, 351
Mars, assume the port of, 207
Martial, bawdy, 471
Martlet, guest of summer, 314
Martyr, thou fall'st a blessed, 243
Mary-buds begin to ope golden eyes, 433
Mask of night is on my face, 272
Masks for faces and for noses, 154
Masons building roofs of gold, 208
Mass of things to come at large, 251
Mast be now blown overboard, 230
   nor tackle, sail, nor, 4
   upon the high and giddy, 200
Master, Cacaliban has a new, 9
   calls me, I must not say no, 396
   I am meat for your, 198
   of what is mine own, be, 124
   that which I would call, 376
Masters, noble and approved, 399
   to their females, 33
   we cannot all be, 398
Mastiff, greyhound, mongrel grim, 388
Mastiffs of unmatchable courage, 214
Match, learn me to lose winning, 278
   sun ne'er saw her, 267
Matron's bones, mutine in a, 358
Matter deep and dangerous, read, 181
   if thou consider rightly of, 301
   unmixed with baser, 341
Matters, intending other serious, 285
May, full of spirit as month of, 190
   winds do shake buds of, 450

S

*S